Mealtimes & Memories

FOND REFLECTIONS OF FAMILY, FRIENDS AND FOOD

BY

Thelma L. Carlile

by

Thelma Carlile

Additional copies of *Mealtimes and Memories* may be obtained at a cost of $16.95 plus $3.00 postage and handling, each book. Texas residents add $1.40 sales tax, each.

Send to:
Sunline, Inc.
P. O. Box 1287
Big Spring, TX 79720
(915) 263-1281

ISBN 0-9644579-0-3

1st Printing   February, 1995

Printed in the USA by

The Wimmer Companies, Inc.
Memphis • Dallas

2

DEDICATION

This book is lovingly dedicated to —

- my husband, Cleo, who will cheerfully try any food once and often has, and whose encouragement and prodding helped bring my dream to reality.

- my children, by birth and choice, Cyndee, Beverly, Deanna and Joey, who endured all the "weird" stuff I served them in the interest of variety and health and still loved me.

- and to the memory of my Uncle Everett Yerden, whose lavish praise of my first cake helped me believe I could be a good cook.

ACKNOWLEDGEMENTS

Many thanks to—

- *Cleo, my husband, the love of my life, who kept encouraging me to "get on with it", and provided much emotional and financial support.*

- *Larry Stuart, graphic artist and nephew-in-law, for cover design and other artwork and for advice on many topics relating to the publication of this book.*

- *Cyndee, my eldest, who willingly tested recipes while in the middle of a weight-loss program.*

- *Deanna, my youngest daughter, who helped proof and made suggestions on the narrative part of this book while awaiting the birth of grandchild number six.*

- *David, my son-in-law, for cheerfully responding to my cries for help when the computer wouldn't cooperate.*

- *Rita Jo, my sister-in-law, who spent hours proofreading and making suggestions.*

- *all my friends and relatives from North to South, East to West, who willingly and lovingly shared their recipes and lives with me. Your encouragement has filled my heart with warmth and joy.*

INTRODUCTION

Writing a cookbook is no small task!! Even though it was written in my mind long before it was ever put on paper, when I finally got down to business, my house fell apart around me and my husband began to feel neglected. My friends got tired of me saying "Not until the cookbook is finished", the granddaughters wondered if they would ever get their doll clothes sewn, and the grandsons excused me more than once from watching them play ball.

This book is a gift of love—to my children and grandchildren, nieces, nephews, other relatives and friends who through the years have said, "I want that recipe". And it is a gift to myself—a collection of my favorites so I don't have to keep saying, "Now, where is that recipe?"

I think I was born with a love for food and cooking. As a child growing up on a Western Michigan farm, I dearly loved to play house and especially play restaurant. Oh the wonderful hamburgers we made from mud and sawdust. We tucked them between cinnamon bush leaves and served them with soft drinks made from the juices of poke berries or water tinted ridiculous colors from crêpe paper scraps.

By the time I went to college, cakes were my specialty. I loved decorating Christmas cookies, the cornbread recipe was committed to memory, and I had captured a red ribbon for my muffins at the county fair. Those muffins were baked in a stove-top oven setting on the burner of a kerosene stove.

In 1957 I graduated from college and married Gary Smock, all in the same week. Our honeymoon was spent driving to Lawton, Oklahoma for a stint with the U. S. Army. I quickly learned the meaning of frugal. I think our monthly income was $126.00, which seems totally impossible. My favorite company meal was inexpensive (translate that to cheap) and easy to prepare—spaghetti with meat sauce, a garden salad with carefully ringed onion and carrot curls adorning the top (I had more time than money in those days.), butter biscuit sticks, and ambrosia made with canned pineapple chunks and coconut. That meat sauce is still my favorite and the favorite of my family. It was during those days that I became a clipping addict, beginning to compile my own recipe file from recipes I tried from the women's magazines.

When the army time was over, we moved back to Michigan, I finished my Masters Degree (Yes Dad, I finally decided that it was OK to be a teacher.), gave birth to two babies (girls) and became a widow at the early age of 29. During those years in Michigan I kept cooking, clipping and trying anything and everything that held promise. If I ate something delicious, I wasn't hesitant about asking for the recipe.

In 1969, I added on to my small bungalow in Plymouth, Michigan, making my kitchen more efficient and roomy. That same year, my

5

parents, Elmer and Adah Yerden, visited with some friends, Clifford and Eula Carlile, while on a Western trip with me. In the early 1930's, my father and Clifford had been roommates at Anderson College and Theological Seminary in Anderson, Indiana. During their conversation, they discovered they had children in the same position— single with two children. The next thing I knew, my White Knight rode up in a black and white Grand Prix. To be more exact, I flew to Texas on an American jet to meet the White Knight who had driven up to Dallas in a black and white Grand Prix. This wonderful man, a widower with a little girl and boy and a teenage foster boy, swept me off my feet and into his heart and home. Once again I spent my honeymoon driving—this time with 4 children, a teenager and a dog, and it was Christmas!

So the little girl from Western Michigan moved to West Texas. Talk about change!! Big house, big family, new husband and no maple trees!! Those first months in Big Spring were a real challenge for me. It was like cooking for guests for a while. Cooking the same food in the same way all the time was boring to me, so I gave the family plenty of variety. My efforts were not always met with enthusiasm, but I had enough success to keep cooking and clipping. About the time I got used to my new kitchen, we decided to take the kids camping. Now cooking on a camp stove and planning menus to prepare on-the-go is another story, but for 10 years we camped (and I cooked) our way through 46 of the 50 states.

Though times have changed and cooking methods and philosophies along with them, some things haven't changed and never will. The preparation of good food served attractively is one of the ways I show my love to family and friends, and the limitless creativity involved in this process gives me great joy. Good meals are still central to family life and critical to contentment. I enjoy sharing with others that cooking, meal planning and entertaining can be easy and fun as well as healthful and delicious. You may think—"What's the use, I spend all this time and it will be gone in minutes." Just remember, the food may be gone, but the memories linger on.

Memories. Aren't they wonderful? They're important, too. The pain of the bad ones seems to dull with time as the joy in the happy ones increases. We make them every day, all year long, and no one can take them away from us—they are ours forever. It is amazing how many of my memories are centered around food—birthdays, deaths, gradua-tions, weddings, family gatherings, holidays, special celebrations, a special restaurant. Times have changed. The simple, quieter, even safer days of my childhood and youth are gone forever—except in my memory.

My hope is that my memories will cause you to remember a special time in your past and that my recipes will get you into the kitchen to create some new ones.

TABLE OF CONTENTS

TLC* Tips 10

Appetizers, Snacks and Beverages...................... 23

Breads, Spreads and Breakfast 49

Condiments and Sauces...................................... 92

Salads and Dressings...................................... 101

Soups, Stews and Sandwiches 141

Main Dishes.. 181

Vegetables and Other Side Dishes 249

Cakes and Pies 271

Cookies and Candies... 329

Desserts.. 375

* Whenever you see TLC in this book, it means by Thelma Lois Carlile with Tender Loving Care

TLC Tips

TLC EQUIPMENT TIPS

A kitchen is a very personal thing. Though I tend to be a pack rat in other areas of the house, I keep my kitchen stocked with things I really use. That is not to say I don't like gadgets, but they must hold their weight. You will have your own favorites—here are some of mine and why I like them.

WOODEN SPOONS - all shapes and sizes. Fun to collect when traveling. I have found some very nice Teflon ones I enjoy using, also.

TONGS - great for turning pieces of chicken or meat and for picking up most anything.

SPATULAS - I prefer the rubber ones with the wooden handles in various sizes—Rubbermaid makes good ones.

SIEVES - treat yourself to several sizes of these. The small ones are nice for draining pimientos or pouring tea; the larger ones for making yogurt cheese or draining crushed pineapple.

WHISKS - the heavy duty kind are worth the money—aim for all the sizes from small to large.

STAND MIXER - I don't know how anyone can bake without one, though my first cakes were of the "beat 300 strokes" variety and my mother made the most wonderful angel food cakes with a flat whisk. She didn't have a copper bowl either. I baked a lot of years before I got my Kitchen Aide, but it sure has spoiled me.

ZESTER - For years I struggled with trying to grate orange and lemon peel, always ending up with a mush, and often I would leave out the zest because of the mess. The zester solves that problem perfectly.

SALAD SPINNER - A great gadget for getting the water out of your salad greens when you want to use them right away.

MEASURING CUPS - have plenty. Tupperware and Foley are my favorites for dry ingredients. For liquids I love the Pyrex with the open handles. Get the set—1 cup, 2 cups, 4 cups and 8 cups—great for use in the microwave.

MEASURING SPOONS - At least 3 sets—one for use at the stove and 2 for use in baking. The sets with ½ tablespoon and ⅛ teaspoon are helpful.

PARCHMENT PAPER - great for lining baking pans and cookie sheets. If you have a hard time finding it, try a paper supply. Go in with some friends to purchase a box. The flat sheets are a plus.

WAXED PAPER - measure dry ingredients or grate cheese and vegetables on a square of this, then toss when finished. Cheap PAPER PLATES can be used the same way.

MIXING BOWLS - as many as you have room to store and all sizes. There is a set of 9 nesting bowls that is nice, and you need at least 1 really large bowl for big batch mixing.

BLENDER - an oldie but goodie. For milk shakes (of course), breakfast drinks, reconstituting frozen beverages, puréeing soups, mixing flour and liquids for fat-free gravies. In my opinion, if you have to choose between a blender and a food processor, keep the blender.

Twelve-inch SKILLET - even if you cook for 1 or 2, I think you need this size! I can't believe I raised 4 kids without one. And make sure it has a good non-stick surface and a lid. A handle that allows you to put it in the oven is another plus.

SLICER - with grater and julienne attachment—yes, even though I have a food processor I find I reach for my trusty slicer often for small jobs.

KNIVES - the best you can afford. A paring knife, boning knife or utility knife, French chef knife and bread knife are a good basic set and will suffice for most tasks. Store and handle them carefully and keep them sharp. I've found an ELECTRIC KNIFE to be useful for far more than the Thanksgiving turkey. Delicate cakes, quick and yeast breads, slicing chicken breast or steak for stir-fry are a few of the jobs I use mine for.

STIR-FRY PAN - deep with a flat bottom and a domed lid. I like it much better than an electric wok, which never seemed to get hot enough and was hard to store.

STEAMER - you pick your favorite. I have both the collapsible kind that fits various size pans and the kind that fits one certain size pan like a double boiler insert. Vegetables just taste and look better cooked that way. and many other foods benefit from this method of preparation.

PEPPER MILL - inexpensive and you'll be surprised at the punch freshly ground pepper has. Indulge in more than one and try various blends of peppercorns.

WAFFLE SLICER - hand held, this nifty tool makes quick work of slicing carrots, summer squash, potatoes and any other thing where a decorative, waffle edge would be appropriate. I love it for the change of appearance it makes in cooked vegetables or raw vegetable platters.

KITCHEN SHEARS - get a sturdy pair. These are great for cutting small game hens in half, trimming the fat from poultry and meat, cutting pizza into slices. If you can only afford or wish to store one pair, get these and not the regular scissors.

SCALES - I find them invaluable. There are just so many times when you

11

need to know how much something weighs. Ideal if you like to purchase the large economy size and re-package.

TIMERS - Yes, more than one. I know there are times when you have two or three things going at once. I use mine to remind me to do things or go places and help schedule my day.

Now for some things you may not have thought about keeping in your kitchen.

REGULAR SCISSORS - these need not be expensive, but they sure save aggravation when trying to open bags. It eliminates the mess that occurs when you pull on a bag to separate it, it pops oven and half the contents spill all over. Also useful for cutting paper into shape to line baking pans, etc., etc. You'll develop your own list.

TWEEZERS and/or small PLIERS - Very useful in pulling out tiny bones from fish, pin feather remains on chicken and other small pulling jobs where a fine, tight grip is needed.

Large, plastic coated PAPER CLIPS - great for holding bags closed.

Transparent or masking TAPE - use to re-seal packages, stick menus, memos, etc., at eye level on cupboard doors for temporary reference.

PERMANENT MARKING PEN - use to label packages for the freezer or other storage.

PLASTIC RULER - necessary for measuring the thickness of dough and other baking projects—you'll be surprised how many times you use it.

COTTON STRING - Useful for tying up roasts, trussing the turkey, making those little seasoning pouches for spiced drinks, etc. The kids and grandkids will always be cutting off a length for their projects, too.

TLC INGREDIENT TIPS

We are fortunate today to have such a wide variety of ingredients from which to choose. In some ways that makes it even more difficult, as we seek to make wise decisions about what we put on the table.

A good general rule is to always use the highest quality you can afford. That doesn't always mean it will be the most expensive.

I believe that fresh is best whenever possible. I like to use fresh vegetables. I generally use fresh onion and fresh garlic. I prefer fresh lemon and fresh lime juice. Life is not perfect, however, so I also use what is available. While we are on the subject of freshness, do make sure that all the ingredients you use are not beyond their prime. Even if properly stored, everything has a shelf life, and one bad apple really does spoil the bushel. Check the dates on your ingredients, use your eyes and nose, and above all, common sense. Not only do you want your food to look and taste appetizing, but you want to stay healthy also.

In my kitchen, and in these recipes, FLOUR is all-purpose, unbleached unless specified otherwise. Try to find one that has not been processed with chemicals. If you have difficulty with that, check the sources elsewhere in this book. It is not necessary to sift the flour before measuring, but do stir the flour and spoon lightly into the cup, leveling the top by drawing a spatula across it. Never shake or pack flour. There are certain cakes that seem to do better if the four has been sifted, and I have tried to indicate where this is necessary.

When SUGAR is called for, I mean granulated white. BROWN SUGAR and POWDERED SUGAR are always called for by name. Remember that brown sugar is always packed in the cup; powdered is spooned in and leveled off. If your powdered sugar seems a little lumpy, sift before measuring. Usually I find that isn't necessary these days.

The BAKING POWDER I use is double-acting, without aluminum. You may need to purchase this at a health food store. Baking powder measurements are always level.

I use regular, all-purpose SALT for baking, and usually a Kosher or sea salt for general cooking. I have reduced our consumption of salt drastically in the last several years, and most recipes reflect that. Feel free to omit or reduce even further for your life style. I like to grind my PEPPER from peppercorns—the taste is so much better.

I always use large EGGS, and like to get those that are from chickens that hunt and peck. Here again, that isn't always possible, but I try.

When my recipes call for VANILLA, I use pure vanilla extract. I especially like the Cook's brand. (See sources) They have a wide variety of other excellent flavorings also.

My recipes call for BUTTER. I prefer unsalted for baking and cooking and salted for table use. Margarine can always be substituted, but I strongly recommend you avoid it for health reasons. Margarine has been hydrogenated and contains trans fatty acids. If SHORTENING is called for, I always use a name brand such as Crisco.

I use canola OIL for general use, in cooking, baking and dressings. I also use olive oil where appropriate.

The MILK in my kitchen is skim these days. Occasionally I find a recipe where it just won't do, and I have indicated that fact. SOUR CREAM, CREAM CHEESE and CHEDDAR CHEESE are the reduced-fat variety. I find the nonfat versions a little harder to work with, but you certainly can give them a try if you wish.

I use all kinds of NUTS and use them interchangeably unless a specific kind is called for.

When a recipe calls for VINEGAR, usually you can use whatever you'd like. Apple cider is a good basic one to keep on hand, but there are so many others to choose from today. I like rice wine vinegar because of its mildness. Balsamic is another excellent mild vinegar. If I have a preference, I mention it in the recipe.

SPICES are ground and HERBS are dried unless otherwise specified.

TLC HEALTH TIPS

Goodness knows I don't cook like I used to!! Does anyone? I've learned that it just isn't necessary to brown ground beef in 2 tablespoons oil, that most dishes can do with less salt, and even sugar can be reduced. My philosophy is to be moderate in my consumption, to use the widest possible variety of foods, and to be wise in the way I prepare them. Admittedly, there are some dishes that appear rarely for those reasons. I prefer not to think of foods as good or bad, but there is such a thing as a good or bad diet.

The recipes in this book have not been compiled with any health condition in mind. As these are family treasures, they reflect an era prior to the knowledge we have today. I have in some cases made some changes from the original to reflect lighter cooking styles. If you wish to alter the recipes, you can probably do so using the tips that follow and the ones in various recipes. Don't be afraid to experiment. The taste may be a little different, but you can probably come up with an end product that will please you.

Keep these things in mind when making changes:

- part whole wheat flour can be substituted in baked goods. Often you will find that whole wheat pastry flour will give a more acceptable product.

- reduce the sugar by ⅓ to ½ in baked goods. Trial and error is the key here. Be careful with cakes—they can be a little tricky.

- substitute 2 egg whites for each egg or use a commercial egg substitute.

- oil can be substituted for melted butter in breads and muffins with some loss of flavor.

- undiluted evaporated skim milk can be substituted for cream in soups and white sauces for richness without fat.

- nonfat yogurt can be substituted for sour cream. Whisk in 1 tablespoon cornstarch per cup to help stabilize it in heated dishes. If the nonfat is more tart than you like, go with a lowfat.

- yogurt cheese (see index) is a good substitute for cream cheese or use reduced fat cream cheese.

- substitute cocoa for chocolate. For each 1 ounce of chocolate, use 3 level tablespoons of cocoa plus 1 tablespoon oil.

- use a sharp cheese in toppings and sauces. You can use less and still have good flavor.

- toast nuts before chopping. The toasty flavor allows you to use less.

- sauté in a non-stick skillet and use water, broth or fruit juice instead of oil.

- drain ground beef in a colander. If you want to reduce the fat even further, blot with paper towels. You can even go a third step and rinse the meat with hot water. This last step is a good idea if you are adding it to a casserole or creamy mixture. It practically insures that the finished dish will not be greasy.

- be aware that ground turkey may not be any less fat than a very lowfat ground beef. If you want really lowfat ground turkey, make sure you get ground turkey breast.

- become a label reader. There are many lower fat versions of your favorite products on the market today. You might be just as pleased with them as the regular version.

TLC MEAL PLANNING TIPS

My experience has been that planning meals reaps many benefits. There is nothing worse than the family converging on you at 5:30 saying, "What's for dinner?" and you don't know. Planning menus is not restricting, it's liberating, and it does not mean you are totally committed. Since we eat approximately 750 meals a year, planning ahead assures variety, and helps us to obtain adequate nutrition. You know what to shop for when you go to the store, and what you are going to do with it when you bring it home. Planning menus is economical, too. I helps you see just how much of something you will need so you are not making reckless purchases.

After a little trial and error, you will decide what method is best for you— a week at a time, 2 weeks or a month. If you can sit still long enough to do a month, you can repeat it over and over. Your family may not even remember. Or the month of menus can be used as a skeleton, adding a few different meals.

For weekly menu plans, I like to use an 8 x 10" sheet of paper divided into 8 equal boxes. That way I have one box for each day plus one left over for notes. I use a separate sheet for breakfast, lunch and dinner (supper). This method gives me enough room to list each dish and the source of the recipe if necessary. I make a master and run the menu sheets off on a copying machine so they will be available when I need them. I've heard that if you skip lunch and use the time to plan your menus, it won't take you long as everything will sound good. So, plan when you're hungry; shop after you've eaten.

As you plan, keep a calendar handy so you will have some idea of the family's schedule, when guests are expected, when you will be away from the house and may want to eat out, and when the children have activities. Should something unforeseen occur, that meal can always be rescheduled at a later time. Keep in mind your family's tastes and preferences, but aim for the widest variety of foods possible. I try to include one or two non-meat meals each week, some new things and some comfortable favorites. If you are trying something new, it's a good idea to keep the rest of the meal familiar.

Once the menus are planned, check your pantry and refrigerator for the food you will need to prepare the meals. What needs to be purchased will comprise your shopping list. I have a master list of all the things I normally purchase at the grocery store and I run off a stack when I do my menu pages. Stick one on the refrigerator with a magnet and check items as you run out. Just reading over the list will help you remember that something is needed.

Depending upon your stage in life, you may need less structure. If you are single or an empty-nester, perhaps you have the freedom to shop more frequently and are less hampered by others' schedules. In that case, a simple Monday - pasta, Tuesday - broiled fish, Wednesday -eat out, etc., will suffice.

TLC HOSPITALITY TIPS

Having people share your home and food is a warm and rewarding experience. It can be as simple as a cup of coffee or tea shared at the kitchen table or as grand as a formal sit-down dinner with several courses. The main thing to remember is to RELAX and enjoy the process. Do only what you are comfortable with. If that means picking up a roasted chicken from the deli to go with your famous Caesar salad and fabulous cheesecake, so be it. Or perhaps you bring in dessert to compliment the pasta dish you enjoy preparing. Maybe it means incorporating some shortcut that only you know about (the stuffing started with a mix, you added little extras). Just remember to serve everything in an imaginative way, put on some good music, light the candles and smile.

You do not need a fancy home or accessories for people to enjoy your company. General cleanliness is understood, but a little dust never hurt anyone. A good imagination is helpful, as is an adventurous spirit and a willingness to try new and different things.

There are times when we don't know ahead of time that we will be feeding extra people. That's where a sense of humor and a little creativity are helpful. A well-stocked pantry and freezer don't hurt either. But when I know ahead of time that I am going to entertain people in my home, I consider these things:

THE MENU - The menu is the first thing I tackle. The occasion and the season often dictate the kind of food I'll serve and what the table will look like, as does my schedule at the time. I list everything I'll serve, from pre-dinner beverage to after-dinner coffee, and where each recipe can be found. I plan my menu with an eye to how it will look on the plate as well as incorporating a variety of tastes and textures, aiming not to duplicate. There is comfort in serving tried and true dishes, but I've been known to try something new and haven't been surprised many times.

THE TABLE - In recent years we have seen a trend toward less formal table settings. We no longer feel uncomfortable combining patterns, textures and colors. This certainly allows us a lot more flexibility with our tableware, especially if entertaining a large group. If I find myself wanting to seat a larger number of people than I have napkins, I'll often alternate napkins of different patterns and/or colors. At least that way it looks like you did it on purpose—more so than if you put 8 napkins of one pattern and 2 of another. You can do the same thing with china or crystal.

Speaking of CHINA, I really like dishes, and my collection includes everything from formal to casual, expensive to downright cheap, and dishes that pick up different ethnic themes. I have one set of plain, white dishes, and I think you should too. There's no end to the tables you can set when your dishes are white and your color comes from linens and center-pieces. And there's nothing quite so elegant as an all white table—dishes, linens and centerpiece!! Try it sometime.

I love pretty table LINENS, and have found the majority of mine in discount stores and on sale tables. I like to use cloth napkins, and with today's easy-care fabrics, I find myself doing so more and more often. Don't be limited by the usual—be inventive and imaginative. I've used bandanas, guest towels and wash cloths for napkins and tea towels, hand towels, and small rugs for place mats. Inexpensive table covers can easily be cut from regular sewing fabrics—the sky's the limit here. If you are covering card tables, you probably won't even have to sew a seam, and a simple hem finishes them nicely. If you're in a real hurry, pink the edges.

CENTERPIECE - Rarely do I purchase fresh flowers, but prefer instead to combine what I can find around the house and yard to work with the theme for the occasion. I have been known to fashion an all green display of vegetables and fruit in a rustic basket, filling in the spaces with curly endive or kale. Or fill a basket with all things Italian for a pasta meal. I've used an arrangement of seashells on a mirror for a fish fry, small hatboxes filled with plants, tulle and ribbons for a bridal luncheon, a toy truck filled with stuffed toys and wrapped candies for a child's birthday dinner and gold gift bags stuffed with foil tissue to hold a bud vase for a 50th anniversary celebration. I hope these ideas will inspire you to be creative in your own special way.

SERVICE - For groups of six or eight, we usually sit around the table and the meal is served family style. Occasionally I will have a first course soup or salad at the places when I announce that dinner is ready, then put the rest of the food on the table after the soup or salad plates are cleared. Dessert can be served at the table or elsewhere, if you wish to leave the dishes until later

For a group larger than 6 or 8, I like sit-down buffets—the tables are set, grace is said, each person picks up his plate and serves himself from the buffet table.

Perhaps you don't have a formal dining room, or a large enough one to seat even six or eight around one table. Please don't let that discourage you from feeding your friends. Clear off the coffee table, set up some tray tables, use your card table, or let your guests hold the plates on their laps. Being together is the important thing.

PLACE CARDS - I think using place cards is a nice touch for special family meals, and for larger affairs. It helps to avoid confusion when it is time to sit down. File cards folded over and decorated with a seal are easy enough for a child to make, and attractive too! Use your imagination and you'll think of other things you can use. Try a shiny Christmas ball tied with a ribbon bow and the name written on with glitter. A tiny wrapped package holding take-home favors with the name written on the package tag, small photos in unusual frames, writing the name on a clip clothespin and using it as a napkin holder as well as a place card are just some ideas you may want to use.

I hope it is evident that feeding my family and friends is a joy to me, and a task I can get very excited about. Just remember to find your own style and take it from there.

TLC PREPARATION TIPS

It's flattering to have someone ask for the recipe for something you have prepared. It has happened to me many times. But there are so many variables in the preparation of food, that sometimes a dish with the same title bears little resemblance to the original. One of my favorite authors, Erma Bombeck, devoted an entire column to that thought. It seems that she begged for a cake recipe that her friend raved about. She left out the mashed potatoes, substituted mint for cloves, used three eggs instead of four, chocolate chips instead of cocoa, and baked it in a sheet cake pan instead of a bundt pan. She said she was embarrassed for her friend when she removed the cake from the oven.

Of course recipes are really only guides—that's why each dish is so unique—but if you want your dish to taste like my dish, then you must prepare it with the same ingredients, in the same amounts, in the same way and for the same length of time. If you make any changes, it is no longer my recipe, it's yours—just as good, probably, perhaps even better. There's not a thing wrong with that concept—variety is the spice of life.

I would hate for you to be embarrassed for me when you prepare my recipes, so keep these things in mind:

1. Please read the recipe in its entirety before starting to put it together. We all know to do this, but even I slip up at times. That will inevitably be the time I get halfway through the recipe and lack an ingredient. Though I may improvise, I have changed my recipe. See? Also, by reading the recipe ahead of time, you will know if there are preliminary steps which need to be taken—like letting something set or chill for a length of time.

2. After you have read through the recipe, gather all the ingredients together before you start measuring. You're right, I don't always do this, but it sure saves time and mistakes if you do. Set them on one side of you before you measure and move them to the other side after you measure. That way, if you get called to the phone or have some other interruption, you will know that you have added when you come back.

3. I believe in accurate measurements. You may get away with throwing things together if you are making a casserole, but especially in the area of baking, accuracy contributes greatly to the outcome of the dish.

19

Level means level, packed means packed. I measure my dry ingredients in cups designed for that purpose, and I measure liquids in my glass measuring cups. Always bend down to read the measurement at eye level.

4. Perhaps we all have our own idea of what constitutes a large onion or small apple. Use good judgement here. If exactness is critical, exact measurements are usually given.

5. Pans are in different sizes for a reason. Here again the size of the pan is important to how the dish looks when it comes out of the oven, and how it cooks while in the oven. Usually the size is inscribed somewhere on the baking dish or pan. If not, take the time some weekend day to measure all of yours and write down the measurements in your recipe file. Volume is also important. While you're measuring, use a standard measuring cup to fill each with water and see how much it holds. Record this information also. You'll only have to do it once. With this information at hand, you can save yourself from many a recipe failure.

6. Oven temperatures do vary. Your 350 degrees may not be as hot as my 350 degrees. A good oven thermometer is an inexpensive purchase. When a recipe gives a baking time range, always set your timer for the minimum time and check for doneness. You can always add a few more minutes, but you can never take them away. If no range is given, I recommend you set your timer 5 minutes before the suggested cooking or baking time and check for doneness. A little forethought sure can save an overcooked, if not burned, dish.

7. When I bake cakes that are going to be removed from the pan, I always line the bottom of the pan with waxed or parchment paper, then grease and flour the paper. This insures that the cake comes out nicely. Baking cookies on parchment-lined baking sheets is nice also— no greasing and the cookies are easily removed. My recipe directions may say "greased and floured" or "lightly greased", so you do have that option.

Appetizers, Snacks and Beverages

After a day filled with swinging in the rope swing hanging from one of the beautiful, large maples in the front yard, building a playhouse, helping with the haying or bringing up the cows from the "back 40", we certainly didn't need an appetizer to get us ready for the main event. My mother never served appetizers when I was growing up—not for "company meals" or farm hands and certainly not for the family. I can't remember when this word crept into my culinary vocabulary, but somewhere along the way it did and I collected some recipes for tasty ones that have become family favorites. A selection could serve as a light meal.

As for snacks, we kids would grab a juicy tomato, warm from the vine, sprinkled with a little salt, cookies from Grandmother's cookie jar, or a couple of graham crackers. Actually, sometimes it was more than a couple. My sister says she can remember a time when she and our brother polished off nearly a box between them along with a half-gallon of milk. Popcorn was a great Saturday night treat, popped in melted shortening in a heavy pan on the range, poured into mom's aluminum dishpan, and liberally doused with melted butter. What comfort to open the oven door, pull up a couple of chairs, place the pan of popcorn on our outstretched legs, and indulge. I think about the time I was in high school, Aunt Virginia Yerden introduced us to Nuts and Bolts—the cereal and nut mixture that is still popular today under many different names.

Beverages meant good, Jersey milk or water. Neither mom nor dad were coffee drinkers in my early years. Hot tea was served when you were under the weather, and since serving iced tea meant chipping away with an ice pick at the block of ice in the ice box, it was reserved for special occasions. Lemon and orangeade were wonderful, cooling drinks made with real fruit, juiced by hand and the rinds dropped into the pitcher, or five-gallon milk can, depending on the size of the crowd.

CYNDEE'S LO-CAL CHEESE DIP

This dip is a popular accompaniment to a vegetable platter, and often finds its place on an appetizer table or buffet menu. It does need to be made a few hours ahead so the flavors can blend, overnight is even better.

2 cups low-fat cottage cheese
2 teaspoons beef bouillon
   granules

2 teaspoons dried minced
   onion
2 teaspoons lemon juice

Place knife blade in processor bowl. (Or use the blender.) Add all of the ingredients. Process until smooth, about 1 minute. Chill several hours before serving. If mixture seems too thick, add a little milk. Serve with veggies or crackers.

SPINACH DIP

My sister, Ruth, thinks this is the greatest. Its popularity seems to run in cycles, but you really can't go wrong with it on your table.

1 package vegetable soup mix
   (Ruth uses Knorr)
1 cup mayonnaise
1½ cups sour cream
1 (10-ounce) package frozen
   chopped spinach, thawed
   and well drained

1 can water chestnuts,
   drained and chopped
⅛ teaspoon garlic powder
Round loaf of French bread

Combine all ingredients except the French bread. Chill to blend flavors. Slice off the top of the bread, and pull out the center to make a bowl. Serve the dip in the bread bowl, using the cubes and/or pieces of bread as dippers.

GARLIC YOGURT DIP

This is a great dip for fresh vegetables or steamed tiny new potatoes. Next time you are asked to bring something to nibble on, try this—I'm sure it will be a hit.

4 to 5 cloves garlic
1 teaspoon salt
¼ cup yogurt

1½ cups low-fat ricotta or
cottage cheese
½ cup olive oil

Peel the garlic cloves and squeeze through a garlic press onto a chopping board. Add the salt, and combine to a paste using a metal spatula. Place the yogurt and cheese in a blender container and purée. Add the garlic/salt mixture and pulse to combine. With motor running, add the oil in a slow steady stream. Chill until ready to serve with boiled shrimp, cooked tiny new potatoes, hard-boiled eggs or blanched and/or raw veggies. Some I like to use are mini-carrots, cauliflower and broccoli flowerettes, zucchini spears and cherry tomatoes. (Don't blanch the tomatoes, of course.) Jícama slices, turnip wedges, fresh mushrooms, pepper strips of all colors, pea pods—the list goes on and on. I strive for a variety and plenty of color so it will be a feast for the eyes as well as the body.

TLC Tip: *Sometimes I use a large sweet pepper—green, red or some other color—as a container for this dip.*

DEVILED HAM DIP

This is an oldie that I have used on many occasions. I like it so much I can almost make a meal out of this and crackers.

½ cup mayonnaise
1 (8-ounce) package cream
cheese, softened
1 (5-ounce) can deviled ham
½ teaspoon onion juice (you
can buy it bottled, but if
you don't have any on
hand, hold your breath,
and use a sharp knife to
scrape a cut onion until
you get ½ teaspoon)

¼ teaspoon Worcestershire
sauce
Dash of salt
A few grindings black pepper
2 tablespoons chopped
pimientos

Blend mayonnaise and cream cheese until smooth. Add the remaining ingredients, mixing well. Chill. Serve with assorted crackers.

MEXICANA BEAN DIP

When you serve this dip, you take the chance that your guests will be too full to eat the main course! I like it best served with the large Fritos, but when I listen to my heart and not my mouth, I use no-fat tortilla chips. You'll like it either way.

½ pound bulk sausage (regular, lite or turkey will work here)

1 (28-ounce) can pork and beans, or baked beans
½ cup barbecue sauce
⅓ cup chopped onion

Brown the sausage; drain well on paper towels. Purée the pork and beans in the food processor or blender. Combine all ingredients in a large saucepan. Heat slowly over medium-low heat, stirring often. Serve warm with your choice of chips.

TLC Tip: *It seems to me that can sizes have a way of changing. If you can't find the exact weight, use one as close to it as possible. If you think there is more liquid on the pork and beans than necessary, pour some of it off before you purée the mixture. You can always add some back if the mixture is too thick.*

RIO GRANDE DIP

I could make a meal of this. It's perfect to serve while you are waiting for the steaks or chicken to cook on the grill or as part of a Mexican Fiesta.

1 (20-ounce) can pork and beans, sieved or puréed in the food processor
½ cup shredded sharp Cheddar cheese
1 teaspoon garlic salt
1 teaspoon chili powder
½ teaspoon salt

Dash cayenne pepper
2 teaspoons apple cider vinegar
2 teaspoons Worcestershire sauce
½ teaspoon liquid smoke
4 slices bacon, cooked crisp and crumbled

Combine all ingredients except the bacon in the top of a double boiler. Heat until very warm. Top with the crumbled bacon. Serve hot with corn chips or tortilla chips.

TLC Tip: *You can heat this in a saucepan over direct heat, but you will have to stir often and watch carefully. It can also be heated in the microwave.*

BEVERLY'S GUACAMOLE

Daughter Beverly serves this as an accompaniment for her chicken fajitas (see index) or a dip for chips. This dip will wake up your taste buds.

2 large ripe avocados, mashed
  with a fork
1 tablespoon garlic salt (more
  if needed)

1 to 2 tablespoons lemon juice
1 cup HOT picante sauce, or
  to taste
1 cup low-fat plain yogurt

Blend all ingredients in a food processor, pulsing just to combine. Beverly says to taste and adjust the various ingredients to your liking.

CAVIAR PIE ROMANOFF

This sensational appetizer recipe was given to me by Kathy Velas. We stopped at their place in Syndey, British Columbia, when we were cruising the San Juan Islands with our friends Barbara and Colin Taylor. Kathy served us a delightful meal of fresh crab legs, caught in traps near their home, with local berry cobbler for dessert. She served this appetizer as we watched the sun set over the water. Thanks, Kathy.

6 hard-cooked eggs, chopped
  fine
3 tablespoons mayonnaise
1 to 1½ cups finely chopped
  onions, to your taste
  (Kathy says you can use
  any kind, but I usually
  use yellow, or when I can
  get them, some type of
  sweet onion)

8 ounces cream cheese,
  softened
⅔ cup sour cream
3½ to 4 ounces caviar,
  drained, rinsed and
  patted dry

Mix the eggs and mayonnaise. Spread evenly in a well-greased 8" spring form pan. Sprinkle with the onion. Mix the cream cheese with the sour cream until smooth. Spread over the onion with a wet spatula. Cover; chill 3 hours or overnight. Top with caviar just before serving. Run knife around side of pan edges, loosen spring form and lift off. Place on a plate and garnish with lemon wedges and parsley. Serve with tiny slices of rye bread, plain melba toast, or a cracker of your choice. Fabulous!!

TLC Tip: *After I rinse and drain the caviar, I usually place it on a paper-towel lined plate to dry a little. Sometimes I find those little eggs hard to deal with. Using the tip of your vegetable peeler makes the task of arranging them a little easier.*

SMOKY BACON CHEESE SPREAD

I think you'll enjoy the smoky flavor of this tasty cheese spread. Provide plenty of cocktail bread slices or plain crackers with this one.

1 (8-ounce) package cream
   cheese, softened
¼ cup butter, softened
1 (5-ounce) jar sharp cheese
   spread

⅛ to ¼ teaspoon liquid smoke
7 slices bacon, cooked crisp
   and crumbled
2 teaspoons fresh or frozen
   chopped chives

In a medium bowl, combine the cream cheese, butter, cheese spread and liquid smoke. Blend well. Add the bacon and chives. Cover and chill well to blend flavors. Remove from refrigerator about 30 minutes before serving.

SEAFOOD CHEESE SPREAD

This is an adaptation of a recipe I found in Country Home *magazine. It is wonderful served with small slices of bread, melba toast or plain crackers.*

2 (8-ounce) packages cream
   cheese, softened
1 cup shredded Swiss cheese
1 teaspoon horseradish
1 teaspoon chili powder
1 (6-ounce) can crab meat,
   drained and flaked (don't
   forget to look it over
   carefully for stray pieces
   of shell)

1 (4½-ounce) can tiny shrimp,
   drained
½ cup chopped green pepper
⅓ cup sliced green onion
¼ cup sliced almonds, toasted

Combine the cheeses, horseradish and chili powder. Stir in the remaining ingredients except the almonds. Line a 4 x 8" loaf pan (or other similar container) with plastic wrap, letting the edges hang over. Spoon in the cheese mixture. Cover; chill several hours or overnight. When ready to serve, fold back the plastic wrap, unmold onto serving plate, and peel off the plastic wrap. Sprinkle with the almonds. Garnish with parsley sprigs, lemon slices and cherry tomatoes, if desired.

HAM AND CHEESE BALL

Surrounded with melba toast or buttery crackers, this cheese ball makes an attractive presentation and will delight your guests with its savory taste.

2 (8-ounce) packages cream
   cheese, softened
½ pound sharp cheese,
   shredded
2 teaspoons grated onion
2 teaspoons Worcestershire
   sauce
1 teaspoon lemon juice
1 teaspoon mustard
½ teaspoon paprika
½ teaspoon salt
1 (2¼-ounce) can deviled ham
2 tablespoons finely chopped
   parsley
2 tablespoons chopped
   pimiento
⅔ cup chopped pecans

In a large bowl, combine all the ingredients except the pecans. Mix thoroughly. Chill until nearly firm. Shape into a ball, roll in the pecans and wrap in plastic wrap. Refrigerate overnight. To serve, unwrap, place on serving plate, sprinkle with additional paprika, and garnish as desired.

SMOKY SALMON AND CHEESE BALL

The flavor of smoked salmon comes through in this delectable spread. Do try it.

¾ cup sliced almonds, toasted,
   divided use
1 (7¾-ounce) can red salmon,
   drained and flaked
1 (8-ounce) package cream
   cheese, softened
2 tablespoons chopped green
   pepper
1 tablespoon chopped fresh
   parsley
1 teaspoon chopped pimiento
⅛ to ¼ teaspoon liquid smoke

Coarsely chop ¼ cup of the almonds; reserve remaining almonds for garnish. In a medium bowl, combine salmon, cheese, green pepper, parsley, pimiento, liquid smoke and ¼ cup chopped almonds; mix well. Cover, refrigerate at least 1 hour until firm. Shape mixture into a ball, roll in reserved sliced almonds. Cover with plastic wrap and refrigerate. Serve with rye snack bread or crackers.

CHUTNEY AND CHEESE

This couldn't be easier, but the taste is anything but ordinary.

1 (8-ounce) package cream
   cheese (lite is just fine)

Chutney, your choice of
   flavor, I like Major Gray's
Assorted crackers

Unwrap the cream cheese and place in the center of a pretty serving plate. Cover lightly and let come to room temperature. Spoon chutney over the top—use plenty, it doesn't hurt if it runs down the sides. Surround with your favorite crackers—an assortment is nice. Serve with pride.

CHILI CHEESE SQUARES

These delicate squares have a zesty flavor that will perk up your next appetizer buffet.

1 (4-ounce) can diced green
   chilis, drained (you select
   the heat)
8 ounces shredded Monterey
   Jack or sharp Cheddar
   cheese (2 cups)

1 cup biscuit baking mix
1 cup half-and-half
4 eggs
¼ teaspoon salt
¼ cup sliced pimiento-stuffed
   olives

Sprinkle the chilis and cheese in the bottom of a lightly greased 9" square baking pan. Combine the biscuit baking mix, half-and-half, eggs, and salt in a medium-size bowl; beat until thoroughly blended. (You could use your blender for this job.) Pour over the chili/cheese mixture. Bake in a 375 degree oven for 30 minutes or until puffed and golden and a toothpick inserted in the center comes out clean. Let stand 10 minutes before cutting into squares to serve. Garnish each square with a green olive slice if desired.

CHEDDAR PUFFS

Tender morsels that just melt in your mouth. You can eat these by the handful.

½ cup butter	1¼ cups flour
1 cup grated sharp cheese	¼ teaspoon salt

Cream the butter with the cheese until smooth. Blend in the flour and salt, then knead lightly with hands to form a soft dough. Roll by teaspoonfuls into balls, place on greased cookie sheet and bake at 400 degrees for 12 minutes. This should make about 3 dozen.

SPINACH PARMESAN QUICHES

Club meetings are great places to trade recipes. You know how it is, someone brings a dish for refreshments, you taste, your face lights up and you just have to have the recipe. This recipe, from Liz Edwards, came to me in that way. Years ago we were both part of the local AAUW and both enjoyed cooking. These yummy little tarts will disappear almost as fast as you can put them on a plate.

1 (8-ounce) package cream cheese, softened	2 eggs, beaten
½ cup butter, softened	1 cup whipping cream
1½ cups flour	1⅔ cups grated Parmesan cheese
1 teaspoon nutmeg, divided use	1 (6-ounce) can pitted ripe olives, sliced
1 (10-ounce) package fresh spinach, cooked, drained well and chopped	½ red onion, sliced and sautéed

Mix the cheese, butter, flour and ½ teaspoon nutmeg to form a soft dough. Chill thoroughly at least 1 hour. (You can even let it chill overnight.) Shape into 24 small balls, and press into tiny greased tart pans. Place back in the refrigerator while you prepare the filling. Combine the spinach, eggs, cream, cheese, olives, onion and the remaining ½ teaspoon nutmeg. Spoon filling into prepared tart shells. Bake in a 350 degree oven for 30 minutes. Cool slightly in pans before removing. Garnish with a bit of parsley or additional sliced olives, if desired. May be served warm or at room temperature.

CRAB MEAT APPETIZERS

This tidbit is very popular with our family, and has been served at many a family get-together. They disappear quickly, so make plenty.

Triscuit crackers
1 tube garlic cheese spread,
  softened
1 can crab meat (the best you
  can afford)

Dash of salt, if desired
  (I usually don't add any)
¼ cup finely chopped onion
1 (3-ounce) can mushrooms,
  drained and finely
  chopped

In a shallow bowl, mash the cheese spread with a fork. Pick over the crab meat carefully to remove any bits of shell. Combine as much as possible with the cheese spread. Mix in the chopped onion. Spread on the crackers and sprinkle the top with a bit of chopped mushrooms. Place under the broiler for a few minutes until slightly brown. Serve warm. (You might want to sample one as you remove them from the oven because there won't be any left when you start passing them around.)

SAUSAGE BALLS

A regular for brunches and showers, these simple appetizers are so easy to eat! They can be frozen before baking—just place on a baking sheet, freeze, then place in a heavy freezer bag to store. Bake from the frozen state. You might have to add a minute or two to the baking time.

1 (10-ounce) package Cheddar
  cheese (I like sharp)

1 pound hot bulk sausage
  (you can use some other
  variety if you wish)
2½ cups biscuit baking mix

Cut cheese into cubes; place in top of double boiler. Heat over hot water, stirring frequently, until melted. Place sausage, biscuit mix and cheese in a large mixing bowl; mix well. Shape into small balls, place on cookie sheet and bake in a 350 degree oven for 15 minutes. Cool on a wire rack. You can serve these at room temperature, or reheat briefly in the microwave to serve warm.

SPICY APPETIZER MEATBALLS

These little meatballs make a real hit on a buffet table. I usually serve them in a chafing dish, garnished with a dusting of finely chopped parsley.

1 pound lean ground beef
¾ cup seasoned dry
   breadcrumbs
2 tablespoons finely chopped
   onion
1 tablespoon catsup
4 drops hot sauce

½ teaspoon prepared mustard
2 eggs, well beaten
½ teaspoon salt
¼ teaspoon pepper
1 tablespoon grated Parmesan
   cheese

Combine all ingredients in a large mixing bowl; mix well and shape into 1" balls. (Keep the size small, as they aren't as attractive if too large.) Sauté in a large non-stick skillet until browned. You can also place them on your broiler pan and bake at 425 degrees for about 12 minutes. I have even cooked them in the microwave (follow the directions for your particular brand), as being brown isn't important because they are served in a sauce. Set aside while you prepare the sauce.

Sauce:

½ cup catsup
½ cup chili sauce
¼ cup cider vinegar
½ cup packed brown sugar
2 tablespoons finely chopped
   onion
1 tablespoon Worcestershire
   sauce

4 drops hot sauce
½ teaspoon dry mustard
3 drops Angostura bitters
   (look for this in the
   section where drink
   mixers are sold)
1 teaspoon salt, less if desired
¼ teaspoon pepper

Combine all ingredients in a large saucepan; bring to a boil. Reduce heat, and simmer 5 minutes. Add the meatballs and simmer an additional 10 minutes. Transfer to chafing dish to keep warm. Makes about 3½ dozen meatballs.

BARBECUED PECANS

The robust barbecue flavor of this snack makes it a real winner.

2 tablespoons butter
¼ cup Worcestershire sauce
1 tablespoon catsup

2 dashes hot sauce
4 cups pecan halves

Melt the butter in a large saucepan. Mix in the Worcestershire sauce, hot sauce and catsup. Stir in the pecans; then spread in a glass baking dish. Toast in a 400 degree oven for about 20 minutes, stirring frequently. Turn out on paper towels and sprinkle with a bit of salt.

AUNT VIRGINIA'S NUTS AND BOLTS

Aunt Virginia Yerden was a school teacher. She taught for years in the Kalamazoo, Michigan, area. She loved to entertain and fix food, which she did into her 80's. This is her version of the ever-popular cereal snack mix. Hers was the first of this type snack I tasted, and I always thought the name was so cute. I think the reason it was called Nuts and Bolts had something to do with the Cheerios and stick pretzels.

2 pounds mixed nuts
1 (12-ounce) box Wheat Chex
1 (12-ounce) box Rice Chex
1 (10-ounce) box Cheerios
1 (6½-ounce) bag pretzel
   twists

1 (6½-ounce) bag pretzel
   sticks
2 cups oil
2 tablespoons Worcestershire
   sauce
1 tablespoon garlic salt
1 tablespoon seasoned salt

Combine the nuts, cereal and pretzels in a large roasting pan. (You can see by the ingredient list that it must be a very large pan.) Combine the oil and seasonings. Pour over the cereal mixture and mix gently but thoroughly with a wooden spoon. Roast in a 250 degree oven for 2 hours, stirring every 15 minutes. Cool, store in tightly covered containers.

TLC Tip: *Times change, and product packages with them. If you can't find cereals and pretzels in exactly the right size container, just come close. Two cups oil is a LOT of oil, so you might want to cut down there a bit, and usually I find that garlic powder can be substituted for the garlic salt— there is enough salt elsewhere in the recipe to help you meet your daily limit!!*

THEL'S TEXAS TRASH

I have tried many recipes for this snack mix, and this is the version I most often make.

2 cups Wheat Chex
2 cups Cheerios
2 cups tiny cheese crackers
  (or goldfish)
2 cups pretzel sticks (or rings
  or twists)
2 cups Corn Chex

2 cups Rice Chex
1 pound mixed nuts
¾ cup butter
1 teaspoon Worcestershire
  sauce
½ teaspoon garlic powder
½ teaspoon celery salt

Combine the cereal, crackers, pretzels and nuts in a large roasting pan. Melt the butter (I usually use the microwave) and add the seasonings. Stir well and pour over the cereal mixture. Mix gently but thoroughly. Bake at 250 degrees for 1 hour, stirring every 15 minutes. Cool, and store in tightly covered containers or self-seal bags.

CYNDEE'S PARTY SNACK

Another great munchie from daughter Cyndee's kitchen.

4 ounces shoestring potatoes
1 can French fried onions
2 cups Corn Chex
2 cups mixed nuts

2 cups cheese crackers
½ cup butter
1 package taco seasoning mix

Combine the shoestring potatoes, French fried onions, Corn Chex, nuts and crackers in a large baking pan. Melt the butter and pour over the dry mixture. Stir gently to combine. Sprinkle the dry taco seasoning mix over all and mix gently but thoroughly. Bake in a 250 degree oven for 30 minutes, stirring every 10 minutes. Cool, store tightly covered.

DOWN ON THE RANCH MIX

The flavor of ranch dressing makes this mix different and tasty.

1 (1-ounce) package ranch-
    style dressing mix (don't
    use reduced-fat)
2 tablespoons dried dillweed

6 cups corn and rice cereal
6 cups oyster crackers
4 cups small pretzel twists
½ cup oil

Combine the salad dressing mix and the dillweed in a large self-seal bag (2-gallon size). Add the cereal, crackers and pretzels. Close the bag and shake gently. Drizzle the oil over the cereal mixture; close bag and shake gently. Place 2 paper towels in the plastic bag, close bag securely and let stand 2 hours, shaking occasionally. Store in an airtight container—I usually use the bag I mixed it in, removing the paper towels. Makes about 16 cups.

TLC Tip: *Need I say, this, or any of these snack mixes, would make a nice gift? Package in freezer bags—I like to use the kind that come with twist ties—tie with yarn, raffia or "binder twine" (rough cord), label and present with love. An assortment would be even better.*

SPICED HOLIDAY (OR ANY DAY) NUTS

If you are blessed with your own pecan tree, you might want to make a quantity of this mix for sharing with all your friends who like "hot stuff". The flavor combination is unusual and habit-forming.

½ teaspoon ground cumin
½ teaspoon chili powder
½ teaspoon curry powder
½ teaspoon garlic salt
¼ teaspoon cayenne pepper
¼ teaspoon powdered ginger

¼ teaspoon ground cinnamon
2 tablespoons olive oil
2 cups whole shelled almonds
    or pecans
1 tablespoon Kosher salt
Extra garlic salt, if desired

In a small bowl, mix the dry spices. Set aside. Heat the oil in a non-stick skillet over low heat. Add spice mixture and stir well. Continue cooking over low heat for 3 to 4 minutes to mellow the flavors. Place the nuts in a bowl. Scrape the spice mixture onto the nuts and toss well. Spread the nuts in one layer on a baking sheet. Bake for 15 minutes, shaking the pan once or twice. Remove from oven. With a rubber spatula, toss nuts with any spices and oil on bottom of the pan. If desired, sprinkle with coarse salt and a bit more garlic salt. Let rest for 2 hours to cool.

SUGARED AND SPICED NUTS

If you can't keep your hands out of the nut bowl, you won't stand a chance with these.

3 cups pecan or walnut halves, or half of each	1 tablespoon cinnamon
	½ teaspoon ground cloves
1 cup sugar	½ teaspoon salt
⅓ cup water	1½ teaspoons vanilla

Spread the nuts on a greased cookie sheet. Bake in a 275 degree oven for 10 minutes. In a medium saucepan, combine the sugar, water, cinnamon, cloves and salt. Bring to a boil; cook 2 minutes, stirring occasionally. Remove from heat; stir in vanilla and nuts. Using a slotted spoon, place nuts on foil or waxed paper. Separate with a fork; let dry. Store in an airtight container in a cool, dry place.

CRUNCHY TOPPING MIX

This mix is not only great when the munchies strike, but also makes a good substitute for croutons in a salad.

1 (6-ounce) package tiny fish-shaped Cheddar cheese crackers	1 tablespoon grated Parmesan cheese
	½ teaspoon Italian seasoning
2 cups oyster crackers	¼ teaspoon garlic powder
1 cup chow mein noodles	½ teaspoon Worcestershire sauce
½ cup oil	

Spread the crackers and noodles in a single layer in an ungreased jelly roll pan. In a small bowl, combine the oil, cheese, Italian seasoning, garlic powder and Worcestershire sauce. Blend well and pour over the crackers and noodles; stir to coat. Bake at 325 degrees for 10 to 15 minutes, stirring once. Cool completely before storing in an airtight container.

CRUNCHY PARTY MIX

A wonderful blend of everyone's favorite snacks.

6 tablespoons butter	¼ teaspoon hot pepper sauce
1 tablespoon Worcestershire sauce	6 cups air-popped popcorn
1 teaspoon chili powder	2 cups thin pretzel sticks
½ teaspoon garlic salt	2 cups bite-size rice cereal
½ teaspoon salt	1 cup small cheese crackers
	½ cup salted peanuts

In a small saucepan, melt the butter. Stir in the seasonings and keep warm. In a large bowl, combine the remaining ingredients. Pour the butter mixture over the popcorn mixture and stir gently to coat. Spread in a large roasting pan and bake in a 300 degree oven for 1 hour, stirring every 15 minutes.

TLC Tip: If you like, and I often do, you can toss the warm mixture with ⅓ to ½ cup grated Parmesan cheese after you take it out of the oven. Um-m, good!

JEAN'S CHRISTMAS PUNCH

My cousin, Jean Tufts, is the most delightful lady! We have had so many fun experiences through the years, everything from spending part of our summer vacation together to sharing some college years. She was a "city girl" while I grew up in the country, so we had a lot to teach each other. We share a love of shoes and shopping, and she has a wonderful sense of humor. She never ceases to bring a smile to my face each time I see her. She told me that this recipe was born out of a desire to serve something different when entertaining one Christmas.

1 cup liquid piña colada mix	1 quart ginger ale
1 (46-ounce) can pineapple juice	1 quart pineapple sherbet

Combine the piña colada mix and pineapple juice. Add the ginger ale. Spoon sherbet into punch bowl, and pour the punch mixture over. Stir gently to mix slightly. This would be pretty garnished with maraschino cherries and fresh mint leaves.

TLC Tip: You can also serve this by the glass if you wish. Just spoon some sherbet into a tall glass, fill about half full of colada/juice mixture and fill to the top with ginger ale. Stir gently to mix. Garnish with a pineapple cube and cherry on a pick.

SWIMMING

In spite of all the wonderful things that growing up on the farm provided us with, swimming was not one of them. I guess we kids always felt a little cheated because on those gloriously warm Michigan summer days, we couldn't go to the lake—take your pick, we lived within a stone's throw of several. Dad took the saying "make hay while the sun shines" literally, and going swimming in the rain never really appealed to us. The next best thing was Mom's wash tubs—the forerunner of the plastic wading pool! We would select the sunniest part of the yard, drag out the tubs (one was always square), fill them with water, and then drive Mom crazy asking her if the water was warm enough yet. The size of the tubs certainly didn't limit us to the fun we had. We would run and jump into the water, sit in the tubs with our bottoms submerged and our feet and legs hanging over the side, dunk our heads and hold our breath. Finally there would be more water out of the tubs than in them, mom would bring out the towels and say we had had enough. We would wrap the towels around us and run shivering into the house.

SPARKLING LEMONADE

After our "backyard swim" our thirst was usually at a peak. Mom would often serve lemonade, made with freshly-squeezed lemon juice and our good well water. This Sparkling Lemonade will satisfy your backyard swimmers or barbeque guests admirably. Perch a lemon slice on the edge of each glass as an added touch.

1 (12-ounce) can frozen lemonade concentrate, thawed
1 (12-ounce) can frozen pink lemonade concentrate, thawed
1 (2-liter) bottle lemon-lime sparkling water, chilled
1 (1-liter) bottle ginger ale, chilled
1 large bottle sparkling cider, chilled
1 large bottle club soda, chilled

Mix all ingredients in a large bowl or beverage container. Add ice cubes and lemon slices if desired. Makes 22 (½ cup) servings.

TEA SYRUP

My sister, Ruth, is a natural at entertaining with flair and grace. I attended a reception she hosted for a college graduate where she served iced tea in the punch bowl, with lemon slices floating on the top! What a clever idea. This is her recipe for Tea Syrup. If you are going to prepare enough tea for a punch bowl, and you like your iced tea sweetened, this is a nice way to do it. The syrup can be stored for several days in the refrigerator.

1 cup loose tea leaves	**4 cups sugar**
4 cups plus 1 cup water	

Put 1 cup tea leaves and 4 cups water in a medium saucepan. Bring to a boil, remove from heat and let set for 20 minutes. Put the sugar in a large container, preferably glass. Strain the tea over the sugar. Add the remaining cup of water to the leaves, stir around a bit, and strain into the sugar and tea mixture. Stir to dissolve. To make tea, stir 1 cup tea syrup into 4 cups water.

AUNT MÁCO'S LUSCIOUS PUNCH

My Aunt Máco and Uncle Harve lived in Pryor, Oklahoma, the town where my mother grew up. Occasionally they would make the trip to Michigan to visit us on the farm. I can still remember how we watched the driveway for their arrival. Aunt Máco always sent the neatest presents. One year she sent my sister and me red velvet Christmas dresses. Alas, mine didn't fit!! Oh, well. Aunt Máco loved to hostess, and her Luscious Punch graced many a reception table.

1 (6-ounce) can frozen lemonade concentrate	**1 (46-ounce) can pineapple juice**
1 (6-ounce) can frozen orange juice concentrate	**1 large bottle Collins mix**
	½ gallon pineapple sherbet

Combine the frozen juices with the pineapple juice in a large punch bowl. Add the sherbet by large spoonfuls. Stir in the Collins mix. Ladle into punch cups to serve.

TLC Tip: *For an added touch, spear mandarin orange slices and pineapple cubes on a cocktail pick. Place in each cup, pour punch over.*

RUBY PUNCH

This punch is a favorite whenever and wherever it is served. Simple to put together, the ingredients can easily be kept on hand. The vibrant color makes it a natural for the holiday season. Cleo was principal at Airport Elementary for nine years. One unusually warm December evening we entertained his staff. This punch was so popular, I had to send the kids to get more ingredients.

1 cup grenadine syrup
2 cups water
1 (12-ounce) can frozen pink
   lemonade concentrate,
   undiluted

2 (28-ounce) bottles black
   cherry soda

Stir the grenadine into the water in a large punch bowl. Add the lemonade concentrate. Stir in the black cherry soda. Add ice cubes or an ice ring. Makes about 25 punch cup servings.

TLC Tip: Occasionally I have a difficult time finding the large bottles of black cherry soda. Not to worry, just use an equivalent amount of canned soda.

FRUIT SMOOTHIE

A breakfast in a glass, this drink will get you going in a hurry. Just add a muffin or a slice of toast and you're on your way.

1 cup skim milk
1 cup fresh or frozen
   unsweetened
   strawberries
½ cup pineapple chunks,
   fresh or unsweetened
   canned, drained

½ cup plain lowfat yogurt
¼ cup instant nonfat dry milk
1 teaspoon granulated sugar
½ teaspoon vanilla
4 ice cubes (You can omit
   these if you use frozen
   strawberries.)

Place all ingredients in a blender and purée until thick and smooth. Pour into glasses for two lucky people.

KAY SHAW'S PINK PUNCH

Kay has catered many a party, shower, wedding and dinner here in Big Spring, and I suppose her Pink Punch has made an appearance at many of those, including our daughter, Deanna, and David's wedding reception. It makes a large quantity, the base can be made ahead, and it tastes so refreshing with a variety of food. She graciously shares it with us.

3 cups plus 2 cups water
1 cup sugar
1 (3-ounce) package raspberry
    gelatin
1 (46-ounce) can pineapple
    juice
2 (12-ounce) cans lemonade
    concentrate, undiluted
1 (6-ounce) can orange juice
    concentrate, diluted as
    directed
Cranberry juice for color,
    up to 1 quart
1 small bag of crushed ice
1 large bottle (1 liter) ginger
    ale

Boil the 3 cups water and sugar together to make a simple syrup. Remove from heat and add the gelatin. Stir until dissolved. Add the 2 cups cold water and the juices. Chill. One hour before serving, pour the bag of crushed ice into the punch bowl; add the punch. At serving time, add the ginger ale. Stir gently before serving.

TLC Tip: *Kay always made beautiful ice rings to garnish her punch. I don't know how she did hers, but this is how I do mine.*

Pour a small amount of distilled water into a ring mold. Lay one layer of fruit in the bottom of the mold, remembering that the bottom will be the top. (It doesn't necessarily have to be that way—just give it some thought.) Place the mold in the freezer and let freeze solid. Remove from freezer, and put on some more fruit, then a little more water. Return to freezer to anchor that layer. Repeat process until mold is full. Cover with foil and hold in freezer until serving time. To unmold, dip very briefly in hot water. I find it easier, and safer, to place the ice ring in the punch bowl before adding the punch. You can use just about any type of fruit, but orange, lemon and lime slices are nice, along with clusters of grapes, red or green. Mint leaves add a nice touch, pieces of pineapple would work also. Be creative, and devise your own masterpiece.

LAURA HORN'S FROZEN FRUIT PUNCH

My friend, Laura, is from Fort Worth. She adds a special touch to every-thing she does, and you should see her house!! Right out of Country Living. This punch is absolutely delicious, and keeps well in the freezer, allowing you time to attend to all those last minute details of your open house or party. This was the punch we served at our daughter, Cyndee, and Darell's wedding reception.

4 cups sugar
6 cups water
5 bananas
1 (46-ounce) can pineapple
juice

1 (6-ounce) can frozen
lemonade concentrate,
diluted
1 (6-ounce) can orange juice
concentrate, diluted
2 to 3 liters chilled ginger ale

In a medium saucepan, combine the sugar and water. Bring to boiling, stirring until sugar is dissolved. Boil gently, uncovered, for 3 minutes; remove from heat and cool. In a blender container, combine the bananas and part of the pineapple juice. (You may have to do this in 2 steps.) Cover and blend until smooth. Pour the mixture into a large container. Stir in the cooled syrup, the remaining pineapple juice, the orange juice and lemonade. Stir to mix well. Pour into large containers (clean, empty milk cartons work well here) and freeze. To serve, remove from freezer 2 hours ahead of serving. Peel off milk cartons, place in punch bowl. At serving time, add the ginger ale. Stir gently to combine.

TLC Tip: *If you freeze the base in something other than milk cartons, be sure the container has a top wide enough to allow you to use a large metal spoon to scoop the frozen mixture into the punch bowl. If you have frozen it in a gallon water jug, you're on your own!*

PEPPERMINT EGGNOG PUNCH

A different eggnog drink for your holiday entertaining. Niece Cynthia and her husband Shane toasted their marriage with this one.

1 quart peppermint ice cream
1 quart commercial dairy
eggnog

4 (12-ounce) cans ginger ale,
chilled

Spoon the ice cream into a punch bowl. Add the eggnog and stir to combine. Pour in the ginger ale and stir gently. This should make about 4½ quarts.

TLC Tip: *When serving small groups, it's fun to garnish each cup with a peppermint stick.*

CELEBRATION PUNCH

We celebrated Cleo's mother's 80th birthday with this cooling beverage.

3 cups apricot nectar
3 cups pineapple juice
4 cups orange juice

4 cups 7-Up
4 cups ginger ale

Combine all the juices in a punch bowl and stir. Add some ice cubes or an ice ring. Gently mix in the sodas.

YVONNE'S ALMOND TEA

Often served when Yvonne Ivy hosts the 1970 Hyperion Club, this refreshing tea always gets rave reviews. Try it for your next get-together.

2 cups sugar
4 cups water
Juice of 4 lemons (about ¾ cup)

1 cup strong tea (use 6 to 8 tea bags)
1 tablespoon vanilla
1 tablespoon almond extract
1 to 2 quarts ginger ale

Combine sugar, water and lemon juice in saucepan. Place over low heat, bring to a boil and boil for 3 minutes. Cool. Stir in the flavorings. When ready to serve, add the ginger ale.

LIME PUNCH

A pretty citrus punch perfect for any celebration.

2 cups boiling water
2 (3-ounce) packages lime flavor gelatin
¾ cup sugar
1 (6-ounce) can frozen orange juice concentrate
1 (6-ounce) can frozen lemonade concentrate

5½ cups cold water
2½ cups pineapple juice, chilled
2½ cups grapefruit juice, chilled
1 (28-ounce) bottle (3½ cups) ginger ale, chilled

In a medium saucepan, bring water to a boil; remove from heat. Add gelatin and sugar, stirring until dissolved. Pour into a 5-quart non-metal container. Stir in the orange juice and lemonade concentrates, cold water, pineapple juice and grapefruit juice; refrigerate. Just before serving, gently stir in the ginger ale. This will make 36 (½ cup) servings.

SHIRLEY'S HOT GRAPE PUNCH

Shirley Beauchamp has worked for Cleo for many years, first as a PE aide, then as a library aide, finally as a secretary while he was a principal. She became his administrative assistant in 1981 when he started StarCom, an electronics distribution company. Besides all that, she has been a good friend. This punch is a nice change from spiced cider. I think you'll like it.

10 cups boiling water
1½ tablespoons loose tea
1 teaspoon allspice
2 cups grape juice

4 lemons, juiced (about ½ cup juice)
2 oranges, juiced (about 1 cup juice)
¾ cup sugar

Pour the boiling water over the tea and allspice. Steep for 5 minutes. Strain into a large pan and add the juices and sugar. Heat until steaming hot. Serve in mugs.

TLC Tip: *This punch can also be served cold.*

DEE'S FAVORITE COCOA MIX

Daughter Deanna keeps this on hand for those times she needs a comforting cup of hot cocoa. She also gives it as gifts, placed in a plastic freezer bag and covered with a fabric bag tied with cord or ribbon. Including a special mug and a small bag of marshmallows is a nice touch.

5 cups (3-quart package) instant nonfat dry milk
1¼ cups instant cocoa mix

¾ cup non-dairy powdered creamer (try to find one that doesn't contain palm or coconut oil)
⅓ cup powdered sugar
Dash of salt

In a large bowl, combine all ingredients; mix well. Store in a tightly covered container. For each serving, place 3 to 4 tablespoonfuls of mix in each cup; fill with 1 cup boiling water and stir well. This makes about 7 cups of mix.

44

HOLIDAY WASSAIL

This is a good beverage to serve while trimming the tree or after caroling or while watching the Christmas specials on TV. With a pot of this simmering on the back burner, the house will smell wonderful.

2 quarts apple juice
2 cups orange juice
1 cup lemon juice
18 ounces pineapple juice
  (3 of those little cans
  will do it)

1 stick cinnamon
1 teaspoon whole cloves
¼ to ½ cup sugar

Place all ingredients in a large saucepan and bring to a boil over medium-high heat. Reduce heat, partially cover pot, and simmer 1 hour. Serve hot.

SPICED CRANBERRY PUNCH

Fragrant with spices, tangy with citrus and colorful with cranberry, what more could you ask from a punch? The fact that it can be served hot or cold makes it versatile as well.

1 cup sugar
4 cups water
12 whole cloves
4 (3") cinnamon sticks
2 tablespoons minced ginger
  root

8 cups cranberry-apple juice
  cocktail
2 cups orange juice
1 cup fresh lemon juice

In a large saucepan, combine the sugar, water, cloves, cinnamon sticks and ginger; mix until sugar dissolves. Bring to boiling; simmer 10 minutes. Remove from heat, cover, let stand 1 hour. Strain into a large serving container. Stir in the cranberry cocktail, and juices. Serve hot, or chill to serve cold. If you serve this cold, you might like to add 1 quart ginger ale at serving time.

TLC Tip: *I am especially fond of this served hot. Served in clear glass cups or mugs, it looks pretty garnished with a cranberry and a small wedge of lemon speared on a pick.*

SPICED RUSSIAN TEA

The Christmas after Cleo and I were married, we piled the four kids into the car and joined our friends, the Max and Jean McAdams family, on a trip to Ruidoso, New Mexico. We all stayed in a huge cabin nestled in the woods near the river that runs through town. We spent our days sledding, trying on skis (we didn't really ski), browsing the quaint shops and investigating the area. While we were there, the lady who owned the cabins invited Jean and me for Spiced Russian Tea. I doubt that any Russians ever drank this tea, but we loved it then and still do.

4 cups water, divided use	**Juice of 4 large oranges**
2 cups sugar	**Juice of 4 lemons**
2 teaspoons whole cloves	**1 quart strong tea**
1½ sticks cinnamon	

Boil 2 cups of water and the sugar together to make a thin syrup. Bring the remaining 2 cups of water and the spices to a boil and simmer for 5 minutes. Strain into the sugar syrup. Add the juices and the tea. Heat and serve steaming hot, with a cinnamon stick stirrer perhaps?

TLC Tip: *I really don't recommend using frozen orange juice or bottled lemon juice in this recipe.*

MOCK SANGRÍA

Add some sparkle to your next Mexican meal with this fruity grape beverage.

1 quart grape juice, chilled	**Slices of fruit, such as**
1 quart club soda, chilled	**oranges, lemons or**
	nectarines

In a large pitcher, combine the grape juice and club soda. Add ice cubes, if desired, and slices of fruit. Olé.

TLC Tip: *You may use purple, red or white grape juice for this beverage; personally I like either red or white—it seems to show off the fruit better.*

Breads, Spreads and Breakfasts

The bread I experienced as a child was hearty and rough, made from freshly-ground wheat flour, and prepared by hand. I can still remember when my mother got a bread mixer—a large contraption that fit in a bucket-type container. You turned the handle on top, which kneaded the bread. This was a definite help to someone who made several loaves at one time. As a child, I used to wish I had sandwiches made from "city bread". Funny how our tastes change. Muffins were common—we called them Graham Gems. The many and varied kinds we know today were not a part of our menus. Cornbread was served often. In fact, that is one of the first things my grandmother taught me to bake. I use the same recipe today, and it is one of the few I have committed to memory. The only special bread I remember mother making was Date Nut, which she made around the holidays.

We always ate breakfast when I was growing up. Mother usually cooked cereal, often wheat similar to Ralston, but sometimes we had oatmeal. We kids were influenced by commercials even then and begged for Cocoa Wheats—a cereal similar to chocolate cream of wheat. I'm sure we ate some eggs, usually poached, but I don't remember having what you would call large farm breakfasts. As dry cereal came on the market, it was included in our breakfast menus. Dad was a fan of corn flakes. We had waffles occasionally with real maple syrup made from the sap from our own maple trees. We had a large grove of maple trees that dad would tap when it began to warm up, sometime in March. Little buckets hung on the tap to catch the clear, sweet liquid. The pails would be emptied into enormous flat pans that rested on an open fire. The sap was boiled for hours until it became thick and golden. What a way to crown a waffle! Pancakes were often made with cornmeal.

JENNIE BRINK'S GRAHAM GEMS

Jennie Brink was the Junior Class Sunday School teacher when I was a child attending the First Church of God in Allegan, Michigan. Miss Brink was a dedicated teacher. My brother says we gave her a hard time. I don't know about this "we" business—it must have been him, I don't think I ever gave her a hard time!! This is her recipe for whole wheat muffins. The original recipe called for more salt and sugar than I have listed, and also used melted lard instead of oil. I think whole wheat pastry flour gives a lighter, more tender muffin, but try it either way.

2 cups whole wheat flour	1 cup buttermilk
½ teaspoon salt	1 teaspoon soda
⅓ cup sugar	2 tablespoons canola oil
1 egg	1 tablespoon molasses

Measure the flour, salt and sugar onto a square of waxed paper. Whisk the egg in a large bowl. Mix the soda into the buttermilk, and add to the egg along with the oil and molasses. Blend well. Add the dry ingredients all at once. Stir only until combined. Pour into muffin cups that have been greased on the bottom only, filling each cup ¾ full. Bake at 400 degrees for 20 minutes. This recipe will make 10 to 12 muffins depending on size.

TLC Tip: *I really like this muffin. It is hearty, not overly sweet, and very good to serve with a soup or stew. If you are feeling adventurous, you might want to add some raisins or chopped nuts to the batter before spooning into the muffin cups.*

HONEY BRAN MUFFINS

The bran muffins from my childhood were straight off the Kellogg's All Bran box. That still isn't a bad idea—my mouth waters when I think about them. This version uses honey instead of sugar—now you have a choice.

1½ cups whole bran cereal	1¼ cups flour
(not flakes)	1 tablespoon baking powder
1¼ cups milk	½ teaspoon salt
1 egg, slightly beaten	1 cup raisins or chopped
½ cup honey	dates, optional but
⅓ cup butter, melted	worth it

Mix the cereal and milk in a small bowl; let stand 5 minutes. Stir in the egg, honey and butter. Combine flour, baking powder, salt and fruit, if using. Stir into the bran mixture just until blended. Fill greased muffin cups ⅔ full. Bake in a 400 degree oven until toothpick inserted in center comes out clean—15 to 20 minutes. Will make 10 to 12 muffins, depending on size.

PRUNE WHEAT MUFFINS

These muffins are so easy to make in the food processor, so there is absolutely no excuse for not serving a good, hot bread for breakfast often.

1 cup flour	½ cup pitted prunes
¾ cup whole wheat flour	2 eggs
⅓ cup packed brown sugar	¾ cup milk
1 tablespoon baking powder	⅓ cup cooking oil
¼ teaspoon salt	

Combine flours, brown sugar, baking powder and salt; set aside. Into a food processor fitted with the steel blade, add the prunes and eggs. Cover; process with 2 or 3 on-off turns or until prunes are coarsely chopped. Add the flour mixture. Combine milk and cooking oil. With processor motor running, quickly add the milk mixture through feed tube. Process until ingredients are just combined. Do not overmix. Grease 12 muffin cups; fill ⅔ full. Bake in a 400 degree oven for 15 to 20 minutes. Remove from pan and cool slightly on a wire rack.

TLC Tip: *If you don't have a food processor, combine the dry ingredients in a large bowl. Snip the prunes into small pieces and toss with the dry ingredients. Beat the eggs in a small bowl and combine with the milk and oil. Pour the wet ingredients into the dry ingredients, stirring just until mixed. Bake as directed above.*

BEST BANANA MUFFINS

There is no doubt about it—these are THE BEST banana muffins. When you read the list of ingredients, you'll know why. Though you may not want to prepare these on a regular basis, do fix them for that special breakfast or brunch. They are worth the splurge.

2 cups flour	2 eggs
½ cup sugar	½ cup milk
½ cup chopped nuts	½ cup butter, melted
1 tablespoon baking powder	(don't substitute)
½ teaspoon nutmeg	Toasted wheat germ
½ teaspoon salt	for garnish
1 large banana, diced	

Mix the flour, sugar, nuts, baking powder, nutmeg and salt. Add the banana; toss to coat. In a small bowl, beat the eggs with a fork; beat in the milk and butter. Add to the flour mixture; stir just until blended. Fill greased muffin cups ⅔ full. Sprinkle tops with wheat germ. Bake in a 400 degree oven until toothpick inserted in center comes out clean, about 20 minutes.

APRICOT SUNBURST MUFFINS

These muffins are chock full of wonderful flavors and other good things. Enjoy to your heart's content.

1 cup flour	¼ cup honey
1 cup whole wheat flour	¼ cup canola oil
1½ teaspoons baking soda	1 egg
1 teaspoon grated orange peel	½ cup chopped dried apricots
¼ teaspoon salt	1 tablespoon unsalted
1 cup plain lowfat yogurt	sunflower nuts
¼ cup orange juice	

In a large bowl, combine dry ingredients and orange peel. In a small bowl, combine yogurt, juice, honey, oil and egg; beat well. Stir in apricots. Add to dry ingredients, stirring just until moistened. Divide mixture into 12 greased muffin cups. Sprinkle the tops with the sunflower nuts. Bake at 375 degrees for 20 minutes.

TLC Tip: *You may substitute ¼ cup melted butter for the oil if you wish. The flavor is wonderful, but usually good sense prevails, and I use the oil.*

OATMEAL RAISIN MUFFINS

A slightly fancier version of oatmeal muffins, with the addition of raisins and a crumb topping.

1 cup quick oats	1 cup flour
½ cup raisins	3 teaspoons baking powder
¾ cup milk	1 teaspoon salt
½ cup cooking oil	½ teaspoon cinnamon
⅓ cup brown sugar, packed	¼ teaspoon nutmeg
1 egg, beaten	

Combine oatmeal, raisins, milk, oil, brown sugar and egg in a large mixing bowl; mix to blend. Stir together the flour, baking powder, salt, cinnamon and nutmeg. Add dry ingredients to oatmeal mixture, stirring just to moisten. Spoon batter into greased muffin cups. Sprinkle crumb mixture on top. Bake at 400 degrees for 20 minutes. Should make 10 to 12 muffins, depending on size.

Crumb Topping:

6 tablespoons flour	1½ teaspoons cinnamon
3 tablespoons packed brown sugar	3 tablespoons butter

Combine flour, brown sugar and cinnamon. Cut in the butter until crumbs form.

CHOCOLATE CHEESECAKE MUFFINS

Almost a dessert, these muffins probably are more suited to tea time than breakfast. But for those of you who are chocolate fans, go for it!!

6 ounces cream cheese, softened	1 teaspoon soda
¼ cup sugar	½ teaspoon salt
2 eggs, divided use	½ cup sugar
⅛ teaspoon salt	⅓ cup oil
¾ cup chocolate chips, divided use	1 teaspoon vanilla
	1 cup water
1½ cups flour	Powdered sugar

Combine the cream cheese, sugar, 1 egg and salt; beat until creamy. Stir in ¼ cup chocolate chips. Set aside. Melt ½ cup chocolate chips over simmering water, stirring until smooth. Remove from heat; cool slightly. In a small bowl, combine flour, soda and salt; set aside. In a large mixing bowl, combine sugar, oil, 1 egg and vanilla; beat well. Stir in chocolate. Beat in the flour mixture alternately with the water. Fill greased muffin cups ⅓ full. Spoon 1 tablespoon cream cheese filling over batter. Cover with remaining batter, filling each cup no more than ⅔ full. Bake in a 350 degree oven for 20 to 25 minutes. Cool slightly, remove from pans. Sprinkle with powdered sugar before serving.

CYNDEE'S OATMEAL MUFFINS

Daughter Cyndee is an elementary school teacher in Azle, Texas, so getting herself and the twins out of the house each morning doesn't leave much time for fancy morning meals. Come Saturday, however, breakfast is special, and these muffins are a favorite of her family. I love muffins, so these were a good addition to my file.

1 cup oatmeal	3 teaspoons baking powder
1 cup milk	½ teaspoon salt
1 cup flour	1 egg, well beaten
⅓ cup sugar	¼ cup oil

Combine oatmeal and milk in a large bowl. Let set to soften oatmeal. Combine flour, sugar, baking powder and salt on a square of waxed paper. Add egg and oil to the oatmeal mixture. Mix well. Stir in the flour mixture, mixing lightly and only until no dry ingredients are visible. Divide into 12 muffin cups that have been well greased. Bake at 425 degrees for about 20 minutes. Remove from pan immediately after baking. Cool on a wire rack or put directly into your napkin-lined bread basket to serve.

PUMPKIN STREUSEL MUFFINS

A wonderful muffin with a surprise center. These muffins don't even need a spread, but of course you can add one if you wish.

1 egg, beaten	3 teaspoons baking powder
½ cup milk	1 teaspoon cinnamon
½ cup canned pumpkin	½ teaspoon salt
⅓ cup oil	½ teaspoon nutmeg
1¾ cups flour	3 ounces cream cheese
½ cup sugar	

Combine the egg, milk, pumpkin and oil in a large bowl; mix well. Stir in the remaining ingredients except the cream cheese, mixing only until dry ingredients are moistened. Batter will be lumpy. Fill greased muffin cups about ½ full. Divide the cream cheese into 12 equal pieces. Place one piece in the center of each partially filled cup. Cover with the remaining batter to ¾ full. Sprinkle tops with topping and bake in a 400 degree oven for 15 to 20 minutes or until golden brown. Serve warm.

Streusel Topping:

¼ cup packed brown sugar	¼ cup finely chopped nuts
½ teaspoon cinnamon	1 tablespoon butter

Combine dry ingredients; cut in the butter to make crumbs.

SUPER CHEESE MUFFINS

The muffins I entered in the Allegan County Fair as a 4-H project were just plain muffins, probably much like these minus the cheese. Does anyone make a plain muffin anymore? I mean with white flour and no nuts, fruit, wheat germ, oat bran or oatmeal? I don't think so. These are the closest I come. These are savory with the addition of cheese and do wonders for a soup or salad meal.

2 cups flour	1 cup milk
2 tablespoons sugar	¼ cup butter, melted, or
2 teaspoons baking powder	canola oil, if you prefer
1 teaspoon salt	½ cup shredded, sharp
1 egg, beaten	Cheddar cheese

Combine the flour, sugar, baking powder, salt and cheese in a medium-size bowl. Make a "well" in the center of the dry ingredients. Combine the egg, milk, and melted butter or oil in a small bowl; add all at once to the flour mixture. Stir lightly just until liquid is absorbed. (Batter will be lumpy.) Spoon into 12 greased muffin cups, filling each ⅔ full. Bake in a 400 degree oven 25 minutes or until golden brown. Remove from pan and serve hot.

DEE'S FAVORITE BLUEBERRY MUFFINS

Deanna doesn't like her Blueberry Muffins fussed with, so don't try to add whole wheat flour or other strange ingredients. These are her favorite and they just might well turn out to be yours, too.

2 cups flour	1 cup milk
⅓ cup plus 1 tablespoon sugar	¼ cup butter, melted
3 teaspoons baking powder	1 cup dry-pack frozen
1 teaspoon salt	blueberries
1 egg, well beaten	1 teaspoon grated lemon peel

Combine flour, ⅓ cup sugar, baking powder and salt in a large bowl. Mix egg, milk and melted and cooled butter in a small bowl; add all at once to flour mixture. Stir lightly with a fork just until liquid is absorbed. (Batter will be lumpy.) Fold in the blueberries. Don't fret if the batter turns slightly blue. Spoon into greased muffin cups, filling each ⅔ full. Combine the 1 tablespoon sugar and lemon peel. Sprinkle on top of the muffin batter. Bake at 425 degrees for 20 minutes or until golden brown. Remove from pans and serve hot. This should make 12 medium-size muffins.

TLC Tip: Deanna says she never puts the lemon/sugar mixture on the top and they are still yummy.

MINI BRUNCH PUFFS

These little gems have been around for years—I know I started making them when I was first married. These delicate morsels are perfect for coffees or brunches.

⅓ cup soft shortening or	½ teaspoon salt
butter	¼ teaspoon nutmeg
1 cup sugar, divided use	½ cup milk
1 egg	⅓ cup melted butter
1½ cups flour	1 teaspoon cinnamon
1½ teaspoons baking powder	

Mix the shortening, ½ cup sugar and egg thoroughly. Measure flour, baking powder, salt and nutmeg onto waxed paper. Stir into shortening mixture alternately with the milk. Fill greased mini muffin cups ⅔ full. Bake at 350 degrees for 15 to 20 minutes. Immediately remove from pan and roll in the melted butter, then in a mixture of ½ cup sugar and cinnamon. Serve hot. Makes 36 puffs.

TLC Tip: These can be baked in regular-size muffin pans if desired—about 20 to 25 minutes.

CLOUD BISCUITS

Nothing dresses up a simple meal like hot bread. If you make these, you just might be able to get away with leftovers. This is one of my two favorite recipes for biscuits, I've made them many, many times, and have never been disappointed.

2 cups flour	½ cup shortening
1 tablespoon sugar	1 beaten egg
4 teaspoons baking powder	⅔ cup milk
½ teaspoon salt	

Combine dry ingredients in a large bowl; cut in the shortening with a pastry blender until mixture resembles coarse crumbs. Combine egg and milk; add to flour mixture all at once. Stir until dough follows fork around the bowl. Turn out onto a lightly floured surface; knead gently 20 times. Roll or pat dough to ¾" thickness. Cut with a 2" (or whatever size you prefer) cutter, pressing straight down. Don't twist the cutter, or your biscuits won't rise as high. Place close together on an ungreased baking sheet. Bake at 450 degrees for 10 to 14 minutes, until golden. If necessary, you can chill the unbaked biscuits 1 to 3 hours before baking. Cover with a cloth so they won't dry out. Cleo eats these with plenty of honey.

BISCUITS SUPREME

This is my other favorite biscuit recipe. Tall and flaky, these are worthy of your favorite spread or equally as good smothered with chicken a la king or creamed chipped beef.

2 cups flour	2 teaspoons sugar
4 teaspoons baking powder	½ cup shortening
½ teaspoon salt	⅔ cup milk
½ teaspoon cream of tartar	

Mix together the flour, baking powder, salt, cream of tartar and sugar in large bowl. Cut in the shortening until mixture resembles coarse crumbs. Add the milk all at once. Stir with a fork until dough follows the fork around the bowl. Turn out on lightly floured surface; knead gently ½ minute. Pat or roll ½" thick; cut with biscuit cutter. Place on an ungreased baking sheet, placing biscuits close together. Bake in a 450 degree oven for 10 to 12 minutes. Serve hot.

ONION PARSLEY BUTTERFINGERS

Like breadsticks without the yeast, these are so-o good with just about any meal—soup, pasta, salads.

2 cups buttermilk baking mix	**½ cup butter**
1 egg	**2 tablespoons onion flakes**
⅓ cup milk	**2 tablespoons parsley flakes**

Combine mix, egg and milk and beat vigorously 20 strokes. Turn dough out on lightly floured surface and knead lightly ½ minute. Roll or pat into a 9 x 13" rectangle. Heat the oven to 450 degrees. Place the butter in a 9 x 13" pan and melt in the hot oven. Cut the dough into 12 strips with a sharp knife or pizza cutter. Cut each strip in half. Place strips evenly atop butter in pan. Combine the onion and parsley and sprinkle over the strips. Bake in hot oven for about 8 minutes, until golden brown. Recut strips and serve hot to your delighted guests.

TLC Tip: *Mackie Bobo, cooking teacher in Lubbock, Texas, sprinkles her strips with a mixture of 1½ teaspoons Italian seasoning, ½ teaspoon paprika and ⅓ cup grated Parmesan cheese.*

BUTTER BISCUIT STICKS

My sister and I have made these since the beginning of our homemaking days. They never cease to impress.

¼ cup butter	**2 teaspoons baking powder**
1¼ cups flour	**1 teaspoon salt**
2 teaspoons sugar	**⅔ cup milk**

Heat the oven to 450 degrees and melt the butter in a 9 x 9" square pan. Remove pan from oven as soon as butter melts. Do not let it brown. In a large bowl, stir dry ingredients together. Add milk. Stir 30 strokes with a fork until dough clings together. Turn out on floured surface. Knead lightly about 10 times. Roll or pat to an 8" square, about ½" thick. With floured sharp knife, cut into strips 4" wide, then cut crosswise to make 18 sticks. Dip sticks in butter; place in 2 rows in pan. Bake for 15 to 20 minutes; serve hot.

TEA PARTY SCONES

Some of my favorite times are the tea parties I have with our twin grand-daughters, Kimberley and Rebekah Eastin. The goodies may vary—sometimes tiny sandwiches, brownies or even purchased cookies—as well as the attire and guest list. But we always serve hot tea with milk and party sugar, and use their treasured china tea cups. Sometimes we have these tasty scones with preserves and fake clotted cream.

2 cups flour	¼ cup butter, cut up
4 tablespoons sugar, divided use	⅔ cup buttermilk
	1 egg
2 teaspoons baking powder	1 tablespoon poppy seeds
½ teaspoon baking soda	½ teaspoon grated lemon rind
½ teaspoon salt	1 tablespoon lemon juice

Combine flour, 2 tablespoons sugar, baking powder, baking soda, poppy seeds and lemon rind in a large bowl. Cut in the butter with a pastry blender until mixture resembles coarse crumbs. Beat buttermilk and egg in a small bowl. Pour onto dry ingredients and stir with a fork until mixture comes together. On a lightly floured surface, knead the dough 5 or 6 times. Pat into an 8" circle on a lightly greased cookie sheet. Cut into 8 wedges with a long, sharp floured knife. Bake 14 to 16 minutes, until golden. Transfer to wire rack. Combine the remaining 2 tablespoons sugar with the lemon juice in a small bowl. Brush over the top of the warm scones. Serve warm.

TLC Tip: *You can also make round scones by patting dough ¾" thick, and cutting with a 1½" or 2" biscuit cutter. Bake and finish as above.*

Fake Clotted Cream:

In a chilled bowl, beat ½ cup whipping cream until soft peaks form, then add 2 tablespoons powdered sugar and continue beating until almost stiff. Fold in ½ cup sour cream.

AUNT MÁCO'S FEATHERBED ROLLS

*When I was a child, I thought this name was so cute. I remember these rolls just melting in my mouth. These are batter rolls so those of you who have a fear of kneading, or don't think you have the time to knead, can still surprise your family with yeast rolls—soft as a featherbed!! When my aunt died, I was given one of her cookbooks—*The Household Searchlight Cookbook *published in 1935. The only evidence that she had used the book was the many special recipes she had copied on the blank pages. What a treasure. This recipe was one of them.*

½ cup warm water
1 envelope active dry yeast
2 cups lukewarm milk
½ cup shortening (Aunt Máco
    said that part butter was
    good)

2 tablespoons sugar
2 teaspoons salt
5 cups flour

Dissolve the yeast in the warm water. When it has dissolved, add it to the warm milk. Cream the shortening in a large mixer bowl. Gradually add the sugar and salt. Stir in the flour alternately with the yeast/milk mixture, beating well after each addition. Continue beating until dough is smooth and well blended. Cover bowl with damp cloth and let rise in a warm place until double in bulk, about 1 hour. Stir the dough with a wooden spoon, and divide into greased muffin cups (about 30). Cover and let rise again until double in bulk, about 20 minutes this time. Bake in a 425 degree oven for 18 to 20 minutes. Remove from pans and serve warm.

TLC Tip: *If you have a heavy-duty mixer it takes a lot of the work out of mixing this bread. Even if your mixer isn't heavy-duty, you might use it to begin, then finish by hand.*

DEAN'S HONEY WHEAT BREAD

My cousin, Dean Yerden, lives in the Columbus, Ohio, area. He is a blond dynamo, electronics and computer whiz, tennis player, bread baker, and the ONLY person who gets by with calling me Tilly!! Dean is a consultant and works out of his home, so he likes to put this bread in the bread machine so the aroma greets his wife, Ginny, when she walks in the door from the office. We think this bread is wonderful. You will feel so nourished after you eat a slice.

1 cup warm water	**1½ cups bread flour**
5 tablespoons pure honey	**1½ teaspoons bread machine**
½ teaspoon salt	** yeast**
1½ cups whole wheat flour	**2 tablespoons wheat gluten**

Place the ingredients in your bread machine in the order directed by your manual. In mine, I place the liquids first, the dry ingredients next, and the yeast on top. If you use the timed cycle, be sure the yeast does not come in contact with the honey or salt. I always set my machine for light crust.

TLC Tip: This will be a short dense loaf, delicious eaten warm with honey, jam or jelly.
TLC Tip Two: Dean always uses the rapid bake cycle. I've made it both ways, and it turns out about the same.

MOM MIZELL'S HOT ROLLS

Ruth Mizell is the mother of my sister-in-law, Rita Jo. She lives in Bristow, Oklahoma. With this recipe in hand, you can serve rolls often, as they are so quick and easy to make. These rolls were served at niece Debbie's bridal luncheon.

½ cup shortening
6 tablespoons sugar, rounded
2 teaspoons salt
2 cups hot water

2 packages active dry yeast
½ cup warm water
2 eggs, slightly beaten
7 cups, or a little more, flour

Pour the hot water over the shortening, sugar and salt in a large bowl. Let cool to lukewarm. Soften the yeast in the warm water. Add to the shortening mixture with the beaten eggs. Stir in flour to make a soft dough. Let rise 1 hour. Punch down, spoon into greased muffin cups, cover and let rise again until double, about 1 hour. Bake in a 400 degree oven for 15-20 minutes.

MY MOTHER'S PARKERHOUSE ROLLS

These rolls were my mother's specialty. She made them for Sunday dinners when guests were expected, the New Year's Gathering, and entertaining visiting ministers. I can still remember the slightly salty taste of the tops that had been brushed with melted butter. They were light and tender and nearly melted in your mouth. Now that's a memory!!

½ cup shortening
1 cup milk, scalded
1 teaspoon salt
¼ cup sugar
2 packages active dry yeast

2 eggs, well beaten
5 cups flour (use bread flour
    if you have it)
4 tablespoons butter, melted

Add the shortening to the hot milk; then add the salt and sugar and stir until dissolved. Cool to lukewarm. Put the yeast into a large bowl. Add the lukewarm milk mixture gradually and stir until dissolved. Add the eggs and blend. Add flour, mixing well. Knead until smooth. Place in a greased bowl, cover, and let rise until double in bulk. Punch down, roll dough ½" thick, brush with melted butter, and cut with floured biscuit cutter. Crease with the dull edge of a knife a little to one side of center. Fold over and press together. Brush with butter. Place rolls 1" apart on a greased pan. Cover and let rise until light. Bake in a 425 degree oven for 20 to 25 minutes. Makes 2 dozen.

LONDA'S WHOLE WHEAT ROLLS

The flavor of these rolls is so good. I'll bet your guests will never guess the secret ingredient. Londa Henry prepared these for Deanna's bridal luncheon—I don't think there was a crumb left.

½ cup scalded milk
2 tablespoons oil
2 tablespoons plus 1 teaspoon
    honey
2 teaspoons vegetable salt (try
    your health food store for
    this if you can't find it on
    your supermarket shelf)

½ cup warm water
1 package active dry yeast
1 egg, beaten
2 cups whole wheat flour
2 tablespoons wheat germ
1 medium sweet potato,
    cooked, peeled and
    mashed

Combine the scalded milk, oil, honey and salt. Set aside to cool. Mix the yeast and warm water with 1 teaspoon honey. Let soften. Add the yeast mixture, flour, wheat germ and mashed sweet potato to the milk mixture. Mix well; turn out on heavily floured surface (use whole wheat flour). Knead five minutes, adding more flour as necessary, but try not to add too much. Let rise in warm place until double in bulk. Shape into rolls; let rise until almost double. Bake in a 400 degree oven for 20 minutes.

TLC Tip: *Cook the sweet potato in the microwave—no muss, no fuss.*

GARLIC HERB BREAD

This is by far my favorite garlic bread. The aroma is heavenly, and matches the taste. You can get this ready ahead of time and pop it in the oven 20 minutes before you sit down to eat. This is a natural with Italian main dishes, but also goes well with foods cooked on the grill or soup suppers.

1 large loaf French bread
½ cup butter, softened
1 teaspoon dried parsley
    flakes
½ teaspoon dried oregano,
    crushed

¼ teaspoon dried dillweed,
    crushed
1 clove garlic, crushed or
    finely minced
Freshly grated Parmesan
    cheese

Mix all the ingredients except the cheese and bread. Slice bread into thick slices. Spread each slice generously with butter mixture. Reassemble into loaf shape. Spread remainder of butter mixture over the top. Sprinkle generously with cheese. Place on a sheet of foil, and wrap halfway up loaf, leaving top exposed. Bake at 400 degrees for 20 minutes.

SWEDISH TEA RING

This is another of my "parent" recipes, this one from the mother of a student at Farrand School in Plymouth, Michigan. I can't even remember the lady's name, but I thank her every time I make this mouth-watering pastry—usually during the holidays. These make nice gifts, decorated with a vanilla glaze and red and green candied cherries.

1 package active dry yeast	1 cup butter, softened
¼ cup warm water	(this may seem like a lot
2¼ cups flour	of butter, but trust me,
2 tablespoons sugar	it's worth it)
1 teaspoon salt	¼ cup evaporated milk
	1 egg

Soften the yeast in the warm water; let set to dissolve. Stir together the flour, sugar and salt in a large bowl. Add the dissolved yeast. Beat in the butter; add the milk and egg. Roll into a ball, wrap in plastic wrap and chill overnight or at least 2 hours. When ready to finish, divide dough into 3 parts. Roll each part into a 12 x 6" rectangle on a lightly floured surface. Spread each with 2 tablespoons soft butter, 2½ tablespoons brown sugar and 2½ tablespoons chopped nuts. Roll up from the long side pressing the seam and ends to seal. Place on an ungreased cookie sheet, make slits along one edge and shape into a crescent shape. Cover lightly and let rise in a warm place 45 minutes. Bake in a 350 degree oven for 20-25 minutes. Frost while warm and decorate as desired.

Vanilla Glaze:

Melt 2 tablespoons butter. Add 1 cup powdered sugar, ½ teaspoon vanilla and 3-4 teaspoons milk. Blend well to a spreading consistency.

EASY AND ELEGANT KOLACHES

Another sweet treat that will look and taste like you spent hours in the kitchen.

2 (10-ounce) cans refrigerated flaky biscuits	2 tablespoons butter, softened
½ cup butter, melted	3 tablespoons flour
Canned pie filling, your choice	¼ cup sugar

Separate dough into 20 biscuits. Dip one side of biscuit into melted butter. Place butter-side-up on ungreased cookie sheet. Make a large deep thumbprint in center of each biscuit; fill with heaping teaspoonful pie filling. Combine remaining ingredients; mix well. Sprinkle mixture evenly on each roll. Bake at 375 degrees for 15 to 20 minutes or until golden brown. Serve warm.

NORWEGIAN HOLIDAY BREAD

This makes such a pretty loaf to share with family and friends. It is well worth the time and energy it takes to prepare it.

½ cup butter
½ cup milk
1 packet active dry yeast
½ cup warm water
¼ cup sugar
1 teaspoon salt
1 cup raisins

½ cup chopped candied
   cherries or mixed fruit
½ cup blanched slivered
   almonds
1 egg, slightly beaten
3½ to 4 cups flour

Heat the milk and butter in a small saucepan over low heat until butter melts. Cool to lukewarm. Soften the yeast in the warm water in a large mixing bowl. Stir in the sugar, salt, raisins, candied fruit, almonds and the egg and milk mixture. Add the flour gradually, mixing to form a stiff dough. Beat well after each addition. (If you have a heavy duty mixer with a dough hook, you have it made. Otherwise you will have to rely on your own muscle.) Cover bowl with plastic wrap and let rise in a warm place until doubled in size, about 1½ to 2 hours. Turn out on a floured surface. Toss lightly until coated with flour and not sticky. Shape as desired. I like to divide it into 3 parts, shape into round loaves and place in three well-greased (don't skimp here) 1-pound coffee cans. Or you can divide into 2 parts, shape into round loaves and place on a well greased cookie sheet. Either way, cover lightly and let rise again until doubled, about 1 hour. Bake in a 350 degree oven for 30 to 35 minutes. Remove from pans to a wire rack to cool. You can brush the tops with a little butter when you take them out of the oven if you wish.

TLC Tip: If I am giving these away, I like to make a very thick glaze and pour over the top, letting it drip down the sides—looks neat. A sprinkle of finely chopped candied fruit or cherries on the glaze really finishes it off nicely.

PAT'S CINNAMON ROLLS

Pat Anderson and I are charter members of the 1970 Hyperion Club. We have been friends for 25 years. I also had the privilege of teaching 3 of her 4 children. When she prepared these rolls for club meeting, we savored every bite!

1 package yellow cake mix	4 cups warm water
with pudding	Melted butter
4 packages dry yeast	1 cup sugar
6 to 8 cups flour, divided use	1 to 2 teaspoons cinnamon

In a large bowl, mix together the cake mix and yeast. Add 4 cups flour and stir together until blended. Stir in the water, and add 2 to 4 cups more flour. Let rise until doubled. Punch down; divide dough into four parts. Roll each part into a rectangle. Brush with melted butter. Combine the sugar and cinnamon. Sprinkle dough with ¼ of the sugar mixture. Roll up from the long side. Cut into 12 slices. Place in a greased 9 x 13" pan. Repeat rolling and cutting process with remaining 3 parts of the dough. Bake in a 350 degree oven for 15 to 20 minutes. Invert onto a cookie sheet while still warm. Frost with a powdered sugar glaze when cool, if desired.

CHOCOLATE CHIP PARTY ROLLS

These tasty rolls can almost double for a cookie and just might find their place at your next shower or party.

⅓ cup mini chocolate chips	1 (8-ounce) package
¼ cup granulated sugar	refrigerated crescent
½ teaspoon cinnamon	dinner rolls
	1 egg, beaten (optional)

In a small bowl, combine the chips, sugar, and cinnamon; set aside. Unroll the crescent dinner rolls. Separate into triangles. Sprinkle the morsel mixture evenly on each triangle. Press mixture into dough. Starting at shortest side of triangle, roll up dough. Place crescent point-side down on lightly greased cookie sheet. Brush with beaten egg, if desired. Bake at 375 degrees for 9-11 minutes. Serve warm. You won't like these—you'll love them!

TLC Tip: A sprinkle of powdered sugar might be a nice touch.
TLC Tip Two: Use any leftover sugar mixture to make cinnamon toast.

FRUIT AND CHEESE DANISH

These showy and delicious treats will impress your friends. Don't reveal how easy they are to put together!

1 tablespoon plus ½ cup sugar	1 (10-biscuit) can refrigerated
3 ounces cream cheese	flaky biscuits
¼ teaspoon cinnamon	¼ cup melted butter
	Jam or preserves, your choice

Blend the cream cheese and 1 tablespoon sugar. Mix together the ½ cup sugar and the cinnamon. Separate the biscuits and dip in melted butter, then in cinnamon/sugar mixture. Place on a greased cookie sheet. With thumb, make a 1½" indentation in each. Fill with rounded teaspoon of cream cheese mixture. Bake in a 375 degree oven for 15 to 20 minutes or until golden brown. Remove from pan immediately and top with your choice of jam or preserves. These are best served the day they are made.

AUNT LODEMA'S BUFFLE LOAF

When my aunt hosts overnight guests, she often delights them with this delicious coffee ring the next morning. She didn't reveal how this recipe got its name, but I think someone somewhere along the line hit the "f" instead of the "b" when they were typing it. What do you think?

1 cup butter, divided use	1 cup granulated sugar
½ cup brown sugar	1 teaspoon cinnamon
Pecan halves	18 to 24 frozen dinner rolls
Maraschino cherries, if	
desired	

Melt ½ cup butter and the brown sugar together in a small saucepan. Pour mixture into an ungreased 12-cup bundt pan. On top of this, place pecan halves and cherries. Set aside. In a small bowl, combine the remaining ½ cup sugar and the cinnamon. Melt the remaining ½ cup butter. Dip each of the frozen rolls in the melted butter and then in the cinnamon/sugar mixture. Place in the prepared pan. After all rolls have been dipped, mix together any remaining sugar and butter. Drizzle over the top of the rolls. Cover with a sheet of plastic wrap that has been sprayed with cooking oil spray. Let this set on the counter overnight. In the morning, bake in a preheated 350 degree oven for 20 to 25 minutes. Let set in pan about 20 minutes before turning out onto a plate.

TLC Tip: *My aunt says she often uses the lesser amount of rolls with good results.*

PECAN COFFEE RING

If you keep a couple of cans of refrigerated biscuits on hand, you can whip up this coffee ring on short notice. This is a nice addition to that morning coffee with your best friend or a brunch with special friends.

¾ cup packed brown sugar
2 tablespoons grated orange
   peel
1 cup chopped pecans

2 packages refrigerated
   biscuits, separated
⅓ cup butter, melted
2 tablespoons orange juice
1 cup powdered sugar

Mix the sugar, orange peel and nuts in a shallow dish. Dip the biscuits in the melted butter, then roll in sugar/nut mixture. Arrange the biscuits slightly overlapping in a greased 6-cup ring mold. Bake in a preheated 350 degree oven for 30 minutes or until lightly browned. Invert onto a serving plate; remove mold. In a small bowl, gradually mix the juice with the powdered sugar until smooth. Drizzle over the hot biscuit ring. Serve warm.

FRENCH APPLE COFFEE CAKE

I've found there are many occasions when a good coffee cake is appropriate—certainly it isn't restricted to the morning hours. This one has been used not only for coffees and such, but also for evening refreshments. Since apple is a popular fruit, I'm sure you will find a good time to serve it too.

¾ cup granulated sugar
¾ cup brown sugar, packed
⅔ cup buttermilk
2 eggs
2½ cups flour
2 teaspoons soda

2 teaspoons cinnamon
½ teaspoon salt
1 can French apple pie filling
Topping
½ cup melted butter

Mix the sugars, buttermilk, eggs, flour, baking soda, cinnamon and salt. Fold in the pie filling and spread in a greased 9 x 13" pan. Sprinkle the topping on the top. Bake at 350 degrees for 40 to 50 minutes. When cake is done, pour the melted butter over the hot cake.

Topping:
1¼ teaspoons cinnamon
¼ cup white sugar

¼ cup brown sugar, packed
½ cup chopped walnuts

Combine all ingredients in a small bowl.

TLC Tip: *If you have a hard time finding the French apple pie filling, just add ¼ cup raisins to a can of apple pie filling.*

CRUNCHY COFFEE KUCHEN

This is a very satisfying coffee cake that will please your friends and family. Try serving it with a scoop of vanilla or cinnamon ice cream for dessert.

1¾ cups flour	1 cup granola, divided use
2 teaspoons baking powder	2 eggs
½ teaspoon salt	⅔ cup evaporated milk
¼ teaspoon cinnamon	1 apple, peeled and sliced thin
⅛ teaspoon nutmeg	2 tablespoons granulated
⅔ cup packed brown sugar	sugar
½ cup butter, divided use	

Mix the flour with the baking powder, salt, cinnamon and nutmeg in a large bowl. Stir in the brown sugar. Cut in 6 tablespoons butter with pastry blender until mixture is crumbly. Measure out ½ cup, add ¼ cup granola and set aside. Combine the eggs and milk in another bowl. Add the flour mixture and mix just until flour is moistened. Stir in remaining granola. Pour into a greased 9" round cake pan. Arrange apple slices in overlapping pattern on top of dough. Sprinkle with reserved cereal/crumb mixture. Dot with remaining 2 tablespoons butter and sprinkle with the granulated sugar. Bake at 350 degrees for about 45 minutes or until cake tester inserted in center comes out clean. Cool 10 minutes; cut in wedges and serve warm.

BAKED DOUGHNUT TWISTS

Doughnuts have got to be about the unhealthiest thing on earth—all that sugar and fat. But they taste so good!! I was delighted to find a recipe that delivers the taste but leaves out much of the fat. These may win you over too.

2 cups biscuit mix	1 teaspoon grated orange peel
2 tablespoons + ½ cup sugar	Melted butter
1 teaspoon instant coffee	½ cup sugar
crystals	1 teaspoon cinnamon
¼ cup milk	¼ teaspoon nutmeg
1 beaten egg	

Combine the biscuit mix and the 2 tablespoons sugar; set aside. Dissolve the coffee crystals in the milk; add egg and orange peel. Add to the dry ingredients; stir just until moistened. Turn out onto a well-floured surface; knead gently 10 to 12 strokes. Roll to ½" thickness. Cut with floured doughnut cutter. Holding opposite sides of each doughnut, twist. Bake on ungreased baking sheet in a 400 degree oven for 10 to 12 minutes. Brush liberally (or lightly) with melted butter. Dip in mixture of ½ cup sugar and spices. Best served warm.

FRUIT SWIRL COFFEE CAKE

The ease with which this coffee cake goes together makes it a natural as your contribution for the next club bake sale. It is also perfect for brunches and breakfasts where a crowd is expected. I served it for a graduation brunch I hosted for my niece, Cynthia.

4 cups baking mix (like Bisquick)
½ cup sugar
¼ cup butter, melted
½ cup milk
1 teaspoon vanilla

1 teaspoon almond extract
3 eggs
1 can pie filling, your choice (I've used cherry, apple, blueberry and apricot)
Glaze

Combine all ingredients except pie filling and glaze. Beat vigorously for 30 seconds. Spread ⅔ of the batter in a greased jelly roll pan, 15 x 10". Spread pie filling over the batter. (The filling won't cover the batter completely.) Drop the remaining batter by spoonfuls onto the pie filling. Bake in a 350 degree oven for 20 to 25 minutes, until light brown. Drizzle with glaze while still warm.

Glaze:
1 cup powdered sugar   **1 to 2 tablespoons milk**

Beat powdered sugar and milk until smooth and of desired consistency.

TLC Tip: This can also be baked in two 9 x 9" square pans. Divide batter and filling accordingly.

RAISIN COFFEE CAKE

I found this recipe on the back of a calendar page years ago. It makes a large cake, and I've taken it to the teachers' lounge at school, committee meetings at church and served it at club meetings in my own home. It goes well with coffee and tea, and might even double as a light dessert. I hope you won't wait too long before you try this.

¾ cup butter, softened
1½ cups sugar
3 eggs
3 cups flour
2 teaspoons baking powder
1 teaspoon salt
1 teaspoon soda

1 cup buttermilk
1 tablespoon grated orange
   peel
Streusel mixture
1 cup dark or golden raisins,
   divided use
Orange glaze

Cream the butter and sugar together until light and fluffy. Add the eggs, one at a time, beating well after each addition. Measure the dry ingredients onto a square of waxed paper. Add them alternately with the buttermilk, mixing just until blended. Stir in the orange peel. Pour half of the batter into a greased and floured 10" tube pan. Sprinkle with half of the streusel mixture and ½ cup raisins. Top with the remaining batter and streusel mixture. Bake in a 350 degree oven for 50 to 60 minutes, or until a toothpick inserted in the center comes out clean. Top with orange glaze and sprinkle with the remaining ½ cup raisins. Serve warm.

Streusel Mixture:
½ cup brown sugar
⅓ cup flour

2 teaspoons cinnamon
¼ cup soft butter

Blend together until crumbly brown sugar, flour, cinnamon and butter.

Orange Glaze:
1 cup powdered sugar

2 tablespoons orange juice

Blend powdered sugar with orange juice until smooth.

BUTTERSCOTCH COFFEE RING

I got this recipe from Laura Furney, one of my sister's friends from Anderson, Indiana. I think Laura likes recipes about as much as I do. Though there are many variations of this floating around, this is the one of the best. I predict it will be one of your favorites, too.

1 package frozen dinner rolls	¾ cup brown sugar, packed
1 small box instant	¾ teaspoon cinnamon
butterscotch pudding	½ to 1 cup chopped pecans
½ cup butter, melted	

Before you go to bed, butter a 12-cup bundt pan. Sprinkle with some of the pecans. Layer the frozen rolls in the pan, filling pan about ½ full. Resist the urge to add more rolls—remember they are going to rise. Sprinkle with the pudding mix. Combine the melted butter with the brown sugar and cinnamon. Pour over the rolls. Sprinkle with more nuts. Cover loosely with plastic wrap that has been sprayed with cooking spray. Let set on the counter overnight. In the morning, bake in a 350 degree oven for 20 to 25 minutes. Immediately invert onto a plate. These are out-of-this-world when slightly warm, but I've never had any problem eating them when they get cold.

APPLESAUCE OATMEAL BREAD

Less sweet than some fruit breads, this hearty loaf is wonderful with a cup of herb tea. Plain or with your favorite spread, one slice just may not be enough!

1½ cups flour	2 eggs, well beaten
1 teaspoon baking powder	1 cup applesauce
1 teaspoon baking soda	¼ cup butter, melted
1 teaspoon salt	1½ cups rolled oats
1 teaspoon cinnamon	1 cup raisins
⅔ cup brown sugar	½ cup chopped nuts

Stir the dry ingredients together in a large mixing bowl. Add the brown sugar. Mix in the eggs, applesauce and butter; blend thoroughly. Stir in the oats, raisins and nuts. Turn into a greased 9 x 5" loaf pan. Bake at 350 degrees for 1 hour or until toothpick comes out clean. Remove from pan and cool on a wire rack.

CHOCOLATE ZUCCHINI BREAD

There's something about chocolate bread that seems a little crazy. But is it good!! Not quite a cake but more than just a bread, and so easy to slice and serve. This one is from my mother's files.

3 eggs
1¾ cups sugar
¾ cup oil
6 tablespoons cocoa
1 teaspoon vanilla
2 cups grated zucchini

3 cups flour
1 teaspoon salt
1 teaspoon cinnamon
¼ teaspoon baking powder
1 teaspoon soda
1 cup chopped almonds

Beat the eggs with the sugar in a large bowl. Stir in the oil, cocoa, vanilla and grated zucchini. Combine the dry ingredients on a square of waxed paper. Stir into the egg/oil mixture; mix thoroughly. Stir in the nuts. Pour into 2 greased 8 x 4" loaf pans. Bake at 350 degrees for 60 to 70 minutes. Let rest for 10 minutes, then remove from pans to wire rack to cool.

CHERRY NUT BREAD

My sister has so many talents! She does her own decorating, she looks fantastic in anything she wears, (I don't think she's tried a gunny sack, but I'm sure she would turn it into a fashion statement.), and she knows how to put a meal on the table quickly and with flair. This is one of her delicious recipes.

¾ cup sugar
½ cup butter
2 eggs
2 cups flour
1 teaspoon soda
½ teaspoon salt

1 cup buttermilk
1 cup chopped pecans
1 (10-ounce) jar maraschino
  cherries, drained and
  chopped
1 teaspoon vanilla

Cream the sugar, butter and eggs until light and fluffy. Stir the dry ingredients together on a square of waxed paper. Add to the creamed mixture along with the cherries, pecans and vanilla. Pour into a greased 9 x 5" loaf pan. Bake at 350 degrees for 55 to 60 minutes. Remove from pan to a wire rack to cool. Need I add that this is a very pretty bread, and looks wonderful on a tray of teatime goodies.

GRANDMA'S CORNBREAD

This is the cornbread my grandma taught me to bake, and I've been baking it ever since. I've been told it is Northern cornbread, as it is sweeter than the cornbread the South is famous for. This is one of the few recipes I have committed to memory. When grandma was baking this bread, she used melted lard or shortening or even bacon grease in the batter. These days we know better, so I use oil. My grandma and I baked this in a granite pan of a rather unusual size, but I find it works very nicely in my 10" cast iron skillet. This will also make 12 muffins or 16 corn sticks. I hope you enjoy it as much as I have all these years.

1 cup flour	⅓ cup sugar
1 cup yellow cornmeal (stone	1 teaspoon salt
ground makes a heartier	1 cup milk
cornbread)	1 egg
4 teaspoons baking powder	¼ cup oil

Combine the dry ingredients in a large mixing bowl. Make a "well" and stir in the milk, egg and oil. Mix thoroughly. Pour into a greased pan or muffin cups and bake at 400 degrees for about 20 minutes. This is probably best served hot—we liked the addition of honey or maple syrup, but served cold with milk and sugar, it brings back wonderful memories.

TLC Tip: Always one to economize with dishes and steps, I measure the milk in a 2-cup measure, add the ¼ cup oil in the same cup, drop in the egg, whisk a bit, then pour all into the flour mixture. Easy.

TLC Tip Two: When I use a cast iron skillet or corn stick pans, I grease the pan and place it in the oven to heat for 5 to 10 minutes. This insures a nice, crispy crust.

72

DOROTHY MASON'S HOBO BREAD

I have no idea how this bread got its name—maybe because it is baked in a coffee can or because of its rustic taste. Do save some 1-pound coffee cans or large vegetable cans to use for baking. The resulting round slices are pretty and different.

2 cups raisins	½ cup brown sugar
1½ cups boiling water	2 eggs
2 teaspoons soda	1 teaspoon salt
4 tablespoons soft butter	1 teaspoon vanilla
1½ cups granulated sugar	4 cups flour

In a large mixing bowl, pour the boiling water over the raisins and let cool. Add the remaining ingredients; mix thoroughly. Pour the batter into 3 well-greased (don't skimp) 1-pound coffee cans, filling each half full. Bake 45 to 60 minutes at 350 degrees. Remove from cans and cool on a wire rack.

BANANA WHEAT QUICK BREAD

I think the combination of ingredients in this banana bread makes it a real winner. I have been using this recipe for many years, with slight variations, always with good results.

1¼ cups flour	1½ cups (about 3 medium)
½ cup whole wheat flour	mashed or thinly sliced
1 cup sugar	bananas
1 teaspoon soda	2 tablespoons orange juice
1 teaspoon salt	1 egg
	¼ to ½ cup raisins

In a large mixer bowl, blend all ingredients. Beat 3 minutes at medium speed. Pour batter into greased 9 x 5" loaf pan. Bake 60 to 70 minutes or until toothpick inserted in center comes out clean. Remove from pan to cool on a wire rack. You can also bake in three 5 x 2½" pans or soup cans. Bake these 35 to 40 minutes.

TLC Tip: *If you aren't a raisin lover, you can omit them. When I do that, I usually add ¼ to ½ cup chopped nuts. There have been times when I was caught without orange juice, and substituted 2 tablespoons milk. The bread was fine, but I think the orange juice makes it a little more special.*

CRANBERRY CHEESE BREAD

Who would think, cranberries and cheese? A surprising combination, but a good one.

2½ cups flour
1 cup milk
½ cup granulated sugar
½ cup brown sugar
¼ cup butter or shortening
2 eggs
3 teaspoons baking powder
1 teaspoon salt
½ teaspoon baking soda

1 cup chopped nuts
1 cup chopped fresh or frozen
  cranberries
2 teaspoons grated orange
  peel
2 tablespoons orange juice
1 cup shredded sharp
  Cheddar cheese

Blend the flour, milk, sugars, butter, eggs, baking powder, salt, soda and nuts in a large mixer bowl on low speed for 15 seconds. Beat on medium speed 30 seconds, scraping bowl once or twice. Mix the cranberries, orange peel and juice. Add to the bread mixture along with the cheese. Pour into a greased 9 x 5" pan and bake at 350 degrees for 1 hour and 10 minutes. Remove from pan and cool completely on wire rack. For better slicing, refrigerate bread overnight, but who can resist the wonderful aroma of a freshly baked nut bread? Go ahead, use an electric knife, and treat yourself!

ZUCCHINI OATMEAL BREAD

Another good use for zucchini and oatmeal.

2 cups flour
1 cup uncooked quick oats
½ cup sugar
½ cup brown sugar, packed
1 teaspoon baking powder
1 teaspoon baking soda
¾ teaspoon ground cinnamon

½ teaspoon salt
3 large eggs
¾ cup salad oil
3 cups shredded zucchini
1 teaspoon vanilla
1 cup walnuts, chopped

In a large bowl, mix the flour, oats, sugars, baking powder, baking soda, cinnamon, and salt. In a medium bowl, beat the eggs slightly with a fork; stir in the salad oil, shredded zucchini, vanilla and walnuts; stir into the flour mixture just until flour is moistened. Spoon batter evenly into a greased 9 x 5" loaf pan. Bake bread 50 minutes or until toothpick inserted in center comes out clean. Cool bread in pan 10 minutes, then remove from pan and finish cooling on wire rack.

TLC Tip: *You can also bake this bread in two 4 x 8" loaf pans. Adjust the baking time accordingly.*

FIG AND HONEY LOAF

This bread dates back to my introduction to "healthy" foods. It is a hearty loaf, and full of nutrition, but good tasting too. Do try it with the Honey-Lemon Butter.

1 cup whole wheat flour	1 cup buttermilk
1¼ cups unbleached flour	1 tablespoon oil
1 teaspoon salt	2 eggs, well-beaten
¼ teaspoon baking soda	½ cup snipped dried figs
2 teaspoons baking powder	1 cup finely chopped walnuts
⅔ cup mild honey	

Combine the flours, salt, soda and baking powder in a large mixing bowl. In a smaller bowl, combine the honey, buttermilk, oil and beaten eggs. Add to the dry ingredients, mixing only until moistened. Fold in the figs and nuts. Spoon the batter into a greased 9 x 5" loaf pan. Bake at 350 degrees about 1 hour or until a toothpick inserted in the center comes out clean. Remove from pan and finish cooling on a wire rack.

HONEY-LEMON BUTTER

½ cup butter, softened	2 tablespoons fresh lemon
¼ cup mild honey	juice
	1 teaspoon grated lemon peel

In a small bowl, cream the butter until fluffy with a hand mixer or whisk. Continue creaming while adding the honey in a fine stream. Add lemon juice and sprinkle in the lemon peel, stirring until all ingredients are evenly blended. Chill until ready to serve.

TLC Tip: *To make this a truly "healthy" bread, use sea salt, raw buttermilk, farm eggs, and nonsulphured figs. Either way, your body will thank you for serving it this bread.*

RUTH'S PUMPKIN RAISIN NUT BREAD

If it comes from Ruth's kitchen, it's bound to be good! Great for those cool fall days with a cup of hot spiced cider.

1 cup oil	1½ teaspoons salt
4 eggs, beaten	1 teaspoon nutmeg
⅔ cup water	2 teaspoons cinnamon
1 (16-ounce) can (2 cups)	3 cups sugar
pumpkin	½ cup raisins
3⅓ cups flour	½ cup chopped nuts

Combine the oil, eggs, water and pumpkin in a small bowl. Stir together the flour, salt, nutmeg, soda, cinnamon and sugar in a large mixing bowl. Make a "well" in the center of the dry ingredients and add the pumpkin mixture. Blend only until dry ingredients are moistened. Add raisins and nuts. Pour into 3 greased and floured 8 x 4" loaf pans. Bake in a 350 degree oven for 1 hour. Remove from pans, and cool on a wire rack.

TLC Tip: *Though my sis says 3 pans, I usually bake the mixture in two. I find the loaves are taller. You can also bake this bread in 3 (1-pound) coffee cans. It will take about 1 hour and 20 minutes this way.*

CHERRY CHIP BREAD

What could be bad about a bread filled with chocolate chips and cherries? I think you'll love this combination.

2 cups flour	¾ cup water
1 cup sugar	1 egg, slightly beaten
1½ teaspoons baking powder	¾ cup dried tart red cherries
½ teaspoon soda	½ cup miniature chocolate
½ teaspoon salt	chips
¼ cup butter	

In a large bowl, combine flour, sugar, baking powder, soda and salt. Using a pastry blender, cut in the butter until particles are the size of coarse meal. Stir in the water and egg just until dry ingredients are moistened. Fold in the cherries and chocolate chips. Pour batter into a greased 9 x 5" loaf pan. Bake at 350 degrees for 50 to 60 minutes or until a toothpick inserted in center comes out clean. Cool upright in pan 10 minutes, then remove and cool on wire rack. Wrap tightly to store.

TLC Tip: *You may substitute ¾ cup chopped maraschino cherries, drained, for the dried cherries if you wish.*

GLORIA'S DATE BREAD

Another treasured recipe from my friend, Gloria South. I think the addition of coffee gives a full-bodied taste to this loaf.

1 cup sugar	1 teaspoon vanilla
1 tablespoon butter, softened	½ teaspoon salt
1 egg	1 cup chopped nuts
1½ cups flour	1 cup strong coffee
1 cup chopped dates	1 teaspoon baking soda

Cream the sugar, butter and egg. Add the flour, vanilla, salt and nuts. Mix the coffee, dates and baking soda together in a small bowl. Add to the creamed mixture. Blend well. Bake in a greased 8 x 4" loaf pan at 375 degrees for 60 to 75 minutes. Remove from pan to wire rack to cool.

ALMOND PUDDING LOAF

What a delicious and easy bread this is, so perfect for the holidays and sharing with the neighbors.

1⅓ cups toasted and finely chopped almonds, divided use	1 small package vanilla instant pudding, dry
2½ cups biscuit baking mix	⅔ cup milk
¼ cup sugar	¼ cup oil
	4 eggs

Generously grease four 4 x 6" loaf pans. Sprinkle with ⅓ cup of the almonds. Beat the remaining almonds with the rest of the ingredients in a large mixer bowl on low speed for 30 seconds; then beat on medium speed for 3 minutes, scraping the bowl occasionally. Pour into the prepared pans. Bake at 350 degrees for 50-55 minutes or until wooden pick inserted in center comes out clean. Immediately remove from pans; cool completely on wire rack. Spread with Creamy Glaze.

Creamy Glaze:

1 cup powdered sugar	1 to 2 tablespoons milk
1 teaspoon rum, almond or vanilla extract	

Combine all ingredients in a small bowl. Beat until smooth and of spreading consistency.

CRANBERRY OATMEAL BREAD

When the first cranberries of the season appear in the supermarket, treat yourself to this moist, quick bread. You'll probably like it so much, you'll want to keep some berries in the freezer so you can prepare it all year long.

1 cup quick rolled oats	2½ cups flour
1¼ cups hot water	2 teaspoons baking powder
¾ cup butter, softened	½ teaspoon baking soda
1¼ cups brown sugar	½ teaspoon salt
½ cup sour cream	1½ teaspoons cinnamon
2 tablespoons grated orange peel	1 cup chopped fresh cranberries
1 egg	½ cup chopped walnuts

In a small bowl, soak the oats in hot water for 5 minutes. In large bowl, cream the butter and brown sugar until fluffy. Add oat mixture, sour cream, orange peel and egg. Blend well. Measure the flour, baking powder, baking soda, salt and cinnamon onto a square of waxed paper. Add to creamed mixture; blend well. Fold in the cranberries and walnuts. Spoon mixture into two greased 8 x 4" loaf pans. Bake at 350 degrees for 55 to 65 minutes or until toothpick inserted in center comes out clean. Cool 15 minutes; remove from pans and cool completely on wire rack. Wrap tightly and store in the refrigerator.

90'S BUTTER

For years my mother-in-law has been combining butter with oil to use as a table spread. I never paid much attention until I started being more careful about putting fat into my body and even more important, the kind of fat. 90's Butter combines butter (for flavor) with the unsaturated fat of a good quality oil. The result is a spread that is as low in saturated fat as margarine, but without hydrogenation, processing, and additives. 90's Butter can be used at the table or in the sauté pan. Even though this is "better butter", that doesn't give one the license to use it with abandon. Spread thinly, and use only the smallest amount on vegetables or in cooking.

1 cup canola oil	1 cup (½ pound) butter

Use butter that is soft but not melted. Blend in the oil, a small amount at a time, until mixture is smooth. You can use a mixer, blender, spoon or, as I do, a wire whisk. Pour into small covered containers and keep refrigerated. You will be able to spread this right from the refrigerator, but the mixture will get soft and runny if left at room temperature too long.

TLC Tip: *90's Butter is not meant to be used for baking.*

YOGURT CHEESE

Yogurt cheese is a delightful and lowfat substitute for higher fat cream cheese. You can use it in recipes, or for dips and spreads. Just remember to start draining the yogurt 24 hours before you wish to use it.

Line a colander or large strainer with a double layer of cheesecloth or a couple of coffee filters. Spoon in the yogurt. Be sure that you use a yogurt that does not contain starch, gums or gelatin. You can find this type of yogurt at a health food store, or use Dannon from the supermarket. I use either nonfat or lowfat—the nonfat is quite tangy. Cover the bowl with plastic wrap and set in the refrigerator overnight. The yogurt will become thick as the liquid drains away. Transfer the cheese to a separate container, and discard the liquid. Use as desired. It will keep in the refrigerator for up to 1 week. Three cups of yogurt will make about 1 cup of cheese.

PEACH CONSERVE

My mother-in-law, Eula Carlile Phillips, grew up in the panhandle of Oklahoma. She loved "club work" in her younger years, and had a talent for taking care of elderly people. When Cleo's father became ill, we moved them close to us in Big Spring. After his death, she married C. D. Phillips. Eventually we moved them even closer—right next door. It has been especially nice to have her close since the death of Mr. P. in 1990. She's quite a lady! At 86 she still drives her car, crochets afghans, helps Cleo a little in the garden, is an active participant in her Sunday School class and plays a mean game of dominoes. She enjoys reading and pampering her little dog, Bebe. This colorful spread was a prize-winner for her at the Texas County Fair. She came away with a Blue Ribbon. We "younger people" aren't used to preparing jams and jellies this way, and I do think this method requires patience and a special touch. But the appearance and flavor is so incredible you might find it worth one of your summer afternoons.

25 peaches	2 lemons
1 (20-ounce) can crushed pineapple	10 red plums
	Pinch of salt
1 pound white grapes, halved and seeded	¾ cup sugar for each cup of fruit
3 oranges	4 ounces slivered almonds

Grind the peaches, oranges and lemons with rind, seeded grapes and plums. Add the salt. Measure the fruit and add ¾ cup sugar for each cup of fruit. Bring to a boil, reduce heat to low, and cook, stirring occasionally until consistency of jelly. Add the almonds. Fill jelly glasses and seal with paraffin.

ORANGE MARMALADE SPREAD

1 (8-ounce) package cream   ½ cup orange marmalade
   cheese, softened

In a small bowl, combine the cream cheese and marmalade; beat until smooth. Use as a spread for muffins or bread. This spread is also good on gingersnaps, purchased or homemade. If you can find those thin Swedish kind, all the better.

TLC Tip: You can substitute apricot jam for the orange marmalade for a different but equally delicious spread.

CRANBERRY STRAWBERRY JAM

The beautiful red color of this jam just shouts "Christmas", and the sweetness of the strawberries compliments the tartness of the cranberries.

1 pound fresh cranberries   5½ cups sugar
2 (10-ounce) packages frozen   ½ bottle liquid fruit pectin
   strawberries (the kind
   with sugar added)

Grind the cranberries (or chop finely in the food processor) and combine with the strawberries. Measure 4 cups into a large pan. Add the sugar and mix well. Bring to a rolling boil and boil for 5 minutes, stirring constantly. Remove from heat and add pectin. Skim off foam, then stir and skim by turns for 5 minutes to cool slightly and prevent floating fruit. Ladle into hot jars and seal at once. Store in the refrigerator.

APPLE CINNAMON JELLY

A cinnamon raisin bagel topped with cream cheese and this jelly is a wonderful way to start the day—or end it, for that matter. Stir up a batch of this jelly and share with a friend.

1 package powdered fruit   4 cups sugar
   pectin   1 to 2 tablespoons red
1 quart apple juice   cinnamon candies

In a large pot, dissolve the powdered fruit pectin in the apple juice and bring to a boil. Add the sugar and candies. Return to boil, stirring occasionally. Boil 2 minutes, stirring constantly or until mixture drips with jelly-like consistency from the stirring spoon. Remove from stove and skim. Ladle into sterilized jars and seal. Cool completely, label, and store in the refrigerator.

RAZZLE-DAZZLE JAM

Such a pretty spread, perfect for gift giving. Deanna makes this to share at Christmas.

3 cups fresh or loose-pack
  frozen raspberries,
  thawed, drained
1 (16-ounce) can sweet
  cherries, drained,
  reserving liquid
½ cup corn syrup

1 tablespoon lemon juice
5 cups sugar
Reserved liquid plus water to
  make ¾ cup
1 package powdered fruit
  pectin

Crush the raspberries; measure 2 cups. Finely chop the sweet cherries; measure 1 cup. In a large bowl, combine the raspberries, cherries, corn syrup, lemon juice and sugar; mix well. Let stand 10 minutes. In a small saucepan, combine liquid and powdered pectin. Heat to full rolling boil, stirring constantly; boil 1 minute. Pour hot pectin mixture into fruit mixture; stir vigorously 3 minutes. Ladle jam into eight (8-ounce) clean jelly jars. Cover with tight-fitting lids; label. Let stand several hours at room temperature or until set. Store jam in refrigerator up to 3 weeks or in freezer up to 3 months.

JEWEL JAM

Jars filled with this jam truly do look like jewels. Another great combination for those of us who don't live in the Fruit Belt.

1 (16-ounce) can water packed
  pitted red cherries
1 (10-ounce) package frozen
  sliced strawberries,
  thawed

3 tablespoons fresh lemon
  juice
4½ cups sugar
½ bottle liquid fruit pectin

Drain cherries, reserving juice. Chop the cherries, then measure and add enough juice to make 1 cup. In a large pan, combine them with the strawberries, lemon juice and sugar; mix well. Place the mixture over high heat, bring to a full rolling boil, then boil hard 1 minute, stirring constantly. Remove from heat and stir in the pectin all at once. Stir and skim for 5 minutes to cool slightly and prevent floating fruit. Ladle into jars and seal at once. Store in the refrigerator.

PINEAPPLE-ORANGE MARMALADE

Pineapple and orange is a great tasting flavor combination—one that will really perk up your breakfast or bedtime toast, English muffins or bagels.

1 package powdered fruit
  pectin
1 (20-ounce) can crushed
  pineapple

1 (6-ounce) can frozen
  concentrate for orange-
  pineapple juice
3 cups sugar

Combine fruit pectin, pineapple and juice, and orange-pineapple juice concentrate in a large saucepan. Heat, stirring often, to a full rolling boil. Stir in sugar; heat to boiling again, then cook rapidly, stirring constantly, 1 minute. Remove from heat. Stir and skim, alternately, 5 minutes. Ladle into hot, sterilized jars. Seal, cool completely, label and store in the refrigerator.

MOM'S PEACH MARMALADE

My mother was known for her peach marmalade. I must confess that I have never been as consistently successful at getting it to turn out as she was. Mine is usually a little thin or too thick. Since it doesn't contain fruit pectin, it is neither quick nor easy, but if you have patience, the end result is delectable.

12 good-size peaches
1 orange

Sugar

Peel the peaches, remove pits and mash to a pulp. Squeeze the juice from the orange and add to the peach pulp. Put the orange rind through a food grinder (or use your food processor) and add to the pulp. Measure the fruit mixture and add an equal amount of sugar. Pour into a large pan. Cook slowly until desired thickness is reached. Stir often to prevent sticking. Pour into sterilized jars, seal, and either process in a hot water bath or store in the refrigerator.

GARNETTA'S CHERRY PRESERVES

Garnetta Vaughn is a friend from my Michigan days. She was a teacher, too, as was her husband, Don. Living in Michigan, you have plenty of beautiful, tart red cherries to use in recipes such as this. If you aren't so blessed, use the loose pack frozen cherries, but do try these preserves.

5 cups pitted ripe tart red cherries	1 package powdered fruit pectin
5½ cups sugar	¾ cup water

Measure fruit by firmly packing without crushing. Combine the cherries and the sugar in a large saucepan. Bring to a boil, stirring constantly. Remove from heat and let stand at room temperature 4 to 5 hours. Return to heat, and bring to a full rolling boil for 2 minutes, stirring constantly. Remove from heat. Mix powdered fruit pectin with water in a small saucepan and bring to boiling; boil hard one minute, stirring constantly. Add to hot fruit and mix well. Skim off foam and stir and skim about 10 minutes to prevent floating fruit. Ladle into hot sterilized jars or glasses and seal immediately. Store in the refrigerator.

MULTI-GRAIN PANCAKES

These hearty pancakes are filling and delicious. I often serve them with vanilla yogurt and fresh fruit, such as peaches, strawberries or blueberries. A breakfast fit for a king—or queen!!

⅔ cup whole wheat flour	¼ teaspoon salt
⅓ cup unbleached flour	1 cup buttermilk
¼ cup oat flour	¼ cup skim milk
2 tablespoons wheat germ	1 whole egg
2 teaspoons sugar	1 egg white
1 teaspoon baking powder	1 tablespoon oil
½ teaspoon baking soda	¼ teaspoon vanilla

Mix all dry ingredients in a large bowl. In a second bowl, combine all wet ingredients, whipping them enough to beat the egg white and whole egg slightly. Add these to the dry ingredients, stirring just to combine them. The batter can stand for about 10 minutes out of the refrigerator or for an hour or more refrigerated. Bake on a preheated griddle.

TLC Tip: *Instead of the oat flour, you can use the same amount of cornmeal, or buckwheat.*

SIMPLY WONDERFUL PANCAKES

These are the pancakes my kids grew up on. They are light and airy, and the perfect background for additions or embellishments.

2 cups buttermilk	2 tablespoons sugar
¼ cup oil	2 teaspoons baking powder
2 eggs	1 teaspoon soda
1¾ cups flour	1 teaspoon salt

In a large bowl, combine the milk, oil and eggs. Beat well. Measure the dry ingredients onto a square of waxed paper; add to liquid mixture and stir just until lumps disappear. If necessary, thicken with a little additional flour or thin with a little more milk. Pour batter about ¼ cup at a time onto a lightly greased griddle that has been heated to 375 degrees. Bake until bubbles break and edges start to dry; turn and bake other side. Serve immediately.

TLC Tip: *Need variety? Add ½ cup shredded apple and ½ teaspoon cinnamon to the batter or add ½ cup chopped nuts. This batter also marries well with blueberries.*

WHOLE WHEAT PANCAKES

Light but hearty, these pancakes are a great way to start your day.

2 cups whole wheat flour	½ teaspoon soda
2 tablespoons sugar	2 cups milk
3 teaspoons baking powder	¼ cup oil
1 teaspoon salt	2 eggs

In a large bowl, combine the dry ingredients. Add milk, oil and eggs, stirring just until lumps disappear. Spoon about ¼ cup batter onto hot griddle (about 400 degrees if you are lucky enough to have one with a temperature gauge) that has been lightly greased. Bake until bubbles break and edges start to dry; turn and bake other side. Serve immediately.

BAKED HONEY WHEAT CAKES

When you make this variation of pancakes, you can sit down to eat with the rest of the family, the oven does all the work.

1 cup bran buds or all bran cereal	¼ cup oil
¼ cup wheat germ (I like to use the toasted honey crunch kind)	¼ cup honey
	1 cup flour
	1½ teaspoons baking powder
½ teaspoon soda	1 cup buttermilk
½ cup hot water	1 egg

In a large bowl, combine the cereal, wheat germ, soda, water, oil and honey. Add the remaining ingredients and beat until well blended. Pour into a greased 15 x 10" jelly roll pan. Bake in a 425 degree oven for 8 to 10 minutes until firm to the touch. Cut into squares and serve immediately with your favorite toppings.

QUICK BUCKWHEAT PANCAKES

Usually buckwheat pancakes tend to be a bit time-consuming, so I was pleased to find this recipe that is, as the name implies, quick and easy. Buckwheat has a distinctive taste that some people don't care for. Too bad, as it has great nutritional value. Cleo likes these, so they are a standard at our house, often served with warmed applesauce and/or maple syrup.

½ cup flour	1 large egg
½ cup buckwheat flour	1 cup milk
2 teaspoons baking powder	2 tablespoons melted butter
2 teaspoons sugar	or oil
½ teaspoon salt	

Stir the dry ingredients together on a square of waxed paper. In a large bowl (I like to use my large Pyrex measuring bowl, as the lip makes it easy to pour the batter onto the griddle), beat the egg slightly, add the milk and beat to combine. Stir in the melted butter. Gradually add the dry ingredients, beating until almost smooth. Ignore any small lumps as they will disappear during baking. Bake on a hot griddle until tops are bubbly and bottoms are browned. Turn to cook the other side. Serve warm with your favorite toppings.

WHOLE WHEAT BANANA PANCAKES

Make your own specialty pancakes with the addition of bananas and nuts. Who needs IHOP!!

1 cup whole wheat pancake mix (Aunt Jemima has a good one)	½ teaspoon salt
	2 beaten eggs
	1½ cups milk
½ cup wheat germ	1 teaspoon vanilla
2 tablespoons nonfat dry milk powder	4 drops lemon extract
	1 banana, coarsely mashed
2 teaspoons baking powder	½ cup chopped nuts

In a large mixing bowl, combine the dry ingredients. Whisk together the eggs, milk and flavorings. Stir into the flour mixture just until blended. Fold in the banana and nuts. Using ¼ cup batter, bake on a preheated, lightly-greased griddle until bubbles break on the surface and the edges are dry. Turn, (these are tender cakes, so handle carefully) bake until done.

TLC Tip: *I've used macadamia nuts in this recipe—the ultimate indulgence! Serve with a pineapple sauce and a sprinkle of coconut and save the plane fare to the islands.*

BUTTERMILK WHOLE WHEAT WAFFLES

There's just something special about waffles. When I was a kid, I loved filling each little dent with syrup. Now I ration it a bit more. My mother's waffles were wonderful. She just didn't make them often enough. She had a plain round waffle iron, Belgian hadn't been heard of. Now waffle irons come in many shapes, from square to rectangle to heart and Mickey Mouse shape. Whatever shape you like, these waffles will leave a smile on your face.

2 eggs, separated	1½ teaspoons baking powder
2 tablespoons oil	½ teaspoon baking soda
2 cups buttermilk	½ teaspoon salt
2¼ cups whole wheat flour	

Beat the egg yolks with the oil, then add the buttermilk. Combine the dry ingredients and add to the buttermilk mixture. Beat the egg whites to stiff peaks in a separate bowl. Carefully fold into the batter. Bake in a preheated waffle iron following the directions for your particular baker.

OAT WHEAT WAFFLES

The addition of oats gives these waffles a slightly nutty taste.

¾ cup flour
¾ cup whole wheat flour
½ cup quick oats
4 teaspoons baking powder
1 tablespoon sugar

¼ teaspoon salt
6 tablespoons oil
2 large eggs, separated
2 cups milk

Combine the dry ingredients in a large bowl. Add the oil, egg yolks and milk; beat until smooth. In a small bowl, whip the egg whites until stiff peaks form. Fold into the batter. Half fill a heated waffle iron. Cook until crisp and golden. Serve hot with your favorite toppings.

EGGNOG FRENCH TOAST

This French toast is so tasty, and perfect for weekends when guests are expected. You make it ahead and freeze it, ready to bake at a moment's notice. A light dusting of powdered sugar sends it to the table in style.

6 eggs
2 cups half-and-half
¼ cup sugar
¼ teaspoon nutmeg
1½ teaspoons vanilla

¾ teaspoon rum extract
16 to 18 slices firm white
or whole wheat bread
(I like to use French)
Butter, melted

Grease two cookie sheets. Use ones with sides to prevent a mess. In medium bowl, combine eggs, half-and-half, sugar, nutmeg, vanilla and rum extract; beat until well blended. Dip each slice of bread in egg mixture; place on prepared cookie sheets. Cover lightly with foil; freeze 1 to 2 hours or until completely frozen. To store, remove from freezer, stack slices, placing waxed paper between, and wrap stack in foil or place in heavy self-seal freezer bags. When ready to serve, heat oven to 425 degrees. Remove bread slices from freezer; brush 1 side with melted butter. Place buttered side down on ungreased cookie sheets. Bake for 10 minutes. Brush top with butter; turn buttered side down. Continue to bake an additional 10 to 15 minutes or until golden brown. Can't you just taste this served with fresh strawberries?

HOT THREE-GRAIN CEREAL

Hot cereal is a breakfast stand-by in our household. I especially like this one. It's tasty, hearty and sticks with you. I eat mine without added milk.

1½ cups water
1½ cups skim milk
¼ to ½ teaspoon salt
⅔ cup quick oats
1 tablespoon raisins
¼ cup Cream of Wheat

2 tablespoons unprocessed
  bran
2 tablespoons maple syrup
1 tablespoon sliced, toasted
  almonds

Bring water, milk and salt to a boil in a small heavy saucepan. Reduce heat to low. Mix in the oats and cook 3 minutes, stirring occasionally. Add raisins, Cream of Wheat and bran and stir until thickened, about 1½ minutes. Divide among 2 bowls. Drizzle each with 1 tablespoon syrup and sprinkle with ½ tablespoon almonds. This makes two very large servings.

FRUITED OATMEAL

This is a delicious version of an old favorite.

2⅔ cups water
1⅓ cups quick oats
½ teaspoon salt
1 apple, finely chopped

¼ cup raisins
¼ teaspoon cinnamon
  (more if you like)

Place the water, salt, apple, raisins and cinnamon in a medium saucepan. Bring to a boil. Stir in the oats. Boil one minute, stirring constantly. Remove from heat; cover; let stand at least 1 minute. Serve with milk and sweeten with brown sugar or maple syrup, if desired. Makes 4 servings.

CORNMEAL MUSH

Sunday night supper was always a simple affair when I was a child. Often it would be cornmeal mush, sometimes freshly cooked and eaten with milk and maple syrup much like a cereal, and at other times, fried, also eaten with maple syrup. Today people add some extra ingredients and call it polenta. Whatever you call it, it's good, and comforting as well.

1 cup yellow cornmeal
1 teaspoon salt

1 cup cold water
3 cups boiling water

Combine cornmeal, salt and cold water. Gradually pour into boiling water, stirring constantly. Return to boil, stirring constantly. Reduce heat; cover. Continue cooking over low heat about 5 minutes, stirring frequently. Spoon into bowls to serve.

FRIED MUSH

Line an 8 x 4" loaf pan with strips of waxed or parchment paper, letting the ends hang over the sides of the pan. Pour in one recipe of Cornmeal Mush. Cool slightly, then refrigerate several hours or overnight. Remove from pan, with the aid of the paper strips. Slice into 12 slices. Pan-fry over medium heat in a small amount of butter or oil about 10 minutes per side, or until golden. I like to use my cast iron skillet for this. This is delicious served with maple syrup, but applesauce is good too. You can also serve this as a side dish instead of potatoes or rice.

BRUNCH EGG CASSEROLE

I guess I serve this most often on Christmas morning, but it is certainly appropriate for any morning occasion where a group is expected. This is especially nice because you can put it together the night before.

¼ cup + 2 tablespoons butter, divided use
¼ cup flour
1 cup milk
1 cup evaporated skim milk
4 cups shredded sharp Cheddar cheese (about 1 pound)
¼ teaspoon dried thyme
¼ teaspoon dried basil
18 hard-cooked eggs, sliced
¼ cup minced fresh parsley
1 pound turkey bacon, cooked and crumbled
1½ cups fresh breadcrumbs

Melt ¼ cup butter in a heavy pan over low heat; stir in the flour, stirring until smooth. Cook 1 minute, stirring constantly. Gradually add both milks; cook over medium heat, stirring constantly, until mixture is thickened and bubbly. Add cheese and herbs, stirring until cheese melts. Layer half each of the egg slices, parsley, bacon, and cheese sauce in a lightly greased 13 x 9" baking dish. Repeat layers and ingredients. Melt the 2 tablespoons butter; combine with the breadcrumbs and sprinkle over the casserole. Cover and refrigerate overnight or at least 8 hours. Remove from refrigerator; let stand 30 minutes. Bake, uncovered at 350 degrees for 30 minutes. Should serve 8 to 10.

IMPOSSIBLE BREAKFAST PIE

An easy and savory breakfast or brunch entree. Try substituting 1 cup cubed ham for the sausage for a change of pace.

1 pound bulk pork sausage (turkey sausage works fine)
1 small onion, chopped (about ½ cup)
2½ cups frozen loose-pack hash brown potatoes
1 cup + ¼ cup shredded Cheddar cheese, divided use

¼ cup chopped green onions, with tops
1¾ cups milk
1 cup Bisquick baking mix
4 eggs
¼ teaspoon salt
⅛ teaspoon pepper

Cook sausage and onion in a large skillet, stirring often until sausage is fully cooked; drain. Mix sausage mixture, potatoes and 1 cup cheese in a well-greased 10" pie plate. Beat remaining ingredients except ¼ cup cheese with wire whisk or hand beater until smooth. (I usually use my blender for this job.) Pour mixture into the pie plate. Bake in a 400 degree oven about 40 minutes or until golden brown and knife inserted in center comes out clean. Sprinkle with ¼ cup cheese. Bake about 2 minutes longer or until cheese is melted. This makes 6 to 8 servings.

CHRISTMAS MORNING SAUSAGE RING

Certainly this can be served any morning, but for us, it usually was/is Christmas Morning Brunch. These days I tend to use lite or turkey sausage, but the fat content still relegates this to an occasional treat. The way it is prepared makes it a natural for serving to a crowd.

2 pounds bulk sausage
2 eggs, beaten
2 tablespoons grated onion

1½ cups fine dry breadcrumbs
¼ cup chopped parsley, optional but nice

Mix ingredients well and pack into a lightly oiled 9" ring mold. Bake at 350 degrees for 20 minutes, take from oven and drain off accumulated fat. Return to oven and bake 20 minutes more. Turn onto heated serving dish. Fill the center with scrambled eggs or scrambled Egg Beaters.

Condiments
and Sauces

AUNT EDNA HITSMAN'S CRISP PICKLES

Aunt Edna's Crisp Pickles were as pretty to look at as they were good to eat. They were, as the name indicates, very crisp and a vibrant green. Her recipe called for a large amount of ingredients, and the directions were a bit ambiguous, as old recipes sometimes are. This is a slightly modified version that I feel keeps the same flavor and texture. These pickles are great alongside a tuna salad sandwich.

3½ quarts 2" pickling
   cucumbers (about
   4 pounds)
1 cup coarse pickling salt
4 quarts boiling water,
   divided use

½ teaspoon powdered alum
5 cups vinegar
4½ cups sugar, divided use
4 (2") sticks cinnamon
2 teaspoons whole cloves

Wash the cucumbers carefully; cut in half lengthwise and place in a glass or enamel-lined pan. Dissolve the salt in 2 quarts boiling water; pour over the cucumbers. Weight the cucumbers down with a plate almost as large as the container and lay something heavy on the plate to keep the cucumbers under the brine. Let stand 1 week. On the 8th day, drain; pour 2 quarts fresh boiling water over the cucumbers and let stand 24 hours. On the 9th day, drain; pour 2 quarts boiling water mixed with alum over the cucumbers. Let stand 24 hours. On the 10th day, drain; pour 2 quarts fresh boiling water over the cucumbers. Let stand 24 hours. The next day, drain. Combine vinegar, 3 cups sugar, cinnamon and whole cloves; heat to boiling point and pour over the cucumbers. For the next 3 days, drain, retaining the liquid. Reheat this liquid each morning, adding ½ cup sugar each time. After the last heating on the 14th day, pack pickles into hot, sterilized jars. Remove cinnamon and cloves; pour boiling hot liquid over the pickles and seal at once. This should make 5 to 6 pints.

TLC Tip: *For an unusual but tasty tea sandwich, chop some of these pickles very fine and mix into cream cheese. Spread on dark bread; cut as desired.*

BREAD AND BUTTER PICKLES

My mother made THE BEST bread and butter pickles. I loved them when I was living at home, and they are still my favorite pickle. I cannot be positive that this recipe from an old Farm Journal *magazine was the one she used, but it sure comes close. Whether you grow your own cucumbers, or purchase from a farmer's market or stand, do try these.*

4 quarts sliced cucumbers
    (40 to 50 small)
½ cup salt
Ice cubes
2 quarts sliced onions
1 quart vinegar

4 cups sugar
1 tablespoon celery seeds
2 tablespoons mustard seeds
1 tablespoon ginger
1 teaspoon turmeric
    (optional)

Gently stir the salt into the thinly sliced cucumbers. Cover with the ice cubes; let stand 2 or 3 hours or until cucumbers are crisp and cold. Add more ice if it melts. Drain and add the onions. Combine the remaining ingredients in a large stainless steel pan. Bring quickly to a boil and boil 10 minutes. Add cucumber and onion slices and bring to boiling point. Pack at once into hot jars. Process in boiling water bath for 30 minutes. Remove jars from canner and complete seals unless closures are self-sealing type. This should make 8 pints.

TLC Tip: *These pickles are a wonderful addition to hamburgers and as an accompaniment to other sandwiches and potato salad.*

BUTTER RUM SAUCE

You'll love this rich sauce and probably find it difficult to save for special occasions. End a simple meal with scoops of vanilla ice cream topped with this sauce. No other embellishments are needed, but chopped nuts can be added if you like.

1 cup firmly packed light
    brown sugar
⅓ cup butter-flavored
    shortening

½ cup dark corn syrup
¼ cup milk
1 to 2 teaspoons rum flavoring

Blend brown sugar, shortening and corn syrup in a medium saucepan. Cook and stir over medium heat until mixture comes to a boil. Boil 1 minute. Remove from heat. Gradually blend in milk until smooth. Stir in flavoring. Cool slightly before serving. Leftovers, if you have any, keep well in the refrigerator, but reheat over low heat, stirring constantly, before serving.

BRANDIED APRICOT SAUCE

A versatile sauce to serve over pancakes, waffles, or ice cream. Easy to make, and low in sugar.

1 cup apricot nectar
2 tablespoons cornstarch

1 teaspoon brandy extract

Combine nectar and cornstarch in small saucepan. Heat to boiling over medium-high heat, stirring constantly. Remove from heat, add flavoring. Cool slightly before using.

HOT APPLESAUCE

This is a great glorified applesauce. The addition of butter elevates it from the ordinary to the special. Try serving this atop or alongside your favorite spice cake or spooned over vanilla ice cream. Yum-m-m!

5 pounds apples
½ cup water
2 tablespoons butter
½ cup brown sugar

1½ teaspoons cinnamon
½ teaspoon nutmeg
½ cup raisins

Peel, core and slice apples. Combine apples in saucepan with water, butter and brown sugar. Cook over medium-low heat until apples are soft. Add cinnamon, nutmeg and raisins.

TLC Tip: *The amount of spices can be adjusted to your taste.*

APPLE SYRUP

A very good topping for pancakes or waffles. Or try it warm spooned over slices of your favorite apple pie.

¾ cup frozen apple juice
  concentrate
¾ cup water
2 tablespoons vanilla

½ teaspoon pumpkin pie spice
1 tablespoon cornstarch
1½ tablespoons water

Mix apple juice concentrate, ¾ cup water, vanilla and pumpkin pie spice in small saucepan. Simmer 5 minutes. Mix cornstarch and 1½ tablespoons water; stir into simmering apple juice. Cook until thick and clear.

TLC Tip: *This syrup can be made in the microwave by combining all ingredients in a microwave-safe bowl. Cook on full power 2-4 minutes, stirring every minute, until thick and clear.*

SANDERS HOT FUDGE SAUCE

Sanders was a restaurant chain in the Detroit area. It still may be going strong, and probably is if it serves this sauce. You could purchase it to take home so you could savor the delicious, smooth taste between visits to the shop. Of course, this is my version, but good enough to make you famous.

1 (12-ounce) can evaporated
  milk
1 pound Kraft caramels,
  unwrapped

½ pound butter
12 ounces Nestle's milk
  chocolate (don't
  substitute)

Put all ingredients in top of a double boiler over simmering water. Stir until smooth. Continue to cook 30 minutes, stirring once or twice to scrape down pan. Remove from heat, beat with an electric mixer or process in a pre-warmed blender for a few minutes. Keep sauce in the refrigerator; warm before serving. I have known people to eat it by the spoonful right from the refrigerator—I wonder who?

THEL'S FAMOUS CHOCOLATE SAUCE

I found this recipe in a small cookbook back in the 1960's. It was a hit right from the start. I have changed it a little since then, but my kids think this is the chocolate sauce to end all chocolate sauces. I predict you'll love it too, and find many uses for it.

4 ounces unsweetened
  chocolate
2 tablespoons butter
1 cup sugar

1 (12-ounce) can evaporated
  milk, divided use
1 teaspoon vanilla

Place chocolate and butter in a heavy saucepan. Melt chocolate over low heat. In a small mixing bowl, combine sugar and 1 cup evaporated milk. Add to melted chocolate. Stir over medium heat until sauce reaches boiling point. Reduce heat; add remainder of milk, continue to cook until sauce thickens slightly. Remove from heat, stir in vanilla. Serve hot or cold.

TLC Tip: *The original recipe called for cream. Once when I wanted to make this sauce I didn't have any cream so I used evaporated milk. I can't see that it tastes any better with the cream, so I nearly always use the evaporated milk. Also, be reminded that chocolate is packaged differently sometimes, so make sure you use 4 ounces, not necessarily 4 pieces.*

THICK HOT CHOCOLATE SAUCE

This is probably the first homemade chocolate sauce I tasted. It is a simple sauce, not as rich as the others, but excellent for those times when something less indulgent is desired.

⅓ cup cocoa
1 tablespoon flour
½ cup sugar
1 cup boiling water

½ teaspoon vanilla
1 tablespoon butter
⅛ teaspoon salt

Blend the cocoa, flour and sugar. Add the boiling water and stir until smooth. Cook slowly for 2 minutes. Remove from heat and stir in the vanilla, butter and salt. Serve as desired.

BLUEBERRY SAUCE

In our household, this is a real favorite with whole grain pancakes or waffles. Sometimes we spoon a little plain or vanilla nonfat yogurt over the pancakes before pouring on this sauce. You certainly won't miss the butter and syrup!

1 cup fresh or frozen
    unsweetened blueberries
1 tablespoon cornstarch

1½ tablespoons sugar
½ cup unsweetened grape
    juice

If using frozen blueberries, microwave blueberries in a microwave-safe bowl 1 minute on high. Set aside. In a 4-cup measure, combine cornstarch, sugar and grape juice. Stir in the blueberries. Microwave on high 2½ to 3 minutes or until syrup is clear and thickened, stirring every minute during cooking.

TLC Tip: I like to keep those little individual boxes of juice on hand to use in this recipe. Be sure to get the ones that are 100% juice, and not a juice drink. I have used various juices in this recipe, even water on occasion when I didn't have any juice on hand.

VANILLA SAUCE

This Vanilla Sauce and the Lemon Sauce that follows were the sauces of choice for the Cottage Pudding that was served frequently for dessert when I was growing up. These are simple sauces, but very good. The Vanilla Sauce is a favorite of mine.

¾ to 1 cup sugar	1 cup boiling water
2½ tablespoons flour	1 tablespoon butter
¼ teaspoon salt	1 teaspoon vanilla

Blend the sugar, flour, and salt. Add the boiling water and stir until smooth. Heat over medium heat until mixture comes to a boil; boil 3 minutes, stirring constantly. Remove from heat, add the butter and vanilla. Serve over Cottage Pudding (see index) or as desired.

TLC Tip: The original sauce called for 1 tablespoon flour. Since I prefer a thicker sauce, I have increased the amount to 2½ tablespoons. DON'T omit the butter. It makes the sauce.

LEMON SAUCE

Prepare the Vanilla Sauce, adding 3 tablespoons lemon juice and 2 teaspoons grated lemon rind. Omit the vanilla. You lemon fans will love this version.

TLC Tip: I guess we were a little creative in "the good ole days", as I remember making a peach sauce by substituting boiling peach juice for the water in the Vanilla Sauce recipe. If you try this variation, add a cup of sliced peaches after the sauce is removed from the heat.

OLD FASHIONED LEMON SAUCE

This is a wonderful sauce, and glorifies gingerbread superbly. It is rich, containing both egg and butter, so you will probably want to reserve it for special occasions.

½ cup butter	1 egg, well beaten
1 cup sugar	3 tablespoons lemon juice
¼ cup water	Grated rind of 1 lemon

Combine all ingredients in a medium saucepan. Cook over medium heat, stirring constantly, just until mixture comes to a boil. Serve warm or cold.

COFFEE BUTTERSCOTCH SAUCE

Our son, Joey, especially likes this sauce. It is best served warm, and delicious over butter pecan ice cream, squares of spice cake or pecan waffles.

1 cup firmly packed light brown sugar	¼ cup half-and-half
¼ cup light corn syrup	1 teaspoon instant coffee powder
¼ cup butter	

Combine sugar, corn syrup, butter, half-and-half, and coffee powder in a saucepan. Bring to a boil over medium-low heat, stirring constantly, and boil for 2 minutes. Sauce will thicken as it cools.

LITE AND EASY WHITE SAUCE

I've learned that white sauce doesn't have to be fat-laden to taste good. I know you probably have a favorite of your own, or could find one in a cookbook, but since it is so useful and the necessary ingredient of many dishes, I decided to include the one I use most often.

1 tablespoon 90's Butter (see index)	½ teaspoon salt (or less, to your taste)
2 tablespoons flour	⅛ teaspoon white pepper
	1 cup skim milk

Microwave the butter in a large microwave-safe bowl. Whisk in the flour, salt and pepper. Whisk in the milk. Microwave on high 2-4 minutes, stirring after each minute, until thick and bubbly. Use as desired.

LITE AND EASY CHEESE SAUCE

To the Lite and Easy White Sauce recipe, add ½ teaspoon dry mustard with the dry ingredients. When sauce is thick, add ⅓ cup grated, reduced-fat sharp Cheddar cheese. Whisk until cheese is melted.

TLC Tip: *Sometimes I add freshly grated Parmesan cheese, instead of Cheddar, and serve it with pasta.*

Salads and Dressings

Salads? Well, we ate a lot of tender, fresh-picked leaf lettuce during the growing season. My father always sprinkled his with sugar! We had large, vibrant tomato rounds. He sprinkled those with sugar too. If we got fancy, there was Perfection Salad, a mixture of grated cabbage and carrots held together in a jelled substance, probably lemon or orange. And who could forget cottage cheese and crushed pineapple in lime Jello. We had coleslaw with a simple dressing of mayonnaise thinned with a little milk and sweetened with sugar. We never served salad as the main course.

LISA'S LAYERED SALAD

Lisa Hancock is my niece. Invariably when we get together to plan a communal meal, someone will say, "See if Lisa will bring her layered salad". This is a salad for large groups, and very attractive made and served in a clear glass trifle dish so you can see the various layers.

1 (10-ounce) package fresh spinach, chopped	12 hard-cooked eggs, chopped
1 pound bacon, cooked crisp, drained and crumbled	1 cup mayonnaise
1 (10-ounce) package frozen English peas, uncooked	1 cup salad dressing (like Miracle Whip)
1 head lettuce, chopped	Grated Swiss cheese—Lisa is generous here

Layer the vegetables and eggs in a large bowl in the order listed. Combine the mayonnaise and salad dressing and spread over the salad mixture like you were frosting a cake. Sprinkle liberally with the cheese. Cover with plastic wrap and refrigerate at least 12 hours. Do not toss to serve.

TLC Tip: Lisa never puts onions in her salad. If you would like to, chop 1 bunch of green onions (include some of the green) and add between the peas and head lettuce. If you prefer another type of cheese, such as Parmesan or Cheddar, feel free to substitute.

FRESH VEGETABLE SALAD

This recipe was submitted by my mother for a cookbook published by the Allegan News, I don't know what year, but probably the early 1940's. Personally, I think the salad was a little ahead of its time, composed as it was. My mother confessed to me in later years that she never prepared this salad!! Don't let that fact stop you. It will make a stunning addition to your next cookout. If beets aren't your thing, why not substitute matchsticks of zucchini or summer squash?

Cabbage	Carrots
Beets	Lettuce leaves

Shred cabbage, uncooked beets and carrots, keeping each separate. Chill until cold and crisp. Arrange in separate piles on lettuce-lined platter or individual plates. Serve with your favorite dressing. The Creamy Italian or Honey Mustard (see index) would be good.

CREAMY BROCCOLI AND CAULIFLOWER SALAD

Often served when the family gets together, but wonderful anytime. This is a delicious way to get your quota of these two healthful vegetables.

1 cup mayonnaise
1 cup sour cream
½ teaspoon dried parsley
   flakes
½ teaspoon dried dillweed
½ teaspoon onion salt

½ teaspoon Beau Monde
   seasoning
1 bunch broccoli
1 head cauliflower
10 ripe olives
10 green olives
1 small onion, chopped

Combine the first 6 ingredients; mix well and set aside. Trim off large leaves of broccoli, remove tough ends of lower stalks, and wash broccoli thoroughly. Remove flowerettes and cut stems into thin slices. Remove outer leaves of cauliflower. Break cauliflower into flowerettes, and wash thoroughly. Bring a large pot of water to a boil. When it is boiling rapidly, add the broccoli and cauliflower. Boil for two minutes. Drain, and immediately place in a bowl of ice water. Drain, and combine the vegetables and olives in a large bowl. Spoon dressing mixture over the top; toss gently to coat. Refrigerate 8 to 10 hours or overnight. Makes 8 to 10 servings.

TLC Tip: I'm always a little amused when the number of servings is listed for this type of dish. It all depends—on how fond people are of the dish, the proportion of adults to children—there are any number of variables, but at least you have some idea.

FOUR BEAN SALAD

I have made any number of bean salads through the years. I like them for their ease of preparation, combination of flavors and the way they keep. This version has no oil, and interestingly enough, you don't miss it. This recipe just may become one of your favorites.

1 (16-ounce) can garbanzo
   beans
1 (16-ounce) can red kidney
   beans
1 (16-ounce) can cut green
   beans
1 (16-ounce) can wax beans
2 large stalks celery, sliced
1 large red onion, halved and
   sliced thin

1 green bell pepper, chopped
1 red bell pepper, chopped or
   a small (2-ounce) jar of
   pimientos, drained
¾ cup vinegar (I like apple
   cider)
¾ cup sugar
1 teaspoon lite salt, or to taste
¼ teaspoon freshly ground
   black pepper

Drain the liquid from all canned beans. Mix beans with vegetables in a large bowl. In a small saucepan, heat the vinegar, sugar, salt and pepper until steaming hot. Pour the hot dressing over the beans and vegetables. Mix. Chill several hours or overnight before serving. This will keep 1 to 2 weeks in the refrigerator. In fact, the flavor just keeps getting better and better.

TOSSED SALAD WITH CREAMY BUTTERMILK DRESSING

If you are bored with the usual combination of ingredients in your tossed salads, try this one. The dressing compliments it nicely.

4 cups torn mixed salad
   greens
1 to 2 tomatoes, cut in wedges,
   or a like amount of
   halved cherry tomatoes
½ cup thinly sliced cucumber

½ cup sliced mushrooms
¼ cup sliced radishes
2 tablespoons sliced green
   onions
1 tablespoon sliced ripe olives

Toss all ingredients together in a large bowl. Serve with Creamy Buttermilk Dressing.

Creamy Buttermilk Dressing:
⅔ cup mayonnaise
½ cup buttermilk
1 clove garlic, crushed

1 teaspoon parsley flakes
1 teaspoon chives
1 teaspoon seasoned salt

In a small bowl, combine all ingredients, mixing well with a wire whisk. Refrigerate several hours to blend flavors.

GOOD AND EASY CAESAR SALAD

It always seemed to me that Caesar Salad was a bit complicated to make and best left up to those showy waiters in fancy restaurants that did it tableside. But the taste of a good Caesar Salad is so wonderful that I was always on the lookout for a dressing that delivered that taste without the work. This is what I found. It doesn't require any raw eggs, either, so you can enjoy it to your health's content.

1 large head romaine lettuce	Freshly grated Parmesan
1 cup seasoned croutons	cheese
	Caesar Salad Dressing

Separate, wash and thoroughly dry the romaine. Tear the larger leaves into smaller pieces, and place them in a large bowl with the croutons. Just before serving, shake the dressing very well, pour it over the salad and toss to distribute the dressing evenly. Sprinkle with Parmesan cheese.

Caesar Salad Dressing:

¾ cup oil	½ teaspoon salt
¼ cup lemon juice	¼ teaspoon pepper
¼ cup freshly grated	1 tablespoon anchovy paste or
Parmesan cheese	mashed anchovies
2 cloves garlic, finely minced	(optional, but I think it
½ teaspoon Dijon mustard	makes the dressing)

Place all the ingredients in a jar with a tight-fitting lid and shake vigorously. Store the dressing in the refrigerator and shake well before serving. Makes about 1 cup.

TICKLED TROUT HOUSE SALAD WITH HONEY MUSTARD DRESSING

When we started vacationing in San Diego, we stayed in hotels on Hotel Circle. One of the hotels had a restaurant called The Tickled Trout. It was decorated in the English manner, and served good seafood and this salad that we thought was the best thing we had ever eaten. It was here that we tasted Honey Mustard Dressing for the first time, and it fast became my husband's favorite dressing. This is my rendition of that salad and dressing.

Romaine lettuce	**Raisins**
Grated carrots	**Honey Mustard Dressing**
Sunflower seeds	

Thoroughly wash and dry the lettuce, then tear into bite-size pieces. Arrange a generous amount on each salad plate. (The Tickled Trout uses clear glass ones that have been chilled.) Sprinkle the carrots, sunflower seeds and raisins over the lettuce, the amount decided by you. Pour Honey Mustard Dressing over all.

Honey Mustard Dressing:

⅓ **cup honey**	**2 tablespoons fresh lemon**
¼ **cup Dijon mustard**	**juice**
1 clove garlic, minced or	¼ **cup rice wine vinegar**
crushed	**1 cup canola oil**
	½ **teaspoon sesame oil**

In a blender or food processor, combine honey, mustard, garlic, lemon juice and vinegar. Process until well mixed, about 1 minute. With motor running, add canola oil and sesame oil in a slow, steady stream, processing until dressing is smooth with a creamy texture. Store covered in the refrigerator.

RENA FARNUM'S BEAN AND VEGETABLE SALAD

Harold and Rena Farnum were our neighbors across the road from the farm in Michigan. Harold wasn't a true farmer, having a full-time job elsewhere, but they were friends of our parents and long-time members of our church in Allegan, Michigan. They allowed us to use their hills for sledding in winter, and Rena made a to-die-for chocolate fudge—the old-fashioned, slightly-grainy kind, slow cooked, and beaten to death by hand. This salad is colorful and good—a slightly different variation of the bean salad.

1 (16-ounce) can kidney beans
1 (16-ounce) can cut green
   beans
1 (16-ounce) can wax beans
1 onion, sliced thin
1 to 2 carrots, shredded

Green pepper strips,
   if desired
½ cup salad oil
½ cup vinegar
½ cup sugar

Drain the beans well. Combine with other vegetables in a large bowl. Thoroughly mix the oil, vinegar and sugar. Pour over the vegetables and stir well. Chill several hours or overnight. Will keep for several days in the refrigerator.

ARTICHOKE RICE SALAD

This was the salad that our daughter, Deanna, requested for her celebration buffet when she graduated from high school. It is very tasty—when you try it you'll know why it is a favorite of hers. Sherri Key, fellow Hyperion, shared this recipe with me.

1 package chicken-flavored
   rice mix
4 green onions, sliced thin
½ green pepper, chopped
12 pimiento-stuffed olives,
   sliced

2 (6-ounce) jars marinated
   artichoke hearts
¾ teaspoon curry powder
⅓ cup mayonnaise
Lemon juice to taste (I usually
   use about 2 tablespoons)

Prepare rice as package directs; cool. Transfer to a large bowl. Add onions, pepper and olives. Drain the artichoke hearts, saving marinade from one jar. Cut the artichoke hearts in half and add to rice. Combine marinade with curry powder and mayonnaise. Pour over rice mixture, toss gently. Chill several hours or overnight.

TLC Tip: *You can substitute ¾ cup regular rice cooked in 1½ cups chicken broth if you wish.*

GARBANZO BEAN SALAD

If you like Mexican food, you will love the flavor of this salad. Because the main ingredient is beans, it can easily be used as the main dish of a meatless meal.

4 ounces small, fresh mushrooms	**1 (15-ounce) can garbanzo beans, drained**
½ medium green pepper, cut into thin strips	**Yogurt Dressing (recipe follows)**
½ cup sliced pitted ripe olives	**Lettuce leaves**
¼ cup sliced green onions, with tops	**Tomato wedges**

Mix mushrooms, green pepper, olives, onions and beans. Refrigerate until chilled, at least 2 hours. Just before serving, toss salad with Yogurt Dressing. Serve on lettuce leaves; garnish with tomato wedges. Will serve 4 as a side dish, plan on 2 servings as the main course.

Yogurt Dressing:

½ cup plain yogurt	**¼ teaspoon garlic juice**
¼ cup mayonnaise	**¼ teaspoon garlic salt**
½ teaspoon ground cumin	**⅛ teaspoon ground turmeric**
1½ teaspoons lemon juice	

Thoroughly mix all ingredients.

SCARECROW COUNTRY INN BROCCOLI SALAD

During a business trip to Cookeville, Tennessee, my husband, Cleo, was lucky enough to eat supper at this quaint bed and breakfast. Not only did he eat there once, but he was so impressed he ate there a second time during his short stay. He came home raving about this house salad, and nothing would do but I find out how it was made. With a quick phone call, they graciously shared the recipe. The salad is as good as he described. Cleo says the broccoli is chopped so fine that it doesn't look like broccoli. You decide how you like it best.

8 cups chopped broccoli (cut the flowerettes with a knife, and chop the stems in the food processor)
½ cup onions, chopped (green onions are good but white or yellow will work)
1 cup raisins
1 cup unsalted dry roasted peanuts (chopped or not, your preference)
1 cup mayonnaise
⅓ cup sugar
¼ cup red wine vinegar

In a large bowl, toss the vegetables, raisins and nuts together. In a small bowl, combine the mayonnaise, sugar and vinegar. Pour over the salad ingredients and mix well. Chill 1 to 4 hours before serving.

TLC Tip: This salad must be eaten fresh; it does not hold over well. (I still do it, and enjoy the leftovers myself, but perhaps it isn't company quality.)

HUSH PUPPY COLE SLAW

I guess everyone has a different opinion about what makes a good cole slaw. Some like it chopped, some like it grated, some like it sliced. Some like a clear dressing, others like a creamy dressing. No matter what your preference, do try this one. It will really complete your next fish and chips dinner.

1 quart coarsely chopped green cabbage
¼ cup coarsely chopped carrots
¼ cup coarsely chopped purple cabbage
¼ cup + 2 teaspoons sugar
¾ teaspoon garlic powder
1 tablespoon vinegar
1 cup salad dressing (such as Miracle Whip)

Combine vegetables in a large mixing bowl. Combine remaining ingredients for dressing. Mix until smooth; add to salad, toss well. Better if chilled before serving.

MY GRANNY'S COLESLAW

Granny Crabtree lived in Pryor, Oklahoma, right next door to the water tower. Her little home was on a quiet, tree-lined street. I suppose that it was in this house that I first ate fried okra. We used to visit Granny and Grandpa infrequently, as it was a long way from Michigan to Oklahoma in a Model A Ford. We loved to go there—to walk to the corner gas station for a pop or slow poke, to play with the cousins, go to Saturday night "singin's", or have Aunt Máco "beat the bats" for us!! Granny's food was simple food, but hearty and good. Her coleslaw was great.

3 tablespoons sugar	¾ cup evaporated skim milk
1 tablespoon flour	2 tablespoons cider vinegar
½ teaspoon dry mustard	2 egg yolks
¾ teaspoon salt	6 cups shredded cabbage
Few grains pepper	

Combine dry ingredients in a heavy saucepan. Slowly whisk in the milk and vinegar until smooth. Cook over medium-high heat for 2 to 3 minutes, stirring constantly, until mixture thickens and comes to a boil. In a small bowl, beat the egg yolks, then whisk some of the hot mixture into the yolks to warm them. Scrape the sauce back into the pan; reduce the heat to medium-low, and cook without boiling, stirring constantly, for 1 or 2 minutes, until the sauce is thickened and smooth. Pour the hot dressing over the cabbage and toss to mix thoroughly. Let cool, then refrigerate at least 1 hour or up to 24 hours before serving.

TLC Tip: *I don't remember my granny ever adding carrots, green peppers or such, but sometimes I do.*

PICNIC PARTY POTATO SALAD

This salad has been prepared for many occasions and is always at home where a good potato salad is needed. It makes a large quantity, but keeps well if kept properly chilled.

5 pounds potatoes
1 cup sliced green onions
½ cup Italian dressing
1 cup mayonnaise
1 tablespoon prepared
    mustard, can use more if
    you wish

1 teaspoon salt or to taste
2 cups sliced celery
4 hard-cooked eggs, diced
½ cup chopped sweet pickles

Cook potatoes just until tender, about 20 minutes, in boiling salted water. Drain, cool until they can be peeled, then dice into a very large bowl. (I use my Tupperware mix and fix bowl for this.) Add the green onions and Italian dressing; toss to coat. Cover bowl and chill at least 1 hour. Combine mayonnaise, mustard and salt in a small bowl; pour over potatoes and combine gently but thoroughly. Add celery, eggs and pickles; toss again. Cover and refrigerate several hours before serving.

TLC Tip: I usually wear clean rubber gloves to hold the hot potatoes while I peel them. I keep a pair labeled FOOD just for occasions such as this. One of the secrets to the wonderful flavor of this salad is having the potatoes hot when they are coated with the Italian dressing and mixed with the green onion. I have used sweet pickle relish instead of chopped pickles and find it seems to work just as well. An alternative serving suggestion is to pack the salad in a ring mold before chilling, then unmold to serve. Sometimes I cook an additional egg to slice and use as a garnish.

STAUFFER'S SPINACH AND EGG SALAD

This salad, or one similar, was served at the restaurant atop the Stauffer Hotel in the Detroit area back in the 60's. It was a special place to eat, as there was a spectacular view of the city, and the food was always good. I've served this salad often.

1 (10-ounce) package fresh
   spinach
3 hard-boiled eggs, chopped
6 slices bacon, cooked crisp
   and crumbled
¼ cup + 2 teaspoons vinegar
   (I like apple cider here)
¾ cup salad oil

4 teaspoons spicy brown
   mustard
¼ cup + 1 tablespoon chopped
   green onion
½ teaspoon salt
¼ teaspoon pepper
2 tablespoons sugar

Wash and drain spinach, tear into bite-size pieces; add eggs and bacon and toss lightly. Combine dressing ingredients and mix well with a wire whisk. Pour just enough dressing over salad to coat lightly. Enjoy!!

TLC Tip: *Sometimes I arrange the spinach on individual salad plates, sprinkle the chopped egg and crumbled bacon over the top, and drizzle with a little dressing. This makes a nice salad to serve as a first coarse, already on the table when your family and / or guests are seated.*

AUNT ELSIE'S CANDLE SALAD

Aunt Elsie and Uncle Ivan Yerden were pastors at the Allegan Church of God during my growing-up years. They lived "in town" and their house had a basement with a ping-pong table and was totally modern! When we ate Sunday dinner there, Aunt Elsie would often serve this salad. As a child, I thought it was really special.

Lettuce leaves
Pineapple slices
Bananas, peeled and cut in
   half crosswise

Mayonnaise, thinned with a
   little milk or juice and
   sweetened, if desired
Maraschino cherries
Green pepper strips, optional

Arrange a lettuce leaf on each serving plate. Place a pineapple slice in the center of each leaf. Stand the banana half in the hole of the pineapple slice so that it is upright. Drizzle the mayonnaise dressing over the tip of the banana, letting it drip down naturally. Place a cherry on the very tip, perhaps removing a bit of the banana to make it stay in place. Carry carefully to the table. You can fashion a handle for your "candle holder" from the green pepper strip if you wish.

GREEK SALAD

I just love this salad!! Something about the combination of ingredients really makes a hit with me. I usually use the feta cheese, I like the sharp flavor. Though this salad doesn't hold over well, I have been known to eat it for lunch the next day, never minding the slightly wilted vegetables. I think you'll find numerous occasions to serve this salad.

1 (6-ounce) jar Greek or black olives, drained
10 radishes, sliced
1 medium cucumber, sliced
6 green onions, cut in ½" slices
½ cup vegetable oil
⅓ cup wine vinegar
1½ teaspoons salt

1½ teaspoons dried oregano leaves
1 medium bunch romaine lettuce, torn into bite-size pieces
1 medium bunch leaf lettuce, torn into bite-size pieces
¼ cup crumbled Bleu or feta cheese

Place olives, radishes, cucumber and onions in a large bowl. Mix oil, vinegar, salt and oregano in a covered glass container; shake well. Pour salad dressing over olives and vegetables. Place romaine and leaf lettuce on top; arrange cheese on lettuce. Cover and refrigerate at least 2 hours. Just before serving, toss salad. Should serve 8 people generously.

CRISP AND TANGY SALAD

This is a good salad to serve with a casserole meal. Its great texture and tangy bite are especially good with Italian food, such as lasagne, manicotti or stuffed shells.

1 head lettuce, romaine preferred
1½ cups pitted ripe olives
4 ounces Monterey Jack cheese, cut in strips

1 cup halved cherry tomatoes
½ cup sliced cucumber
½ cup sliced onion
Oregano Vinaigrette Dressing (recipe follows)

Rinse and thoroughly drain the lettuce; spin or pat dry, refrigerate in a plastic bag. At serving time, tear lettuce into salad bowl. Top with remaining ingredients; drizzle with dressing. Toss gently before serving.

Oregano Vinaigrette Dressing:
½ cup salad oil
6 tablespoons vinegar
2 tablespoons sugar

2 teaspoons dried oregano
½ teaspoon garlic salt

Mix or shake ingredients together until well blended.

GLENDA'S SALAD

My friend, Glenda Hendrickson, is a "crafty lady", fond of antiques and country things, and has a quick sense of humor. Her husband, Darrell, is the pastor of our church here in Big Spring, and my husband's tennis partner. Glenda says that someone shared with her many years ago that a "tossed" salad should have at least seven vegetables. That is the principle upon which Glenda builds her great salads. She credits her trusty salad shooter with helping her achieve such tasty results, but you can use a knife, grater, food processor, slicer or some other handy gadget as well. Her ingredient list is flexible, depending on what is in season and/or what happens to be in her refrigerator. The nice thing about this salad is that it is very personal, but to be authentic, just be sure to use seven vegetables. Some possible combinations are listed below.

Salad one:

Green leaf lettuce	Thinly sliced cucumbers
Romaine lettuce	Thinly sliced radishes
Shredded purple cabbage	Wedges of tomato
Grated carrots	

Salad two:

Green leaf lettuce	Julienned zucchini squash
Purple leaf lettuce	(Glenda would not use
Fresh spinach leaves	this!)
Julienned summer squash	Thinly sliced cauliflower
	Slivers of raw jícama

I think you can get the idea, so be creative and toss up a salad you can eat to your heart's delight. Glenda likes to serve her salads with a lite dressing, either one of the good bottled ones now on the market, or the Lo-Fat Ranch (see index).

RUTH'S KOREAN SALAD

This salad, from my sister's recipe file, is a great way to consume all the vitamins and minerals that spinach provides. It is easy to prepare and goes with a variety of entrées. Note that the dressing should be mixed 24 hours before serving. I think you will find this a salad you will serve often.

1 cup vegetable oil
¼ cup vinegar
¾ cup sugar
⅓ cup catsup
1 tablespoon Worcestershire
    sauce
1 medium onion, finely
    chopped

1 pound fresh spinach,
    washed, stemmed and
    dried
5 strips bacon, cooked crisp
    and crumbled
1 can water chestnuts,
    drained

Combine the first six ingredients in a jar, cover tightly and shake thoroughly. Chill for 24 hours. Place spinach, bacon and water chestnuts in a large salad bowl. Pour dressing over salad, toss lightly, sprinkle with salt and freshly ground pepper if desired. Garnish with fried Chinese noodles, if desired.

TLC Tip: This recipe makes more dressing than is necessary for the salad—at least for my taste. Usually I prepare half the amount of dressing. The dressing does keep well in the refrigerator, however, so you can use it on another salad or as a basting sauce for chicken or pork chops.

CORNBREAD SALAD

This is a very tasty, hearty salad that is great to take to church dinners, club luncheons, reunions or anywhere else a large dish is needed. For family meals, it can be easily cut in half. It does make a lot, so be sure you have a large dish to prepare it in. A clear dish makes a pretty presentation.

1 (1-ounce) package dry ranch
    dressing mix
1 cup sour cream
1 cup mayonnaise
1 (9") pan Tex-Mex cornbread,
    crumbled
2 (16-ounce) cans pinto beans,
    drained
3 large tomatoes, peeled and
    chopped

½ cup chopped green pepper
½ cup chopped green onions
8 ounces (2 cups) Cheddar
    cheese, grated
10 slices bacon, cooked and
    crumbled
2 (17-ounce) cans whole
    kernel corn, drained

Combine salad dressing mix, sour cream, and mayonnaise. Set aside. Place half of the crumbled cornbread in the bottom of a large serving bowl. Top with half of the beans. In a medium bowl, combine tomatoes, pepper, and onions; layer half of this mixture over the beans. Layer half of the cheese, bacon, corn and reserved salad dressing. Repeat layers using remaining ingredients. Garnish as desired. Cover and chill 2 to 3 hours before serving.

TLC Tip: *Tomatoes are most easily peeled if placed in a pan of boiling water for 30-40 seconds, then plunged into cold water to stop the heat. Whenever I fail to take the time to do this step, I always regret it. I have prepared this salad using reduced-fat sour cream and mayo and frankly, I couldn't tell the difference.*

SPINACH ORANGE SALAD

I like this salad for its fresh taste and good dressing. If you want to break from tradition, it would compliment a meal of Tex-Mex food.

1 large bunch spinach, stems
   removed
2 oranges
½ small jícama, peeled and
   cut into matchstick-like
   pieces (about 1 cup)

¼ cup toasted pecan halves
Lime Vinaigrette (recipe
   follows)

Wash and dry the spinach; chill until very crisp. Tear into bite-size pieces; place in large bowl. Pare oranges, removing white membrane. Cut segments between membranes to remove; chop. Add oranges, jícama and pecans to spinach. Prepare dressing; pour over spinach mixture and toss gently until well mixed.

Lime Vinaigrette:
3 tablespoons lime juice
2 tablespoons vegetable oil
2 tablespoons sour cream
2¼ teaspoons sugar

¼ teaspoon salt
⅛ teaspoons crushed red chili
   pepper
Dash of white pepper

Whisk ingredients in small bowl until well blended.

TLC Tip: *Jícama is a root vegetable with a crisp, mild, slightly sweet taste. Look for it in the produce section, near the mushrooms, chilis, and snow peas.*

SUMMERTIME DELIGHT

As the title hints, this salad is a delight to serve for those bridal luncheons in June, your backyard cookouts in July and light suppers during the dog days of August. Since fresh fruit is available nearly all year long these days, you can even enjoy this salad when summer is a mere memory. It is very easy to prepare, pretty to look at, and absolutely delicious.

1 pint fresh strawberries
1 (20-ounce) can pineapple
   chunks, drained
1 can mandarin oranges,
   drained
1 can dark, pitted cherries,
   drained
2 apples, diced

2 bananas, sliced
2 cups miniature
   marshmallows
1 cup pecan pieces
Confectioner's sugar
Cinnamon
1 (8-ounce) container
   whipped topping, thawed

Combine all the fruit and nuts in a large bowl. Sprinkle with sugar and cinnamon. Fold in whipped topping. Chill before serving.

MOM'S FAMOUS OVERNITE SALAD

Holiday dinners just never were complete without this salad, lovingly put together the night before, sometimes very late into the night, by my mother. My sister and sister-in-law carry on the tradition now, serving it often at special holiday dinners when their families gather. I think my mother found this recipe in one of her farm magazines. It is lovely to look at and delicious to eat.

3 egg yolks	1 cup whipping cream,
2 tablespoons lemon juice	whipped
2 tablespoons pineapple	2 cups drained pineapple
syrup (saved from fruit)	tidbits
2 tablespoons sugar	2 cups miniature
Dash of salt	marshmallows
1 tablespoon butter	¼ cup blanched slivered
1 large can Queen Anne	almonds
cherries	2 oranges

Combine egg yolks, lemon juice, pineapple syrup, sugar, salt, and butter in small saucepan. Cook over medium heat until thick, stirring constantly. Set aside to cool. Drain the cherries, and pit if necessary. In a large bowl, combine cherries, pineapple tidbits, marshmallows and almonds. Fold whipped cream into cooled dressing. Pour over fruit mixture and fold gently to combine. Chill 24 hours to allow the flavors to blend. Near serving time, peel the oranges with a sharp knife, keeping the peel in one long strip. Use the resulting corkscrew swirl to decorate center of the salad. Remove the membrane from the oranges and cut into sections. Arrange the sections around the swirl. This salad should serve 8-10 lucky people.

CITRUS AVOCADO SALAD

This is a wonderfully refreshing salad and good for you if you don't overdo the avocado. It makes a pretty salad platter for a buffet table or composed on salad plates for individual servings.

Dressing:
½ cup lowfat vanilla yogurt   ½ medium ripe banana, sliced
½ teaspoon lemon juice

Salad:
2 oranges, chilled   Lettuce leaves
1 grapefruit, chilled   ¼ cup thinly sliced green
1 ripe avocado   onions
1 tablespoon lemon juice   1 teaspoon poppy seed

In a blender or food processor, combine dressing ingredients; process until smooth. Pour into a small bowl; cover, and refrigerate at least 30 minutes. Using a sharp knife, peel oranges and grapefruit. Cut each crosswise into ¼" thick slices. Peel and pit avocado; cut into ¼" thick wedges. Sprinkle the lemon juice over the avocado wedges to prevent browning. Arrange fruit and avocado as desired on lettuce-lined platter. Sprinkle with green onions. Sprinkle poppy seed over the dressing. Serve on the side.

TLC Tip: Keep your poppy seed in the freezer as it can become rancid easily.

PISTACHIO PUDDING SALAD

This salad and all of its variations goes by many names but this particular one came from my mother. It is so simple to put together, and tastes out of this world. It is hard to stop eating it. I like to take this to potluck dinners or serve it with a simple meal when there is no dessert waiting in the wings.

1 (3-ounce) package instant   1 (8-ounce) can crushed
   pistachio pudding mix   pineapple, undrained
¾ cup pineapple juice   1 (8-ounce) carton whipped
                                    topping, thawed

Combine pudding mix, pineapple juice and crushed pineapple. Stir until it begins to thicken. Fold in the whipped topping. That's all there is to it!! Put into one of your prettiest glass bowls and chill for an hour or two (or more, if you want).

TLC Tip: Sometimes I add a handful or two of miniature marshmallows. That is the way daughter, Deanna, likes it best. She says it is better if it chills a while so the marshmallows have time to soften. Some flaked coconut and/or additional chopped pistachio nuts create yet another taste. One could get carried away here, but you get the idea.

SOUTHERN CITRUS SALAD

This is a good salad to serve in the winter when oranges and grapefruit are plentiful. It can be created in a large bowl for family-style service, or composed on individual plates. Either way you'll like it.

3 cups torn leaf lettuce
3 cups torn romaine lettuce
2 grapefruit, peeled, sectioned
3 oranges, peeled, sectioned

1 avocado, peeled, sliced
¼ cup slivered almonds,
   toasted

Toss lettuces together in a large bowl. Arrange fruit, avocado and almonds over greens. Serve with dressing.

Southern Citrus Dressing:
⅓ cup sugar
3 tablespoons vinegar
1 teaspoon finely chopped
   onion

½ teaspoon salt
½ teaspoon dry mustard
½ cup oil
2 teaspoons poppy seed

Combine sugar, vinegar, onion, salt and mustard in a blender container. Cover and process until blended. With machine running, add oil in a slow, steady, stream, processing until thick and smooth. Add poppy seed, process a few minutes until blended. Chill.

CHRISTMAS SALAD

I don't know where this salad got its name, as it certainly isn't limited to the holiday season. In fact, it is so easy to make you will find yourself preparing it for all sorts of occasions. It looks pretty served in a trifle dish. If you don't have one, why not put it on your wish list? It isn't expensive, and can be used in many ways.

1 (14-ounce) can condensed
   milk
1 (20-ounce) can crushed
   pineapple, undrained
2 cups miniature
   marshmallows
1 cup drained sour pie
   cherries or sliced fresh
   strawberries

1 cup coconut
1 can mandarin oranges,
   drained
1 cup chopped pecans
1 (8- or 12-ounce) container
   whipped topping, thawed

In a large bowl, combine the condensed milk and pineapple. Gently mix in the marshmallows, fruit, coconut and pecans. Fold in the whipped topping. Chill overnight. This makes a large salad. If you wish to serve it to your family, why not divide it in half and share with a friend?

THE NEW YEAR'S GATHERING

I think the New Year's Gathering was the highlight of the Yerden holiday season. Instead of getting together at Christmas, all of Grandma's children and grandchildren congregated on New Year's Day to enjoy each other and a community meal.

It was all planned very carefully—on a rotation basis. If it was at your home, you provided the meat, potatoes and gravy. The year after it was at your house, you provided the dessert. Sometime in the years in between, you provided the vegetables, salads and bread, butter and pickles.

On the day of the event, we began to gather as soon as daily routine could be finished, and the drive to the respective home made. Such fun to see everyone, some we hadn't seen in quite a while, though there really wasn't much distance between the families. Of course there would usually be some additions to the family group, as people married or had babies. Naturally we had to endure the "My, this can't be little Thelma!" and the "You certainly are getting BIG!"

I guess good cooks have always run in the Yerden family, as I remember the food to this day. Always a variety of things, but some things never changed—mashed potatoes, turkey, someone's yeast rolls (Mom's Parkerhouse were like feathers.), a fruit bread of some kind, probably the more ordinary kinds of vegetables like peas, corn and green beans— sometimes Harvard beets, and Aunt Evelyn's molded salads were a picture! I thought they were so neat.

When we were little, we kids didn't do much but get off to ourselves, catch up on the kid gossip, and play with some new Christmas game or toy. We were pretty good at inventing things to do, too. Naturally as we got older, the kinds of things we amused ourselves with changed. Our talk switched from dolls and trucks to boys and dates and college and careers.

Sometime after lunch we would all gather around Grandma's chair and present her with her Christmas presents—chocolates, a new dress or sweater—one year a TV! Then it would be time for the Grab Bag. Each family brought a small useful/funny gift for each member of the family. The collection would be passed around, and you took the package that appealed to you. If you didn't like it or couldn't use it, you were allowed to trade. Somehow we kids usually got the dish scratchers and the dust cloths!!

After the Grab Bag would come the highlight of the day—the program. There would be singing, piano solos or duets, poems, jokes and anything else one could think up for fun. One year we kids made up an original song, using the names of family members, to the tune of the currently popular

120

"Somebody Snitched on Me." It was a big hit. I'm sorry the words weren't written down for posterity.

Usually after the "program" we would start to think about disbanding. Of course in our case, there were chores crying to be done. Everyone would gather up their dishes, the leftovers, the grab bag gifts. There would be reminders not to forget boots and mittens, of where the gathering would be held the next year, and who was to bring what. Then we would pile into our cars and make our way home in the winter dusk, full of wonderful food and memories.

NEW YEAR'S GATHERING SEAFOOD MOLD

As a little girl, I thought Aunt Evelyn Yerden was terribly sophisticated. She, and my uncle Orrin, lived in Plainwell, Michigan. She taught school, always dressed up, wore make-up and she and my uncle played golf at the Country Club!! Besides all that, she played The Glow Worm on the piano when we got together for the New Year's Gathering. The dishes she prepared were always special. I think way back then I decided I would present food like she did. She made a jelled seafood salad that was in the shape of a fish. I was so impressed! This recipe is for you, Aunt Evelyn.

2 envelopes unflavored gelatin	2 tablespoons chopped fresh dill
1 (14¼-ounce) can chicken broth	½ teaspoon salt
¼ cup lemon juice	¼ teaspoon white pepper
1 (16-ounce) can red salmon	½ cup mayonnaise
1 cup finely cut celery	½ cup sour cream
2 tablespoons grated onion	Lettuce leaves
2 tablespoons chopped fresh parsley	1 pimiento-stuffed olive for garnish

Soften the gelatin in the chicken broth over low heat, stirring constantly until gelatin dissolves. Add the lemon juice. Drain the salmon, remove all bones and skin, and flake with a fork. Add to gelatin mixture along with the celery, onion, parsley, dill, salt, pepper, mayonnaise and sour cream. Spoon into a fish mold. Chill until set. Unmold on lettuce-lined plate. Use the olive slice for the fish's eye. Garnish with additional fresh dill sprigs and lemon wedges, if desired.

TLC Tip: *Grating onion is not much fun. The important thing here is that the onion be in very fine pieces. If you prefer to chop finely or use the food processor, I'm sure no one will know the difference.*

121

LINDA'S FAMOUS STRAWBERRY PRETZEL SALAD

Sister-in-law Linda comes through with another delicious recipe, this one often served as a salad, but could easily double as a dessert. Linda is always asked to bring this for church dinners and family get-togethers.

¾ cup butter, softened
5 tablespoons brown sugar
2½ cups crushed pretzels, not too fine
1 (6-ounce) package strawberry Jello
2 cups boiling water

2 small packages frozen, sweetened strawberries
8 ounces cream cheese
1 cup sugar
8 to 12 ounces whipped topping, thawed

Combine butter, sugar and pretzels. Press into a 9 x 13" buttered dish. Bake at 350 degrees for 10 minutes. Cool. Dissolve Jello in boiling water. Add frozen strawberries, stirring often until berries are thawed. Chill until slightly thickened. Cream the cheese and sugar well; beat in the whipped topping. Spread on the cooled crust, then top with gelatin mixture. Refrigerate. Cut in squares to serve.

TLC Tip: *Linda says that 8 ounces of whipped topping is enough, but if you like a really fluffy texture, use 12 ounces.*

CHERRIES JUBILEE FRUIT SALAD

I have served this salad often for its festive look and good taste. I think you will like the combination of flavors.

1 (16-ounce) can pitted dark sweet cherries
1 (3-ounce) package cherry gelatin
1 (16-ounce) can pear halves, drained, juice reserved

2 teaspoons sherry or vanilla flavoring + enough reserved pear juice to equal ½ cup
1 (3-ounce) package cream cheese, cut in small cubes
¼ cup chopped pecans

Drain cherries, reserving syrup. Add water to syrup to make 1½ cups. In medium saucepan, combine gelatin and syrup mixture. Heat and stir until gelatin dissolves. Remove from heat; stir in flavoring and juice mixture. Chill until partially set. Reserve 2 pear halves; slice and set aside for garnish. Chop remaining pears; fold into gelatin along with cherries, cheese cubes and pecans. Turn into a 4½-cup mold. Chill until firm. Unmold, garnish with lettuce leaves and pear slices. Makes 8 servings.

CHRISTMAS RIBBON RING

It is easy to see why this is a Christmas salad, with its red, white and green layers. Though it is a bit time-consuming to prepare, the end result is worth it for the oh's and ah's you will hear when you serve it.

1 (3-ounce) package
  strawberry gelatin
1 (16-ounce) can whole berry
  cranberry sauce
1 (3-ounce) package lemon
  gelatin
1 (8-ounce) package cream
  cheese, softened

1 (8-ounce) can crushed
  pineapple
¼ cup chopped pecans
1 (3-ounce) package lime
  gelatin
2 tablespoons sugar
1 (16-ounce) can grapefruit
  sections

Dissolve strawberry gelatin in 1¼ cups boiling water. Add cranberry sauce, mixing well. Chill until partially set. Pour into an 8-cup ring mold. Chill until almost firm. Dissolve lemon gelatin in 1¼ cups water; add cream cheese, beating smooth with electric beater. Add pineapple with juice; chill until partially set. Stir in pecans, then pour over the cranberry layer. Chill. Dissolve lime gelatin and sugar in 1 cup boiling water. Add grapefruit with juice. Chill until partially set; pour over cheese layer. Chill salad overnight. Unmold; garnish with curly leaf lettuce or endive. Because of the vivid colors in the salad, that will probably be all the garnish needed.

CRAN-RASPBERRY MOLD

This is a cheery red salad perfect for Thanksgiving or Christmas entertaining, but good any time of year. Try it with a dressing of mayonnaise and sour cream sweetened with a little sugar. It is simple to make—a plus for the holidays when we are all stretched to the limit.

2 (3-ounce) packages
  raspberry gelatin
1¾ cups boiling water

1 (16-ounce) can whole
  cranberry sauce
1 (20-ounce) can crushed
  pineapple, undrained

Dissolve gelatin in boiling water. Stir in cranberry sauce and undrained pineapple until cranberry sauce melts. Chill in a flat serving dish or your prettiest bowl. Garnish with dressing suggested above, mint leaves and sugared cranberries, if desired.

APRICOT SALAD RING

The next time you are called upon to bring a salad to a club luncheon or church dinner, try this one. It is a large salad and very good. For a garnish, I like to shape small cubes of cream cheese into balls, then roll them in chopped nuts and place them in canned apricot halves, arranging them on lettuce leaves around the ring mold. Serve the dressing from a container that sits in the center of the ring mold.

2 (3-ounce) packages lemon gelatin	1 (20-ounce) can crushed pineapple, drained
1 (3-ounce) package orange gelatin	½ cup chopped nuts
3 cups boiling water	1 can apricot or peach pie filling, divided use
2 cups cold water	

Dissolve gelatins in boiling water. Stir in cold water. Chill until gelatin is syrupy and thickened. Add pineapple, nuts, and all but ½ cup pie filling. Pour into oiled 6-cup ring mold and chill until set. Turn out on serving plate and garnish as desired.

CREAMY APRICOT DRESSING

1 (3-ounce) package cream cheese, softened	1 cup whipping cream, whipped
Reserved pie filling	½ cup powdered sugar
2 to 3 tablespoons milk, if needed	½ teaspoon vanilla
	¼ teaspoon almond extract

Blend cream cheese with reserved pie filling, adding milk to thin if necessary. Fold sugar and flavorings into whipped cream. Combine with cream cheese mixture. Serve with the salad.

JELLED PEACH MOLD

I've made this salad so-o many times!! I love the flavor and it goes with so many different kinds of meals. It is prepared ahead, which is always a plus, and great for Sunday dinners and a special treat for family suppers.

1 large can sliced peaches or 2 (16-ounce) cans	1 (6-ounce) package orange gelatin
2 to 4 tablespoons vinegar (to your taste)	Walnut halves
1 teaspoon whole cloves	Additional peach slices
1 (4") stick cinnamon	Mayonnaise

Combine the peaches, vinegar, and spices in a medium saucepan. Heat to boiling, remove from heat, cover and let stand 6 minutes. Remove peach slices and chill. Strain hot syrup and measure, adding enough boiling water to make 2 cups. Dissolve gelatin in the hot liquid; add 1¾ cups cold water. Chill until partially set. Add the peaches; pour into decorative mold or flat dish. Chill until firm. Unmold on serving plate; decorate with peach slices, mayonnaise and walnut halves, if desired. Or cut into squares, place on a lettuce-lined plate and decorate as desired.

AUNT MÁCO'S DELICIOUS SALAD

This salad was a favorite of my Aunt Máco, and no doubt it will become one of your favorites too. It lends itself well to lady-like luncheons or buffet tables, and can be served with a spoon or cut into squares and placed on a lettuce-lined plate. An additional sprinkling of cheese on the top makes for an attractive presentation.

1 (3-ounce) package lemon gelatin	1 cup chopped pecans
1 cup boiling water	8 ounces Cheddar cheese, grated
1 (20-ounce) can crushed pineapple	1 cup whipping cream, whipped
½ cup sugar	

Dissolve gelatin in boiling water. Combine pineapple and juice with the sugar in a small saucepan. Heat 3 minutes over low heat; add to dissolved gelatin; cool. Stir in the pecans and grated cheese and chill until mixture begins to set. Fold in the whipped cream. Chill until firm. Serve as desired.

TLC Tip: *Personally, I don't find it necessary to add additional sugar if I use sweetened pineapple. If you use the canned-in-juice variety, you might want to add some, but still not ½ cup perhaps. I see no reason not to use reduced-fat Cheddar or 2 cups whipped topping to replace the whipped cream.*

STRAWBERRY SALAD

I have made this salad more times than I can recall and it is always a big hit, especially with the young people. I must confess that most times I prepare it without the sour cream and no one seems to mind, but the addition of the sour cream step elevates it a bit to a more sophisticated level. Either way you do it you'll like it.

2 (3-ounce) packages strawberry Jello	1 (14-ounce) package frozen, sweetened strawberries
2 cups boiling water	4 bananas, mashed
1 (8-ounce) can crushed pineapple, drained	1 cup chopped pecans
	1 pint sour cream

Pour the boiling water over the Jello and dissolve well. Add the strawberries and stir until they separate and are mostly thawed. Add pineapple, bananas and pecans. Pour ½ the mixture into a 9 x 13" pan. Chill until firm. Spread sour cream over the top; carefully pour the remaining gelatin over the sour cream and chill again. Cut into squares to serve.

TLC Tip: *If you would prefer to spoon-serve the salad, chilling it in a trifle dish makes a pretty presentation. For a special luncheon, I might chill the salad without layering the sour cream, cut into squares, place on lettuce-lined plate, top with a dab of sour cream and garnish with fresh strawberry half, green top included.*

GINGERED PEAR MOLD

I really like the flavor of this salad, and the fact that it is not heavy on the sugar. It has a light, refreshing taste, and is a good addition to your Sunday dinner.

1 cup ginger ale	¼ cup sugar
½ cup cranberry juice cocktail	½ teaspoon ginger
	½ cup water
1 teaspoon cider vinegar	1 (16-ounce) can pear halves,
1 envelope unflavored gelatin	well drained and sliced

In a medium bowl, combine ginger ale, cranberry juice and vinegar; set aside. In small saucepan, stir together gelatin, sugar, ginger and water. Stir over medium heat until gelatin and sugar dissolve. Stir into ginger ale mixture. Chill until consistency of unbeaten egg white. Fold in pears; pour into 3- to 4-cup mold. Chill several hours or overnight. Unmold to serve.

TLC Tip: *When I'm in a hurry, or not feeling very creative, I put the sliced pears in a pretty glass bowl, pour the gelatin mixture over and chill and serve in the same bowl. If you choose to unmold, reduce the ginger ale by ¼ cup.*

FROSTED 7-UP SALAD

This is an oldie but goodie from my files—the type that you aren't quite sure whether to call salad or dessert. I like to serve a salad of this type as part of a luncheon plate with a straightforward kind of sandwich such as sliced turkey or roast beef or as part of a salad plate that also might include Southwest Couscous Salad (see index) and soft breadsticks. In this case, I probably would forgo dessert. This salad is also great to carry to a potluck dinner—I guarantee you won't carry any of it home!

2 small packages lemon gelatin	2 bananas, mashed
2 cups boiling water	½ cup sugar
2 cups 7-Up	2 tablespoons flour
1 (20-ounce) can crushed pineapple, drained	1 cup pineapple juice
1 cup miniature marshmallows	1 egg, beaten
	1 tablespoon butter
	1 cup whipping cream, whipped

Dissolve the gelatin in the boiling water, stirring until completely dissolved. Add 7-Up; chill until syrupy. Add the drained pineapple, marshmallows, and bananas. Pour into 9 x 13" or similar serving dish, place in refrigerator and continue chilling until firm. Meanwhile, combine sugar, flour, pineapple juice and beaten egg. Cook over medium heat until thick, stirring often. Remove from heat and stir in butter. Cool. When completely cool, fold in whipped cream. Pour over firm gelatin, smoothing attractively. Cut into squares to serve.

TLC Tip: *I like to keep on hand the small cans of pineapple juice to use in cases like this where a small amount is needed. Of course you can use the juice drained from the crushed pineapple, but will need additional. Though the small cans are more expensive, quantity wise, I consider it a saving in the long run as I would probably end up throwing out most of the large economy size.*

HEAVENLY PINEAPPLE MOLD

These days it seems that molded, gelatin salads have gone out of style—I guess in part due to the time element and also because this type of salad tends to be higher in sugar, fat and calories. I feel that there is still a place for them in our recipe files, however, and this one from my mother is a good one. When you read this recipe, I think you will be able to see how it could be lightened up a bit and feel free to do so.

1 (3-ounce) package lemon
    gelatin
1 cup boiling water
¾ cup pineapple juice
1 tablespoon lemon juice
1 (20-ounce) can crushed
    pineapple, drained
    (about 1¼ cups)

1 cup shredded sharp cheese
    (I like the Cracker Barrel
    brand)
1 cup whipping cream,
    whipped

Pour the boiling water over the gelatin and stir until thoroughly dissolved. Add the pineapple and lemon juices, and chill until slightly thickened. Fold in the drained pineapple, shredded cheese and whipped cream. Pour into a mold and chill until firm. Unmold onto a serving platter and garnish as desired. I sometimes circle the mold with leaf lettuce, pineapple slice halves with a small dollop of whipped cream in the hole and sprinkled with additional shredded cheese.

TLC Tip: *This salad can easily be chilled in a serving dish for a simpler presentation. The salad can then be cut into squares or served with a spoon.*

CHICKEN AVOCADO SALAD

This is a wonderful main-dish salad. The next time you host a luncheon, try serving this after a cup of tomato soup and before Chocolate Cups Olé (see index). You'll be the Hostess with the Mostest!!

2 cups cut-up chicken
4 ounces hot pepper cheese,
   cut in strips
1 (16-ounce) can kidney
   beans, drained and
   rinsed
2 stalks celery, thinly sliced
10 cherry tomatoes, cut in
   half

1 small onion, finely diced
Chili Mayonnaise (recipe
   follows)
1 medium avocado
1 head lettuce, torn into
   pieces (I prefer romaine)
Tortilla chips

Place the chicken, cheese, beans, celery, tomatoes and onion in a large bowl. Cover and refrigerate 4-6 hours. Prepare the Chili Mayonnaise. Just before serving, peel the avocado and cut into thin slices. Add to the salad with the lettuce; toss with the dressing. Top with 1 cup broken tortilla chips. Garnish with additional avocado, if desired, and serve with additional whole chips.

CHILI MAYONNAISE

½ cup salad dressing
¼ cup chili sauce

½ teaspoon salt
2 drops red pepper sauce

Mix all ingredients. Cover and refrigerate at least 1 hour.

TLC Tip: If making tomato soup from scratch seems too time-consuming, and opening a can too plain, do try this variation. Dilute canned tomato soup with half water and half milk. Add some canned, chopped green chilis (to taste) and heat slowly. Top each serving with a little grated cheese.

J. L. HUDSON'S MAURICE SALAD

During the years I lived in the Detroit area, it was always a treat to eat in the dining room of Hudson's department store. This salad was one of their trademarks and a particular favorite with "ladies who lunched". As you can see by the ingredient list, this was BC—before cholesterol. I have the fondest memories of this salad.

2 raw egg yolks (always use
    raw eggs with care)
¼ cup lemon juice
¼ cup non-dairy creamer, dry
¼ cup sugar
1 teaspoon onion salt
1 tablespoon Dijon mustard
1 cup canola oil

1 cup sour cream
1 tablespoon dry minced
    parsley
Shredded salad greens
Matchsticks of Swiss cheese,
    lean boiled ham and
    turkey breast

Put egg yolks, lemon juice and creamer into blender and blend on high speed 1 minute. Turn to medium speed while adding sugar, onion powder and mustard. Add canola oil very gradually, about 1 spoonful at a time. Transfer to mixing bowl and add sour cream and parsley, which has been rubbed to a fine dust between your fingers. Fill a salad plate with a generous amount of salad greens; arrange the cheese, ham and turkey attractively on top. Pour desired amount of dressing over all. Extra dressing will keep in the refrigerator about a week.

SOUTHWESTERN COUSCOUS SALAD

Somehow preparing this salad causes me to pause and reflect on the place I live—Big Spring, Texas. Big Spring is a small town that some would say has seen better days. But you can't beat the weather—our really cold days are few in number. Most years we don't get enough rain, but we have magnificent sunsets. Our trees are scarce and small, but the blooming cactus is a sight to behold. This is the Southwest, and it has a beauty all its own that I've come to love very much. This main-dish salad has a wonderful flavor. It also has the plus of providing complex carbs and non-animal protein. It keeps well, travels well, looks attractive and is good for you. Need I say more?

1½ cups water
1 cup uncooked couscous
2 cups frozen corn with red and green peppers, thawed and drained
1 (15-ounce) can black beans, drained and rinsed
¼ cup chopped, seeded tomato

2 tablespoons sliced green onions
2 tablespoons chopped fresh cilantro or parsley
⅓ cup olive oil
¼ to ⅓ cup fresh lime juice
¼ teaspoon salt, if desired
¼ teaspoon garlic powder
¼ teaspoon cumin
⅛ teaspoon cayenne pepper

Bring the water to a boil in a small saucepan; remove from heat. Stir in couscous; allow to stand 5 minutes. Cool completely. In large bowl, combine couscous, corn and peppers mixture, black beans, tomato, green onions and cilantro; toss to combine. In small jar with tight-fitting lid, combine olive oil, lime juice, salt, garlic powder, cumin and cayenne pepper; shake well. Pour over salad; toss to coat. Cover and refrigerate at least 1 hour to blend flavors. Line a serving platter with leaf lettuce leaves; spoon salad over leaves. Garnish with lime slices and fresh cilantro if desired. Should make 12 (½ cup) servings, less if using as the main course.

TLC Tip: Cilantro seems to be a seasoning you either like or dislike, no middle ground. Personally, I love it for its pungent, slightly spicy flavor. If you don't care for it, be sure to use the chopped fresh parsley. The color contrast is a nice addition to this dish.

BEST OF THE SOUTHWEST TACO SALAD

One taste and you will know how this salad got its name. Filling enough to serve as the main course, it is especially tasty with the Avocado Dressing.

1 pound ground beef
1 (10-ounce) can tomatoes and
   green chilis
½ teaspoon garlic powder
½ teaspoon salt (or to taste)
1 teaspoon chili powder
1 bunch romaine lettuce, torn
   into pieces

3 tomatoes, chopped
1 cup sharp, reduced-fat
   Cheddar cheese
3 green onions with tops,
   chopped
Sliced ripe olives
Crushed tortilla chips

In a large non-stick skillet, brown meat and pour off any accumulated fat. Mix in the tomatoes and green chilis, garlic powder, salt and chili powder. Simmer for 10 minutes. To serve, layer lettuce, meat, tomatoes, cheese, green onions, olives and chips. Top with Avocado Dressing.

AVOCADO DRESSING

2 avocados, mashed
2 tablespoons lemon juice
1 cup lite sour cream
⅔ cup salad oil

1 teaspoon sugar
½ to 1 teaspoon garlic salt
1 teaspoon chili powder

Combine all ingredients, blending until smooth.

TLC Tip: *As with dishes of this nature, feel free to adjust the seasonings to your liking. As an option, you might like to omit the tortilla chips and serve the salad in a tortilla bowl. These can be purchased in the Mexican food section of most supermarkets, or you can easily make your own. Soften flour or corn tortillas by wrapping them in foil and heating in a 350 degree oven for 10 minutes. Remove from foil, spray both sides with vegetable oil spray, and press into oven-proof bowls to shape, one to each bowl. Bake for 15 minutes or until crisp.*

GREAT CHICKEN SALAD

There are all kinds of wonderful chicken salad recipes. Some with fruit, some with nuts, others with olives, marinated artichoke hearts, and on and on. You probably have a favorite in your own files that you use over and over. This one has less fat than most, and tastes so good you won't miss the fat—I promise!

3 cups cooked, diced chicken
   breast (grilled chicken
   gives a really good
   flavor)
1½ cups diced celery
½ cup diced green onions
¼ cup minced fresh parsley
1 cup diced water chestnuts
1 apple, diced
2 tablespoons whole-grain
   mustard

½ cup lowfat buttermilk
2½ tablespoons plain nonfat
   yogurt
2½ tablespoons reduced
   calorie mayonnaise
1½ tablespoons lemon juice
Pinch of salt
Freshly ground black pepper,
   to taste

Mix first 6 ingredients together and set aside. Combine remaining ingredients in a separate bowl; add to chicken mixture. Combine gently but thoroughly. Serve as desired.

TLC Tip: *Serve this as part of a salad plate, perhaps choosing one of the jelled salads and/or pasta salads from the index. Or mound on a lettuce leaf and serve with your choice of rolls or crackers. This makes an equally good sandwich—wonderful on a great mixed grain bread or try it on raisin bread.*

DE-LITE-FUL TUNA SALAD

This is a spa-type salad—it fills you up, not out. The ingredient list may be longer than the tuna salad you are used to, but the combination of fruit and vegetables is really good. The dressing is lite and tasty. This salad does not hold very well, so plan on serving it soon after it is made.

1 (6½-ounce) can water-
    packed tuna
1 stalk celery, diced
2 tablespoons fresh minced
    parsley, optional
2 tablespoons diced onion
¼ cup diced apple
2 tablespoons sweet pickle
    relish

½ cup halved grapes
2 tablespoons grated carrots
¼ cup plain, nonfat yogurt
2 tablespoons reduced-calorie
    mayonnaise
1 tablespoon sesame seeds
¼ teaspoon dried dillweed
Freshly ground pepper, to
    taste

Mix all ingredients together, chill and serve.

TLC Tip: *This is a versatile salad. You can serve it between two slices of bread—hearty whole wheat is especially good. You can stuff it into a pita pocket. You can mound it on a lettuce leaf and serve breadsticks, crackers, or melba toast alongside.*

BARB TAYLOR'S PASTA SALAD

Barb and Colin Taylor live in Spokane, Washington. We became acquainted with them on a trip to Denmark and Sweden that we won for our efforts in the electronics distribution business. Some of our loveliest vacation times have been spent with them touring their beautiful Pacific Northwest. One year we were guests on their boat for a trip through the San Juan Islands. Barb put together this salad for one of our lunches during that trip. It is a favorite of her family—we like it too.

8 to 12 ounces rainbow rotelli pasta (or other favorite shape)

4 cups mixed vegetables, lightly steamed (I especially like broccoli, cauliflower and carrots)

1 onion, chopped

Sliced black olives—as much as you like

¾ cup creamy Italian dressing

¼ to ⅓ cup green peppercorn or similar dressing

Freshly grated Parmesan cheese

Dillweed, to taste (I like a lot)

Cook the pasta until just tender in salted water. Drain, rinse briefly in cold water and combine with remaining ingredients. Add salt and pepper if necessary; adjust other seasonings to your taste. Serve at room temperature or chill before serving.

TLC Tip: Use your imagination and special favorites in choosing the vegetables. Besides those mentioned, others that are good are green peas, red, yellow or green pepper strips, or sugar snap peas.

CHICKEN PASTA SALAD

Lynda Elrod is a very busy lady. She is a former Home Ec teacher who has turned her talents to decorating, running a furniture store with her husband, Dee, here in Big Spring, and keeping up with two teenage daughters. Thanks to her recipe file, this was the salad served for the Symphony Guild Luncheon and Fashion Show one spring when I was in charge. We prepared enough of this salad to serve about 70 people. It is a great tasting salad, hearty yet not heavy, and a wonderful summer meal. We served the salad on a lettuce leaf and garnished each plate with green and black olives, cherry tomatoes and marinated artichoke hearts. We started the meal with Parmesan Mushroom Soup (see index) and served breadsticks alongside. Dessert was Tortoni Delight (see index again). My own family has requested this dish on several occasions.

2 cloves garlic
1 cup olive oil, divided use
3 chicken breast halves, boned and skinned
Salt and lemon pepper for seasoning
16 ounces dried pasta (a combination of tortellini and corkscrew is nice)
3 ounces cooked ham, cut into thin strips

3 stalks celery, diced
1 green pepper, diced
1 small red onion, thinly sliced
⅓ pound smoked Gouda cheese, cut into thin strips
2 tablespoons Dijon mustard
1 teaspoon dry mustard
¾ cup tarragon vinegar
¾ cup honey

Heat 1 tablespoon olive oil in large non-stick skillet over medium-low heat. Add the garlic cloves and sauté until garlic is fragrant, then remove. Turn heat to medium-high, add the chicken breasts, sprinkle with salt and lemon pepper and sauté 5 minutes or so on each side, until lightly browned and cooked through. (Cut into the thickest part of one breast to check for doneness.) Remove and reserve. Cook pasta as directed on the package in salted water. If using two different types of pasta, cook separately. Drain and toss with 2 tablespoons olive oil. Cool. Cut the chicken breast into bite-size strips or chunks. In a large bowl, combine the chicken, pasta, celery, pepper, onion, cheese and ham. In a small bowl, combine remaining olive oil, mustards, vinegar and honey to make a vinaigrette. Pour over salad and toss well to combine. Chilling overnight is best. Should make 12 (1-cup) servings.

TLC Tip: *For optimum flavor, it really is best to sauté the chicken breast rather than poaching it. You can even grill the breast if desired.*

POPPY SEED DRESSING A LA BARB TAYLOR

This dressing will make you love eating your raw cabbage! Of course the hefty amounts of sugar and oil might cancel the benefits of the cabbage, but once in awhile, go for it!!

1½ cups sugar	2 tablespoons onion juice or
2 teaspoons dry mustard	grated onion
2 teaspoons salt	2 cups salad oil
	2 to 3 teaspoons poppy seed

Blend the sugar, mustard, salt and onion juice or onion. Whisk in the oil gradually until well combined and smooth. Stir in the poppy seed. Serve over fresh fruit or grated or shredded cabbage. This makes a quart so share with your friends.

LITE RANCH DRESSING MIX

This dressing tastes so much fresher than the light dressings that come in a bottle, and certainly doesn't contain the chemicals. Since you can mix the dry ingredients ahead and keep on hand, it is extremely simple to make fresh dressing as needed. A package of the dry mix makes a nice little token gift for friends and family.

¼ cup dried parsley	½ teaspoon garlic powder
3 tablespoons dried minced	½ teaspoon ground celery
onion	seed
2 teaspoons dried chives	½ teaspoon dried dillweed
1 teaspoon salt	¼ teaspoon black pepper

Combine the dressing mix ingredients in a small jar and mix well. Store in a dry place. To make the dressing, combine 1 tablespoon of the dressing mix with ¼ cup light mayonnaise in a small bowl. Mix thoroughly with a wire whisk. Add 1 cup buttermilk slowly, stirring constantly until well mixed. Refrigerate in a tightly-covered container to blend flavors.

TLC Tip: *Be sure to stir the dry mix well before measuring out the 1 tablespoon.*

THOMAS' RESTAURANT ROQUEFORT DRESSING

Thomas' Restaurant was THE place to dine in Pryor, Oklahoma. We have had many an evening meal there while visiting the relatives or used it as a stopping-off place for coffee after a morning of shopping. If Uncle Harve and Aunt Máco weren't home, you could be reasonably sure you would find them at Thomas'. The restaurant served a wonderful Roquefort Dressing. It made even plain head lettuce taste good. This recipe comes from my Aunt Máco.

1 wedge Roquefort cheese, (about 4 ounces) crumbled	2 cups mayonnaise
	1 clove garlic, put through garlic press
1 cup buttermilk	¼ to ½ teaspoon onion salt

Combine all ingredients well with wire whisk or electric mixer.

TLC Tip: *Sometimes I add a little more buttermilk if the dressing is thicker than I like.*

DENNIS' CREAMY ITALIAN DRESSING

Dennis is my daughter, Cyndee's, brother-in-law. He has made a career in the food business, managing several different restaurants and delis, and doing a fair amount of catering in the Dallas/Fort Worth area. This recipe comes from his files.

1 cup well-mixed Italian dressing	1 cup mayonnaise
	¼ cup sour cream

Combine well with a wire whisk.

Soups, Stews and Sandwiches

The soup I enjoyed during my childhood was simple and straightforward—no exotic ingredients or fancy names. We liked Potato Soup and Beef Rice Soup, which was more hearty and similar to a stew. Mock Oysters was a soup made with cabbage. When I was older we enjoyed chili. Michigan Bean Soup was another favorite, always with ham hocks or snippets of leftover ham. Soup was served at the evening meals always with saltine crackers and sometimes with a hot bread such as cornbread or muffins.

We nearly always carried sandwiches to school, but I don't remember much about what they contained. What I do remember is that my mother always spread the butter, mayonnaise, and/or filling to the edge of the bread, so whatever kind we had was delicious. I know we had peanut butter, and often with the addition of long, thin slices of mom's home-canned dill pickles added. We would have meatloaf if there happened to be any leftovers, and my brother and I would sometimes make an onion sandwich if we were hungry at bringing-up-the-cows time. As I got older, we had cheese sandwiches, and my mother made Pimiento Cheese spread, which I didn't develop a taste for until much later. Today it is my favorite sandwich. We also had Egg Salad occasionally.

I don't think we consumed sandwiches as part of regular meals—only for picnics, snacks, school lunches, and those times when dad was working at the back of the farm and didn't want to take the time to come to the house for lunch.

NAVY BEAN SOUP CARLILE

This is my version of a soup made with Michigan navy beans. Hearty and satisfying, it keeps well for warming over the second day. Try it served with cole slaw and corn sticks.

1 pound dry navy beans	1 large carrot, chopped
Water	4 sprigs fresh parsley
2 to 3 smoked turkey legs	½ lemon, sliced
1 tablespoon oil	1 bay leaf
2 onions, chopped	¾ teaspoon dried thyme
1 clove garlic, minced	Salt to taste
½ cup sliced celery	Grindings of black pepper

Sort and wash the beans, cover with plenty of cold water and let set overnight. Place the turkey legs in a large stew pot and cover with 6 cups water. Bring to a boil, reduce heat and simmer gently for 1 hour. Remove turkey legs, strain and reserve liquid for broth. Skin the turkey legs, remove meat from bone and chop coarsely. Drain the beans, return to stock pot and cover with the reserved broth and enough boiling water so liquid is about 2 inches above the beans. Bring to a boil, reduce heat and simmer 1 hour. While beans are simmering, heat the oil in a non-stick skillet. Sauté the onion, garlic, celery and carrot until vegetables are crisp-tender. After the beans have simmered 1 hour, add the sautéed vegetables, parsley sprigs, lemon slices, bay leaf and thyme. Continue cooking for another 1-2 hours until beans are tender, adding more boiling water if soup becomes too thick. Remove the lemon slices, parsley sprigs, and bay leaf. Purée 2 cups of beans with liquid in the blender or food processor. Return to soup kettle, taste and season with salt and pepper. Add the reserved turkey meat. Heat gently for a few minutes more.

MEXICAN CHICKEN SOUP

In 1992, Cleo's competitive spirit drew him, and his tennis partner, Darrell Hendrickson, to the Cowtown Open in Fort Worth. Of course I tagged along to cheer them on, and Cyndee and Darell and the girls drove over to lend their support. Between matches, we ate lunch at Water Street Seafood Restaurant. Cyndee and I enjoyed this great soup. Right off we knew we just had to have the recipe. At the cash register they had recipe coloring books for sale and luckily the soup was a part of the collection. Here it is, for you to sample too, with our own variations.

1 (2½-pound) chicken, cut up and skinned
13 cups water
2½ tablespoons chicken stock base
1 teaspoon white pepper (this might be too much for your taste; feel free to adjust)
2½ teaspoons ground cumin
1 sprig fresh basil
2 bay leaves
3 whole cloves

2 teaspoons oregano leaves
2 cloves garlic, minced
⅓ bunch fresh cilantro, chopped
6 carrots, sliced
1 small onion, diced
2 (16-ounce) cans garbanzo beans, drained and rinsed
¾ pound zucchini, sliced
Cooked rice
Sliced avocado
Pico de gallo or picante sauce

In a large pot, bring the chicken and water to a boil, reduce heat and simmer until the chicken is tender, about 30 to 45 minutes. Remove chicken from pot, cool; then remove meat from bones; set aside. To the broth, add the chicken stock base, white pepper, ground cumin, basil, bay leaves, whole cloves, oregano leaves, and minced garlic. Add the cilantro, carrots and onion to the pot; cook until vegetables are tender. Add the garbanzo beans, zucchini and reserved chicken; cook just briefly—zucchini should be tender-crisp. Spoon rice into serving bowls, top with soup. Garnish with avocado slices and pico de gallo, then enjoy!!

TLC Tip: *You can serve this soup in small bowls as an appetizer or larger ones as the main dish. I think warm tortillas are great to serve with it and how about a caramel custard for dessert? Olé!*

TURKEY SOUP

This is the soup to make with the turkey carcass after the holidays. Talk about frugal—this is it, but no one will complain because it tastes so good. After the carving is done, and the bones are picked, scoop all the carcass and skin into a large 2-gallon self-seal bag and refrigerate right away, or even freeze, depending on the after-holiday schedule. When soup day arrives, I'm ready. This soup is made in two parts—the stock first, then the soup. I've made this soup without the leeks, but I do think they add a special taste, so I always try to include them.

Stock:

Turkey carcass, skin included	2 cups chopped celery tops
16 cups water	1 cup scrubbed and chopped
½ cup or more turkey gravy	carrots
1 bay leaf	1 cup chopped, peeled onion
6 sprigs fresh thyme or 1	1 cup chopped green part of
teaspoon dried	leek

Put carcass and skin in large stock pot. Add water, gravy and rest of ingredients. Bring to a boil and let simmer 1 hour. As the broth cooks, skim off and discard any scum, foam and fat that rises to the surface. Strain the broth into a clean kettle; chill. Remove fat from the top. Note: No salt is not a mistake; salt is added in the soup step. The stock can be frozen at this point if you aren't in the mood for turkey soup.

Soup:

Reserved turkey stock	½ cup orzo or other small
2 cups sliced carrots	pasta
2 cups diced celery	1 cup fresh or frozen corn
½ cup finely chopped onion	kernels
2 cups tomatoes, peeled and	1 cup cooked turkey meat
cubed (fresh is best, but	(or more if you wish)
canned, drained will do)	¼ cup finely chopped parsley
1 to 2 teaspoons salt	½ cup freshly grated
2 cups cubed zucchini	Parmesan cheese
½ teaspoon minced garlic	

Bring the stock to a boil; add the carrots, celery, leeks, onion, tomatoes, zucchini and garlic. Let simmer about 10 minutes, then add the pasta. Continue cooking 5 minutes and add the corn kernels and turkey meat. Season with the salt and continue cooking 15 minutes. Stir in the parsley. Serve with the cheese on the side.

TLC Tip: *A hot loaf of French or Italian bread makes a good accompaniment to the soup.*

143

ITALIAN VEGETABLE SOUP

Anything Italian makes me sit up and take notice, so this recipe really made a hit with me. Though it is not a last-minute recipe and the ingredient list is long, it is well worth the trouble and excellent to serve to a hungry crowd of football fans or skiers that are chilled to the bone. As with all recipes, be sure to read through the entire recipe before beginning to ensure that you have all the ingredients and become familiar with the procedure.

1 pound great Northern beans
1 tablespoon olive oil
1 tablespoon butter
1 large carrot, peeled and
   diced
2 cups diced celery
1½ cups sliced leeks, white
   part only
1 (16-ounce) can tomatoes,
   undrained
3 quarts beef stock,
   homemade or canned
¼ pound sliced prosciutto, or
   lean ham, cut into bite-
   size pieces

1½ teaspoons salt (optional)
1 clove garlic, peeled and
   crushed
3 sprigs fresh parsley
1 teaspoon dried basil leaves
1 tablespoon dried oregano
2 cups coarsely diced raw,
   peeled potato
2 (9-ounce) packages Italian
   green beans
4 small zucchini, sliced
2 cups shredded cabbage
½ cup uncooked elbow
   macaroni

Wash the beans and soak in cold water overnight. Drain; place beans in large pot, cover with water and cook, covered, about 1 hour, or until beans are soft. Drain. Combine butter and oil in another large pot. Heat over moderately-low heat. Add the carrot, celery and leeks and cook about 5 minutes, stirring occasionally. Stir in the tomatoes, mashing slightly with spoon. Simmer 10 minutes. Add the beef stock, ham and white beans. Simmer 30 minutes, covered. Add salt, garlic, parsley, basil and oregano. Stir in the potatoes and Italian beans. Simmer, uncovered, 10 minutes. Add the zucchini, cabbage and macaroni. Simmer 8 minutes longer. Serve in large bowls; sprinkle each serving with freshly grated Parmesan cheese if desired. Should serve 12 as the main dish.

TLC Tip: You can substitute cut green beans for the Italian beans if necessary.

TINA'S POTASSIUM BROTH

Tina is a nutritionist we knew in San Diego, California. She is a lovely lady and very dedicated to helping people live a healthy lifestyle. She gave us the recipe for this soup, which I think will do everything a Jewish Mother's Chicken Soup will do. It is nourishing and satisfying, and healing too, I do believe. I don't tinker with the ingredients in this one, because I figure Tina knew what she was doing when she combined things just this way. This recipe will be a real asset to your repertoire.

About 2 quarts water,
    perhaps more
2 to 3 carrots, cut up
2 to 3 stalks celery, cut up
1 to 2 parsnips, cut up
    (optional)
2 to 3 cloves garlic, minced

1 to 2 sprigs fresh parsley
2 to 3 medium potatoes,
    scrubbed, skins left on,
    cut into chunks
3 to 4 chicken legs (or thighs
    or breasts) skinned but
    left whole

Place all ingredients in a large pot. Bring to a boil, and simmer 30 to 45 minutes until everything is tender. Add natural herbs and seasonings as desired, a little salt if you wish and pepper to taste. Reheats well.

TLC Tip: *If you feel the need for seasoning, 1 bay leaf, 1 teaspoon dried basil, 1 teaspoon dried thyme and 1 to 2 teaspoons salt is a good combination.*

ASPARAGUS SOUP

This soup has become a favorite of ours in recent years. It is easy to make, low in calories, high in nutrition and the ingredients can be kept on hand for an instant addition to lunch or supper. Save an asparagus tip to garnish each serving, if desired.

2 cups cut asparagus, drained
    (2 10½-ounce cans)
3 cups defatted chicken broth
2 cups skim milk, part
    evaporated, if desired

4 tablespoons flour
¼ to ½ teaspoon curry
    powder, optional
Salt to taste

Purée asparagus in blender or food processor with some of the broth. Transfer to saucepan and heat to almost boiling. Dissolve flour in milk and add to asparagus purée. Add seasoning and continue to heat over low heat until mixture returns to boiling and thickens, stirring constantly. Um-m, good!!

TLC Tip: *Some folks don't like curry, so choose another favorite seasoning if you wish. I happen to like the curry, and always add it to my portion even if I don't season the whole recipe with it.*

BEEF RICE SOUP

We always carried this soup on our trips to visit mother's family in Oklahoma. Mother would pack it into blue glass canning jars, and she would heat it up for our supper in the cabin, always somewhere after we had crossed "the bridge" over the Mississippi River. "The bridge" was the Chain of Rocks Bridge. She used beef from cows we had raised on the farm. As we didn't have a freezer, she cut the beef into chunks and canned it. I do have good memories of this soup, hearty and thick with rice. I don't think mother used a recipe, so this is my rendition. All you need is a simple salad and some good bread or even saltine crackers for a supper that will stick to your ribs.

2 pounds good quality stew
    meat
2 onions, halved and sliced
2 (14-ounce) cans beef broth
4 cups water
1 bay leaf

⅓ cup long grain rice
1 tablespoon Worcestershire
    sauce
Salt to taste (I use maybe ½
    teaspoon)

Spray a large Dutch oven or soup pot with cooking spray. Brown the meat with the onions over medium-high heat, stirring often. Add the broth, water and bay leaf and bring to a boil. Lower heat and simmer slowly 3 hours. Add the rice, Worcestershire sauce and salt, if necessary, and continue cooking 1 hour more.

PARMESAN MUSHROOM SOUP

This is a wonderful, rich soup, best served as a first course, in my opinion.

2 cups sliced fresh
    mushrooms
½ cup chopped onion
1 clove garlic, minced
2 tablespoons butter
3 cups chicken broth
3 tablespoons tomato paste

¼ teaspoon salt
4 slightly beaten egg yolks
¼ cup grated Parmesan
    cheese
3 tablespoons snipped parsley
1 teaspoon sherry flavoring,
    optional

Melt the butter in a medium saucepan and cook the mushrooms, onion and garlic about 5 minutes, or until tender but not brown. Stir in the chicken broth, tomato paste, salt and a few grindings of pepper. Bring to boiling; reduce heat. Cover and simmer 5 minutes. Combine egg yolks, Parmesan cheese, and parsley; stir in about 1 cup of the hot mixture. Return to remaining hot mixture in pan. Cook and stir until mixture almost comes to a boil. Cook and stir 2 minutes longer. Remove from heat, add sherry flavoring if desired. This will make about 6 small servings.

TORTELLINI VEGETABLE SOUP

Cleo's eyes always light up when he hears this soup is on the menu. It is very good, easy to make and filling without being heavy. A spoonful of freshly grated Parmesan cheese and a loaf of good garlic bread compliments this soup perfectly.

1 cup chopped onions
1 cup chopped carrots
1 cup chopped zucchini
1 tablespoon plus 1 teaspoon
   olive oil
2 small garlic cloves, minced
4 cups thoroughly washed
   and stemmed spinach
   leaves

4 (14½-ounce) cans low-salt
   chicken broth
2 cups water
2 tablespoons chopped fresh
   Italian parsley (optional)
2 tablespoons chopped fresh
   basil (optional)
1 (9-ounce) package
   refrigerated cheese
   tortellini

In a large kettle, heat the olive oil over medium heat. Add the chopped vegetables and garlic, and stir well to coat with oil. Sauté for 5 to 10 minutes. Add remaining ingredients except tortellini. Bring to a boil, turn down the heat and simmer about 20 minutes until vegetables are tender. Add the tortellini, bring to a boil and simmer for 9 to 10 minutes, until tortellini is tender. Serve in flat soup bowls garnished with Parmesan cheese, if desired.

TLC Tip: *Sometimes I omit the Italian parsley and basil. They do add a nice dimension to the soup, however. Taste for salt, especially if omitting the herbs. I find it usually needs just a little. I personally do not like dried tortellini in this soup, but it might do in a pinch.*

147

MOCK OYSTERS

I have no idea where this soup got its name. It certainly doesn't look like oyster stew or taste like oyster stew. Perhaps it is the fact that it has a milk base. Don't let the ingredients put you off—it is really quite good, and certainly simple to make. These days we know it is good for us, especially if made with skim milk, which I like to do so I can add a dab of butter on the top of each serving—for looks and unbeatable flavor. As a child, this soup was probably a dish I might have said "Yuk" about, if that word had been allowed.

1 tablespoon oil
1 small head cabbage,
   coarsely chopped
1 medium onion, sliced (I
   don't think mother ever
   added this, but I do)

4 (14-ounce) cans chicken
   broth or 2 quarts
   homemade
1 teaspoon salt, or to taste
¼ teaspoon pepper
3 cups skim milk (or use
   regular, if you prefer)

In a large saucepan, cook the cabbage and onion in the oil until lightly browned over medium heat, about 7 minutes, stirring frequently. Add the chicken broth. Cover and simmer about 30 minutes, until cabbage is very tender. Add the seasonings and the milk; heat thoroughly but do not boil. Ladle into bowls to serve; top with a tiny bit of butter.

TLC Tip: *If dark flecks of pepper seem unappetizing to you in this soup, use white pepper.*

POTATO SOUP

There is something comforting about potato soup. It was a staple in our farm household, but simply made and seasoned. I do remember mother adding butter to it—I can still see it floating on the top. I have tried a number of potato soups during my cooking years. The addition of crisp, crumbled bacon pieces is definitely a plus, as are onions or leeks. Cooking the potatoes in chicken broth instead of water adds good flavor also. Around our house these days, this is the one I most often prepare.

4 leeks, thoroughly washed and cleaned	1½ cups skim milk
4 medium potatoes, peeled and diced	Freshly ground black pepper
3 cups chicken broth	Salt, optional
	1 teaspoon dried dillweed

Cut off the green tops of the leeks and reserve; slice the white part thinly. In a covered pot, simmer the whole leek tops, sliced bottoms and the potatoes in the chicken broth until very soft, about 45 minutes. Remove the leek tops, and mash the vegetables with a potato masher or purée somewhat in a blender or food processor. Return to pot, add the milk and heat through. Just before serving, add the seasonings. Should make 6 (1-cup) servings.

TLC Tip: *Sometime you may want to prepare this soup when you don't have any leeks on hand or you may have trouble finding them. I have had good success with this soup by substituting 1 large onion, chopped, for the leeks. As a nice variation, you might omit the dillweed and garnish the soup with crumbled crisp bacon.*

FAVORITE LENTIL SOUP

Lentils were not something we consumed when I was a child. I don't think I even knew what a lentil was. In the 70's, when I began to think more about what I put in my body and the bodies of my family, I found out about lentils. They are very nutritious, cook quickly and are a good base for a meatless meal. Just add a bit of cheese and/or some good bread and you have complete protein. As the title says, this is our favorite lentil soup. Maybe it will be yours too.

1 tablespoon oil
2 large onions, chopped
   (about 2 cups)
3 carrots, coarsely chopped
¾ teaspoon marjoram,
   crumbled
¾ teaspoon thyme leaves,
   crumbled
1 (28-ounce) can tomatoes
   with their juice, coarsely
   chopped

7 cups broth (beef, chicken, or
   vegetable)
1½ cups dried lentils, rinsed
   and picked over
½ teaspoon salt, if desired
¼ to ½ teaspoon freshly
   ground black pepper
⅓ cup chopped fresh parsley
   or 2 tablespoons dried
4 ounces Cheddar cheese,
   grated, optional

Heat the oil in a large saucepan, and sauté the onions, carrots, marjoram, and thyme, stirring the vegetables frequently, for about 5 minutes. Add the tomatoes, broth, and lentils. Bring the soup to a boil, reduce the heat, cover the pan, and simmer the soup for about 1 hour or until the lentils are tender. Add the salt, pepper, parsley, and simmer the soup for a few minutes to blend the seasonings. Serve with cheese sprinkled on each portion.

TLC Tip: I like to prepare my own chicken stock and freeze in small 1 and 2 cup portions for use as I need it. When I do, I do not salt the stock. When I use canned stock, I usually use the kind that does not need water added and is the reduced-salt variety. Adjust the salt in the recipe according to the kind of broth you use. If you use a salted stock, don't add any additional salt until you taste.

LENTIL SOUP

This version of Lentil Soup has no tomatoes. I have made it often and it has always been well-received. It tastes great even if made without the ham bone or hocks, and it just simmers away while you busy yourself with other things.

2 cups lentils, rinsed
   thoroughly
Meaty ham hock or leftover
   ham bone
2 medium onions, peeled and
   sliced
2 carrots, cleaned and
   chopped
1½ cups celery, coarsely
   chopped
1 medium potato, peeled and
   chopped

3 cloves garlic, peeled and
   minced
3 sprigs parsley
2 bay leaves
2 sprigs fresh basil or 1
   teaspoon dried
¼ teaspoon cayenne pepper,
   optional
3 quarts water
Freshly ground black pepper
Salt to taste

In a large soup pot, combine the lentils, ham, onions, carrots, celery, potato, garlic, parsley, bay leaves, basil, and cayenne. Add the water. Bring to a rapid boil, skim, cover and lower heat to a simmer. Allow to bubble 3 to 4 hours. Remove the bay leaf, parsley, and fresh basil, if used. Add black pepper and adjust for salt. Strip meat from ham bone; discard bone and return meat to soup pot. Bring back to a boil. Serve in large soup bowls with a hearty bread.

TLC Tip: *If I am making this soup without the ham bones, I like to substitute beef broth for part of the water. As with most soups, the exact amount of vegetables is not critical.*

CREAM OF CAULIFLOWER SOUP

When you need a soup to serve as a first course, this is a good one. Naturally there isn't much color, so a garnish of chopped parsley or a sprinkling of sharp Cheddar cheese spices things up a little. I have used this soup as part of a luncheon plate with ham and cheese croissant sandwiches and a garnish of orange slices, kiwi slices and a fresh strawberry with the stem left on.

4 cups chicken stock, fresh or canned	2 tablespoons butter or oil
2 (10-ounce) packages frozen cauliflower	3 tablespoons flour
1 medium onion, chopped	1 cup evaporated milk or light cream
1 bay leaf	¼ to ½ teaspoon white pepper
1 sprig fresh parsley	¼ teaspoon salt
	Dash of nutmeg

Combine the cauliflower, onion, bay leaf and parsley with chicken stock in a large saucepan. Cover and simmer for 15 minutes or until vegetables are tender. Remove and discard bay leaf and parsley. Melt butter or heat oil in a heavy skillet over low heat . Blend in the flour and stir for 5 minutes. Do not brown. Add to the soup and stir to blend. Cool. Pour in small quantities into blender container and purée. Return to saucepan. Add milk or cream, pepper, salt and nutmeg. Heat, but do not boil. This makes 8 servings.

TLC Tip: *I would advise adding the smaller amount of pepper at first, adding more if it doesn't suit your taste.*

CURRIED AVOCADO SOUP

I first served this soup as part of an anniversary dinner I fixed for Cleo. I served it another time when my nephew, Chris Mason, was spending the summer with us. I don't think he has ever forgotten that "cold, green soup". I'm sure it must have been a shock to his teenage tastebuds. It is a delicious soup, nice served as a first course or as part of a sandwich or salad meal. I suppose some would say it does have an "adult taste".

1 medium ripe avocado, peeled and cut up	¾ teaspoon curry powder, more or less
2 cups chicken broth, defatted	1 teaspoon seasoned salt
1 cup sour cream	Lemon slices, sour cream and fresh parsley for garnish
1 tablespoon lemon juice	

Combine the first 6 ingredients in a blender container; process until smooth. You may need to do this in two batches, depending on the size of your blender container. Chill well. Garnish with thinly cut lemon slices, a tiny dab of sour cream, and a sprinkling of finely chopped fresh parsley floated on each serving.

BLACK BEAN SOUP

I first started making this soup when black beans were not easily available. I had to have a relative send them to me from South Florida. Now you can find them in most grocery stores, and certainly health food stores. This is a hearty, delicious soup. Try garnishing it with a lemon slice sprinkled with chopped parsley, or a spoonful of yogurt on the top.

1 pound black beans	3 sprigs fresh parsley
2½ quarts water	2 bay leaves
5 slices bacon, cut in small	2 cloves garlic, minced
pieces	2 carrots, coarsely chopped
2 stalks celery, chopped	2 parsnips, chopped, optional
2 medium onions, chopped	¼ teaspoon ground black
2 tablespoons flour	pepper
2 smoked ham hocks	2 teaspoons salt, or to taste

Wash beans; cover with cold water and soak overnight; drain, and wash again. Place in a large soup pot, cover with the 2½ quarts water, cover and simmer 90 minutes. Meanwhile, cook bacon pieces in a heavy skillet for a few minutes; add the celery and onion and cook until tender but not brown. Blend in the flour and cook, stirring constantly, one minute. Add this mixture to the beans along with the ham hocks, parsley, bay leaves, garlic, carrots, parsnips, pepper and salt. Cover and simmer over low heat about 4 hours, adding more water if necessary. Remove hocks, and purée beans in blender or food processor, in small batches. Remove meat from bones, cut into small pieces, return to soup. Reheat soup, serve hot.

TLC Tip: *I like to purée only half the soup, leaving some of the beans and vegetables intact. This gives a little more texture to the soup. It is probably a little more elegant looking if you purée all the soup, however.*

COUNTRY PEA SOUP

I am sure there are as many variations of Pea Soup as there are cooks to make them. I've tried my share over the years, and think this to be one of the best. I always think of Split Peas with Ham, but smoked turkey also does nicely. If you don't have a meaty ham bone or don't wish to use ham hocks, add some ham pieces, regular or turkey, toward the last of the simmering. Or substitute pieces of smoked sausage.

1 pound split peas, washed and sorted	2 leeks, cleaned and sliced
Ham bone or ham hocks	½ cup chopped carrots
3 quarts water	½ teaspoon thyme or marjoram
1 medium onion, stuck with 2 cloves	1 bay leaf
1 clove garlic, minced	Dash of cayenne pepper, optional
1 cup chopped celery, with leaves	Salt to taste
	Grindings of black pepper

Combine the split peas, ham bone or hocks and water in a large soup pot. Bring to a boil, skim, lower the heat, and simmer uncovered 1 hour, stirring occasionally. Add the onion, garlic, celery, leeks, carrots, thyme or marjoram, bay leaf and cayenne. Cover and simmer 2 hours. Remove bones, strip off meat, and cut into small pieces. Purée soup in blender in small batches. Transfer soup back to a clean soup pot, add pieces of meat and reheat. Taste for seasoning. Add salt if necessary and a few grindings of pepper. This should serve 8 to 12 people, depending on how hungry they are.

TLC Tip: *To get the "good ole ham flavor" without the fat, simmer the ham bone or hocks in the water the day before making the soup. Remove the bones and meat, chill the broth. The next day, remove the chilled fat from the top of the broth, and proceed with the recipe, using the broth for the water, adding additional if necessary to make 3 quarts.*

SOUPS, STEWS AND SANDWICHES

RUIDOSO

When we need a "stress break", we head for the lower Rockies in Ruidoso, New Mexico. From the time we first vacationed there in the winter of 1970, we have been drawn to this Land of Enchantment. In the fall of 1981, Cleo had a dream of someday having a place there. By the summer of 1982 we were touring homes and sites, and by October we had selected a lot and broken ground for our leisure home. It has always been somewhat amazing to me that we were able to build this house, living 300 miles away, and have it turn out exactly as we envisioned. Nestled at the back of a wooded lot, with a gorgeous view of Sierra Blanca, you can just feel the peacefulness overtake you as you proceed up the driveway. It doesn't get much more hectic than that, as each day the only major decisions you have to make are which golf course to play, which tennis court to reserve, where to take your daily walk, which stream to fish or how many shops to frequent. We've listened to the woodpeckers, watched the hummingbirds, counted the stars, felt the gentle mountain breezes and discussed our hopes, dreams and goals as we sat on the deck. We've experienced happiness in sharing our home with family and friends, and always look forward to spending the time between Christmas and New Year's there with our older grandsons, Daniel and Dustyn. We feel blessed and thankful that God has allowed us to experience this paradise on earth.

CABBAGE PATCH STEW

An easy and quick-cooking stew to put together, and a good way to get some of that healthy cruciferous vegetable, cabbage, into our bodies. Try serving it with cornbread or soft breadsticks.

1 pound ground beef	1 cup cooked tomatoes
2 medium onions, sliced	½ teaspoon salt
1 cup shredded cabbage	Dash of pepper
½ cup diced celery	1 teaspoon chili powder
1 (16-ounce) can red kidney beans	2 cups hot mashed potatoes

In a pan sprayed with cooking spray, brown the meat over medium heat. Add onions, cabbage, and celery; cook until soft. Add water to cover (about 2 cups); simmer 15 minutes. Add beans, tomatoes, and seasonings; cook 15 to 25 minutes. Serve in bowls topped with spoonfuls of mashed potatoes. This should serve 4 hungry people adequately, 6 who are less hungry.

CHILLED ZUCCHINI SOUP

I prepared this soup when our son-in-law, David, brought his mother to visit us in Ruidoso, New Mexico. It was part of a lunch I served on the deck, under the towering pines. You may not have a deck or towering pines, but you can fix this soup and use your imagination.

⅓ **cup butter**
1 cup sliced green onion
1 clove garlic, minced
3 cups sliced zucchini
1 cup chicken broth
½ **teaspoon salt**

⅛ **teaspoon pepper**
4 cups milk
2 tablespoons cornstarch
½ **cup finely diced raw**
zucchini

In a large saucepan, melt the butter over medium heat. Add the onion and garlic, and cook 5 minutes or until tender. Add the zucchini slices. Cook and stir 10 minutes or until zucchini is very soft. Add chicken broth, salt and pepper. Cover and simmer 15 minutes. Pour into blender container a little at a time; cover, and blend 30 seconds or until smooth. Return to saucepan. Stir cornstarch into milk. Add to soup. Cook and stir over medium heat until soup boils for 1 minute. Cover and chill several hours or overnight. Before serving, garnish with the diced zucchini.

TLC Tip: If you can find a low-salt chicken soup base, adding 1 teaspoon with the chicken broth intensifies the flavor. Sometimes I use 1 can evaporated skim milk plus enough regular skim milk to equal 4 cups. Somehow this seems to make a richer, smoother tasting soup. Of course, you could use some half-and-half instead, if you dare.

BUCKAROO STEW

I don't remember where I got this recipe, but I have made it often over the years. This is a stick-to-the-ribs kind of stew that goes together easily, looks appetizing in the bowl and tastes great.

1½ pounds ground beef
1 clove garlic, minced
½ to 1 teaspoon salt
⅛ to ¼ teaspoon pepper
1 large onion, chopped
1 tablespoon chili powder
2 (16-ounce) cans tomatoes,
    with juice

1 (16-ounce) can white kidney
    beans
1 (16-ounce) can red kidney
    beans
1 (16-ounce) can whole kernel
    corn
4 ounces cheese, grated

Combine the ground beef, garlic, salt and pepper in a large bowl; mix until lightly blended. Shape into 36 balls. Brown in a non-stick skillet or on a broiler rack in a 400 degree oven. Transfer to a large kettle. Stir in the onion, chili powder, tomatoes, beans and corn with their liquids. Bring to a boil, reduce heat to simmer and cook 15-20 minutes, until heated through and meat is cooked. Serve in bowls topped with the grated cheese.

TLC Tip: This stew can be easily frozen. After combining the meatballs, vegetables and seasonings, spoon into a 12-cup freezer-to-oven container. Wrap, label and freeze. Two hours before serving, place covered dish in cold oven. Bake at 350 degrees for 2 hours or until bubbly hot. Serve as above.

GOOD BROWN STEW

I've made this stew so many times! Of course that was in the days when we all ate more meat than we do now. It still has a place in our diet, perhaps on a chilly winter evening or on a day when something you don't have to watch cook is in order. Buy the leanest beef you can. Though the recipe doesn't call for it, I like to toss a cup of frozen peas in at the last minute for appetizing color.

2 pounds boneless beef, cut in cubes	1 teaspoon salt
4 cups hot water	¼ teaspoon pepper
1 teaspoon lemon juice	Pinch of allspice
1 teaspoon Worcestershire sauce	1 teaspoon sugar
1 clove garlic, minced	6 carrots, cut into chunks
1 medium onion, sliced	8 small onions
1 small bay leaf	3 medium to large potatoes, cut into chunks

Spray a large heavy kettle with cooking spray; brown the meat thoroughly. Add remaining ingredients except carrots, whole onions and potatoes and simmer 1 hour and 45 minutes, adding water if necessary. Add carrots, onions, and potatoes and cook about 30 minutes until vegetables are tender. Thicken liquid with flour and water mixture if desired.

THREE BEAN STEW

This is another quick-to-fix stew that is really delicious, low in calories, fat-free and high in fiber and nutrients. This is a vegetarian stew. If you just have to have meat, add some well drained, already cooked smoked sausage, the turkey or beef kind, or pieces of cooked ham. However, I don't think you'll miss the meat.

2 (16-ounce) cans tomatoes, cut up	2 medium bell peppers, chopped
1 (16-ounce) can red kidney beans	2 large stalks celery, sliced
1 (16-ounce) can great Northern beans	1 medium zucchini, chopped
1 (16-ounce) can garbanzo beans	½ cup water
3 medium onions, chopped	1 to 2 teaspoons chili powder
2 to 3 cloves garlic, minced	2 teaspoons basil, crushed
	¼ teaspoon black pepper
	1 bay leaf

Place the cut-up tomatoes with their juice in a large kettle. Add the undrained beans and all other ingredients. Bring to a boil, reduce heat; cover and simmer for 2 hours. Vegetables will be tender in 1 hour, but you will have a tastier stew after 2 hours of simmering. This makes about 10 (1-cup) servings.

TLC Tip: As with most dishes of this nature, there is nothing too sacred about the ingredients. You can play around a bit with them, substituting one bean for another, leaving out the peppers, adjusting the seasonings to your taste. After all, a recipe is only a guide.

PAUL'S TEXAS RED

My brother-in-law, Paul, is an avid student of history. He is also a teacher in Forsan, Texas. One of his "hidden" talents is cooking, so when the Lindell household gets in the mood for chili, Paul is the one to make it. Not one to be stingy, he also volunteers his services when the youth group has a chili supper for a fund raiser, or the family gathers for a casual evening of food and fellowship. His chili is simple and versatile, good to the last spoonful.

2 pounds lean ground beef	**1 package William's chili mix**
4 (15-ounce) cans ranch-style	**(this brand is Paul's**
beans	**favorite)**
	3 cups tomato juice

Brown the ground beef in a non-stick skillet or large pot sprayed with vegetable oil spray. Stir occasionally and break up the meat as it is browning. Drain off any accumulated juices. Add the remaining ingredients, bring to a simmer, and cook for about 15 minutes. If you like it a little thicker, you can cook a few more minutes. Paul says he likes to serve it over corn chips garnished with grated cheese, chopped onions and picante sauce. He says it is also good served in warmed tortillas like a soft taco. It's even good just served in a bowl with crackers on the side. Leftovers are good spooned over hot dogs.

TLC Tip: *Paul told me he has tried making this with all ground turkey, and it seemed to lack a little something. He has also used deer meat and part pork sausage with success.*

MOM'S CHILI FOR TWENTY-FIVE

Our children loved Grandmother Yerden's chili!! When she came to visit, she nearly always made a pot. I didn't realize at the time that it was Chili for 25. I don't know whether she cut the recipe in half or not but there never was much left, which tells you something, doesn't it? This chili would never win in a chili cookoff—it is much too simple and straightforward. And the original called for browning the ground beef in 1½ cups butter!! I didn't have the heart (no pun intended) to write it that way, and I have also reduced the salt somewhat. You can leave it out altogether if you wish. As with any chili recipe, let your taste buds be your guide as to the amount of chili powder to use.

2 cups chopped onion	1 gallon cooked tomatoes
1 tablespoon oil (optional)	1 gallon cooked kidney beans
4 pounds lean ground beef	2 tablespoons chili powder,
2 teaspoons salt (more or less	or to taste
if you wish)	

Spray a large pot with cooking spray. Heat over medium-high heat. Add oil, if desired, ground meat and onions, stirring occasionally until meat begins to brown and onions soften. Add the remaining ingredients, bring to a boil, reduce heat and simmer at least 1 hour. Ladle into bowls and garnish with chopped raw onion and grated cheese if you wish.

TLC Tip: *This recipe can be cut in half successfully. Be sure to taste for seasoning, and adjust if necessary.*

MICHELLE'S WHITE CHILI

Michelle Dorrington is a friend from my teaching days in Plymouth, Michigan. We both taught 2nd grade at Farrand School. She came there straight out of college. She drove this cute little yellow Ford Mustang and I was driving a sedate Galaxy 500—I guess I was a little envious. She was a born teacher if there ever was one, and our teaching styles were very much alike (though her desk was always neater). We enjoyed combining our classes to put on programs and to do other kinds of projects. Michelle and "Skip" married the same year as Cleo and I. She did not feel very confident in the kitchen when she married, and I presented her with a week's worth of Instant Dinner Kits that I had prepared to help her along. We've chuckled about that since, as she has become World Class in the kitchen. This recipe for chili is one her husband and two sons enjoy. It's really delicious, a great change from the ordinary "bowl of red".

1 to 1½ pounds boneless, skinless chicken breast
2 cups chopped onion (Michelle says she uses white)
2 tablespoons minced, fresh garlic
1 tablespoon olive oil
2 (14-ounce) cans chicken broth
3 (16-ounce) cans great Northern beans (or other white beans)

2 (4-ounce) cans chopped green chilis, juice included
2 heaping teaspoons ground cumin
2 level teaspoons dried oregano
¼ heaping teaspoon cayenne pepper
Dash or two of hot sauce

Bake the chicken breasts in a 350 degree oven for ½ hour. Remove, and set aside until cool enough to handle, then cut into bite-size pieces. Heat the olive oil in a large saucepan over medium heat. Add the onion and garlic, and stir until wilted. Stir in the chicken pieces, broth, undrained beans, chilis and seasonings. Turn the heat to medium-high, and heat until chili is hot. Serve with cornbread.

TLC Tip: This chili will be very spicy. You may want to start with a little less of the seasonings—you can always add more.

BROCCOLI AND CRAB BISQUE

This is an attractive soup to serve and one that will please your taste buds and satisfy your tummy. Add a salad and some good bread for a complete meal. I use the imitation crab easily found in the supermarket. If you live in an area where seafood abounds, you may want to spring for the real thing!

1½ cups chopped onion
2 teaspoons butter or oil
5 cups broth (fish, chicken or
  vegetable)
1 large head broccoli, stems
  sliced, crosswise,
  flowerettes reserved
4 medium potatoes, peeled
  and diced
1½ cups diced carrots
¾ cup chopped celery

¼ to ½ teaspoon freshly
  ground black pepper
1 teaspoon lemon juice
¼ teaspoon thyme leaves,
  crushed
1 bay leaf
¾ teaspoon salt
Dash cayenne, optional
2 cups skim milk
1 pound imitation crab pieces

In a large saucepan, sauté the onion in the butter or oil until it is soft. Add the broth, broccoli stems, potatoes, carrots, celery, pepper, lemon juice, thyme, bay leaf, salt, and cayenne. Bring the soup to a boil, reduce the heat, and simmer the soup for about 15 minutes or until the vegetables are tender. Remove the bay leaf, and purée half the vegetables and broth in a blender. Return the purée to the pan. Add the broccoli flowerettes to the pan, and cook the soup for another 5 to 10 minutes or until the broccoli is tender-crisp. Add the milk and the crab meat and heat the bisque but do not boil. Garnish with croutons, if desired.

NORWEGIAN FISH CHOWDER

My family really likes this soup. I say family, not as in small children, but as adults. It is hearty and delicious.

2 leeks, sliced
2 carrots, sliced
3 tablespoons butter, divided
   use
1½ to 2 pounds cod or
   haddock
2 cups water
1 teaspoon salt
1 can cream of celery soup,
   low-sodium if possible

3 cups frozen O'Brien
   potatoes (you can
   substitute plain hash
   browns if you wish)
1 small cucumber, peeled and
   halved lengthwise
3 cups hot milk
1 tablespoon chopped fresh
   dill

In a large pot, sauté the leeks and carrots in 2 tablespoons butter for 4 to 5 minutes, or until tender but not browned. Cut the fish into serving-size pieces; place in pot, add water and salt. Bring to boiling, lower heat, cover and simmer 15 minutes or until fish flakes easily. Remove fish from pot with a slotted spoon and set aside. Add the celery soup and potatoes to the pot, bring to boiling, cover, lower heat and simmer 5 minutes. Remove the seeds from the cucumber halves. Slice crosswise into ⅛" thick slices. Sauté in a small skillet in the remaining tablespoon butter 3 to 4 minutes. Add to the pot with the milk, fish and dill. Bring just to boiling. Remove from heat and serve hot.

TLC Tip: *90's Butter (see index) may be substituted in this recipe.*

POTATO CLAM CHOWDER

For those of us who don't live near a coast, this chowder prepared with canned clams is very good.

4 teaspoons vegetable oil
2 slices turkey bacon, cut into
  small pieces
1 cup chopped onion
1 teaspoon salt
¼ teaspoon dried savory
¼ teaspoon dried thyme,
  crushed
⅛ teaspoon pepper
2 (6½-ounce) cans minced
  clams

4 medium potatoes, peeled
  and cut into small cubes
  (about 4 cups)
2 cups skim milk (I like to use
  evaporated for the added
  richness but no fat),
  divided use
2 tablespoons flour
2 tablespoons snipped fresh
  parsley

In a large saucepan, heat the oil. Cook the bacon until almost crisp, add the onion and cook until tender. Stir in the salt, savory, thyme and pepper. Drain the clams, reserving the liquid. Set clams aside. Blend reserved clam liquid and 1 cup water into the mixture in the saucepan. Add potatoes. Bring to boiling; reduce heat, cover and simmer 15 to 20 minutes, stirring occasionally. Stir in the clams, 1½ cups milk and parsley. Whisk the flour into the remaining ½ cup milk. Add to the chowder. Heat gently until mixture thickens. Serves 4 to 6.

JEAN'S BROCCOLI SAUSAGE CHOWDER

This chowder is a great way to warm up a chilly evening. This recipe comes from my cousin, Jean Tufts. Living in Kalamazoo, Michigan as she does, she has plenty of chilly evenings to warm up. I can see this as part of a soup supper, where you also serve some kind of clear soup, such as a chicken noodle or chicken vegetable and a chili-type soup. Serve a variety of breads such as buttered French, cornbread and perhaps a hearty whole wheat, add a green salad, a warm apple pie, and you're entertaining like a queen!!

2 (14-ounce) cans chicken
broth
2 large stalks celery, sliced
1 large onion, chopped
1 red pepper, chopped
1 pound red potatoes,
scrubbed and cut up
½ pound smoked sausage,
sliced and browned

1 (16-ounce) bag frozen
chopped broccoli
2 (16-ounce) cans shoe peg
corn, drained
2 cans cream of broccoli soup,
undiluted
1 cup half-and-half

Simmer the celery, onion, pepper and potatoes in the chicken broth until tender. Brown the sausage in a skillet or heat between paper towels in the microwave. Blot thoroughly. Cook the broccoli until crisp-tender. Add the broccoli, corn and sausage to the cooked vegetables. Blend the soup with the half-and-half. Stir into vegetable mixture. Heat slowly just to boiling point. Serves 4.

TLC Tip: *You can lighten this soup considerably by substituting evaporated skim milk for the half-and-half. Also be sure to blot the browned sausage well to remove as much fat as possible.*

PRAIRIE CORN CHOWDER

I love a good corn chowder. I can't say that my family shares my enthusiasm, so this one's for me. I think you'll find the combination of corn and chipped beef a good one.

4 slices bacon, cut in pieces
4 ounces dried beef, finely
    sliced
2 medium onions, peeled and
    minced
1 medium potato, cut in fine
    pieces
¼ cup minced green pepper
½ teaspoon paprika

¼ teaspoon savory
⅛ teaspoon pepper
½ cup water
1 (16-ounce) can cream style
    corn
1 quart milk
½ to 1 teaspoon salt, or to
    taste

Cook the bacon over moderately high heat until crisp; remove and reserve. Toss the dried beef with the bacon drippings and heat until edges begin to curl, 1 to 2 minutes. Remove and drain on paper towel. Reduce heat to moderate; add onions and potato and brown lightly, 8 to 10 minutes. Add green pepper and sauté, stirring constantly, 2 to 3 minutes. Mix in paprika, savory and pepper; add water, cover and simmer 5 minutes. Mix in corn, milk, bacon and dried beef; turn heat to low, cover and simmer—do not boil—20 minutes. Taste before adding salt. This should serve 4 people nicely.

TLC Tip: *You can use more or less bacon, but do use a little for the taste. You might even try turkey bacon. Use the kind of milk you feel comfortable with. I like to use half skim milk and half skim evaporated.*

SALMON CHOWDER

When we were young, mom served a salmon soup. I remember it being one of dad's favorites. She certainly didn't call it "chowder", nor was it fussy. She probably opened a can of salmon, tossed it in a pot, added that rich Jersey milk and seasoned it a little. That couldn't be easier, and I remember it tasting good. I always ate mine with saltine crackers—the big square kind, not those tiny little ones we know as chowder crackers. I still like "salmon soup" but I call mine chowder, and I do a few more things to it. You take your choice.

¾ cup diced celery
½ cup chopped onion
  (1 medium)
2 tablespoons butter
4 tablespoons flour
4 cups milk
1 teaspoon dried dillweed

1 (16-ounce) bag frozen mixed
  vegetables
2 (14-ounce) cans salmon,
  drained and boned
2 cups cooked, diced potatoes
1 to 2 teaspoons salt, or to
  taste
Chowder crackers

Sauté the celery and onion in the butter until soft. Blend in the flour; stir in the milk and continue cooking and stirring until mixture thickens and boils 1 minute. Stir in the frozen vegetables, heat to boiling and simmer 12 minutes or until the vegetables are tender. Add the salmon, potatoes, salt and dillweed. Heat slowly to boiling. Ladle into soup bowls. Serve with chowder crackers.

TLC Tip: *You certainly can use oil instead of butter, half oil and half butter or spray a non-stick pan with cooking spray and omit the fat altogether. You can also use skim milk if you wish—evaporated skim will make a richer chowder.*

RITA JO'S COUNTRY CHICKEN CHOWDER

My brother and sister-in-law, Paul and Rita Jo Yerden, make a great musical team. They have used their talents at the piano and organ in many churches and for many occasions across this country and other places in the world. Rita Jo also has a beautiful soprano voice, and taught piano lessons for many years. She is an avid reader, great homemaker, and keeps her flower beds picture perfect. Rita Jo and I were roommates at Anderson College during my senior year—her junior year—and we both became engaged that year. Like me, she has never been shy about trying new and different recipes, and we have exchanged many over the years. One of Rita Jo and Paul's favorite holiday fêtes is a Soup and Carols party, where they serve a variety of soups and then sit around and sing carols. This soup is one that is always requested. Rita Jo doesn't mind, as it is so simple to put together!! Her guests think she slaved all day, and so will yours!!

½ cup chopped frozen onion
  (I always use fresh)
2 tablespoons butter
2 cans chicken noodle soup
1 soup can water
⅛ to ¼ teaspoon white pepper
1 cup diced, cooked chicken

1 (16-ounce) can cream style
  corn
1 small can (⅔ cup)
  evaporated milk
2 tablespoons chopped
  parsley

Sauté the onion in the butter in a large saucepan. Add the remaining ingredients except the parsley. Heat to boiling but do not boil. Pour into soup bowls; garnish with parsley. Serves 6.

TLC Tip: *When I prepare 1 recipe, I sometimes use the canned white meat chicken. That enables you to have all the ingredients on hand for a last minute meal. If you double or triple the recipe, you might want to cook your own chicken ahead instead of buying canned, as the canned gets a little expensive. Also, do not automatically double or triple the pepper. Start with the regular amount and work up from there.*

TURKEY BURGERS

I've fixed this recipe dozens of times since using ground turkey instead of ground beef has become popular. If you use ground turkey meat, you probably aren't consuming any less fat than using a lean ground beef. But I like the flavor of these burgers. If you want a truly lean burger, make sure you use ground turkey breast. When you have the time, try the special dressing.

1 pound ground turkey	**½ teaspoon salt**
⅓ cup dry breadcrumbs	**½ teaspoon poultry seasoning**
1 tablespoon finely chopped	**⅛ to ¼ teaspoon pepper**
fresh parsley or 1	**1 egg**
teaspoon dried	

Combine all ingredients in a medium bowl. Shape into 4 patties. Cook in a large non-stick skillet that has been sprayed with vegetable oil spray. I like to serve these on whole wheat buns with mustard and/or mayonnaise, a lettuce leaf and slice of tomato or the following sauce.

Special Sauce:

¼ cup Creole-type mustard	**¼ teaspoon all vegetable**
¼ cup mayonnaise	**no-salt seasoning**
Juice of 1 lime	

Combine mustard, mayonnaise, lime juice and all vegetable no-salt seasoning. Use as a spread with turkey burgers.

TLC Tip: *Personally, I think the best way to combine mixtures of this kind is with your hands. Naturally you will make sure they are freshly washed, or even better, I keep a supply of disposable plastic gloves on hand for occasions such as this.*

PIZZA BURGERS

This is another of my sister's great recipes. I can remember one year, the two of us, plus my sister-in-law, prepared enough of these to serve a very large group of people. The fact that they can be prepared ahead and heated at the last minute was a plus in that situation. That they are very tasty doesn't hurt a bit either.

1 pound sausage	¼ cup chopped green pepper
1 pound ground beef	1 pound Velveeta cheese,
1 teaspoon dried oregano	cubed
flakes	7 to 8 English muffin halves
1 onion, chopped	Salt and pepper, if desired

Brown the sausage, ground beef, onion and pepper in a large skillet. Drain and add the seasonings. Stir in the cheese and heat over low heat until cheese is melted. Spoon on English muffin halves. Heat in a 350 degree oven until bubbly.

TLC Tip: *You can use any type of sausage you like—hot, mild, sage, turkey, and I have had good results with using a natural Cheddar cheese. The muffins can be topped with the meat mixture ahead of time, refrigerated, and heated later. You will probably have to adjust the baking time a little if the mixture is cold.*

DALLAS

When we owned StarCom, we spent a lot of time in Dallas. It seemed like Cleo was always needing to be at the Arlington office, or flying through DFW or Love Field to one of the other offices. He practically had his own room at the Arlington Radisson Hotel. So in June of 1989 we purchased a "business" house in Irving—halfway between the airports and 15 minutes from the office. It was an ugly-duckling sort of house, but it was great fun to see it blossom under the decorating skills of Cassandra Johnson. We love the Dallas area. We think it is one of the most exciting cities in the country. We enjoy the restaurants and the bookstores, I enjoy the shopping centers and the grocery stores. It's a big change from our usual small-town life. Our house has served its purpose. It has been the site for managers' meetings and informational seminars. We've housed friends, family and business associates. And being close to Texas Stadium, it has been the perfect place to meet before or after going to see the Cowboys play their special brand of football. I love cooking in the "Dallas house". The kitchen is large, with plenty of counter space, and the variety of food that is available makes it more of a pleasure than a task.

ATHLETE'S BURGERS

One of our favorite things to do in the Dallas area is go to one of the Whole Foods Markets. Such an array of untreated vegetables and fruits, tempting baked goods, fresh fish, and poultry and meats without hormones. If you're thirsty, they have a juice bar. If you're hungry, they have a deli. If you need a neck massage, they have that, too. They sell a meat mixture we are very fond of. It is called Athlete's Blend, and it is composed of 50% very lean ground beef, 40% ground turkey breast and 10% lamb. It makes a delicious burger, and we always try to prepare one while we are there. You may not be able to get to Whole Foods Market, but now that you know the formula, perhaps you can mix your own. Shape the mixture into ¼-pound patties, handling gently, season as desired, and grill or pan-fry in a non-stick skillet until done to your liking. Place in a whole-grain bun with a garnish of leaf lettuce and whatever other veggies you like, spread on your choice of spread, sit back and enjoy. Your body will thank you.

DEANBURGERS

Deanburgers were originated by the people who promoted Jimmy Dean sausage. I can't count the number of times I've made these burgers, often putting them in the freezer to have on hand when the mood for a cookout hit. Of course that was before "lowfat" became part of our vocabulary. When using a grill, a lot of the fat drips off, but they are probably still something for a special occasion and not on your weekly menu. These have a wonderful flavor.

3 pounds ground beef
1 pound pork sausage
3 teaspoons dried parsley
    flakes

1½ teaspoons garlic powder
1 package dried onion soup
    mix
¼ cup Worcestershire sauce

Mix all ingredients together thoroughly. Shape into ¼-pound patties. Cook on the grill until well cooked but still juicy. If not cooking right away, wrap tightly in plastic freezer wrap, freeze solid, then place in a self-seal freezer bag for storage. Makes 16 good-sized burgers.

TLC Tip: *We are especially fond of the wheat buns with the seeds on the top. If that isn't your thing, they'll taste good on whatever you choose.*

SLOPPY JOES

As members of the Allegan High School band, we were "privileged" to help out at the Band Booth at the County Fair each September. We always served these Sloppy Joes. The recipe was distributed to all the members, and supposedly, we came up with a fairly uniform product. It was fun working the booth, meeting the people, and getting out of school for a few hours during fair week. This is still my favorite Sloppy Joe recipe. Don't try to double this recipe. It would take too long to cook down to the right consistency. If a large quantity is needed, better to make several batches.

2 pounds ground beef	1 cup water
1 medium onion, chopped	½ cup catsup
½ cup chopped celery	1 can condensed tomato soup,
2 tablespoons brown sugar	undiluted
2 tablespoons prepared	Salt to taste, if needed
mustard	

Brown the ground beef, chopped onion and celery in a medium saucepan over medium-high heat. Add the remaining ingredients; simmer until thick. Serve on buns.

TLC Tip: *These delicious Sloppy Joes are in their glory served with potato chips, raw veggies and a crispy dill pickle spear.*

FLANK STEAK SANDWICHES

I guess you could say that these sandwiches are my version of the Philly Steak and Cheese Sandwich. They are almost a meal in themselves, though perhaps a little messy. Do try them—just provide plenty of napkins.

Grilled flank steak (see index	Swiss cheese slices, if desired
for recipe)	Hoagie sandwich buns
1 to 3 large onions, sweet if	Mayonnaise, if desired
possible	

Heat a large non-stick skillet over medium heat. Spray with cooking spray. Add a little oil or butter if you wish but it really isn't necessary. Slice the onions into ¼-inch slices. Spread in the skillet, separating into rings. Cover and cook over medium heat, stirring occasionally, until onions are golden and soft. Sprinkle with a little salt. Split the sandwich buns in half and spread with mayonnaise if desired. Top with slices of the flank steak, plenty of the onions and a slice of Swiss cheese. Cover with the top of the bun, and cut in half for easier handling. If you want, you can place the sandwich with the cheese under the broiler briefly to melt the cheese a little before adding the top. You can see that the ingredients are adjustable to the number of persons you are serving.

BARBECUED BEEF SANDWICHES

There is no way you can duplicate the barbecue beef sandwiches prepared by Al's Barbecue here in Big Spring. They are an institution—the best in the land according to my husband and many others. But this is a good second. Feel free to adjust the seasonings to your particular barbecue taste.

2½ pounds good quality beef
    stew meat
1 large onion, chopped
½ cup chopped celery
1 tablespoon oil
1 (12-ounce) bottle catsup
¼ cup lemon juice
2 tablespoons vinegar

1 teaspoon Worcestershire
    sauce
⅓ to ½ cup brown sugar
1 cup water
1 teaspoon chili powder,
    optional
½ teaspoon dry mustard

Combine the beef with water to cover in saucepan. Bring to a boil, lower heat, cover and simmer until tender, 3 to 4 hours. Drain, saving broth. Shred the meat. Sauté onion and celery in the oil in a saucepan over medium heat. Add the shredded meat and rest of ingredients. Mix well, bring to a boil, reduce heat. Simmer for 1 hour, or until thick as you like. Serve on your choice of buns. If you want to pretend you are at Al's, garnish with an onion slice, a dill pickle spear and a pickled pepper.

BARBECUED BEEF PITA SANDWICHES

This is a take-off on the ever popular Sloppy Joe. You'll find that pita bread makes the perfect holder for this tasty filling.

1 pound ground beef
½ cup chopped onion
2 garlic cloves, minced
¼ cup catsup
2 tablespoons chili powder
½ teaspoon cumin
¼ teaspoon pepper

1 (10-ounce) package frozen
    corn kernels
1 tomato, chopped
6 pocket breads, 6" in
    diameter
1 cup (4 ounces) shredded
    Cheddar cheese

In a large skillet, brown the ground beef with the onion and garlic; drain any accumulated juices. Add the catsup, chili powder, cumin, pepper, unthawed corn and tomato; cover and simmer for 8 to 10 minutes or until corn can be separated by stirring. Continue to simmer for 3 to 4 minutes or until corn is tender. Cut pocket breads in half. Spoon ⅓ cup ground beef mixture into each pocket bread half. Spoon about 1 tablespoon cheese onto top of each sandwich. Wrap each sandwich in foil; place on cookie sheet. Bake in a 350 degree oven for 15 to 20 minutes or until cheese is melted and sandwich is thoroughly heated.

TUNA MELTS

As a young couple in Plymouth, Michigan, we often got together with friends for casual evenings of volleyball and other games. We all brought our children, ate simply and had a great time. My friend, Millie Harder, prepared a sandwich similar to this that we devoured with gusto.

1 (6½-ounce) can tuna, drained and flaked	2 tablespoons mayonnaise
3 hard-cooked eggs, chopped	1 cup shredded Cheddar cheese
⅓ cup sweet pickle relish	6 hamburger buns
¼ cup chopped onion	

Combine filling ingredients, stirring well. Spread on bottom of the bun and cover with the top. Wrap in foil. Place on baking sheet and heat in a 350 degree oven about 20 minutes.

TLC Tip: *It is easy to see that these could be prepared ahead of time, refrigerated and then heated when ready to serve. This recipe can be doubled or tripled for larger groups. You can make open-face sandwiches by toasting the bun halves, spreading with the tuna mixture, then broiling the sandwiches 6 inches from heat until the cheese is melted.*

FRIED EGG SANDWICHES

I guess this is your basic emergency type sandwich—when you can't think of anything else, or the pantry is empty except for some bread and eggs. There is something comforting about this sandwich, and I always think of it as late-at-night food. I don't remember having it on any kind of regular basis as a child, but I have resurrected it from memory on more than one occasion. There are endless possibilities for the spread, but you can hardly beat a good mayo. Of course frying the egg in a little butter helps, too.

1 to 2 eggs, depending on hunger level	2 slices bread, your choice
Butter, optional	Mayonnaise or salad dressing or your choice of spread

Heat a small skillet, preferably non-stick, over medium-high heat. Break the egg/s into a small bowl and beat lightly with a fork. When skillet is hot, add butter, if using, letting it melt and sizzle a little. Carefully pour the beaten egg into the skillet and let it cook undisturbed for a few minutes until set on the bottom. While it is cooking is the time to add your choice of seasoning—salt, pepper, herbs, no-salt seasoning, etc. You will also have time to spread the bread with whatever spread you have chosen. When the mixture is set on the bottom, carefully flip the egg over with a pancake turner, cook briefly, then place on prepared bread slice, top with second slice, cut in half and enjoy.

CHICKEN FILLET SANDWICH

Grilled chicken sandwiches have become very popular in recent years. Most fast food restaurants have a version of this one. There is no doubt that it is healthier than the breaded and fried variety. After you experience the ease with which this can be prepared, you'll pull this out of your culinary hat often.

Boneless chicken breasts　　**Your favorite spread/s**
Your favorite sandwich buns　**Your favorite garnishes**
**　or bread**

Lay the chicken breasts between two pieces of plastic wrap and pound with the side of a meat mallet until flattened slightly. Prepare the breasts as for Amazing Fried Chicken (see index). Spread the buns or bread with your choice of spread, top with the cooked chicken breast and whatever garnish you wish, lettuce, tomato, etc. Now wasn't that easy? And guess what, it's healthy too, if you don't overdo the mayo!!

CHICKEN SALAD SANDWICHES

Use the Chicken Salad recipe from the salad section (see index). Serve between slices of your choice of bread, adding a lettuce leaf or sprouts if you like. Alternately spoon the filling into a pita pocket or roll up in a flour tortilla for a change of pace. Tuna Salad (see index) can be served the same way.

WALDORF CHICKEN SALAD
ON RAISIN BREAD

This is a wonderful combination. You'll wonder why you didn't think of it sooner.

2 cups chopped cooked　　　**⅓ cup mayonnaise, regular or**
**　chicken or turkey**　　　　　**　lite**
½ cup chopped apple　　　　**1 teaspoon lemon juice**
¼ cup chopped celery　　　　**⅛ teaspoon salt, optional**
¼ cup chopped walnuts　　　**8 slices raisin bread**
　　　　　　　　　　　　　　　Leaf lettuce

In medium bowl, combine all ingredients except bread and lettuce. Mix well. Cover, refrigerate ½ hour to blend flavors. Spread scant ¾ cup filling mixture on each of 4 bread slices. Place lettuce leaf on top of filling; top with remaining bread slices. Makes 4 sandwiches.

GETTING THE COWS

A chore that had to be done at least once a day, depending on the time of year, was getting the cows back to the barn so they could be milked. Our farm was a mile deep, with a river running along the back. Most of the time, the cows would be at the end of that mile, much to our dislike, and immature legs. As children do, we tended to make a game of that task, which sweetened our dispositions but aggravated our parents somewhat, as it lengthened the time the job took. Our woods were beautiful, and ideal for using our imaginations to decide that this area was a castle, this one over here someone's house, and the area where the gooseberry bushes were, a candy store. Cows tend to follow each other and the same path each time they traverse an area, but occasionally we would get it into our childish heads that we were going to change their route. We were never very successful. Following the cow paths was such fun—always having to watch out for tree roots that played havoc with our bare feet, wasp or bee nests in the trees and other wild things our minds would conjure up. Sometimes there would be a little excitement, as a cow had a calf, or some animal alien to our herd would have gotten through a break in the fence. Seems like they were always black, which was very apparent among our beautiful registered jerseys. Or perhaps one of the cows would have wandered off, and we would have to hunt for it.

ONION SANDWICHES

One nice thing about going to get the cows was taking along a snack. Sometimes it would be salad dressing on soda crackers or peanut butter and jelly sandwiches. The one that sticks in my mind the most was onion sandwiches. I remember the onions being very sweet then. At certain times of the year, we have access to varieties that are sweet. This sandwich will be even tastier if you can get that kind.

Good, sweet onions　　　　　　　**Butter**
Good bread, preferably whole
　　wheat

Slice the onions thinly. Spread the bread with butter, being careful to spread to the edges. Layer the onions on the buttered bread, as many as you want. Cover with second slice. Cut in half, one for each hand, and enjoy. You may not have cows to bring home, but I am sure you can think of somewhere you can walk while you devour this treat.

PIMIENTO CHEESE SANDWICH

These are the sandwiches I remember my mother preparing for my Aunt Máco and Uncle Harve to take with them on their return trip to Oklahoma. I love pimiento cheese sandwiches, and will choose them from a sandwich tray every time. I always prepare these with whole wheat bread, the heartier the better, but white is passable. I guess you could add all kinds of things to these sandwiches, but I think in this case the simpler the better. These are nice garnished with some potato chips and good black olives.

1 pound mild Cheddar cheese, grated
1 (4-ounce) jar diced pimientos, drained

A little seasoned salt, if desired
½ cup mayonnaise, or to taste

Combine all the above ingredients thoroughly and chill until ready to prepare sandwiches. Be generous with the filling—the sandwiches look better to say nothing of how they taste.

TLC Tip: *Of course you can stop by your friendly market and pick up some pimiento cheese already prepared, most of which are pretty good. But this isn't much more work, and at least you know what is in it. My opinion is not to even bother to make this spread if you aren't going to use real cheese.*

Main Dishes

I still have vivid memories of waking up on Sunday morning to the aroma of mother's roast browning on the stove. She always used a cast iron Dutch oven, and I think, finished cooking it on the stovetop rather than putting it in the oven. Sometimes the aroma would be of chicken. Fried chicken, as people in the South know it, was not part of my culinary past. Though my mother was from Oklahoma, she browned the chicken, then finished it by adding a bit of water, covering the pan and letting it cook at a very low heat. Perhaps part of the reason for this method of preparation was that we used our laying hens for eating, and since they were older, and perhaps less tender, the longer cooking time was necessary. My mother was proficient in catching the chicken, chopping off its head, and everything else necessary to get the chicken ready for the pot. I was never good at the first two, but did learn to pluck the chicken and dress it. I guess that is a lost art, if you can call it that. However, the flavor of chickens that hunt and peck for their food and that have not set in a refrigerated case for days still can't be beat.

Sometimes we enjoyed scalloped potatoes or meatloaf or macaroni and cheese. We knew nothing of grilling steaks, though mother prepared a memorable Swiss steak.

The only fish we ate when I was a child was canned salmon, made into patties or used in soup, or freshly-caught perch or blue gills from one of the many lakes around us. These were prepared by breading in a mixture of flour and/or cornmeal, and lightly sautéed. I don't think I could have told you what seafood was, though I do remember dad having a fondness for oyster stew. These we purchased fresh at the meat market, and carried them home in those little Chinese-restaurant type containers.

SUNDAY MORNING POT ROAST

This is my mother's pot roast, and I have given it this name because of all the Sunday mornings I awoke to the aroma of this roast browning on the stove. Mother always cooked her roast on top of the stove, in a Dutch oven, sometimes adding vegetables and sometimes not. Preparing this dish brings back memories for me; perhaps it will do the same for you.

1 pot roast, size determined
    by the number of people
    you're feeding or the
    amount of leftovers you
    want
Flour

Oil
Onions
Peeled vegetables, if desired,
    such as potatoes and
    carrots

Heat a large Dutch oven over medium-high heat. Add a thin layer of oil. Season the roast with salt and pepper and coat with flour. Brown both sides in the hot oil. Cover with water, add a bay leaf, turn the heat to low, and simmer 2½ or 3 hours or while you are at church and Sunday School. The meat should be very tender. Remove the meat to a platter, and thicken the broth to make gravy. Taste and adjust the seasoning before serving. If you wish to add vegetables, place them on the bottom of the pan after the roast is browned, putting the roast on top. Add water to cover as before.

TLC Tip: *My sister likes to brown sliced onions in the pan before browning the meat. She thinks this gives a good flavor, and I won't disagree with her.*

SAVORY RUMP ROAST

This is an unusual way to prepare roast, but don't knock it until you've tried it. The buttermilk marinade helps to tenderize the roast, and forms the basis of a tangy gravy.

1 (3- to 4-pound) beef rump
   roast
2 cups buttermilk
1 teaspoon salt
½ cup water

Carrots, peeled and cut into
   large pieces
Small, whole onions, peeled
Celery, cut into large pieces

In a shallow dish, marinate meat in buttermilk at least 6 hours, or overnight. Try to turn at least once. Remove meat from buttermilk; refrigerate reserved marinade. In large non-stick skillet or Dutch oven sprayed with cooking spray, brown meat on all sides over medium-high heat. Add salt and water, cover and simmer 2 to 2½ hours or until meat is almost tender. (The same length of time in a 325 degree oven will do the job, too.) Add carrots, onions and celery (you decide the amount depending on the number of people you are serving), and continue cooking for 45-50 minutes or until vegetables are tender. Remove meat and vegetables to a platter and keep warm while preparing gravy.

SAVORY GRAVY

1½ cups pan drippings (add
   water if necessary to
   make this amount)
1½ cups buttermilk marinade
½ cup flour

½ cup water
1 teaspoon grated lemon peel
1 tablespoon lemon juice
1 teaspoon sugar

In skillet or Dutch oven, combine pan drippings and marinade. In separate bowl, mix water and flour to a smooth paste; add to mixture in skillet. Cook over medium heat, stirring constantly, until thickened. Cook 2 minutes more. Add lemon peel, lemon juice and sugar. Serve with meat.

SHIRLEY'S BRISKET

Shirley Beauchamp loves cookbooks almost as much as I do. We both read them like novels and find ourselves drawn to that section of the bookstore. Her brisket is wonderful, and so easy to prepare. I've thanked her many times for sharing this recipe.

1 (4- to 5-pound) brisket, trimmed of fat
1 tablespoon unseasoned meat tenderizer
½ bottle liquid smoke
2 tablespoons Worcestershire sauce
1 teaspoon garlic salt
½ teaspoon pepper

Rub both sides of meat with the tenderizer. Place in a large roasting pan. Mix the remaining ingredients together and pour over the meat. Cover tightly with foil. Bake at 300 degrees for 1 hour, then at 200 degrees for 8-10 hours. Slice across the grain to serve. Great as an entrée and equally as good served on buns.

TLC Tip: Be sure the brisket is table-trimmed of fat. You need a little fat, but not that much. One time I neglected that step, and ended up with a mess. To make an easy sauce to serve with the brisket, thin your favorite bottled BBQ sauce with a little of the pan juices.

BROILED FLANK STEAK

Flank steak is one of the leanest cuts of beef, and is very tasty when marinated, grilled or broiled, and sliced thinly on the diagonal. Unfortunately, it is a bit hard to find. If you ask your meat market attendant or butcher, he can probably get it for you. We love this version, served in any number of ways—as a sandwich (see index), or dinner entrée with oven-fried potatoes.

3 tablespoons teriyaki sauce
½ clove garlic, minced
1 green onion, minced
1 (8-ounce) flank steak (also called London broil)

Combine first 3 ingredients in a small bowl. Score meat on each side with a sharp knife. Pour marinade over meat (I like to use a heavy zip-lock bag for this) and marinate at least 20 minutes—but longer is OK. Broil 8-10 minutes for rare. (Use your oven manual for directions and distance from heat.) You can also grill over hot coals for about the same length of time. When the meat is done to your liking, remove to cutting board and slice thinly across the grain. Across the grain is important. If the meat looks too rare when I slice it, I place the slices over the heat briefly for added cooking.

TLC Tip: Done but not overcooked is the thing to remember here.

SAVORY SWISS STEAK

This is a favorite from my Michigan days. It is a good dish to put in the oven and let simmer away while you are at church or putting the finishing touches on the rest of the meal. I love this version; however, my family prefers the one without tomatoes and peppers. I like to serve this with rice or mashed potatoes.

2 pounds round steak (I have the butcher run it through the tenderizer so I don't have to tenderize it myself)
½ clove garlic, or live dangerously and use the whole clove
Salt and pepper to taste
¼ cup flour
1 tablespoon cooking oil

1 (6-ounce) can tomato paste
1½ cups water
½ teaspoon salt
⅛ teaspoon pepper
1 small bay leaf
¼ teaspoon thyme
¼ teaspoon sugar
1 large onion, sliced
1 green pepper, cut into long strips

Cut steak into serving-size pieces. Trim off all the visible fat. Rub the steak with the garlic; season to taste. Dust the meat with the flour. Heat the oil in a large, non-stick skillet. Brown meat on both sides and place in flat casserole dish. (I like my white Corningware 3-quart one.) Pour off any accumulated fat from skillet, add tomato paste, water and seasonings and heat until bubbly. Arrange onion and green pepper over meat. Pour the tomato mixture over the top. Cover dish tightly and bake in a moderate oven, 350 degrees, for 1½ to 2 hours. Will serve 4 to 6 depending on how hungry everyone is.

THE FAMILY'S FAVORITE SWISS STEAK

This is the Swiss steak my family raves about. I must admit that it is tasty, and a good way to consume your beef allotment. This dish also cooks happily while you do other things, and provides a wonderful aroma when you walk in the door from church. I like this one with mashed potatoes so you have something wonderful to spoon the gravy over.

2 pounds round steak, tenderized	**1 (14-ounce) can beef broth**
¼ cup flour	**¾ cup water**
1 teaspoon lite seasoned salt	**1 bay leaf**
Dash of pepper	**1 large onion, sliced**
1 tablespoon oil	**(optional)**

Cut the meat into serving pieces and trim off all fat. Combine flour, salt and pepper in a flat dish. Heat the oil in a large, non-stick skillet. Lightly coat the meat with the flour mixture, and brown on both sides in the skillet. Place in a large, flat casserole dish. Pour the beef broth and water into the skillet, and scrape up all the brown bits while it heats. Sprinkle the flour left over from breading the meat over the browned meat. Layer the onion over the meat, if you desire, with the bay leaf. Pour the hot liquid over the meat, cover tightly and bake at 350 degrees for 1½ to 2 hours. Or you can bake at 325 degrees for 3 hours, if this helps you out. Serve to 6 or 8 people.

TLC Tip: Sometimes I like to use a package of beef mushroom soup mix. In that case, I omit the seasoned salt and beef broth and add the soup mix to the skillet with 2½ cups water.

CHICKEN FRIED STEAK

Being from the North, Chicken Fried Steak was something I had to learn how to cook when I moved to Texas. As with some other regional foods, I suppose there are as many opinions as to what constitutes a good chicken fried steak as there are people who cook them. What I have observed is that a chicken fried steak is only as good as the meat you start with, so choose the best you can afford. It is mandatory that you serve it with plenty of cream gravy, and potatoes. Here again there is a difference of opinion, some preferring French fries, others thinking mashed potatoes are the only way to go. I prefer the latter, thinking fried potatoes a little bit of fat overkill. Every once in a while, you just have to drag out the old cast iron skillet, roll up your sleeves and declare a Chicken Fried Steak day—no apologies!!

1 pound good quality round steak	**1 teaspoon salt**
1 cup flour	**½ teaspoon pepper**
	½ cup evaporated milk

Remove all visible fat from steak, cut into serving size pieces, and pound to tenderize, if necessary. (I usually have the butcher tenderize it for me.) Combine the flour, salt and pepper. Dip each piece of steak in the flour mixture, then in the milk, and then in the flour mixture again. Lay on a sheet of waxed paper. Reserve flour mixture. Heat ¼ to ½ inch of oil in a heavy skillet. (As I mentioned earlier, I prefer cast iron.) Fry over medium-high heat until lightly browned. Do not overcook. Drain on paper towels. Serve with cream gravy.

Cream Gravy:

3 tablespoons pan drippings (If I don't end up with enough pan drippings, I add oil to make the amount needed)	**3 tablespoons reserved flour mixture**
	1 cup evaporated milk
	1 cup water
	Salt and pepper to taste

After frying the steak, pour off all but 3 tablespoons of the oil. Loosen any browned pieces from the bottom of the skillet and add the flour. Stir flour into drippings until smooth. Combine milk and water. With pan over medium heat, add cold milk mixture all at once, stirring constantly with a wire whisk until thickened. Scrape sides and bottom to loosen any more browned pieces. Taste for seasoning before adding more salt and pepper. Add a little more milk or water if gravy seems a little thick. Makes 2½ to 3 cups gravy.

BEEF STROGANOFF

I've prepared this recipe for years and have always been pleased with the outcome. Though the title sounds a bit fancy, it is really quite a simple dish to make but does look and taste impressive. I like to serve it over noodles, with a green vegetable and a simple green salad. Somehow that seems to compensate for the richness of the sauce.

4 tablespoons flour, divided use	1 cup thinly sliced fresh mushrooms
½ teaspoon salt	½ cup chopped onion
1 pound beef sirloin, cut into thin strips	1 clove garlic, minced
2 tablespoons butter, divided use	1 tablespoon tomato paste (or catsup in a pinch)
2 tablespoons oil	1¼ cups beef broth (canned is OK)
	1 cup sour cream

Combine 1 tablespoon flour and salt; flour meat strips. Heat skillet over medium-high heat; add 1 tablespoon butter and 1 tablespoon oil. When oil is hot and butter is melted, add the meat and brown quickly. Add the mushroom slices, onion, and garlic; cook 3 or 4 minutes or till onion is barely tender. Remove meat from skillet. Add remaining butter and oil to pan drippings. When melted, blend in 3 tablespoons flour. Add the tomato paste. Slowly pour in the beef broth, stirring constantly with a wire whisk. Cook until mixture thickens, still stirring constantly. Return browned meat and mushrooms to skillet. Stir in the sour cream; heat briefly, but do not boil. Serve as desired.

TLC Tip: *This looks nice spooned over noodles or rice and garnished with a bit of chopped fresh parsley.*

CONNECTICUT BEEF SUPPER

This dish has come to my rescue many times over the years. It satisfies the hunger pangs admirably and bakes happily in the oven while you do other things.

½ to 1 tablespoon oil, if
  desired
2 pounds lean beef stew meat,
  cut into 1" cubes
2 large onions, diced
1 cup water
2 large potatoes, pared and
  thinly sliced
1 can cream of mushroom
  soup

1 cup sour cream
1¼ cups milk
1 teaspoon salt (optional)
¼ teaspoon pepper
1 cup shredded Cheddar
  cheese
1½ cups wheat cereal flakes,
  crushed

Cook and stir meat and onion in a large non-stick pan that has been sprayed with cooking spray, using oil if desired. Stir occasionally until meat is brown and onion is tender. Add water, heat to boiling. Reduce heat, cover and simmer 50 minutes. If there seems to be a lot of liquid, remove a little of the juice before pouring the meat mixture into an ungreased 13 x 9" baking dish; arrange potato slices on meat. Stir together the soup, sour cream, milk and seasonings; pour over the potatoes. Sprinkle with cheese and cereal. Bake uncovered at 350 degrees for 1½ hours or until potatoes and meat are tender. Makes 6 to 8 servings.

TLC Tip: This is another recipe where you must adjust the salt to your liking. The kind of soup you use makes a difference.

MEDITERRANEAN STIR-FRIED BEEF

This is a little different twist on the stir-fry as it is served with pasta instead of rice. I think you will like the flavor combination, and the idea that vegetables and linguine are flavored with a modest amount of meat in the 90's style.

½ pound boneless top round
   steak
½ cup water
¼ cup red wine vinegar
2 teaspoons minced dried
   onion
¼ teaspoon pepper
⅛ teaspoon ground red
   pepper (optional)
6 ounces linguine
2 tablespoons butter or extra-
   virgin olive oil

2 teaspoons cornstarch
1 tablespoon olive oil, divided
   use
1 (16-ounce) package loose
   pack broccoli,
   cauliflower and carrots
1 clove garlic, minced
1 cup sliced fresh mushrooms
Freshly grated Parmesan
   cheese

Thinly slice the beef across the grain into bite-size strips. Combine water, vinegar, onion, pepper and red pepper. Add meat; mix well. Marinate 15 minutes at room temperature. Cook pasta according to package directions. Drain, toss with butter or olive oil and keep warm. Drain meat, reserving marinade. Stir cornstarch into reserved marinade; set aside. Heat a non-stick skillet over medium-high heat; add ½ tablespoon olive oil and when oil is hot, add the meat and stir-fry 3-4 minutes. Remove meat from skillet, add remaining ½ tablespoon oil, and stir-fry vegetables and garlic 4 minutes. Add the mushrooms, and continue stir-frying an additional minute. Stir the marinade mixture and add to skillet. Return meat to skillet. Cook and stir until bubbly. Cook two minutes. Arrange pasta on platter, top with meat mixture, sprinkle with cheese. Enjoy!

TLC Tip: Stir-frying is an individual thing. The times listed may be more or less than necessary to achieve the doneness desired, depending on the heat of the skillet and personal taste. Use your own judgment.

FLUFFY MEATLOAF

Meatloaf doesn't seem to rate very high on the family favorite list. I guess it brings up too many memories of school or college cafeterias. However, cooks can think up a number of reasons to serve this homey staple, not the least of which is the fact that it is easy and inexpensive. As meatloaves go, this is a very good one—true to its name, with subtle but tasty seasonings. I've tried many, but always come back to this one. The family tolerates it very well, and so do my last-minute guests.

1½ pounds lean ground beef
3 slices fresh bread, torn into pieces
1 cup milk
1 egg
1 tablespoon dried minced onion (normally I prefer fresh over dried anything, but for some reason, I have always used the dried in this recipe. You can use ¼ cup diced fresh onion if you prefer.)

1 teaspoon salt
¼ teaspoon each pepper, celery salt and garlic powder
1 tablespoon Worcestershire sauce
1 tablespoon horseradish
1 tablespoon catsup

Mix all ingredients thoroughly in a large bowl. I always use clean hands, and think the disposable plastic gloves are great for this purpose. Shape into a loaf in a 9 x 5" pan or shallow casserole dish. Bake in a 350 degree oven for 1½ hours. A coating of your favorite BBQ sauce during the last 30 minutes of baking is a nice touch.

TLC Tip: *This mixture may also be shaped into 8 mini-loaves and placed in a 9 x 13" pan. The baking time will be less, probably about 1 hour. This version is especially nice for a company meal.*

WAIKIKI MEATBALLS

*My Aunt Lodema Crabtree is the loveliest woman. She is kind and gener-
ous, friendly and helpful, and always ready to set another plate on the table
should you appear at her Pryor, Oklahoma, door near mealtime. Her
meatballs go well with steamed rice and perhaps a stir-fry of snow peas
and carrots.*

2 pounds ground beef
¼ cup finely minced onion
⅔ cup cracker crumbs
1 egg
1½ teaspoons salt (less if you
    want)
¼ teaspoon ground ginger
¼ cup milk
1 tablespoon oil
2 (8-ounce) cans pineapple
    tidbits, drained, juice
    reserved

2 tablespoons cornstarch
½ cup brown sugar
⅓ cup apple cider vinegar
1 tablespoon soy sauce
1 (6-ounce) can unsweetened
    pineapple juice
½ green pepper, cut into small
    squares
½ red pepper, cut into small
    squares

Mix the beef, onion, crumbs, salt, egg, ginger and milk. Shape into small
balls, about the size of an English walnut. (A #50 cookie scoop is perfect for
this job.) Brown the meatballs in a large skillet, using the 1 tablespoon oil,
if desired. You can also bake them in a 350 degree oven for about 20
minutes—I find this the easiest way. When the meatballs are cooked,
remove from skillet (or baking pan) and keep warm. Mix the cornstarch
and sugar in the skillet or small saucepan. Measure the reserved juice,
add the can of juice and water, if necessary, to make 1½ cups liquid. Add
the juice, vinegar and soy sauce to the saucepan. Cook over medium heat,
stirring constantly, until mixture thickens and boils. Bring a small pot of
water to the boil. Drop in the pepper pieces and boil for 4 minutes. Remove
with a slotted spoon, rinse with cold water, and add to the sauce. Stir in
the pineapple tidbits. Pour over the meatballs, mix gently to coat with
sauce.

DANIEL'S CHEESEBURGER PIE

What could be more kid-pleasing than a cheeseburger? Our grandson, Daniel Beauchamp, likes this main dish that includes all the best parts of a cheeseburger, even the pickles.

½ of a (15-ounce) package
   refrigerated pie crusts
1 pound lean ground beef
½ cup finely chopped onion
1 clove garlic, finely chopped
½ teaspoon salt
¼ cup flour

⅓ cup dill pickle liquid
⅓ cup milk
½ cup finely chopped dill
   pickles
2 cups shredded Cheddar or
   Swiss cheese, divided use

Place the sheet of pastry in an 8" or 9" pie pan. Flute the edges, prick all over with a fork and bake in a 425 degree oven for 15 minutes. While crust is baking, cook and stir beef, onion and garlic in a large non-stick skillet until brown; drain. Sprinkle with the salt and flour. Stir in the pickle liquid, milk, pickles and 1 cup of the cheese. Spoon into the pie shell. Continue baking for 15 minutes; sprinkle with the remaining 1 cup cheese. Bake until crust is golden brown, about 5 minutes longer. This will serve 6 hungry kids or 4 very hungry ones!!

TLC Tip: *I have known some who like to garnish this with a liberal topping of catsup.*

AFRICAN CHOW MEIN

This recipe comes from Mrs. W. D. Wood. She and her husband were attendants for mom and dad when they married in Anderson, Indiana on June 23, 1933. They married in this couple's apartment in what was then Old Main on the campus of Anderson College. Later that part of the building became the chemistry lab, which is what it was when I attended school there. Now it is a university, and Old Main has been torn down. Fortunately, we have our memories.

1 pound lean ground beef
1 onion, chopped
1 cup regular rice, uncooked
1 can chicken rice soup

1 can cream of mushroom
   soup
1 tablespoon soy sauce
1 cup diced celery

Brown ground beef and onion in a large non-stick skillet. Add the rest of the ingredients, mix well, and transfer to a casserole dish. Bake covered for 45 minutes in a 375 degree oven; uncover and continue baking for another 10 minutes.

TLC Tip: This is nice garnished with chow mein noodles added to the top of the casserole during the last 5-10 minutes of baking.

AUNT MÁCO'S TACO PIE

When you need a Tex-Mex fix in a hurry, my Aunt's Taco Pie should do the trick. Aunt Máco was such fun to be around. She aged gracefully, and kept pace with the times, as this recipe from her files would indicate. The use of extra lean, well-drained ground beef, Healthy Request soup and reduced-fat cheese will bring it into the 1990's in grand style.

1½ pounds lean ground beef	1 small can tomato sauce
1 onion, chopped	1 package corn tortillas (12)
2 cans cream of mushroom	½ pound Cheddar cheese,
soup	grated
1 can enchilada sauce	

Sauté ground beef in a large non-stick skillet with the chopped onion. Drain well. Add both cans of soup, the enchilada and tomato sauces and mix well. Place 2 cups of this mixture in a 9 x 13" baking dish. Place 6 tortillas over the top of this mixture. Add another 2 cups of meat mixture and place the other 6 tortillas over the top. Add the rest of the meat mixture. Cover the top with the grated cheese. Bake until bubbling and hot in a 350 degree oven, about 20-30 minutes.

BEV'S MEXICAN HASH

This recipe came home from school with our daughter, Beverly. They had prepared it in her Home Ec class. Sometimes the simple things are the best, and that is true of this dish. The ingredients are easy to keep on hand for a quick lunch or supper. A salad of avocado and citrus and Chocolate Cups Olé (see index) for dessert dresses it up a bit.

1 pound lean ground beef	2 (16-ounce) cans pinto beans,
1 large onion, chopped	drained
Salt and pepper to taste	Tortilla chips
1 small can chopped green	Grated cheese
chilis	Shredded lettuce
2 (15-ounce) cans tomatoes or	Chopped tomatoes
sauce (we like to use 1 of	
each)	

Sauté the onion and ground beef in a non-stick skillet sprayed with vegetable oil spray. When meat is brown, season to taste, and add chilis, tomatoes and/or sauce and pinto beans. Simmer slowly for 1 hour. Spoon over tortilla chips. Top with cheese, lettuce and tomatoes, as desired.

FIESTA TAMALE PIE

Full of lots of nourishing things and bursting with a combination of spicy flavors, this tamale pie is sure to please. For an even leaner dish, use ground turkey breast instead of the more fatty ground turkey. This is a real family pleaser.

1 pound ground turkey	2 cups tomato sauce
⅛ teaspoon nutmeg	2 cups corn, frozen or fresh
⅛ teaspoon thyme	⅓ cup sliced ripe olives,
⅛ teaspoon garlic powder	optional
⅛ teaspoon sage	1½ teaspoons chili powder, or
1 tablespoon soy sauce	to taste
1 small green pepper,	1 teaspoon salt, divided
chopped	2 cups water, divided
1 small onion, chopped	1 tablespoon butter
1 clove garlic, minced	1 cup stone-ground cornmeal

Season the turkey with the nutmeg, thyme, garlic powder, sage and soy sauce. Brown in a non-stick skillet. When the meat is about half browned, add the vegetables; continue cooking until meat is thoroughly browned and vegetables are wilted. Lower the heat and blend in the tomato sauce, corn, olives, chili powder and ½ teaspoon salt. When heated through, remove from heat and pour into a 9" square pan or 2-quart casserole dish. In a saucepan bring 1 cup water, ½ teaspoon salt and butter to a boil. In a separate bowl, blend the cornmeal and the remaining 1 cup cold water. Gradually stir cold water-cornmeal mixture into boiling water, stirring to thicken, about 2 minutes. Spread cooked cornmeal mixture evenly to edges over top of casserole. Bake uncovered at 350 degrees for 40 to 50 minutes.

TLC Tip: *This looks nice garnished with some lowfat sour cream and sprinkled with additional sliced ripe olives.*

RITA JO'S WESTERN CHILI CASSEROLE

This dish is a favorite of my brother, Paul. He is my "little brother", in years, not necessarily in size, and began entertaining us with his piano playing at the age of three. Mother would get him dressed for Sunday School, and sit him at the piano to keep him busy while she finished getting ready. He developed that talent into his life's work. He is a Minister of Music in Flint, Michigan, and has served in this capacity in churches across the land. He is especially fond of sports, baseball in particular, and took up skiing when he turned 50. My sister-in-law and I prepared this often during our early married years in the late 1950's, and Paul says he still enjoys it after a day on the slopes.

1 pound lean ground beef	**¼ teaspoon pepper**
1 cup chopped onion, divided use	**2 cups corn chips or tortilla chips, slightly crushed, divided use**
¼ cup chopped celery	
1 large can chili (with or without beans)	**1 cup shredded sharp cheese, divided use**

Brown meat; add ¾ cup onion and the celery. Cook until vegetables are just tender. Drain off any accumulated juices. Add chili and pepper; heat. Place a layer of chips in an ungreased 1½-quart casserole. Alternate layers of chili mixture, chips and cheese, reserving ½ cup chips and ¼ cup cheese for topping. Sprinkle center of casserole with reserved cheese and onion. Cover; bake at 350 degrees for 10 minutes or until hot through. Border the casserole with the remaining corn chips before serving.

TLC Tip: *Rita Jo says they always serve this with a green salad and whole kernel corn.*

LINDA'S GREEN BEEF ENCHILADAS

Linda Lindell is my husband's sister. We have had a lot of fun with food over the years, often getting together during the holidays to bake special treats for our families and friends. Linda is a great cook when she can find the time from her busy schedule as high school choir director and other musical duties. This dish does her proud.

1 can cream of chicken soup, undiluted
½ pound Velveeta cheese
1 (4-ounce) can chopped green chilis
1 (2-ounce) jar chopped pimiento
1 (5-ounce) can evaporated milk (⅔ cup)

1 pound lean ground beef
½ pound grated Cheddar cheese
1 cup chopped onions
Garlic powder
Salt and pepper, to taste
1 dozen corn tortillas

Make a cheese sauce by combining the first 5 ingredients in a heavy saucepan. Heat over low heat until cheese melts and sauce is smooth, stirring occasionally. Brown meat in a non-stick skillet. Add the seasonings, remove from heat, stir in Cheddar cheese and onions. Dip tortillas briefly in hot oil or hot water to soften; drain. Fill with meat mixture, roll up and place seam-side down in a 9 x 13" baking dish. Cover with cheese sauce, sprinkle with a little additional grated cheese and bake at 350 degrees for 30 minutes.

TLC Tip: *This dish can easily be modified to reduce the fat and sodium. Use reduced-fat and reduced-sodium soup, reduced-fat Velveeta cheese, evaporated skim milk, very lean ground beef, and reduced-fat Cheddar cheese. You can even omit the Cheddar cheese if you wish.*

HEARTY BEEF AND POTATO CASSEROLE

I love casseroles—for their taste, ease of preparation and serving, and their versatility. I guess we usually think of them as being high in calories and / or fat, and often this is true. They can be lightened up, however, and I try to practice this when preparing them these days. I do this by using Healthy Request soups, skim milk, lean meats, reduced-fat cheeses and alternative toppings. Then I accompany the casserole with vegetables and salads that are low in fat but high in eye appeal and taste. You can do this, too.

**4 cups frozen potato rounds
  or nuggets
1 pound lean ground beef
1 (10-ounce) package frozen
  chopped broccoli, thawed
1 cup French fried onions,
  divided use**

**1 medium tomato, chopped
  (optional)
1 can cream of celery soup
⅓ cup milk
1 cup shredded cheese,
  divided use
¼ teaspoon garlic powder
⅛ teaspoon pepper**

Place the potatoes on the bottom of an 8 x 12" casserole. Bake, uncovered, at 400 degrees for 10 minutes. While the potatoes are baking, brown the beef in a large skillet; drain if necessary. Place beef, broccoli, ½ cup onion rings and tomatoes on top of the potatoes. Combine soup, milk, ½ cup cheese and seasonings; pour over beef mixture. Bake, covered, at 400 degrees for 20 minutes. Top with remaining cheese and onions; bake, uncovered, 2-3 minutes longer. Should serve 6.

TLC Tip: *If you can't find the frozen potato rounds or don't wish to use nuggets, you can substitute 4 cups cooked sliced potatoes.*

197

TATER TOT CASSEROLE

This recipe comes from Jean McAdams. We used to prepare this dish a lot in the 70's when we got together after church for conversation and a game of Rook. If you use lean ground beef, Healthy Request soup and reduced-fat cheese, you can enjoy it still without too much of a guilty conscience.

1½ pounds lean ground beef	1 can cream of mushroom
1 large onion, chopped	soup, undiluted
1 can cream of celery soup,	1 cup grated cheese
undiluted	Tater Tots

Brown the ground beef in a non-stick skillet. Season lightly with salt and pepper or other seasonings of your choice. Place in a 2- to 2½-quart casserole dish that has been lightly sprayed with cooking spray. Sprinkle the onion over the beef. Combine the soups in a bowl and pour over the onion and beef. Top with the grated cheese. Cover the top of the casserole with a layer of Tater Tots. Bake in a 350 degree oven for 30 to 40 minutes.

TLC Tip: When I serve a dish like this, I make sure the rest of the meal has little fat. I would probably serve a green vegetable such as broccoli, green beans or zucchini and a green salad. Dessert would be simple also, perhaps tapioca pudding or sherbet and a simple cookie.

TLC Tip Two: In an effort to make this dish a little more healthy, I have covered the top with cooked potato slices, sprinkled them with fresh breadcrumbs and then sprayed it with butter-flavored spray. Very tasty. If you use the Healthy Request soups, be sure to taste to see if the mixture is seasoned to your liking.

BEEF CHOW MEIN BAKE

This was always a favorite of our family. Now that it is just the two of us, I sometimes prepare this dish, divide it in half before baking, and share with someone or put in the freezer for another meal.

1½ pounds lean ground beef
1½ cups chopped celery
1 medium onion, finely
    chopped
1 can tomato soup
1 can cream of mushroom
    soup

2 to 3 tablespoons soy sauce
1 (4-ounce) can chopped
    mushrooms
2 cups chow mein noodles,
    divided use
½ cup cashew nuts

Brown the beef in a non-stick skillet over medium-high heat. Add the celery and onion; sauté until transparent. Stir in the tomato and mushroom soups (I always use the Healthy Request kind), soy sauce (reduced-sodium, if you prefer) and mushrooms. Add 1½ cups noodles. Place in a 2-quart baking dish. Bake, uncovered, 25 to 30 minutes. Sprinkle with remaining ½ cup noodles and cashew nuts. Bake uncovered an additional 10 minutes.

TLC Tip: *The cashew nuts can be optional, but they add a really nice touch to this dish. They also add fat, but considering the dish serves 6 to 8, not too much. Enjoy!*

YANKEE DOODLE MACARONI

I can't remember how many times I've served this dish during the years when my family was growing up. It is easy to prepare, filling and good tasting. I still use it for potlucks and social gatherings or a casual supper for family or friends.

2 cups chopped onion	1 tablespoon minced fresh
2 cloves garlic, minced	parsley
¾ cup sliced mushrooms	1 teaspoon salt
(optional)	⅛ teaspoon pepper
1 tablespoon oil	8 ounces uncooked macaroni
1 pound lean ground beef	Grated sharp Cheddar or
1 (28-ounce) can cooked	Parmesan cheese
tomatoes (about 3½ cups)	

Sauté onions, garlic and mushrooms in hot oil over medium heat. Add ground beef and cook until brown. Add tomatoes, parsley, salt and pepper; cook slowly, about 45 minutes. Meanwhile, cook the macaroni as package directs. Drain. Arrange the hot, cooked macaroni in a large pasta bowl. Pour the hot sauce over. Top with grated sharp Cheddar or Parmesan cheese. Serve immediately.

TLC Tip: *Often I combine the macaroni and sauce, place in a casserole and keep covered in the refrigerator until near mealtime. When ready to heat, place in a 350 degree oven for 20 to 30 minutes until bubbly. Top with the cheese the last few minutes.*

TLC Tip Two: *Rita Jo says she adds oregano to the basic recipe for a completely different taste. Try 1 teaspoon, more if you like.*

MAÑANA BEEF BAKE

In the 70's and early 80's we had a Radio Shack franchise. This dish was a favorite to serve to our employees during inventory. After the store closed, I would bring in supper, and we would stuff ourselves before the job at hand. This dish makes a generous amount, and is good served with a green or congealed salad, buttered French bread and your favorite cake for dessert.

1 pound lean ground beef
1 large onion, chopped
1 can cream of chicken soup
¾ cup milk
2 tablespoons soy sauce
2 teaspoons Worcestershire
   sauce
⅛ teaspoon pepper
1 (4-ounce) can mushrooms,
   with liquid

1 small green pepper,
   chopped
½ cup sliced ripe olives
5 ounces noodles, cooked and
   drained (this may not
   seem like enough, but it
   is)
1 cup shredded cheese
Chow mein noodles

Cook and stir the ground beef and onion in a non-stick skillet until meat is brown. Drain if necessary. In a medium bowl, combine the soup, milk, soy sauce, Worcestershire sauce and pepper. Combine the soup mixture with the beef and onion; stir in the mushrooms, green pepper, olives, and noodles. Pour noodles and beef mixture into a 2-quart casserole. Bake in a 350 degree oven for about 30 minutes, until bubbly. Top with grated cheese and chow mein noodles. Bake an additional 10 minutes.

TLC Tip: *If you use reduced-sodium soup and soy sauce in this recipe, I think you will need to add a little salt. Try ½ teaspoon—that amount seems to suit our tastes.*

MY OWN SPAGHETTI SAUCE

The recipe card for this sauce is spattered and brown. I began developing this sauce while a new bride in Lawton, Oklahoma. Money was tight, and this was my company dish. The only things I have changed about this recipe over the years are that I now leave out the MSG and use less oil to brown the meat and vegetables. My girls are now carrying on the tradition by preparing this sauce to serve to their family and friends. It freezes beautifully, and makes a satisfying main dish.

½ cup onion slices
⅔ cup chopped green pepper
1 cup chopped celery
1 tablespoon olive oil
 (optional)
1 pound lean ground beef
2 cloves garlic, minced
1 (4-ounce) can mushrooms
 (sliced or chopped,
 depending on your
 budget) or 1 cup sliced
 fresh
1 (28-ounce) can tomatoes
 (about 4 cups) undrained

2 (8-ounce) cans tomato sauce
1 (6-ounce) can tomato paste
1½ teaspoons oregano
½ teaspoon salt (optional)
¼ teaspoon dried thyme
 leaves
1 large bay leaf
⅛ teaspoon nutmeg
A few grindings freshly
 ground pepper
2 tablespoons sugar
1 cup water

In a large saucepan sprayed with vegetable spray, cook the onion, green pepper and celery in the olive oil. Stir often, and when vegetables begin to wilt, add the ground beef and garlic. Brown lightly. Add the remaining ingredients and simmer uncovered 2 to 2½ hours or until thick. Remove bay leaf. (I am notorious for not removing it—then we say the person who winds up with it is in for good luck. Fortunately, I have yet to have someone choke on it. It's best to remove it.) Serve over hot, cooked spaghetti and garnish with freshly ground Parmesan cheese.

TLC Tip: *You can substitute Italian sausage for all or part of the ground beef. If you do so, drain well before adding rest of ingredients. Or you can try turkey sausage—nice change. Daughter Deanna likes to whirl the tomatoes in the blender or food processor briefly before adding to the pot. You can also use your kitchen shears to cut up the tomatoes while they are still in the can. I have occasionally prepared this sauce without meat, and simmered meatballs in the sauce, but I prefer the sauce with the meat.*

EDITH'S CABBAGE ROLLS

Edith Wood and her late husband, Bob, are friends from my days in Plymouth, Michigan. These cabbage rolls are THE BEST, and I have such happy memories of sitting around their table eating them with mashed potatoes. This is a real home-style dish, perfect for the cool days of autumn or chilly days of winter. Besides mashed potatoes, I think cornbread makes a nice addition to this meal and perhaps a salad of grated carrots and raisins.

1 large, solid head of cabbage
1½ pounds lean ground beef
1 large onion, finely chopped
1 handful of rice (not instant)
Salt and pepper to your liking

1 large jar sauerkraut (about
 a quart)
1 (28-ounce) can tomatoes,
 slightly chopped

Remove outer leaves from cabbage, core and carefully peel the leaves away from the head. Place in a large pan, cover with water and boil 3 to 4 minutes until wilted and pliable. Drain. Combine the ground beef, onion, rice, salt and pepper. Place half the sauerkraut in a large Dutch oven. Shape the meat mixture into balls and wrap each in a cabbage leaf; secure with a toothpick. Place the cabbage rolls on top of the sauerkraut; cover with the remaining kraut. Pour the tomatoes over all. Cover the pan, bring to a boil; reduce heat, simmer 2-3 hours.

TLC Tip: *It would be wise to warn your family and friends that they will find a toothpick in their cabbage roll.*

WORLD'S GREATEST PIZZA

I guess whether this title is a correct statement or not is up to the consumer. But one thing I do know, when you make your own pizza it is the greatest because it has on it exactly what you like and the amount of salt and fat can be controlled by you. You will like this crust, with its hearty taste, and the sauce compliments it nicely. When it comes to the toppings, add, subtract, adjust the amounts, whatever, you can't go wrong. Don't let the list of ingredients scare you—it is really quite easy. Prepare the crust first, and let it rest while you are making the sauce and getting the toppings ready.

Quick Pizza Dough:

2½ cups flour (I like half white and half whole wheat)
¾ teaspoon salt

1 package quick-rise yeast
1 cup warm water
1 teaspoon canola oil

In work bowl of food processor, combine flour, salt and yeast. Pulse twice to mix. With machine running, gradually pour warm water through feed tube; then add the oil. Dough should clump together and form ball on top of blade. Process for 45 seconds to knead to a smooth, elastic dough. Form into 2 balls, dust lightly with flour, cover with cloth and set aside while preparing toppings and sauce.

Thel's Special Pizza Sauce:

1 (8-ounce) can tomato sauce
1 (6-ounce) can tomato paste
1 large clove garlic, crushed
2 teaspoons sugar

1 teaspoon oregano
¼ to ½ teaspoon red pepper (optional—I usually do not add this)

Mix all ingredients thoroughly.

Suggested Pizza Toppings:

You decide which ones to use and the amount.

Sweet Italian sausage, ground beef or turkey, browned and well drained
Canadian bacon, cut into small pieces
Pepperoni, sliced thin
Thinly sliced mushrooms
Chopped or thinly sliced onion

Chopped or thinly sliced pepper strips
Sliced black and/or green olives
Grated cheese—mozzarella, Jack, Parmesan—choose one or use a mixture

(World's Greatest Pizza, continued on next page)

204

(World's Greatest Pizza, continued)

When ready to bake, press each ball of dough into a greased 12" pizza pan. Spread with ½ the sauce and sprinkle with desired toppings. Bake on bottom rack of preheated 500 degree oven, 10 to 14 minutes, until crust is golden brown and cheese is melted. Cut into desired size wedges (I use my kitchen shears for this job) and serve.

TLC Tip: *Sometimes I pre-cook the vegetables just a bit before placing on the pizza. I have used zucchini, summer squash, and broccoli flowerettes with yummy success in addition to, or instead of, the other toppings.*

EASY DEEP-DISH PIZZA

The title says it all, except that it is delicious and very kid-pleasing. Add a big green salad and make-your-own sundaes for dessert, and you'll have a winner in no time.

3 cups biscuit mix	1 (15-ounce) can tomato sauce
¾ cup water	1 teaspoon Italian seasoning
1 pound lean ground beef or turkey or a combination of each	1 (4-ounce) jar sliced mushrooms (optional, but good)
½ cup chopped onion	½ cup chopped green pepper
½ teaspoon salt	2 cups shredded mozzarella
2 cloves garlic, crushed	cheese

Mix biscuit mix and water until a soft dough forms. Gently smooth dough into ball on floured surface. Knead 20 times. Pat dough on bottom and up sides of greased 15 x 10" jelly roll pan with floured hands. Cook and stir ground beef, onion, salt and garlic in a non-stick skillet over medium-high heat until beef is brown; drain. Mix tomato sauce and Italian seasoning; spread evenly over dough. Spoon beef mixture over sauce. Top with mushrooms, green pepper and cheese. Bake at 425 degrees until crust is golden brown, about 20 minutes.

TLC Tip: *This can be varied by substituting or adding chopped vegetables of your choice.*

IMPOSSIBLE MAIN DISH PIES

Impossible pies were dreamed up by the Bisquick people. What an invention!! An easy, delicious main dish that can be varied in many ways. Use a deep-dish pie pan and don't fill too full even if it means leaving out a little of the filling. Check baking time carefully—it may take a little longer depending on your oven.

Custard Mixture:

1⅓ cups milk
3 eggs
¾ cup baking mix (such as Bisquick)

¾ teaspoon salt
¼ teaspoon pepper

Beat all ingredients together until smooth, about 15 seconds in a blender, which is by far the easiest way. Pour over filling. (See following recipes.) Bake as directed.

CHICKEN 'N BROCCOLI PIE

1 (10-ounce) package frozen chopped broccoli
3 cups shredded Cheddar cheese, divided use

1½ cups diced cooked chicken
⅔ cup chopped onion

Rinse broccoli under running cold water; drain thoroughly. Mix broccoli, 2 cups of the cheese, the chicken and onion in large, deep-dish pie plate. Pour custard mixture over filling. Bake at 400 degrees for 25 to 35 minutes or until knife inserted in center comes out clean; top with remaining cheese and continue baking just until cheese is melted. Cool 5 minutes before cutting.

TLC Tip: *You can use 2 packages of broccoli and omit the chicken for a meatless dish.*

CHEESEBURGER PIE

1 pound lean ground beef
1½ cups chopped onion
2 tomatoes, sliced

1 cup shredded Cheddar cheese

Cook and stir ground beef and onion in a large skillet over medium heat until beef is brown; drain if necessary. Spread in lightly sprayed deep-dish pie plate. Pour custard mixture over. Bake in 400 degree oven for 25 minutes. Top with tomato slices and cheese. Continue baking until knife inserted in center comes out clean, another 5 to 10 minutes. Cool 5 minutes before cutting.

HAM 'N SWISS PIE

2 cups diced cooked ham   ⅓ cup chopped green onion
1 cup shredded Swiss cheese

Sprinkle ham, cheese and onion in a lightly sprayed deep-dish pie plate. Top with custard mixture. Bake at 400 degrees until golden brown and knife inserted in center comes out clean, about 35 to 40 minutes. Cool 5 minutes before cutting.

SPINACH PIE

1 (10-ounce) package frozen   1 cup shredded Swiss cheese
   spinach, thawed and   ½ cup chopped onion
   drained   ¼ teaspoon ground nutmeg

Mix spinach, cheese and onion in a lightly-greased deep-dish pie plate. Add the nutmeg to the custard mixture. Pour over filling. Bake at 400 degrees about 30 minutes or until a knife inserted in the center comes out clean. Cool 5 minutes before serving.

TLC Tip: You can use one bunch or one 10-ounce package fresh spinach, lightly steamed, in place of the frozen. Great taste!

BOLOGNA WITH KRAFT DINNER

I'm sure this dish was served in my later childhood, and probably invented by us kids. It was popular at the time, today we tend to call such food "junk food". If this strikes your fancy, this is how we prepared it.

1 ring of bologna   1 box Kraft macaroni and
                          cheese

Make small slashes on the outside of the ring bologna. Heat in a small amount of water in a large skillet. Prepare Kraft macaroni and cheese as directed on the box. Remove the bologna from the water and place on a serving plate. Fill the center with the macaroni and cheese. Serve something lean and green with this, please!

TLC Tip: Our son, Joey, reminded me that during his growing up years, we served the Kraft dinner with chunks of smoked sausage—on the side or mixed in. This was one of the dishes I fixed over the camp stove in various campgrounds around the country. He said he fixed it often when he was first on his own. If you choose this variation, I suggest Healthy Choice smoked sausage.

FRANKFURTER SUPPER DISH

This is an oldie I have updated to fit our leaner lifestyles. It goes together in a flash with the help of your microwave, and the 30 minute baking time allows you to toss a salad, heat some rolls and fix a fruit cup for dessert while hubby or the kids set the table.

6 lowfat hot dogs (I prefer Healthy Choice)
2 cups frozen green beans (use what you need from a bag of loose pack, and save the rest for another meal)

1½ cups white sauce (see index)
½ teaspoon Worcestershire sauce
¼ cup grated sharp cheese
½ cup soft breadcrumbs

Drop hot dogs in boiling water and heat 5 minutes. Cut into 1" pieces. Cook the beans about 5 minutes in the microwave. Make cream sauce as recipe directs, stirring in the Worcestershire sauce. Stir beans and hot dogs into white sauce. Pour into a greased 1½-quart baking dish. Sprinkle with cheese and breadcrumbs. Spray with butter-flavored spray. Bake in a 375 degree oven for 30 minutes.

TLC Tip: This dish can be lowfat or higher fat, take your pick. I am sure by now you know how to cut the fat in recipes, but in case you have forgotten, I'll help you out. First of all, find the lowest fat hot dogs that are edible. As I mentioned earlier, I prefer Healthy Choice. Make your white sauce with skim milk. Use reduced fat cheese. Give the crumbs a quick spray with butter-flavored cooking spray instead of buttering them, and there you have it.

JEAN'S SAUSAGE SPAGHETTI PRIMAVERA

I know you'll like this wonderful pasta dish. It's great for quick after-church suppers, or Saturday lunches. You'll probably find yourself preparing it often. I thank my cousin for sharing this recipe.

8 ounces thin spaghetti
1 tablespoon olive oil (you can
    use more if you like)
1 green pepper
1 sweet red pepper
1 large onion, cut into thin
    wedges
1½ pounds smoked sausage,
    coarsely chopped
1 tablespoon chopped fresh
    parsley

1 teaspoon salt
1 small garlic clove, finely
    chopped or
¼ teaspoon garlic powder
1 teaspoon dried marjoram or
    oregano
A good dash cayenne pepper
    (optional)
4 or 5 ounces Parmesan
    cheese, grated

Cook the spaghetti as package directs; drain and keep warm. Heat the olive oil in a large non-stick skillet over medium-high heat. Add the peppers, onions, and garlic, if using fresh. Stir-fry until vegetables are crisp tender. Add the smoked sausage, and heat a few minutes longer. When vegetables are cooked as you like, add the parsley and other seasonings. Mix well. Toss with the spaghetti. Pour into a large bowl; add the Parmesan cheese and toss until coated. Try the Mock Sangría with this. (See index). I would serve a plain Italian or French bread as the dish is quite highly-seasoned. A good romaine lettuce salad with a simple oil and vinegar dressing would be nice, also.

SCALLOPED POTATOES AND
ROASTY SAUSAGES

My mother made THE BEST scalloped potatoes!! I know how she made them—a layer of thin potato slices, salt, pepper, a sprinkling of flour, another layer of potatoes, more salt, pepper and flour, then milk poured over all with a few dots of butter. This would often be her contribution to church suppers. By the time I was in high school, she was adding the roasty sausages, which we thought a great idea. Of course we knew nothing about sodium and fat. To my mother, there was no such thing as a small dish of scalloped potatoes. She prepared hers in a large, oval Dutch oven, enough to feed the thrashers and then some. I guess I didn't pay enough attention to her formula or perhaps I just lack her touch, or maybe it's because I don't use whole milk, but somehow I can never get scalloped potatoes to turn out well preparing them her way. Here is my version.

½ cup chopped onion
2 tablespoons butter
4 tablespoons flour
¾ teaspoon salt
⅛ teaspoon white pepper

2½ cups skim milk
6 medium potatoes, peeled
   and thinly sliced
   (about 6 cups)

For the sauce, cook the onion in the butter in a large microwave-safe bowl about 2 minutes. Add the flour, salt and pepper, along with the milk. Whisk to blend. Return to the microwave and cook on high for 2 minutes. Gently whisk the mixture. Continue cooking on high, stopping every minute to stir, until the mixture thickens and boils, about 5 or 6 minutes. Place half the potatoes in 2-quart casserole that has been sprayed with vegetable spray. Cover with half the sauce. Repeat layers. Bake covered in a 350 degree oven for 40 minutes. Uncover, bake 30 to 40 minutes more or until potatoes are tender. If you wish to add the roasty sausages, place some on each layer. Instead of roasty sausages, I usually will add slices of Healthy Choice smoked sausage that I have microwaved for a couple of minutes between sheets of paper towels to absorb the oil.

TLC Tip: *My mother didn't do this, but sometimes I top the potatoes with some fresh breadcrumbs and give the whole thing a few sprays of butter-flavored vegetable spray before baking.*

BARBECUED BABY BACK RIBS

Ribs like these are served at Hill's Resort on Priest Lake in northern Idaho. We have had some good times on that lake with our friends Barbara and Colin Taylor. Cleo loves ribs, and would eat them often if good sense didn't prevail. For your special occasions, these can't be beat.

5 pounds baby back ribs, not cut apart	½ cup sliced white onion
½ cup red grape juice	2 stalks celery, chopped
1 tablespoon vinegar	1 tablespoon salt
2 tablespoons liquid smoke	½ teaspoon pepper
	Sauce (recipe follows)

Place the ribs in a heavy pan; add water to cover. Add rest of ingredients except the sauce. Bring to boiling, then simmer for one hour or until ribs are tender. Cool in the broth, reserving ½ cup for later use. At this point the ribs can be refrigerated to finish later. To reheat, brown the ribs under the broiler or over a charcoal grill, turning occasionally. Baste with barbecue sauce for the last few minutes. Pass additional sauce when serving.

HILL'S RESORT BBQ SAUCE

1 quart catsup	2 tablespoons honey
2 tablespoons liquid smoke	½ cup defatted broth reserved
½ cup brown sugar	from cooking ribs

Combine all sauce ingredients in a 2-quart saucepan. Cook, stirring constantly, over medium heat until mixture boils. Reduce heat to low, and simmer 20 minutes. This makes more sauce than you will probably use, but it keeps well in the refrigerator.

TLC Tip: This sauce tends to spatter easily, so watch that you don't get burned, and keep heat low when simmering.

LEMON SPARERIBS

Spareribs are one of my husband's favorite meats. Though we ration our consumption, they do tend to appear on birthdays and Father's Day with some regularity.

3 pounds spareribs, cut into
   serving pieces
1 lemon, thinly sliced
1 (6-ounce) can frozen
   lemonade concentrate,
   thawed
2 juice cans water

3 tablespoons soy sauce
½ teaspoon salt (optional)
3 tablespoons catsup
1 to 2 teaspoons vinegar
3 tablespoons packed brown
   sugar

Place the ribs in a flat baking pan, meaty side up. Scatter the lemon slices over the ribs. Roast in a 450 degree oven for 30 minutes. Remove from oven and drain accumulated fat from pan. Combine remaining ingredients. Pour ⅔ of this mixture over ribs. Reduce oven temperature to 350 degrees. Bake the ribs 1½ to 2 hours more, or until tender, adding more of the lemonade mixture if necessary. When ribs are done, remove from sauce. Add any reserved sauce to roasting pan. Thicken with cornstarch to serve with ribs if desired. (Measure liquid, and use 1 tablespoon cornstarch dissolved in a little water for each cup liquid.)

EXTRA POINT PORK CHOPS

This recipe got its name because it was entered in a contest and got the "extra points" needed to win. Makes sense, I guess. I think it will get extra points on your rating scale too.

6 to 8 pork chops, well
   trimmed
6-8 potatoes, peeled and sliced

1 onion, sliced and separated
   into rings
1 can chicken gumbo soup,
   undiluted

Brown chops in a large non-stick skillet over medium-high heat. Place sliced potatoes in a 9 x 13" baking pan. Place the onions on top of the potatoes, then the chops on top. Pour the soup over all. Pour a small amount of water into the browning skillet to loosen up all the good brown bits. Pour over the chops and potatoes. Cover with foil and bake at 375 degrees for 1½ hours.

PORK CHOPS WITH MUSHROOM GRAVY

These pork chops are so good, with their creamy sauce. They go together easily and quickly. I like to serve these with mashed potatoes, zucchini and summer squash combo, an apple and raisin salad, and corn muffins. How about gingerbread with lemon sauce for dessert?

4 to 6 pork chops, your favorite cut
½ teaspoon salt
⅛ teaspoon pepper
1 can cream of mushroom soup

½ cup drained mushrooms
⅓ cup milk or water
¼ cup chopped onion or 1 tablespoon instant minced

In a non-stick skillet, brown chops on both sides. Season with salt, if desired, and pepper. Combine soup, mushrooms, water or milk, and onion. Pour over the chops. Cover; simmer on low heat for 40 to 60 minutes, or until tender.

TLC Tip: *Cooking time greatly depends on the chops you select. If you like a thicker chop, naturally it will take longer. I like to allow at least 60 minutes. I always trim my chops well to reduce the fat content and I use Healthy Request soup.*
TLC Tip Two: *If you like lots of gravy, you'll want to double the soup and water. You may want to double the mushrooms and onions, also.*

CINDY'S PORK CHOPS

Cindy Maddox was Deanna's roommate at Anderson University during her senior year there. These pork chops are really tasty. I like to serve them with baked potatoes or perhaps a rice pilaf.

6 center-cut pork chops, well trimmed
⅔ cup packed brown sugar
1 teaspoon paprika

1 teaspoon sage
1 teaspoon dry mustard
1 tablespoon water

Place the pork chops in a baking dish. Combine rest of ingredients; spread mixture over the chops. Bake at 250 degrees for 1 hour; turn the chops over, increase oven temperature to 350 degrees and continue baking for 15 minutes.

SOUTHERN HAM BAKE

Some of my favorite recipes have come from magazines, and I wouldn't want to guess how many I have clipped over the years! The original of this came from a long-ago issue of Family Circle. *Quick and easy, it is nice served with a cup of some kind of creamy soup to start, cole slaw and cherry cobbler.*

1 large slice ham, cut about ¾" thick	2 cans whole sweet potatoes, drained, or a like amount fresh ones, peeled and cooked
1 (20-ounce) can pineapple chunks	
½ cup packed brown sugar	12 regular-size marshmallows

Cut ham slice into serving pieces; brown in a large non-stick skillet. Drain pineapple over a 2-cup measure; add the brown sugar to the pineapple juice and stir to dissolve. Pour over the ham slices and heat to boiling. Place ham slices in the center of a 2-quart baking dish. Arrange the sweet potatoes around the edge. Tuck the pineapple chunks in between the potatoes; pour hot syrup over. Bake in a 400 degree oven for 15 minutes. Remove from oven, place marshmallows around the edge, return to oven and bake 5 minutes longer or until marshmallows are toasty brown. Makes 4-6 servings.

CREAMY PARMESAN CHICKEN

This is a delicious combination of flavors—oven-fried chicken in a creamy sauce. This is good served with rice or noodles.

¼ cup dry breadcrumbs	1 can cream of mushroom soup
4 tablespoon Parmesan cheese, divided use	½ cup milk
¼ teaspoon dried leaf oregano	¼ cup sour cream
Dash of garlic powder	1 teaspoon chopped chives
Dash of pepper	Paprika, if desired
1 (2½- to 3-pound) frying chicken, cup into pieces and skin removed	

Combine breadcrumbs, 2 tablespoons cheese, the oregano, garlic powder and pepper in a paper or plastic bag. Add the chicken pieces and shake to coat with crumbs. Arrange in a 2-quart baking dish. Bake at 425 degrees for 30-40 minutes or until chicken is nearly done. Combine soup, milk, sour cream and chives; pour evenly over chicken. Sprinkle with 2 table-spoons Parmesan cheese and paprika. Continue baking 10-15 minutes, or until lightly browned.

DUSTYN'S FAVORITE
OVEN-FRIED CHICKEN LEGS

Our grandson, Dustyn Beauchamp, especially likes fried chicken legs. Though these are oven-fried, they always bring a smile to his face when I fix them.

12 chicken legs (This number is not set in stone. I always fix enough for the dinner crowd.)
Skim milk for soaking the chicken
½ cup plain dry breadcrumbs
⅓ cup freshly grated Parmesan cheese
1 tablespoon dried parsley flakes
¼ teaspoon freshly ground black pepper, more or less
½ teaspoon Cavender's Greek seasoning, more or less

Remove the skin from the chicken legs and place in a shallow bowl or pan; cover with milk. Let the chicken soak for 15 minutes. (You can let them set longer, but please put them in the refrigerator if you do.) In a shallow bowl, combine the breadcrumbs, cheese, parsley flakes, pepper and seasoning. Dip each soaked chicken leg in the breading mixture, coating the leg on all sides. Set the coated chicken legs on a greased or non-stick baking sheet. Lightly spray the legs with vegetable-oil, if desired. Bake the chicken in a preheated 375 degree oven for about 45 minutes.

TLC Tip: *Dustyn likes these served with mashed potatoes, cream gravy and green beans.*

AMAZING FRIED CHICKEN

I've found this to be a great way to prepare chicken! I probably prepare this chicken 2-4 times per month. It is good as an entrée, or between buns as a sandwich. I have even sliced each breast thinly and served it in tortillas as a soft taco. Naturally the seasonings can be varied to suit your particular taste. It is great to think that something that tastes this good can be good for you.

⅓ cup flour	¼ teaspoon onion powder or
½ teaspoon salt	garlic powder
½ teaspoon paprika	⅛ teaspoon black pepper
¼ teaspoon poultry seasoning	4 boneless, skinless chicken
¼ teaspoon cayenne pepper	breasts
(optional)	1 tablespoon olive or canola
	oil

Combine flour and spices in plastic bag or in a shallow dish. Coat chicken in seasoned flour, shake off excess and lay on a sheet of waxed paper while you heat the oil in a large, non-stick skillet over medium-high heat. When oil is hot, quickly add the chicken breasts, and cook 5 to 10 minutes per side until golden brown. When chicken is brown, add ½ cup water to skillet, cover and turn heat to low. Continue cooking for about 20 minutes, or until juices run clear when chicken is pierced. Do not overcook. Uncover and continue cooking for a few minutes.

TLC Tip: *The chicken can also be finished in the oven. After the chicken is brown, remove from skillet and place on a baking sheet that has been sprayed with cooking spray. Bake in a 375 degree oven about 20 minutes. Do not add any water if you use this method.*

TLC Tip Two: *Other chicken parts can be prepared in this same way, adjusting the time to suit the part. Just be sure to remove the skin before flouring.*

TLC Tip Three: *For a more elegant presentation, I like to use my electric knife to slice each breast piece on the diagonal. Leave the pieces in place, and lay them on the plate, fanning them out slightly. Add vegetables and garnish, and serve with pride.*

CRUNCHY OVEN FRIED CHICKEN

Being raised in the North, I never learned to "fry chicken" as in Southern Fried Chicken. The way I "fry" my chicken is in the oven. Though not "Southern Fried", it is delicious.

½ cup butter
1 clove garlic, finely chopped
1 cup dry breadcrumbs
1 tablespoon dried parsley
   flakes
¼ cup finely chopped almonds
   (optional)

1 teaspoon salt
¼ teaspoon dried, crushed
   thyme or poultry
   seasoning
⅛ teaspoon pepper
1 (2½- to 3½-pound) frying
   chicken, cut up

Heat oven to 400 degrees. In a 12 x 8" or 9 x 13" baking dish, heat butter and garlic until butter is melted in the hot oven. Combine breadcrumbs, parsley, almonds, salt, thyme and pepper in a shallow dish. Dip chicken pieces in garlic butter; then into crumb mixture to coat each side. Arrange skin side up in baking dish. Sprinkle with any remaining crumbs. Bake at 400 degrees for about 45 minutes, or until juices run clear when chicken is pierced.

TLC Tip: Usually I skin the chicken pieces before proceeding with the dish. I like to serve this with mashed potatoes, and make a cream gravy using the pan drippings as a base.

PARTY CHICKEN

This recipe lives up to its name, perfect for a company meal but simple enough for you to prepare for the family at the end of a busy day. We all know that boning the breasts yourself is the least expensive, but I must admit that most of the time I succumb to purchasing them already skinned and boned. This dish is nice served with a rice pilaf, peas, green salad, and brownies a la mode for dessert.

8 boned, skinned chicken
   breasts
8 slices bacon (use turkey
   bacon if you wish)

2 (6-ounce) packages wafer-
   thin sliced smoked beef
1 can mushroom soup,
   undiluted
1 cup sour cream

Wrap each chicken breast with a strip of bacon. Cover bottom of a greased 9 x 13" casserole with the smoked beef. Arrange the chicken on the beef. Combine the soup and sour cream and pour mixture over chicken. Refrigerate overnight. Bake at 375 degrees for one hour, uncovered.

LEMON ROASTED CHICKEN

I came across this recipe years ago while browsing through cookbooks at the library. This dish never ceases to please, always ending up just as I expect, moist and juicy, and filling the house with the most wonderful aroma while it is roasting!! I have used chickens between 2½ and 4 pounds with success, always removing as much excess fat as possible before placing it in the pan.

1 (2½- to 4-pound) chicken, left whole	1 small lemon, quartered
	1 clove garlic, crushed
Seasoning, as desired	1 teaspoon dried leaf oregano

Remove the giblets from the chicken and discard or save for another use. Remove the excess fat. Rinse chicken well under cold running water, and pat dry with paper towels. (Perhaps here is a good time to remind you that care should always be taken when handling fresh poultry. Make sure any surface the poultry touches is cleaned thoroughly with soap and water, and that includes hands. Always wash knives, cutting boards, etc., well before using again.) Season the chicken inside and out as you wish—salt and pepper, or a special blend you like. I happen to like Greek seasoning. Rub the lemon quarters with the crushed garlic, and sprinkle with the oregano. Place the lemon quarters, garlic pieces and any extra oregano that falls off inside the chicken. Place in a shallow roasting pan or glass baking dish, folding the wings back under the chicken. Bake in a pre-heated 325 degree oven for 1½ hours. Turn the oven off and let the chicken remain inside for another 15 minutes. DO NOT baste the chicken or open the oven door during the cooking time!! Carve as desired.

TLC Tip: *There will be the most delicious juices in the bottom of the pan when the chicken is done. It makes the base for a great gravy. Do pour into a measuring cup and take off the fat first.*

APRICOT GLAZED CORNISH HENS

I think the first time I ever ate Cornish hens was on our first trip to Hawaii in the early 1970's. The "first" of anything is always special, don't you think? I'll never forget hearing my first real Hawaiian music, seeing my first hula, taking my first walk on a black sand beach, experiencing the awe of the volcanoes for the first time, or viewing my first Hawaiian sunset. Cleo and I ate in a cozy little restaurant in Kona during that trip. I guess I have always had an adventurous spirit where food is concerned, so I tried the Cornish hens. They were baked with rice is a cute little clay pot that we got to take with us. It is now part of our decor in Ruidoso, NM, and every time I look at it, I have a flood of wonderful memories. These Cornish hens are not baked in a pot, but they make a spectacular presentation. No one will ever guess just how simple they are to prepare! Arrange them on a large platter surrounded with Cashew Rice Pilaf (see index) and canned apricot halves, and accept the compliments with humility!

¾ cup apricot preserves
2 teaspoons grated orange rind
2 tablespoons orange juice

4 (1- to 1¼-pound) Cornish hens
¼ teaspoon paprika

Combine apricot preserves, orange rind, and orange juice. Set aside. Remove giblets from hens; discard or reserve for other use. Rinse hens with cold water and pat dry. Cut in half. (Your kitchen shears are perfect for this job.) Season as desired (I often use Greek seasoning) and sprinkle with paprika. Place hens, skin side up, in a lightly greased, shallow roasting pan. Bake at 350 degrees for 30 minutes. Remove from oven and baste with apricot mixture. Continue basting, about every 10 minutes, while the hens roast another 30 minutes. Remove from oven. Brush again with apricot mixture after you have arranged the hens on a serving platter.

TLC Tip: *Since there isn't a great deal of meat on a Cornish hen, you may have to allow more than ½ hen per person. This amount should serve 4 to 8, depending on appetites.*

CITRUS GLAZED ROCK CORNISH GAME HENS

1 small lemon, juiced (you should have 1½ to 2 tablespoons)

¼ cup orange marmalade
2 teaspoons soy sauce

Combine the ingredients in a small saucepan. Warm over low heat until marmalade is melted, stirring occasionally. Follow the recipe for Apricot Glazed Cornish Game Hens, substituting this glaze. Wonderful taste!

SIMPLY DELICIOUS FRIED CHICKEN LIVERS

When it comes to eating chicken livers, I guess people feel one of two ways: they either love them or hate them. I happen to be one of those who love them. I don't eat them often, of course, because they aren't supposed to be good for your cholesterol or your heart. But once in a while, I can't fight the urge any longer. When I eat them in a restaurant, I am often disappointed, as the coating is usually overcooked and greasy. But the ones I make in my own kitchen are really good, and well worth the splurge. If you like fried chicken livers, I just know you'll like these!! Be sure to prepare plenty of cream gravy to dip them in. (See index for Chicken Fried Steak.)

1 pound chicken livers (more
   or less, depending on
   how many "lovers" you
   are feeding)

1 cup buttermilk
2 cups self-rising flour

Put the livers in a shallow dish; pour the buttermilk over them, and let set a few minutes. (If you puncture the livers first they won't pop when you fry them.) Measure the flour onto a sheet of waxed paper. Remove the livers from the buttermilk one at a time, letting the excess buttermilk drain back into the dish. Roll in the flour, coating completely. Shake off excess, place on another sheet of waxed paper and let set while you heat your cast iron skillet. When the skillet is hot, add about ¼ to ½ inch of canola oil. (This is one time when spraying with cooking spray just won't do!) When the oil is hot, fry the livers until golden brown on each side. This won't take very long if your oil is the right temperature as chicken livers are tender. Remove from the skillet with tongs, drain on paper towels. Serve with a generous amount of cream gravy for dipping. Actually, I could make a meal on this, but it would be prudent to serve something fresh and green alongside.

BEV'S FAJITAS

Our daughter, Beverly, is well known for her fajitas. I think she devised this method of preparation, and though a bit different from the usual way, the end result is great. Bev's family likes their Mexican food HOT, and this dish reflects that. I hope you'll try it. She provides bowls of sour cream, guacamole, and grated cheese to accompany the fajitas.

8 skinless, boneless, chicken breasts cut into thin strips
2 medium green peppers, cut into strips
2 large onions, sliced and separated into rings
1 large jar HOT picante sauce, about 2 cups
1 dozen flour tortillas
Garlic powder to taste

In a wok or large non-stick skillet, pour ½ to ¾ jar picante sauce. Add the pepper strips and onion rings. Bring to a boil, reduce heat, and simmer until vegetables are tender, about 5 minutes. Stir as needed. Add chicken strips and cook until done. Cover with a lid, when not stirring, to hold in flavor. Sprinkle garlic powder over all when nearly done. Drain off excess liquid before serving. Serve in tortillas, garnish as desired.

CHICKEN FAJITAS

The marinade makes these fajitas so-o good!! I like to put the chicken and marinade in a heavy self-seal bag, then place the bag in a small pan. The bag holds in the flavors and makes the job of turning the meat a simple one. We grill these on our indoor grill, but they could be broiled, charcoaled outside or even sautéed in a pinch.

½ cup vegetable oil
¼ cup red wine vinegar
⅓ cup lime juice
¼ cup finely chopped onion
2 cloves garlic, minced
1 teaspoon dried oregano
½ teaspoon salt
½ teaspoon pepper
3 whole chicken breasts, halved, skinned and boned
Flour tortillas

Combine all ingredients except chicken breasts in non-metal container. Mix well. Add chicken breasts to marinade, turning to coat well. Cover and marinate chicken at least 4 hours in the refrigerator, turning occasionally. Remove chicken from marinade and grill 8 minutes; turn and continue cooking 5 to 7 minutes or until cooked through. Slice chicken breasts into thin slices. Serve in warm flour tortillas garnished as desired. We like chopped tomatoes, grilled onions and pepper strips (I like to use red, green and yellow peppers when available), avocado slices or guacamole, salsa, sour cream and/or cheese.

CHICKEN A LA KING

I remember the first time I heard about this dish. It sounded so sophisti-cated—I couldn't wait to prepare it! This was one of the dishes I prepared while I was in high school. In those days, I think we served it over rice. When I had my own family, they liked those cute little puff pastry cups. Now we think it is pretty special served over homemade biscuits. (See index for a couple of good choices.) Back in the "old days" my recipe called for cream—imagine! Now I use milk, and most of the time skim milk, and we still love it.

¼ cup butter
1 cup sliced fresh mushrooms
⅓ cup flour
¼ teaspoon salt
¼ teaspoon white pepper
1¾ cups milk

1 cup chicken broth
2 cups cubed cooked chicken
¼ cup chopped pimiento
2 teaspoons sherry flavoring
  (optional)
Rice, biscuits, or patty shells

In a saucepan, melt the butter. Add the mushrooms and cook over medium heat until tender. Stir in the flour, salt, and pepper. Add milk and chicken broth, all at once. Cook and stir till thickened and bubbly. Cook and stir for 1 minute more. Stir in chicken, pimiento and sherry flavoring. Heat through. Serve as desired.

TLC Tip: *I think we almost always served this with tiny green peas, but some other colorful vegetable would do as well.*

CHICKEN SPAGHETTI

This is a real crowd pleaser! It can be put together ahead, and baked just prior to serving. If it has been chilled, add a few minutes to the baking time.

1 large chicken
½ cup butter
1 onion, chopped
½ cup chopped celery
1 green pepper, chopped
1 pound spaghetti

1 cup grated American cheese
1 cup grated Colby cheese
1 can cream of mushroom
  soup, undiluted
1 (2-ounce) jar sliced pimiento
2 cups chicken stock

Put the chicken into a large pot and cover with water. Bring to a boil, and simmer until done, about 45 minutes. Cool in the broth, then remove the skin, and take the meat from the bones. Reserve at least 2 cups broth. (Freeze the rest for a later use.) Cut the meat into large chunks; set aside in a large bowl. Melt the butter in a skillet. Sauté the onion, celery, and green pepper until tender. Mix these vegetables, along with the butter they were cooked in, with the chicken. Break the spaghetti into pieces and cook according to package directions. Rinse when done. In a casserole, layer the chicken mixture, spaghetti, and cheeses. Stir together the soup, pimiento, and chicken stock; pour over the chicken and spaghetti. Bake in a 350 degree oven for 1 hour.

TLC Tip: *I find that it is important to break up the spaghetti. It is difficult to mix and serve if left in long pieces.*

HOT CHICKEN SALAD

This really isn't a salad, but a delicious chicken casserole with lots of flavor and crunch. It is great to take to potlucks, but your family will like it too.

4 cups cut-up, cooked chicken
2 cups diced celery
1 (8-ounce) can water
    chestnuts, drained and
    chopped
2 cups cooked rice
¾ cup grated cheese
¼ cup sliced green onion

¾ cup mayonnaise
1 can cream of chicken soup,
    undiluted
1 teaspoon salt
1 tablespoon lemon juice
1½ cups crushed potato chips
½ cup sliced almonds

Mix together in a large bowl, the chicken, celery, water chestnuts, rice, cheese and green onions. In a small bowl, stir together the mayonnaise, soup, salt, and lemon juice. Add this mixture to the chicken mixture and stir to combine. Spoon into a 9 x 13" casserole. Top with crushed potato chips and sliced almonds. Bake in a 375 degree oven for 30 minutes.

TLC Tip: *It takes about 5 chicken breast halves to make the amount of chicken needed for this recipe. If you prefer to cook a whole chicken, it will probably take a little more than one chicken, unless it is very large. I always use reduced-calorie mayonnaise in this recipe, and the lowest fat potato chips I can find—Mr. Phipp's is a good brand.*

RITA JO'S CHICKEN RICE CASSEROLE

I don't know how many times I prepared this during the 60's. It is quick, inexpensive, and tasty. Though this recipe calls for canned, boned chicken, I seldom used it, preferring to cook the chicken myself. However, since all of these ingredients can be kept on your pantry shelf, it is ideal for those times when you need something in a hurry and running to the store isn't an option.

1 can cream of celery soup
1 can cream of chicken soup
1 cup water

1⅓ cups instant rice
1 large can boned chicken

Combine all ingredients in a 1½-quart casserole dish. Cover with foil. Bake at 350 degrees for 30 to 45 minutes.

TLC Tip: *You will need at least 2 chicken breast halves if you cook your own, though the exact amount isn't critical.*

CHICKEN ALMOND STIR-FRY

This is a delicious dish! Once you get everything cut up and measured, it goes together quickly. We like it served with rice and / or Chinese noodles. A salad of fresh orange slices sprinkled with sliced green onions and served with a poppy seed dressing would be a nice accompaniment.

½ pound fresh snow peas, trimmed
2 tablespoons soy sauce, divided use
1 tablespoon water
1 teaspoon sugar
1 teaspoon cornstarch
1 teaspoon vinegar
2 skinless, boneless chicken breasts

2 tablespoons salad oil, divided
½ cup raw, whole almonds
1 teaspoon minced garlic
1 teaspoon grated fresh ginger
¼ pound sliced, fresh mushrooms

Cut any large snow peas in half, crosswise. Set aside. In cup or small bowl, combine 1 tablespoon soy sauce, water, sugar, cornstarch and vinegar; set aside. Cut chicken into small strips. In medium bowl, toss the chicken with the remaining tablespoon soy sauce. In a large, non-stick skillet, heat 1 tablespoon oil over medium heat. Add almonds and stir-fry 2 to 3 minutes or until skins begin to pop. Remove with a slotted spoon; set aside. Add remaining oil. Add garlic and ginger and cook briefly, watching carefully so that they do not burn. Increase heat to medium high and add the chicken strips. Sauté, stirring often, until chicken is opaque. And the mushrooms and continue cooking about 5 minutes. Stir reserved soy mixture and pour into skillet. Add almonds and snow peas. Cook 2 minutes, stirring constantly. Serve immediately.

TLC Tip: If you use low-sodium soy sauce in this dish, you may need to add a little salt. Taste to be sure.

PEPPERIDGE FARM CHICKEN

I got this recipe from Dot Blackwell who is in my garden club. I first sampled this dish at our Christmas Luncheon. It was love at first bite. Dot and I have shared hostessing duties several times, and always have great fun being creative with table settings and favors. Thanks, Dot, for this good recipe. I've served it often to my friends and family since that Christmas luncheon.

1 (8-ounce) package
   Pepperidge Farm herb-
   seasoned dry stuffing
3 cups cubed cooked chicken
¼ cup butter
	½ cup flour
	¼ teaspoon salt
	Dash pepper
	4 cups chicken broth
	6 slightly beaten eggs

Prepare stuffing according to package directions for dry stuffing. Spread in 13 x 9" baking dish. Top with layer of chicken. In a large saucepan, melt butter, blend in flour and seasonings. Add cool broth. Cook and stir until mixture thickens. Stir a small amount of the hot mixture into the eggs, then return to mixture in saucepan. Mix well; pour over chicken. Bake in slow oven, 325 degrees, for 40-45 minutes, or until knife inserted halfway to center comes out clean. Let stand 5 minutes to set. Cut into squares and serve with Pimiento Mushroom Sauce on top.

Pimiento Mushroom Sauce:

1 can cream of mushroom soup ¼ soup can milk	1 cup sour cream ¼ cup chopped pimiento

Mix all ingredients in a small saucepan. Heat, stirring often, over low heat until hot. DO NOT boil.

TLC Tip: *I have put this together the evening before, stored it covered in the refrigerator, and baked just prior to serving. Remember to adjust baking time to allow for chilled mixture.*

RITA JO'S VIVA CHICKEN

This is another of Rita Jo's winners. This casserole will serve 12 generously, must be made the night before, and is a great dish to build a luncheon or supper around. Rita Jo served it for niece Debbie's bridal luncheon. Not overly spicy, you'll find it well received by both men and women.

4 whole chicken breasts,
  skinned and boned
1 can cream of mushroom
  soup
1 can cream of chicken soup
1 cup milk

2 (4-ounce) cans chopped
  green chilis
1 large onion, finely chopped
1 dozen corn tortillas, cut in
  1" strips
1 pound Cheddar cheese,
  grated

Simmer the chicken breasts until tender. Cool in the broth, then remove from the bones, and tear into bite-size pieces. Reserve a small amount of broth. (Freeze the remainder in 1 and/or 2 cup portions. Great to have on hand when you need chicken broth—homemade is always better than canned.) In a bowl, combine the soups, milk, chilis and onion. In a 9 x 13" baking dish that has been sprayed with cooking spray, put 2-3 tablespoons chicken broth. Put in a single layer of tortilla strips, layer of chicken, layer of sauce, layer of cheese. Continue until all ingredients are used. Cover with foil and refrigerate at least 24 hours. Remove foil and bake at 300 degrees 1 to 1½ hours. DO NOT preheat oven.

TLC Tip: *This is also good with Monterey Jack cheese. The heat level of this dish can be altered by the heat of the chilis you choose.*

227

CHICKEN AND MUSHROOM LO MEIN

I found this recipe while looking at a magazine in the car as we were traveling across the Southern U.S. on one of our family camping vacations. I lucked out with this one, as it became a family favorite, and was often requested for birthday dinners and such. I have lightened it up a bit through the years, and I still serve it often.

2 whole chicken breasts, skinned and boned	Boiling water
1 small head bok choy or ½ pound Swiss chard	2 tablespoons oil, divided
½ pound fresh snow peas (frozen will do in a pinch, but fresh is better)	2 tablespoons cornstarch
4 (3-ounce) packages chicken-flavored Ramen noodles	2 cups defatted, low-salt chicken broth
	½ cup sliced water chestnuts
	1 tablespoon soy sauce
	8 ounces fresh mushrooms, sliced

Cut the chicken into thin strips. Wash greens thoroughly; remove the leaves from the stalks. Cut the stalks into thin diagonal slices, cut green tops into 1" lengths. Keep in separate bowls. Trim the snow peas, and cut any large ones in half crosswise. Place the blocks of noodles in a large bowl. Sprinkle with 2 of the seasoning packets and cover with boiling water. Let stand while preparing rest of dish, tossing occasionally to separate noodles. Combine cornstarch and chicken broth with remaining seasoning packets in a 2-cup measure. Heat a large non-stick wok or skillet. Add 1 tablespoon oil. When the oil is hot, add chicken strips to pan. Stir fry until chicken is lightly brown and cooked through, 3-5 minutes. Remove to platter and keep warm. Add remaining oil, snow peas, mushrooms and stalks of greens. Stir fry until just wilted; add greens and water chestnuts, stir-fry 15 seconds. Re-stir cornstarch mixture, pour into pan, bring to boiling. Add soy sauce and chicken. Drain noodles; add to sauce, toss and serve.

TLC Tip: You have to use your eyes to judge the doneness of the vegetables for this dish. You want them crisp-tender, not mushy or dull. I find that if I cover the pan briefly, 1 or 2 minutes, it helps.

TLC Tip Two: This recipe can be cut in half easily—I do it all the time. If you use regular soy sauce you probably won't need any salt. Taste to be sure.

TURKEY TETRAZZINI

This turkey-pasta dish with its creamy sauce really satisfies an appetite. This version is lighter than the usual tetrazzini, yet retains the wonderful taste we've come to associate with this dish. I hope you'll like it as much as we do.

1 (7-ounce) package spaghetti, uncooked
½ tablespoon butter
½ tablespoon vegetable oil
3 cups sliced fresh mushrooms
⅓ cup minced onion
¼ cup diced celery
½ cup flour
1½ cups skim milk
1 (14½-ounce) can reduced-salt chicken broth
¼ cup light cream cheese
¼ cup grated Parmesan cheese, divided use
½ teaspoon salt
½ teaspoon garlic powder
¼ teaspoon pepper
1 (2-ounce) jar diced pimiento, drained
2 cups chopped, cooked turkey breast

Break spaghetti in half, and cook according to package directions, omitting the salt and fat. Drain spaghetti well, and set aside. Coat a large saucepan with cooking spray. Place over medium-high heat, add oil and butter. When butter has melted, add mushrooms, onion, and celery; sauté until tender. Combine flour and milk; stir until smooth. Add flour mixture and broth to vegetable mixture. Bring to a boil over medium heat; reduce heat and simmer 5 minutes, stirring constantly. Remove from heat; add cream cheese, stirring until cheese melts. Stir in spaghetti, 2 tablespoons Parmesan cheese, and remaining ingredients. Spoon turkey mixture into a shallow 2-quart baking dish coated with vegetable cooking spray; sprinkle evenly with remaining 2 tablespoons Parmesan cheese. Bake at 350 degrees for 25 to 30 minutes or until thoroughly heated. Makes 6 generous servings.

CORN 'N TURKEY BAKE

You can stir up this casserole in minutes using leftover turkey or chicken, but it is so good, you may want to cook some turkey just for this dish.

1 (16-ounce) package frozen
   corn and broccoli
   mixture
½ cup finely chopped onion
¼ cup butter
¼ cup flour
¾ teaspoon salt
½ teaspoon dry mustard
½ teaspoon pepper
¾ cup milk
⅓ cup chicken broth
2 eggs, slightly beaten
1½ to 2 cups cubed, cooked
   turkey or chicken
4 ounces (1 cup) shredded
   Cheddar cheese
⅓ cup sliced almonds

Rinse frozen vegetables in warm water; drain well, and set aside. In large saucepan, sauté onion in melted butter over medium heat until onion is tender. Blend in flour, salt, mustard and pepper; stir until smooth. Gradually add milk and chicken broth; cook until mixture boils and thickens, stirring constantly. Gently stir in eggs, turkey, cheese and vegetables. Pour into a greased 12 x 8" baking dish; sprinkle with almonds. Bake at 350 degrees for 25 to 30 minutes or until hot and bubbly.

CRUNCHY TURKEY SUPREME

This is a nice dish to serve for a brunch. It can be put together the day before, leaving you free for those last minute touches the day of your party. This looks attractive garnished with fresh parsley and small strips of pimiento.

2 cups cubed cooked turkey
2 cups cooked rice
1 cup sliced celery
1 can cream of chicken soup
1 (10-ounce) package frozen
   cut broccoli, thawed and
   drained
1 (8-ounce) can sliced water
   chestnuts, drained
¾ cup reduced-calorie
   mayonnaise
1 (2-ounce) jar diced
   pimiento, drained
2 teaspoons lemon juice
½ teaspoon salt
⅛ teaspoon pepper
2½ cups corn flakes cereal,
   crushed to 1 cup
2 tablespoons butter, melted

In a large bowl, combine all ingredients except cereal and melted butter. Spoon into a lightly greased 2-quart casserole. In a small bowl, combine cereal and butter; sprinkle evenly over casserole mixture. Bake at 375 degrees for 30 to 35 minutes or until casserole is thoroughly heated and topping is light brown. Garnish as desired.

TURKEY ENCHILADA BAKE

These are so-o good! Naturally you would think of preparing this dish after Thanksgiving, when you might have some leftover turkey laying around. But I think you will want to have it more often. I usually buy one of those already roasted breast portions to cut into cubes.

½ tablespoon canola oil
½ tablespoon butter
½ cup chopped onion
1 clove garlic, minced
½ cup sliced ripe olives,
    divided use
¼ cup chopped green chilis
½ teaspoon salt

½ cup dairy sour cream
1 can cream of chicken soup
1½ cups cubed, cooked turkey
1 cup (4 ounces) shredded
    Cheddar cheese, divided
8 corn tortillas
¼ cup oil
¼ cup milk

In a medium non-stick skillet, heat the oil and butter. Sauté the onion and garlic over medium heat until onion is tender. Stir in ¼ cup ripe olives, chilis, salt, sour cream and soup; mix well. Reserve ¾ cup sauce. To remaining sauce, fold in turkey and ½ cup cheese. In another skillet, heat ¼ cup oil; lightly fry tortillas until soft. (Or wrap in paper towels or place in a tortilla warmer and heat in the microwave.) Fill tortillas with turkey mixture, roll up. Place seam-side-down in ungreased 12 x 8" baking dish. In small bowl, combine reserved ¾ cup sauce and milk; spoon over tortillas. Cover dish lightly with foil. Bake at 350 degrees for 30 to 35 minutes or until bubbly. To serve, sprinkle with remaining ½ cup cheese and ¼ cup olives.

QUICK GROUND TURKEY STROGANOFF

This is a quick take-off on the classic. Instead of serving it over noodles or rice, try serving as an open-face sandwich over hamburger buns.

½ cup minced onion
1 clove garlic, minced
½ tablespoon oil
1 pound ground turkey (or
    lean beef)
2 tablespoons flour
½ teaspoon salt

¼ teaspoon pepper
1 (8-ounce) can sliced
    mushrooms
1 can cream of chicken soup,
    undiluted
1 cup sour cream

Sauté onion and garlic in the hot oil over medium heat; add meat and brown. Add flour, salt, pepper and mushrooms. Cook 5 minutes. Add soup; simmer, uncovered, 10 minutes. Stir in sour cream. Heat through. Serve as desired.

TLC Tip: *Watch the salt here. If you use regular soup, you may not need any salt. If you use Healthy Request, the salt may be necessary.*

TURKEY RICE CASSEROLE

This is a very tasty way to use up some of that holiday turkey. Of course it is good anytime, and you can substitute chicken for the turkey, if you wish. All you need to round out this meal is a green vegetable and / or salad, some good bread or muffins and Paul's Pumpkin Bars (see index).

½ cup chopped onion
¼ cup chopped green pepper
1 tablespoon vegetable oil
¼ cup flour
2 cups chicken broth, low salt
3 tablespoons diced pimiento
¼ cup sliced, toasted almonds

⅛ teaspoon pepper
2 cups cubed turkey or
    chicken
3 cups cooked rice
½ cup shredded Cheddar
    cheese

Sauté the onion and green pepper in the oil for 3 minutes over medium heat. Stir in the flour; add chicken broth gradually. Stir and cook until thickened. Add pimiento, almonds, pepper, turkey and rice. Stir to combine. Pour into a 2-quart casserole; top with cheese. Bake at 350 degrees for 20 to 30 minutes.

CRISPY BAKED FISH

For those of you who don't like fish any other way but fried, do try this recipe. The flavor is good, the texture is crispy and there is much less fat.

1 pound fish fillets, catfish,
    perch, cod, any white fish
¼ cup oil
½ teaspoon salt

½ teaspoon garlic powder
½ cup dry breadcrumbs
½ teaspoon paprika, if desired

Rinse the fish fillets with cool water and pat dry with paper towels. Mix the oil, salt and garlic powder in a shallow bowl. Add the fish, stir with a wooden spoon or turn with your hands to coat. Let marinate 10 to 30 minutes. Combine breadcrumbs and paprika on a square of waxed paper. Remove the fillets from the oil mixture, let excess drain off, and coat with the crumbs. Place on a greased baking sheet and bake at 400 degrees for 20 to 30 minutes. I like to fix Oven Fried Potatoes (adjust baking time a little to account for the higher temperature) and Granny's Cole Slaw with this.

TLC Tip: *Often I use the catfish nuggets instead of fillets or cut other fillets into strips. Sometimes I will use ½ teaspoon Old Bay seasoning or Cavender's Greek seasoning instead of the salt and garlic powder. Nice change.*

VEGETABLE TOPPED ORANGE ROUGHY

Topping the fish with vegetables insures that the fish will remain moist and flavorful.

1 medium zucchini	2 tablespoons grated
1 small onion, thinly sliced	Parmesan cheese
1 cup sliced fresh mushrooms	¼ teaspoon pepper
3 thin lemon slices	⅛ teaspoon garlic powder
1 tablespoon olive oil	3 pounds orange roughy
1 tablespoon butter	fillets

Cut the zucchini in half lengthwise, then into thin slices. In a non-stick skillet, stir the zucchini, onion, mushrooms and lemon slices in the olive oil and butter over medium heat until tender, about 3 minutes. Remove the lemon slices; set aside. Stir the Parmesan cheese, pepper and garlic powder into the vegetables mixture. Place the fish in a lightly oiled 13 x 9" baking dish. Top with the vegetables; place lemon slices on top. Bake at 375 degrees until fish flakes easily, 30 to 35 minutes.

TUNA ST. JACQUES

If you have some of those cute little scallop shells tucked away in the back of your cupboard, now is the time to take them out, dust them off and use them. This takes ordinary tuna and turns it into an elegant and delicious dish.

3 green onions, finely chopped	White pepper to taste
4 tablespoons butter, divided	Finely chopped fresh parsley
use	2 (6-ounce) cans tuna, drained
4 ounces fresh chopped	and broken into bits
mushrooms	2 tablespoons grated
1 can cream of chicken soup	Parmesan cheese
½ cup chicken broth	⅓ cup fresh breadcrumbs

Sauté the onions and mushrooms in 3 tablespoons butter until tender. Remove from heat. Combine soup and chicken broth in another small saucepan and bring to a boil. Add half of the sauce to the onion/mushroom mixture. Spoon equally into 6 buttered shells or ramekins. Top with parsley and tuna, dividing equally. Spoon on the remainder of the sauce. Combine cheese and breadcrumbs and sprinkle over each serving. Melt the remaining 1 tablespoon butter and drizzle a tiny amount over crumbs. Bake in a 450 degree oven for 10 minutes or until lightly brown.

TLC Tip: I find this mixture makes a rather skimpy serving if divided by six, so I usually make four servings. I most often use water-packed tuna, but I think the tuna packed in oil is more flavorful.

GOLDEN FISH BAKE

Fish fillets bake flaky-tender in a creamy sauce topped with golden crumbs. Prepared this way, my kids ate their fish without complaining while they were growing up. I think I always served it with steamed green peas. Add a green salad and maybe Apricot Pound Cake to round out the meal. For heartier appetites, add oven browned potatoes.

2 pounds white fish fillets, such as cod, haddock, flounder or orange roughy, thawed, if frozen	**¼ teaspoon pepper**
	¾ cup milk
	2 cups fresh breadcrumbs
	2 tablespoons butter
4 tablespoons flour	**1 tablespoon chopped parsley**
2 teaspoons salt (less if you want)	**or 1 teaspoon dillweed**
	1 cup sour cream

Cut the fillets into serving size pieces; coat with a mixture of flour, salt and pepper. Arrange in a single layer in a 13 x 9" baking dish, turning under any thin parts to insure even baking. Pour the milk over. Bake in a 350 degree oven for 45 minutes. Meanwhile, melt the butter in a small non-stick skillet. Add the crumbs and toast lightly. Stir the parsley into the sour cream. Remove fish from oven and spoon the cream mixture over top. Sprinkle with the toasted crumbs. Bake 10 minutes longer or until sour cream is set. Garnish with lemon slices and parsley.

TLC Tip: If using frozen fish, thaw it slowly in the refrigerator for best texture and flavor. Rinse under cold water, and pat dry before proceeding with the recipe.

TLC Tip Two: This recipe can be cut in half, just use a smaller baking dish.

FRUIT OF THE SEA CASSEROLE

I guarantee you've never eaten a tuna noodle casserole like this one!! It just might change your mind about that 50's creation.

4 ounces noodles, cooked and drained
1 can cream of mushroom soup, undiluted
½ cup sour cream
1 (10-ounce) package frozen peas and carrots, cooked and drained

½ cup cooked sliced mushrooms (1 cup fresh)
12 ounces tuna, drained
½ teaspoon salt, optional
¼ teaspoon white pepper
¾ cup dry seasoned breadcrumbs
3 tablespoons melted butter

Combine the noodles, soup and sour cream. Add the remaining ingredients except the breadcrumbs and butter. Place in a lightly greased 1½-quart casserole. Combine breadcrumbs and butter; sprinkle over the top. Bake uncovered at 350 degrees for 25 to 30 minutes or until hot and bubbly.

TLC Tip: Sometimes I sprinkle the top with fresh breadcrumbs and spray with butter-flavored spray instead of using the dry breadcrumbs and melted butter. If you use reduced-sodium soup, I think you will need the salt.

SALMON SUPPER

Like a seafood pot pie, easy on the cook and comforting to the body. You might like to serve this with a green salad, Citrus Delight and Oatmeal Butter Crisps.

3 tablespoons chopped onion
⅓ cup chopped green pepper
1 tablespoon oil (the oil really isn't necessary if you use a non-stick pan and a little water)
½ teaspoon salt, or to taste
¼ cup flour

1 can cream of celery or mushroom soup
1½ cups milk
1 (7-ounce) can salmon, drained
1 cup cooked peas
1 tablespoon lemon juice
Your favorite biscuits, homemade or canned

Sauté the onion and pepper in the oil until soft. Blend in the salt and flour. Gradually stir in the soup and milk. Bring to a boil; boil 1 minute. Add the drained and flaked salmon, peas, and lemon juice. Pour into an 11 x 7" oblong baking dish. Top with biscuits (bake remaining separately to enjoy with your meal). Bake at 450 degrees for 10 to 12 minutes. Will serve 6 to 8 people.

FAVORITE SALMON PATTIES

My father was a hard worker. He was honest, fair, and a firm believer in the power of prayer. He was a man of few words who did not express his emotions freely, but he had a dry sense of humor and enjoyed a good laugh. He never graduated from high school, but went to Anderson College anyway when he was 29. He had to work extra hard to make up for his lack of a high school education, but his desire was strong, and he graduated with a 3-year ministerial certificate when he was 33. We kids never tired of hearing him tell about his college days, and the escapades of which he was a part. He had a lot of musical talent (We loved hearing him sing "The Charming Young Widow I Met On the Train.") but he never had the opportunity to develop it that he provided for us children. Dad really liked salmon, and mother served salmon patties fairly often. I think he would have liked my version. They are quick to put together and light in texture. I'm always pulling this recipe out when I need a quick meal.

1 (16-ounce) can pink salmon
1 egg
1 tablespoon dried minced
  onion or ⅓ cup fresh,
  finely diced

½ cup flour
1½ teaspoons baking powder
2 tablespoons canola oil

Drain the salmon, reserving 2 tablespoons of the liquid. In a medium mixing bowl, combine salmon, egg, and onion until well mixed. Stir in the flour. Add the baking powder to the salmon liquid; mix and stir into the salmon mixture. Form into 6 patties. Heat a large non-stick skillet over medium-high heat; add 1 tablespoon oil. When oil is hot, add the patties. Sauté until nicely browned; turn, drizzle the remaining 1 tablespoon around the patties. Continue cooking until brown. Remove to plates or platter; garnish with parsley sprigs and lemon wedges.

TLC Tip: *This recipe does not call for salt. This is not a mistake; the salmon is salty enough as is.*

SALMON LOAF

Not living near the gulf or ocean makes it difficult to get fresh fish, so we have to make do with the canned and frozen variety a lot of the time. This loaf is a good way to consume part of the fish we need to eat weekly.

1 (16-ounce) can salmon,
  drained and flaked
2 cups soft breadcrumbs
1 tablespoon instant minced
  onion or ¼ cup finely
  chopped fresh

⅛ teaspoon pepper
½ cup cream of celery soup
  (reserve remainder for
  sauce)
2 eggs

In a large bowl, combine all the ingredients; mix well. Place in a well-greased 8 x 4" loaf pan, smoothing the top. Bake in a 375 degree oven for 40 to 50 minutes. Transfer to a platter. Garnish with fresh parsley and lemon wedges and serve with Celery Dill Sauce.

TLC Tip: *When a recipe calls for fresh breadcrumbs, you cannot substitute dry in equal amounts. The moisture in the fresh crumbs contributes to the consistency of the dish. In this case, if you wish to use dry, use only ½ cup; I prefer the fresh as I think it makes a better textured loaf. You can also bake this in muffin cups, filling each ¾ full. Bake for 25 to 30 minutes.*

CELERY DILL SAUCE

¾ cup cream of celery soup
2 tablespoons salad dressing
  (Miracle Whip)

¼ teaspoon dried dillweed

In small saucepan, combine all ingredients. Heat slowly, stirring often until warm. Try not to let it boil. You may also heat this in the microwave on 70% power for about 1 minute, stirring after 30 seconds.

SHRIMP CHOW MEIN

Chinese food is always popular, and this dish will come through for you in grand style. Compliment it with chow mein noodles, of course, but why not provide some rice too? And don't forget the fortune cookies!!

1 medium onion, chopped
1 medium green pepper, seeded and cut into strips
1 cup sliced celery
1 tablespoon oil (half sesame oil is nice)
12 ounces fresh bean sprouts
1 (8-ounce) can sliced water chestnuts, drained

1 (2-ounce) jar diced pimientos, drained
1 cup sliced fresh mushrooms (½ cup canned)
3 tablespoons soy sauce, lite, if you prefer
1½ tablespoons cornstarch
1 pound medium shrimp, peeled and deveined
Chow mein noodles

Sauté the onion, pepper and celery in the oil in a large non-stick skillet or wok about 3 minutes over medium heat. Cover and sauté 3 minutes more. Add the bean sprouts, water chestnuts, pimiento and mushrooms. Stir soy sauce and cornstarch into the chicken broth; add to skillet and cook, stirring constantly, until mixture is thickened. Add the shrimp; cook 3 minutes or until shrimp are tender, stirring constantly. Serve over chow mein noodles.

TLC Tip: *Omit the shrimp and add 3 chicken breast halves (about 1 pound) that you have boned, cut into strips and sautéed, and you have Chicken Chow Mein.*

SEAFOOD THERMIDOR

Bits of fish and shrimp covered with a creamy, cheesy sauce—what a tantalizing late supper for you and your "date" or to entertain some special friends.

1 pound cod fillets, cut into 1"
   pieces
1 cup water
1 small onion, quartered
1 lemon, quartered
1 can cream of shrimp soup,
   undiluted
2 tablespoons flour
¾ cup milk

½ cup shredded Monterey
   Jack cheese
6 ounces cooked shrimp,
   peeled and deveined
1 teaspoon sherry flavoring
Toast points, baked patty
   shells or hot cooked rice
2 tablespoons chopped fresh
   parsley
1 teaspoon paprika

Place the fish, water, onion, and lemon in a large skillet; bring to a boil. Reduce heat, cover and simmer 5 minutes. Drain well, and set aside. Combine soup and flour in skillet; stir in the milk. Cook over medium heat until hot and bubbly. Add cheese, stirring until cheese melts. Stir in the reserved fish, shrimp, and sherry. Cook over low heat until thoroughly heated. Serve over toast points, patty shells (the kids' favorite), or cooked rice. Garnish with a sprinkle of chopped parsley and a shake of paprika.

TLC Tip: *Dishes of this sort are richly satisfying but do lack color, so garnishing is critical. Also, pay attention to what else you serve for the meal, making sure you have plenty of color on the plate.*

SEAFOOD DIVAN

This is a nice dish to serve when your shrimp-loving friends come to share your table. Pop it in the oven, and while it bakes, toss a salad, slice some good bread and set the table. Your family and/or guests will marvel at the ease with which you get a nice meal on the table.

2 cans cream of mushroom
   soup
½ cup grated Parmesan
   cheese
½ teaspoon dry mustard
1 cup sour cream

1 cup cooked, sliced
   mushrooms
½ pound medium shrimp,
   cooked
1 (16-ounce) bag frozen
   broccoli cuts

Combine soup, cheese, mustard, sour cream and mushrooms. Fold in the shrimp. Steam the broccoli until tender-crisp. Place in an 8 x 11" casserole that has been sprayed with cooking spray. Top with the shrimp sauce. Sprinkle with paprika, if desired. Bake in a 325 degree oven about 45 minutes. Serve with rice.

SCALLOPS FLORENTINE

A tasty blend of seafood, vegetable and sauce, this dish looks especially attractive served in individual serving dishes. Don't let not having them keep you from trying it, however.

1½ pound scallops
¼ cup butter
1½ cups milk, divided use
½ cup chicken broth
¼ cup chopped green onion
4 teaspoons cornstarch

1 teaspoon sherry flavoring
   (optional)
1 (10-ounce) package fresh
   spinach, cooked, drained,
   and chopped
Shredded mozzarella cheese

Combine the scallops, butter, 1¼ cups milk, chicken broth and onion in a saucepan; cook over medium-low heat 10 minutes. Combine cornstarch and remaining ¼ cup milk; mix until smooth and stir into hot mixture. Cook until slightly thickened, stirring constantly. Do not boil. Spoon the spinach into a 1½-quart baking dish. Pour scallop mixture over spinach and sprinkle with the cheese. Bake at 350 degrees about 10 minutes or until bubbly.

TLC Tip: *You can easily adapt this recipe to fish fillets in this way: Omit the scallops; prepare the sauce as directed. Poach the fish fillets in a small amount of broth or water for about 5 minutes. Carefully remove and drain well on paper towels. Place the fillets on top of the spinach; top with the sauce and cheese. Bake as directed.*

SEAFOOD SUPPER A LA NEW ORLEANS

A spicy combination of seafood and vegetables served over rice. Wonderful with a salad of avocado and grapefruit sections with Poppy Seed Dressing. One of the chocolate desserts in this book would compliment this menu nicely.

4 slices bacon
2 tablespoons flour
1 teaspoon browning sauce,
   such as Kitchen Bouquet
1½ cups chopped celery
1 medium green pepper,
   seeded and chopped
6 green onions, chopped
2 cloves garlic, crushed
4 medium tomatoes, seeded
   and chopped
1 (4-ounce) can green chilis,
   undrained

2 bay leaves
1½ teaspoons salt
½ teaspoon pepper
½ teaspoon dried whole basil
¾ pound medium shrimp,
   uncooked, peeled, and
   deveined
¾ pound scallops, uncooked,
   rinsed, and drained
½ cup chopped fresh parsley
Hot sauce to taste
Hot cooked rice

Cook the bacon in a Dutch oven until crisp; drain on paper towels, reserving 2 tablespoons drippings in pan. Crumble the bacon and set aside. Add the flour and browning sauce to the reserved pan drippings and cook over medium heat 1 minute, stirring constantly. Add celery, green pepper, green onions and garlic; cook 10 minutes, stirring frequently. Add tomatoes, chilis, bay leaves, salt, pepper and basil; cook, uncovered, 45 minutes, stirring occasionally. Add the shrimp, scallops, reserved bacon, chopped parsley and hot sauce and cook 3 minutes more. Remove and discard bay leaves. Serve over hot cooked rice.

FABULOUS SHRIMP CRAB CASSEROLE

I like this dish so much it is difficult for me to remember that everyone doesn't share my feeling about seafood. I served it for a luncheon once, and much to my embarrassment, found there were a few who ate around the shrimp and crab. Survey your guest list, and if you get a green light, they're in for a treat.

⅓ cup chopped onion
2 tablespoons butter, melted
¼ cup flour
½ to 1 teaspoon salt
½ teaspoon white pepper
1 cup half-and-half
1 cup milk
3 cups cooked, peeled, and
    deveined shrimp

1 (8-ounce) package imitation
    crab meat, shredded (if
    you are where you can
    get the fresh and want to
    spend the bucks, by all
    means do)
1 (5-ounce) can sliced water
    chestnuts, drained
2 cups cooked rice
2 tablespoons lemon juice
2 tablespoons chopped
    pimiento
1 cup shredded Cheddar
    cheese, divided use

Sauté the onion in the butter in a large non-stick skillet. Add the flour, salt and pepper. Cook 2 minutes, stirring constantly. Gradually add the half-and-half and milk; cook over medium heat, stirring constantly, until thickened and bubbly. Remove from heat. Stir in the shrimp, crab meat, water chestnuts, rice, lemon juice, pimientos, and ½ cup cheese. Spoon into a lightly greased 2-quart casserole. Bake at 325 degrees for 25 minutes. Top with the remaining ½ cup cheese; bake 5 minutes or until cheese melts. Serve warm.

TLC Tip: *Steamed asparagus spears and a fresh spinach salad with red onion rings and orange slices are good accompaniments to this dish. Because the casserole is creamy in texture, I usually do not serve a creamy dessert; instead I would choose something light, such as chiffon cake or one of the fruity desserts. (Check the index.)*

PENNE AND PEELED SHRIMP

If pasta and shrimp are your passion, you'll love this combination. Seasoned with garlic and cilantro and vibrant with tomato, all you need is a Caesar Salad and a loaf of unadorned French bread to be in heaven.

2 tablespoons butter
2 tablespoons olive oil
3 cloves garlic, peeled and
   minced
2 medium tomatoes, peeled,
   seeded and chopped
¾ to 1 pound large shrimp,
   peeled and deveined

⅓ cup chopped fresh cilantro
   leaves
Salt and pepper to taste
12 ounces penne or other
   tubular pasta, cooked
   and kept warm

In a large skillet, heat the butter with the oil over medium-high heat. Add garlic and sauté about 30 seconds, watching carefully that it does not burn. Add the tomatoes. Reduce heat to medium-low and cook, stirring occasionally about 5 minutes. Stir in the shrimp and cook 3 minutes longer, tossing occasionally. Stir in the cilantro and season to taste with salt and pepper. Add the penne and stir to combine. Serve immediately to 4 fortunate people.

SCALLOPED OYSTERS

This recipe is a must at Thanksgiving and Christmas, and even the nieces and nephews who wouldn't normally look at an oyster, relish this dish.

4 (8-ounce) cans oysters
1 cup half-and-half
¼ cup butter
5 ounces oyster crackers,
   crushed
¼ cup chopped fresh parsley

½ teaspoon salt
1 teaspoon Worcestershire
   sauce
Dash of liquid hot pepper
   sauce
Paprika

Drain the liquid from the oysters and reserve ½ cup. Combine the liquid with the half-and-half in a 2-cup measure. Melt the butter in a medium size saucepan; stir in the crushed oyster crackers, parsley and salt; mix well. Spread half the buttered crackers in a shallow 6-cup baking dish; spoon drained oysters over the crackers, cover with remaining crackers. Stir Worcestershire sauce and pepper sauce into the cream mixture; pour over the oysters. Bake in a 350 degree oven for 30 minutes or until top is golden. Sprinkle with paprika before serving.

THEL'S TERRIFIC PASTA PRIMAVERA

Pasta dishes are a particular passion of mine. They are so easy to put together at the last minute for a quick, satisfying meal. We try to eat several meals a week that do not contain animal protein. We also try to eat a wide variety of vegetables. This dish covers both of these bases.

1 cup broccoli flowerettes
1 cup thinly sliced peeled
   carrots
½ cup thinly sliced onion
½ cup thinly sliced red bell
   pepper
1 cup thinly sliced mushrooms
1 cup 1" pieces fresh asparagus
1 cup thinly sliced zucchini

6 cups thin spaghetti or
   linguine, cooked (about 9
   ounces uncooked)
2 tablespoons olive oil
2-4 cloves garlic, minced
6 tablespoons freshly grated
   Parmesan cheese
Salt and pepper to taste

Place all the vegetables in a steamer basket and steam for 4 minutes. Remove from heat, and rinse under cold running water. Cook the pasta as package directs omitting the salt. Reserve ¼ cup cooking water, drain and keep warm. In the same large pan you cooked the pasta in, heat the olive oil over medium heat. Toss in the garlic and heat briefly, watching carefully so it does not burn. Add the steamed vegetables and the cooked, drained pasta. Toss gently to combine and heat, adding a little of the reserved pasta water if mixture seems dry. Season as desired. Serve with a dusting of Parmesan cheese.

FETTUCCINE ALFREDO

I think this pasta dish is a favorite among all our family members. The twins loved it long before they could pronounce it properly. When I first started preparing this, I used a recipe that contained egg yolks. I've since revised the recipe and leave them out, which lowers the fat and cholesterol some, though this is by no means a lowfat dish. I've tried many a "healthy" version, some of which were good, but definitely not Fettuccine Alfredo. I would suggest serving this with a lightly-dressed green salad, fresh, warm Italian bread, and a simple dessert, such as fresh fruit or poached pears. Or skip dessert, and sip one of the wonderful flavored coffees available today.

¼ cup butter
1 clove garlic, minced
¾ cup freshly grated Parmesan
   cheese (a must!)

½ cup half-and-half
6 ounces cooked fettuccine

Melt the butter over medium-low heat. Stir in the garlic, and heat briefly. Gradually add the cheese, stirring constantly with a wire whisk. After the cheese is melted, very slowly add the cream, continuing to stir with the whisk. When the sauce is creamy and smooth, combine with the cooked fettuccine. You won't have to make a trip to the Olive Garden with this recipe in your file.

TLC Tip: Should you like to add mushrooms to this dish, sauté 1½ cups sliced, fresh ones in the butter and garlic until tender before adding the cheese.

TLC Tip Two: You certainly don't need any meat with this, but I have been known to add a few cooked shrimp or some ham slivers—good either way.

PASTA WITH HAM

This recipe was my introduction to preparing pasta with an Alfredo-style sauce. I've served it often at our mountain house on winter evenings while beautiful snowflakes were covering the pines and deck and a fire crackled in the fireplace. It is very rich, truly living up to its reputation as a "heart attack on a plate", but a small serving is satisfying.

4 ounces regular fettuccine
4 ounces spinach fettuccine
½ cup butter
½ pound fully cooked ham
    (about 1½ cups, cubed)
1 cup sliced fresh mushrooms
1 cup whipping cream

2 egg yolks, well beaten
½ teaspoon dried basil
½ teaspoon salt
¼ teaspoon ground pepper
1 cup freshly grated
    Parmesan cheese

Cook pasta in a large pot according to package directions; drain, return to pot. Add the butter, ham and mushrooms. In a small bowl, combine the cream and egg yolks; beat well. Slowly stir egg mixture into pasta, mixing well. Add basil, salt, pepper and ¾ cup cheese. Cook over medium heat until thickened, stirring gently. Spoon onto individual serving plates. Sprinkle with remaining cheese.

TLC Tip: *I have used all one kind of pasta, half-and-half instead of whipping cream, omitted the egg yolks and a little less butter (about ⅓ cup) and still ended up with a dish that was acceptable. For a change, seafood can be substituted for the ham.*

Vegetables and Other Side Dishes

We had the most wonderful vegetables when I was a child! My grand-mother tended the garden, arising early, long before I got up, to hoe and weed. There were always green beans, beets, corn, squash (both winter and summer), tomatoes (yes, I know they are technically a fruit), aspara-gus, turnips, potatoes, spinach, lettuce, and cabbage. There were other less common vegetables, too, such as parsnips and kohlrabi. Many of these found their way into our root cellar either canned or in burlap bags to round out winter meals. Grandmother didn't stop with the garden, but went to the fields in search of greens such as lambs quarter, dandelion and poke. We also ate mushrooms (morels) which we gathered from the woods. Mother sliced them, dredged them in flour, and sautéed them in a little butter. Most vegetables were simply prepared, though we did have creamed style and scalloped corn. Grandmother fixed scalloped tomatoes, too. Asparagus was served in small bowls, covered with milk with a little butter added. Potatoes were the starch of choice, but occasionally rice or homemade noodles were served.

Actually, it is hard to improve on fresh vegetables, lightly steamed and seasoned as desired with a final flourish of a tiny dab of butter. The colors are glorious, the texture terrific, and the variety almost endless. We enjoy a wide assortment and I try not to repeat a vegetable any two days in a row.

There is no need for vegetables to be boring, even when prepared simply. First of all, they can be cut in so many different ways—sliced, thick or thin, crosswise or lengthwise, plain or waffled, chunks, strips, grated, mashed, Chinese style, wedges—what have I left out? Then, there are the combinations, and what a feast that is for the eyes. How about carrot strips, zucchini rounds, and cauliflower? Or golden whole kernel corn, green peas, and red peppers? Broccoli, carrot coins and celery slices? I could go on and on, and so can you. These days, you can find various combos right in your grocer's freezer case. If you choose to go this route, just be sure to get the packages that are unseasoned, which allows you to choose the kind and the amount.

In addition to shape and combination, the method of preparation can be varied to suit your time, mood or taste. You can choose from steaming, stir-frying, microwaving and roasting or baking.

Cheese sauce makes a nice addition to some vegetables, and it needn't be terribly high in fat if you make your white sauce with skim milk and use a restricted amount of reduced-fat cheese.

Various nuts and seeds are also good with vegetables—we are all familiar with green beans and sliced almonds. Cashews are another nut that blends easily with veggies. Be adventuresome—create your own favorite combination. Just make sure you "Eat your veggies."

FRIED APPLES

I really like apples fixed this way. Somehow I always think of this dish as fall and winter fare. Though this is good as an accompaniment to roast pork, pork chops or perhaps a sausage and cabbage dish, it could also be served as a simple dessert. If you can find apples that have not been sprayed, do leave the skins on. Otherwise, perhaps it is best to peel them.

6 apples	3 tablespoons pineapple juice
¼ cup sugar	1 tablespoon crushed
1 tablespoon red cinnamon	pineapple
candies	

Core the apples and cut into chunks. Combine with other ingredients in a medium skillet and simmer until apples are tender.

JAN'S SOUTHERN FRIED APPLES

Jan Elston and her husband, Jerry, are friends from way back. We lived in Plymouth, Michigan at the same time, attended the same church, and did many things together. Jerry was my principal at one time during my teaching career. Jan is a terrific housekeeper and cook, just two of her many talents, and always showed the spirit of hospitality. I can remember sitting at her kitchen table, feeling less than wonderful and drinking Constant Comment tea. She was such a good listener. Jan says these apples are so good with a Southern meal of pork chops, baked potatoes, green beans, hot biscuits and strawberry shortcake. Retirement years have taken them to Anderson, Indiana, where she is still spreading sunshine.

2 tablespoons butter (or Jan says, bacon grease)	½ cup granulated sugar
10 Granny Smith apples, cored and sliced	½ cup brown sugar
	½ teaspoon nutmeg
	½ teaspoon cinnamon

Melt the butter in a large skillet; add apples, then pour sugars and spices over apples. Fry slowly, stirring frequently, until apples are light brown in color.

COUNTRY SKILLET APPLES

This is a little different twist on fried apples, but one I think will please. The molasses adds a real homey touch. Try this on Gingerbread or Oatmeal Pancakes, too. (See index.)

¼ **cup butter**	**4 large apples**
¼ **cup molasses (I use the light)**	**Nutmeg to taste**

In a large heavy skillet over low heat, melt butter with molasses until mixture begins to bubble. Meanwhile, cut apples into ½" wide wedges, peeling if you prefer. Transfer to skillet, sprinkle with nutmeg. Simmer, turning apples once or twice with spatula about 8 minutes or until lightly colored. Serve warm in dessert bowls, over ice cream, pancakes, or gingerbread.

ASPARAGUS WITH MILK

When I was growing up, we had a large bed of asparagus. At the time, it was not high on my list of favorite vegetables. In fact, I enjoyed it more as it went to seed. Then I could use the feathery stems as fern in my make-believe bridal bouquets. The way it was always served at our house was in a sauce of milk and butter. Given the cost of asparagus today, and my changing taste, I wish I had access to that asparagus bed.

Fresh asparagus, amount depending on number of people you are feeding	**Salt and pepper to taste**
Milk, whole, lowfat or skim, your choice—we always used whole Jersey milk, "down on the farm"	**Butter—a must and no substitutes**

Wash and trim asparagus, if necessary, and cut into inch-long pieces. Bring a quantity of water to a boil, amount depending on how much asparagus you are cooking. Drop asparagus into boiling water, turn heat down to a simmer, and cook for about 10 minutes. Drain; return to pan, cover with milk, heat until very warm but don't boil. Season with salt and pepper; spoon into serving dishes. Dot each with butter.

CHUCKWAGON BEANS

These beans were just made for barbecue, picnics and potlucks. These can be baked for a long time at a low temperature or for a shorter time at a higher temperature. If you are preparing other foods in the oven, this dish will accommodate you by adjusting to whatever temperature the other dish needs. Just check them from time to time to see that they haven't dried out.

10 slices bacon, cut in pieces (your kitchen scissors do a great job here)	2 (28-ounce) cans pork and beans
2 medium onions, chopped	¾ cup catsup
1 medium green pepper, chopped	½ cup firmly packed brown sugar
	½ cup molasses
	1 teaspoon liquid smoke

Combine the bacon, onion and green pepper in a large skillet. Cook over medium heat until bacon is lightly browned and the vegetables are tender. Drain. Combine the bacon mixture and the remaining ingredients; mix well. Spoon into a lightly greased 12 x 8" baking dish. Bake uncovered at 425 degrees for 30 to 45 minutes or 300 degrees for about 2 hours or temperature of your choice, time will vary. These are great heated the next day—I've even eaten them cold!!

TLC Tip: If there is a lot of liquid in your cans of beans, it is wise to drain off a little (please reserve it) before mixing with the other ingredients. Even after an hour in the oven, they can be runny. You can always add a little of the reserved liquid if you find the beans are getting a bit dry.

JUANITA'S GREEN BEANS

Juanita Harrington is one of the loveliest ladies I have ever known. Though she has developed some health problems in recent years, she never complains, and continues to lend her talents and energies to the work of the church. We love to get together for carry-in dinners at our church, and we always look for Juanita's special green beans. You'll think they're special, too.

5 cans cut green beans (Juanita says to choose beans you know to be of good quality)	7 strips bacon

Cut the bacon into pieces and fry in a large heavy saucepan until very crisp—almost burned!! Drain the beans, and add the liquid to the bacon and drippings. Bring mixture to the boil; add the beans, turn down the heat and simmer for 1 hour. Receive compliments graciously as Juanita does!

251

JOAN'S BROCCOLI CASSEROLE

My friend Joan Beil, and her husband Charles, have joined Cleo and me on a number of Cowboy football weekends in Dallas. Besides rooting for the team in all kinds of weather, we have sampled some of Dallas's finest restaurants and done our share to help the local economy by frequenting the shopping centers. Joan and I were members of the Big Spring Music Study Club and Charles and Cleo started MuTex Sound and Electronics as a partnership in the early 1970's. The Beils love to travel, as we do, so we have plenty to talk about when we get together. Joan loves to entertain and cooks up some great dishes—this is one of hers.

2 (10-ounce) packages broccoli spears	1 small onion, grated
½ stick butter	½ roll garlic cheese spread
1 can cream of mushroom soup	½ cup sour cream
1 small can mushrooms, drained	½ cup soft breadcrumbs
	¼ cup sliced almonds

Cook broccoli until crisp tender. Combine butter, soup, onion, cheese, mushrooms and sour cream; heat over medium heat until cheese is melted. Arrange broccoli in baking dish; pour soup mixture over. Top with breadcrumbs and almonds. Bake at 350 degrees for 30 minutes.

RUTH'S BROCCOLI CASSEROLE

This casserole is really a favorite. I usually serve it as a substitute for potatoes, with main dishes such as ham, the Lemon Roasted Chicken, or mini meatloaves. My sis first served it to us when they were living in New Albany, Indiana. Several years have passed since that time, but the casserole has endured.

½ cup chopped celery	1 (16-ounce) bag frozen, chopped broccoli, thawed
1 medium onion, chopped	1 can cream of mushroom soup
1 cup instant rice	
1 (8-ounce) jar Cheese Whiz	

Sauté the celery and onion in a little butter. (Or better yet, microwave 4-5 minutes until slightly tender.) Prepare instant rice as directed on the package. While rice is hot, stir in Cheese Whiz, and continue stirring until cheese is melted. Add the celery, onion, broccoli and soup. Spoon into a 1½-quart casserole. Bake at 350 degrees 45 to 60 minutes, or until golden and bubbly on top. Do not cover.

TLC Tip: *You can use 2 cups cooked regular rice instead of the instant. If the rice is cold, warm a few minutes in the microwave before adding the cheese. If you forget to take the broccoli out of the freezer in time for it to thaw, just microwave it 2-3 minutes.*

GERMAN RED CABBAGE

This is a colorful side dish that is good to serve with smoked sausage or pork chops.

1 tablespoon butter or
    vegetable oil
1 small onion, sliced
1 small head red cabbage,
    shredded
1 medium tart apple, diced
½ cup raisins

5 whole cloves
3 whole allspice
½ teaspoon salt
3 tablespoons brown sugar
1 tablespoon red wine
    vinegar, or to taste
1 cup water

Heat butter in a large heavy skillet. Add onion and sauté 1 minute. Add cabbage and apple and continue cooking for 5 minutes. Combine rest of ingredients; pour over cabbage mixture. Cook, covered, over low heat for 30 minutes. This is good either hot or cold.

CARROTS AMBROSIA

I got this recipe out of one of my early cookbooks. The sugar heightens the sweetness of the carrots and the orange slices make this dish both delicious and beautiful.

2 cups cooked carrots, coins
    or sticks
¼ cup butter

¼ cup sugar
2 oranges, thinly sliced, seeds
    removed

Combine all ingredients in a medium skillet. Cook over medium heat, stirring often, until heated through and nicely glazed.

GINGER GLAZED CARROTS

Carrots prepared this way will liven up the dullest menu. The marriage of carrots and ginger is a good one.

3 cups sliced carrots, or use
    the tiny ones available
    today
¼ cup sugar

2 tablespoons butter
1 teaspoon finely chopped
    crystallized ginger
Pinch of salt

Steam the carrots over boiling water until crisp-tender, about 4 minutes. Remove to serving bowl. Drain water from pan; combine sugar, butter, ginger and salt in same pan. Heat over medium heat until bubbly. Add the carrots; reduce heat to low and cook, stirring occasionally, until carrots are glazed and heated through. A sprig of parsley makes a nice garnish.

KANSAS CORN SCALLOP

This is a special favorite of my nephew, David Yerden. The recipe came to me via his mother. She told me she found it in a magazine many years ago, we won't tell how many! This is a great dish—I hope you will enjoy it.

2 eggs	¼ cup melted butter
1 (16-ounce) can whole kernel corn	½ teaspoon salt
	¼ teaspoon pepper
1 (16-ounce) can cream style corn	2 tablespoons instant minced onion
1 (5-ounce) can evaporated milk (⅔ cup)	12 ounces Swiss cheese, cubed
	30 saltine crackers, crushed

Beat the eggs slightly. Drain the whole kernel corn, reserving ¼ cup liquid. Mix the reserved liquid and both corns with the eggs. Add the evaporated milk, diced cheese and crackers. Mix gently. Pour into a greased 2-quart casserole. Bake at 325 degrees for one hour or more, until set.

TLC Tip: *My experience has been that it takes a little more than an hour for this to bake and the cheese to become melted and runny, so don't rush the baking.*

EGGPLANT CASSEROLE

This is a dish that will surprise even eggplant haters. It is meant to be "healthy", as you will notice the absence of egg yolks and salt. I usually cheat a little and add some salt, probably about ½ teaspoon. Unless you have a physical condition that severely restricts salt, I suggest you do the same. I sometimes serve this for a meatless meal since it does contain eggs and cheese. Cleo especially likes this.

1 small eggplant (about 1 pound) peeled, diced and cooked	1 teaspoon onion powder
1 cup grated lowfat Cheddar cheese	1 cup coarsely crushed fat-free or regular saltine crackers
¾ cup skim milk	Butter-flavored vegetable oil spray
4 egg whites, beaten	
½ to 1 teaspoon dried dillweed	

Combine first 6 ingredients. Pour into a 9" square glass baking dish. Top with crushed crackers and spray lightly with vegetable oil spray. Bake in a 350 degree oven for 25 to 30 minutes, until golden brown and firm.

TLC Tip: *This is not a colorful dish so keep that in mind when selecting the rest of the meal. I think Glenda's Salad (see index) and one of the quick breads would do nicely.*

HOT FRUIT COMPOTE

This spicy hot fruit combination makes a nice accompaniment to a brunch menu or poultry casserole, perhaps the Crunchy Turkey Supreme or Pepperidge Farm Chicken (see index). It can bake right along with other oven dishes.

1 (20-ounce) can pineapple chunks, drained
1 (16-ounce) can peach slices, drained
1 (16-ounce) can pear slices, drained
1 (11-ounce) can mandarin orange segments, drained

¼ cup butter
½ cup firmly packed brown sugar
½ cup orange juice
2 tablespoons lemon juice
½ teaspoon cinnamon
⅛ teaspoon cloves
⅛ teaspoon nutmeg

Arrange all the fruit in a 13 x 9" baking dish or 1½-quart casserole. In a small saucepan, combine all the remaining ingredients. Cook and stir over medium heat until the brown sugar is dissolved and the butter is melted. Pour over the fruit. Bake at 375 degrees for 25 minutes or until fruit is thoroughly heated. Spoon into small dishes to serve.

TANGY FRUIT COMPOTE

This compote is a good compliment to a breakfast or brunch of pancakes, waffles or French toast. Other fruits can be substituted for those suggested.

1 (6-ounce) can frozen orange-pineapple juice concentrate, thawed
¼ teaspoon cinnamon
1 teaspoon brandy extract
1 (11-ounce) can mandarin orange segments, drained

1 (8-ounce) can pineapple chunks in juice, undrained
1 cup seedless red or purple grapes
1 large tart green apple, unpeeled and cubed

In a large bowl, combine the juice concentrate, cinnamon and brandy extract; blend well. Add the fruit; toss gently. Refrigerate at least 1 hour to blend flavors. Stir gently before serving.

HOLIDAY PEAS

I have served these peas so often, and not just at holiday times. When you read the ingredients, you can see why they are called Holiday Peas. This dish really helps to fill out a plate, especially when the entrée is light colored, such as chicken breast or fish. The recipe is easily doubled for a larger group. If you double the recipe, there probably isn't any need to double the butter, salt and pepper.

1 (10-ounce) package frozen green peas	1 (2-ounce) jar diced pimientos, drained
1 small onion, chopped	½ teaspoon salt, or to taste
½ cup chopped celery	⅛ teaspoon pepper
1½ tablespoons butter	1 (4-ounce) can sliced mushrooms, drained

Steam the peas over boiling water, or cook in the microwave. Drain of any liquid. Sauté the onion and celery in the butter in a medium skillet over moderate heat. Add pimientos, salt, pepper, mushrooms and cooked peas. Stir to combine and heat through.

TLC Tip: *I prefer to use a cup of sliced fresh mushrooms instead of the canned, sautéing them with the celery and onion. Either way, it's good.*

OVEN BLACK-EYED PEAS

This is a very simple and easy way to get your New Year's dose of black-eyed peas, or on any other day of the year, for that matter. Just add a square of hot cornbread, and you will truly feel that good fortune is with you. I have reduced the amount and type of bacon in this recipe to suit our current taste. You could also use only the bacon or only the sausage, if you prefer.

1 pound dried black-eyed peas	1 teaspoon salt
10 slices turkey bacon, cut into pieces	5 cups hot water
2 cloves garlic	¾ pound reduced-fat smoked turkey sausage, cut in pieces
1 tablespoon sugar	

Wash the peas and sort carefully. In a large, ovenware pot with a cover, combine the peas, bacon, garlic, sugar and salt. Add the water; cover and bake in a 350 degree oven 1½ hours. Stir in sausage; cover and bake 45 minutes longer. Check for seasoning; add more salt if necessary. Uncover and bake 45 minutes longer or until peas are tender. Keep peas moist. Add boiling water as needed.

TLC Tip: *I nearly always have to add additional hot water.*

FRIED OKRA

There are people who won't eat okra any other way than fried. However, that almost takes it out of the vegetable category and makes it a snack. I'm not so sure but that the amount of oil needed to give it that properly crunchy texture negates any health value it had to begin with. We like okra fixed in other ways too, but this is a delicious addition to a Southern, or any other, meal.

1 pound okra	1 cup self-rising flour
2 eggs, beaten	1 cup self-rising cornmeal
¼ cup buttermilk	Vegetable oil

Wash and slice the okra into ½" slices; pat dry with paper towels. Combine the eggs and buttermilk; add the okra, and let stand 10 minutes. Combine the flour and cornmeal. Drain the okra in a colander; toss small amounts at a time in the flour mixture, coating well. Heat vegetable oil to 375 degrees in a deep fryer or heavy saucepan. Fry okra until golden brown. Drain on paper towels. Best if served immediately.

TLC Tip: *If you don't have self-rising flour and cornmeal, use the same amount of regular flour and cornmeal and add 1 teaspoon salt and 4 teaspoons baking powder to the mixture.*

TLC Tip Two: *I almost never deep-fry the okra, preferring instead to use my cast iron skillet, adding ¼" to ½" vegetable oil and frying over medium-high heat, stirring frequently until golden to dark brown. Watch carefully, as there is a fine line between done and burned!!*

OUTSTANDING OVEN BROWNED POTATOES

I think you'll really like these potatoes. This is not a lowfat dish, but the wonderful melding of flavors makes a once-in-a-while splurge worth it.

6 medium baking potatoes, peeled and halved lengthwise	2 tablespoons grated Parmesan cheese
½ cup butter	2 tablespoons dry breadcrumbs
½ teaspoon garlic powder	

Generously grease a 13 x 9" baking dish. Cut deep slits in the rounded side of the potatoes at ¼" intervals. Place potatoes slit side up in prepared dish. In a small saucepan, melt butter. Stir in garlic powder. Spoon butter mixture evenly over the potatoes. Bake at 350 degrees for 40 minutes. Baste potatoes with melted butter from bottom of dish; sprinkle evenly with Parmesan cheese and breadcrumbs. Bake an additional 10 to 20 minutes or until potatoes are fork-tender. Yum, yum!!

OVEN FRIED POTATOES

Since I learned how to prepare potatoes this way, fried is a thing of the past. These take about 45 minutes to bake, so you do need to plan ahead, but while they are baking you have plenty of time to put the rest of the meal together. I like to serve these potatoes with such things as salmon patties, baked fish, oven-fried chicken and even hamburgers or turkey burgers.

2 to 4 medium to large potatoes cut as desired (slices, wedges, chunks, french fry cut, peeled, or skins left on)

1 tablespoon salad oil
1 tablespoon water
Seasonings as desired

Measure the salad oil and water into a large bowl or heavy self-seal bag. Add the potatoes, and tumble thoroughly to coat with oil/water mixture. (Hands work wonderfully for this task.) Transfer potato mixture to large baking pan with sides, arranging potatoes so pieces aren't touching. Sprinkle with seasoning/s. Bake in 375 degree oven for about 45 minutes, turning if necessary half way through baking time.

TLC Tip: Seasonings I like are salt and pepper, as well as paprika, garlic salt, and seasoning salt, not necessarily all at the same time. A little dried rosemary is wonderful too, especially if serving with meat dishes. You probably have a combination that will hit the spot with you. Already prepared mixtures are another possibility—how about Cajun? Greek? Chili?

MASHED POTATOES

My family and friends have never complained about my mashed potatoes. There really is no trick to having them turn out creamy and fluffy. Perhaps, as my father was fond of saying when asked about something he did well, "It takes years of experience and lots of practice." I'm not sure about the years of experience, but a little practice wouldn't hurt. There are those who say never to use an electric mixer, but I nearly always do. The old fashioned hand masher will work, it just takes a little more elbow grease. You read that you should always add hot milk; I never do. In fact, I almost always use skim milk, and never add any butter. I guess I prefer to let the potatoes be the blank canvas for whatever you want to "paint" on them at the table. This is how I do them.

Peel enough general purpose potatoes for the number of people you are serving. A good rule of thumb is one medium potato for each person plus one for the pot. Cut into pieces, cover with water, and add a little salt. (This is the only vegetable I salt while cooking, but somehow they just seem to taste better that way.) Bring to a boil over high heat, cover, and reduce heat to a simmer; cook about 20 minutes, until potatoes can be pierced with a fork. Drain the water from the potatoes, recover the pan, and shake a few times to further break up the potatoes. Using a hand-held electric mixer, beat the potatoes until they are mashed and no large pieces remain. If there is a secret to good mashed potatoes, this is probably it—beating the potatoes smooth before adding any milk. After you beat the potatoes until no large lumps remain, then add some milk, continue beating, adding more milk until desired consistency is obtained. I can't tell you how much to add—I guess this is where the experience comes in. I can tell by the feel of the mixture when I have added enough. The potatoes should look fluffy and creamy. Spoon the potatoes into a bowl. Now you can add a little butter if you wish, to melt into a delicious golden pool on the top. Sprinkle with chopped parsley or paprika if desired.

MR. MAC'S POTATO CAKES

Willie McDaniel was the custodian at Moss Elementary here in Big Spring. During the 1970's, I spent seven years teaching third graders there. Mr. Mac, as we called him, was an easy-going fellow, always willing to lend assistance to a teacher who was forever needing some, whether bringing extra chairs for a performance for parents or cleaning up after a messy art project. I don't know how we got around to the subject of cooking, but he volunteered this recipe. I'm glad he did. It always reminds me of a happy period in my life. Next time you prepare mashed potatoes, fix enough extra so you can make these cakes. They are worth the effort.

2 cups mashed potatoes
¼ cup shredded American
    cheese
1 whole egg, slightly beaten
1 egg yolk, slightly beaten

¼ cup dry breadcrumbs
1 teaspoon minced onion
½ teaspoon salt (optional)
¼ teaspoon chili powder

Combine all the ingredients in a medium-sized bowl. Mix until well blended. Heat a large skillet over moderate heat; add oil to cover skillet about ⅛" deep. When oil is hot, drop mashed potatoes by rounded spoonfuls into hot oil; flatten slightly with spatula. Cook 3-5 minutes on each side until golden brown. Drain on paper towels briefly; enjoy!!

SWEET POTATO PUFF

This is a wonderful and different variation of the standard sweet potato dish. This recipe has been lightened up a bit, so you can indulge almost guilt-free. My family really enjoys this and wishes Thanksgiving would come around more often.

3 cups fresh, cooked, sweet
    potatoes
4 egg whites

¼ cup sugar
1 teaspoon vanilla
2 tablespoons flour

Topping:
1½ tablespoons flour
¼ cup brown sugar
1 tablespoon butter

¼ cup chopped nuts (I like
    pecans here)

Using a food processor or mixer, mix together the sweet potatoes, egg whites, sugar, vanilla and flour. Pour into a 1½-quart casserole dish that has been sprayed with vegetable oil spray. Crumble flour, sugar and butter together; stir in the chopped nuts. Sprinkle over the sweet potato mixture. Bake in a 350 degree oven for 30 minutes until golden brown.

TLC Tip: What, no marshmallows? Place a few on the top if you must, but I don't think you'll miss them.

MOM'S CANDIED SWEET POTATOES

My mother's candied sweet potatoes were just that—tender circles of golden orange potatoes coated with a mouth-watering glaze of sugar and butter. It has been years since I fixed sweet potatoes this way, but I can still taste them, right out of mom's cast iron skillet. These potatoes are a special favorite of my nephew, Jay Albright.

Sweet potatoes   **Granulated sugar**
Butter

Scrub the sweet potatoes and place in a large pot. Cover with water, bring to a boil, reduce heat and simmer until the potatoes are fork tender but not too soft. Remove from heat, drain, and place in a bowl or on a flat surface to cool. When cool enough to handle (you can even store them this way in the refrigerator for a while), remove the skins. Slice into thick (about ¾" to 1") rounds. Melt the butter in a heavy skillet over medium heat. (Mom used cast iron and I follow in her footsteps.) Pour some granulated sugar into a shallow dish. When the butter bubbles, dip each slice of sweet potato into the sugar, coating both sides generously. Place in the skillet and sauté until sugar melts and slices are glazed. Arrange attractively on a serving platter. Garnish with a few parsley sprigs if desired.

TLC Tip: Exact measurements aren't critical for this dish. Select the amount of sweet potatoes for the crowd you are feeding, and adjust the amount of sugar and butter accordingly. You may need to add a little butter each time you fill the skillet with potato slices.

TLC Tip Two: Need I say these are glorious with your Thanksgiving turkey?

RATATOUILLE

Cleo fell in love with this dish one summer when we managed to grow eggplant in our garden. We also had tomatoes and zucchini, so we had it made! This dish is worth making even if you can't grow your own veggies, and delicious as a side dish with almost any meat.

1 eggplant, peeled if desired	1 green pepper, cut into
2 tablespoons salt	pieces
2 tablespoons olive oil,	3 to 4 tomatoes, chopped into
divided	coarse pieces
4 cups sliced zucchini	Salt and pepper to taste
2 yellow onions, chopped into	1 teaspoon basil
coarse pieces	½ teaspoon coriander

Cut the eggplant into small squares and toss with the 2 tablespoons salt. Place in a colander, and drain for ½ hour. Heat 1 tablespoon oil in a large heavy non-stick skillet over medium heat. Sauté the zucchini for 5 minutes; add the onion and green pepper and continue cooking for 15 minutes. Remove to a bowl and keep warm. In the same skillet, heat the remaining tablespoon oil and sauté the eggplant for 15 minutes. Remove eggplant to bowl with other vegetables. Add tomatoes to pan and sauté for a few minutes. Put reserved vegetables back into skillet; add seasonings, lower heat and cook for 45 minutes or so. Be careful that vegetables do not get too mushy. Serve and enjoy.

TLC Tip: *This keeps well for a day or two, and reheats easily. I like to have this for a light lunch with a sprinkle of freshly grated Parmesan cheese.*

CASHEW RICE PILAF

An attractive accompaniment to Cornish hens, chicken breasts, or roast turkey, I'm sure you'll find many other ways to serve this delicious combination of rice and seasonings.

½ cup cashews, preferably	½ cup sliced green onions
unsalted	1 (6-ounce) package long
1 tablespoon oil	grain and wild rice mix
1 tablespoon butter	2⅓ cups chicken broth

In a large saucepan, sauté cashews in oil and butter until cashews are golden. Drain cashews, set aside, reserving butter in pan. Sauté green onions in same pan until tender. Add the rice mix to the pan, and prepare as directed on the package, substituting chicken broth for water and omitting salt. Fluff with a fork before serving, and garnish with the cashews and chopped parsley if desired.

RICE-BULGAR PILAF

I like this pilaf because it is a little unusual and compliments chicken, fish, or meat beautifully. The grains can be cooked ahead to save time.

1 tablespoon unsalted butter	2 cups cooked bulgar
½ cup chopped walnuts	2 cups cooked brown rice
4 green onions, cleaned and thinly sliced	Chopped fresh parsley for garnish, if desired

In a medium-size non-stick skillet, melt the butter over medium heat. Add the walnuts and green onions, and sauté, stirring, for 2 minutes. Stir in the cooked bulgar and brown rice and cook until all the ingredients are heated through, about 5 minutes. Transfer to serving dish, and garnish with parsley.

TLC Tip: You may use white rice in this dish if you wish, with a slight loss of nutrition. You may want to add a little salt to taste. I have also used other kinds of nuts, such as pecans and pine nuts, with good results.

SUMMER SQUASH CASSEROLE

I predict this will become one of your favorite side dishes. It certainly is a good way to use up an abundance of zucchini or summer squash.

2 cups water	1 cup sour cream
6 to 8 medium zucchini or summer squash	½ teaspoon dillweed
1 cup shredded carrots	1 can cream of chicken soup
½ cup diagonally sliced celery	4 cups herb-seasoned stuffing mix (6 ounces)
½ cup chopped onion	½ cup butter, melted

In a large saucepan, bring water to a boil. Add zucchini, carrots, celery and onion. Cover; cook over medium heat about 5 minutes or until celery is crisp-tender. Drain. Combine sour cream, dillweed and soup; mix well. Fold in vegetables. In a large bowl, combine stuffing mix and butter. Spoon half of stuffing in bottom of a lightly greased 3-quart casserole. Spoon vegetable mixture over stuffing mixture; sprinkle with remaining stuffing mixture. Bake at 350 degrees for 30 to 40 minutes or until golden brown and thoroughly heated. This should serve 12 people.

SCALLOPED TOMATOES

This side dish was a standby when we lived on the farm. We ate it often in winter, when all the tomatoes we had were home-canned. My mother or grandmother always served these in little dishes next to our dinner plates. This is a great way to use up not-quite-fresh bread, too.

4 cups canned tomatoes, with juice	¼ cup sugar
1 tablespoon minced onion (optional)	¼ cup butter
	¼ teaspoon pepper, or to taste
	4 cups soft bread cubes

Pour the tomatoes into a medium saucepan. Break up the tomatoes slightly; add the onion, sugar, butter and pepper. Heat briefly over medium heat until the butter is melted. Stir in the bread cubes. Continue heating until mixture bubbles. Remove from heat and spoon into dishes to serve.

TLC Tip: *In composing this recipe I have used 4 cups tomatoes because we used a quart of home canned tomatoes. You can easily cut the recipe in half.*

ZUCCHINI CASSEROLE

This method of preparing zucchini makes a large dish that is perfect to take to a church dinner, family reunion or other gathering.

8 to 9 medium zucchini, cut in ¼" slices	2 cups shredded Cheddar cheese
1 cup water	1 teaspoon salt
8 slices bacon, diced	1 teaspoon Italian seasoning
1 large onion, chopped	Dash of pepper
1 large clove garlic, minced	1 (15-ounce) can tomato sauce
4 slices white bread, diced	¼ cup grated Parmesan cheese

In a large saucepan, cook zucchini in a little boiling water until tender, about 5 minutes. (You can also steam the zucchini or cook it in your microwave if you prefer.) Drain. In a medium skillet, cook the bacon until crisp; remove from pan, crumble, and set aside. Add onion and garlic to skillet and sauté until onion is tender; drain. Stir onion mixture and crumbled bacon into zucchini; add remaining ingredients except Parmesan and toss until well coated. Spoon into a 13 x 9" baking dish. Sprinkle with Parmesan cheese. Bake at 350 degrees for 20 minutes or until bubbly.

OPEN FACE SUMMER SQUASH

The next time you fix meatloaf, add this vegetable dish to the oven during the last 30 minutes of baking time.

8 small summer squash	**1 teaspoon seasoned salt**
2 tablespoons butter	**½ cup grated Cheddar cheese**

Cut squash in half lengthwise; steam about 10 minutes. Arrange cut side up in a 3-quart baking dish. Melt butter and add seasoned salt; drizzle over squash. Pierce center of squash so butter is absorbed. Bake at 350 degrees for 20 minutes. Top with cheese; bake about 10 minutes more.

MIXED VEGETABLE STIR-FRY

I love this dish! It is pretty to look at and very tasty—a great addition to any meal with an Oriental theme. Cutting the vegetables is your biggest chore. It's a piece of cake after that.

1 tablespoon oil	**1 small yellow squash, sliced**
1 medium clove garlic, cut in	**1 small zucchini, sliced**
half	**3-4 green onions with tops,**
2 carrots, sliced diagonally	**sliced in 1" pieces**
2 ribs celery, sliced diagonally	**1 tablespoon soy sauce**
3-4 ribs bok choy	**Salt and pepper to taste**
1 green or red pepper cut in	**1 tablespoon sliced almonds**
slices (or ½ of each)	

Separate greens from bok choy ribs; cut the rib into thin slices, and shred the greens. Reserve. In a heavy, non-stick skillet or wok, heat the oil over medium-high heat. Add the garlic and stir briefly to release flavor; remove and discard garlic. Add carrots and celery; stir-fry 3-4 minutes. Add the bok choy ribs, the squash, pepper and the zucchini; continue stir-frying 2-4 minutes. Add green onions, bok choy greens, soy sauce and pepper; taste and add more salt if necessary. Sprinkle almonds over the top.

TLC Tip: Watch carefully after you add the garlic as it is important that you do not let it burn. Usually I finish this dish by turning the heat off, covering the skillet and letting it set on the burner for a couple of minutes. If you do this, don't walk off and forget it, as you want the vegetables to retain their beautiful color and not be overcooked.

ZUCCHINI ROUNDS

Zucchini is very low in calories and actually doesn't have a lot of food value. Perhaps that is why we feel we are justified in preparing it in more caloric ways. This recipe, from my mother's files, uses zucchini to make delightful little patties.

⅓ cup biscuit mix
¼ cup grated Parmesan
   cheese
⅛ teaspoon pepper

2 slightly beaten eggs
2 cups shredded, unpeeled
   zucchini

Stir together biscuit mix, cheese and pepper. Add beaten eggs and stir just until moistened. Fold in the zucchini. Heat a large non-stick skillet and add a small amount of butter or oil. Use about 2 tablespoons of the zucchini mixture to make small cakes. Fry 2-3 minutes on each side. Makes about 12.

WESTERN ZUCCHINI

One year, I presented a program on zucchini for my garden club. Actually, it was a mini-cooking class on the many different roles zucchini can play in your kitchen—everything from appetizers to desserts. I enjoyed doing it and the club seemed to enjoy sampling everything. This is one of the dishes I prepared.

2 slices bacon
2 cups fresh green or yellow
   beans (or use frozen
   beans)
1 small onion, thinly sliced

1 clove garlic, minced
½ cup water
4 small zucchini, sliced (about
   2 cups)
1 tablespoon soy sauce

Fry the bacon until crisp in a medium skillet; set aside. Drain off all but 1 tablespoon drippings from pan. Toss beans, onion and garlic in reserved bacon drippings. Add water. Cover; cook over medium heat about 10 minutes or until beans are crisp-tender. Stir in zucchini and soy sauce. Cover, cook an additional 5 minutes or until zucchini is tender. Spoon into serving dish. Sprinkle crumbled bacon over hot vegetables.

TLC Tip: *For some reason or other, I do not like to use reduced-salt soy sauce in this dish. I'll leave the choice up to you.*

TLC Tip Two: *There is no getting around the fact that bacon adds a lot to the flavor of this dish. If you prefer not to use bacon, use 1 tablespoon oil, sauté the onion and garlic a little, then proceed with the recipe. Hormel packages bacon pieces in a little jar. Sprinkle a small amount over the top of the finished dish. Not a bad variation.*

ZUCCHINI, RICE AND BEANS

This is a variation of a recipe I copied from an old Country Living *magazine. It is a personal favorite of mine, I crave it at times. Simple to put together, it can be used as a meatless main dish, or made a little more hearty with the addition of a small amount of cooked lean ground beef or slivers of cooked ham.*

1 large onion, sliced
1 medium zucchini, sliced
1 tablespoon canola or olive
   oil
½ to 1½ teaspoons chili
   powder
¾ teaspoon salt

1 teaspoon cumin
2 cups, more or less, cooked
   rice, white or brown
1 (16-ounce) can kidney or
   pinto beans, drained and
   rinsed

Heat the oil in a large non-stick skillet over medium-high heat. Add the onion and zucchini; turn heat to medium-low, and cook, stirring often, until vegetables are crisp-tender. Add the rice, beans and seasonings. Mix gently but thoroughly until heated through.

TLC Tip: *This is one of those dishes where ingredient measurements aren't critical. You may prefer more or less of a particular item, so experiment and come up with your own personal version.*

OVEN FRIED ZUCCHINI

This one is a favorite of my husband. It is easy to prepare and doesn't use as much oil as the conventional deep fried. We like this as a side dish, but it is also good served as a first course or appetizer with ranch dressing as a dip.

3 tablespoons herb-seasoned
   breadcrumbs
1 tablespoon grated Parmesan
   cheese
¼ teaspoon salt or garlic salt

⅛ teaspoon black pepper
2 medium zucchini or yellow
   squash, unpeeled
2 teaspoons vegetable oil
2 tablespoons water

Combine breadcrumbs, cheese, salt, and pepper on a sheet of waxed paper; set aside. Quarter the zucchini lengthwise, then cut each spear in half or thirds. Put these in a plastic bag; add the oil and water. Close the bag and shake so spears are lightly coated with oil. Roll each spear in crumb mixture until it is lightly coated. Arrange spears on a cookie sheet that has been sprayed with vegetable cooking spray. Bake at 475 degrees, uncovered, for 7 minutes or until spears are browned and tender-crunchy.

TLC Tip: This recipe can easily be doubled. If you like lots of crunch, you might want to double the crumb mixture anyway.

TLC Tip Two: If you like rounds better, no problem. Slice the zucchini into ¼" thick rounds and proceed in the same manner.

Cakes and Pies

The cakes and pies of my childhood were wonderfully simple and delicious. Birthdays always brought out the wire whisk which produced a beautiful, light angel food. Mother always frosted it with a thin powdered sugar glaze. For Christmas, she made her famous Date Nut Cake, a favorite of my father. Actually, baking cakes was one of my first cooking experiences. Spry shortening put out a cookbooklet containing about a dozen different cakes, and I think I made them all. In the late 1940's and early 1950's the chiffon cake was invented. Each month the women's magazines would feature a different flavor, and somehow I felt duty bound to be the local tester for each flavor.

It seems like pies held more of a place of honor as the sweet ending to a meal, however, especially when we were feeding silo fillers or thrashing hands. Apple was always a favorite, and living close to the orchards near Lake Michigan, we had access to many varieties. Mother made a great Lemon Meringue and a wonderful Graham Cracker Cream.

MOM'S ANGEL FOOD CAKE

Angel food cakes were THE birthday cake when I was a child. Mother always whipped the whites with a flat wire whisk—hard to come by in these days, but even if we had one, I hardly think we would want to expend the time or energy it takes to get the whites just right. Her cakes were a sight to behold—tall and light—and always frosted with a simple powdered sugar glaze. More often than not, we turn to the ones in the box now. They're simple to make, nearly foolproof, and taste good. But sometimes I feel that something is missing. Could it be the love that went into all that whipping?

1 cup cake flour	1 teaspoon vanilla
¾ teaspoon cream of tartar	½ teaspoon almond extract
1 cup egg whites (8 to 10	½ teaspoon salt
large)	1¼ cups granulated sugar

Stir the flour, measure, and sift 4 times. (I think this just may be one of the secrets.) Sift the cream of tartar into the egg whites and beat until the whites will hold a point. (I use an electric mixer on the high speed; if you wish, you can try the whisk method.) Add the flavoring and salt. Add the sugar by sifting it through a strainer into the egg white mixture and folding gently. (Mother's recipe says to "mix the eggs deftly with the sugar so that as little as possible of the air enclosed in the eggs escapes.") Add the flour by sifting through a strainer and fold gently into the egg white mixture. I do my folding by hand—you're on your own if you use your mixer. Turn the batter into a large ungreased tube pan. (Ungreased is important here. In fact, be sure there is no oily residue in the pan. I have even wiped out my pan with a paper towel moistened with a bit of vinegar to be sure.) Bake in a slow oven, 325 degrees, for 1½ hours. When the cake is done, invert the pan to cool, then remove it from the pan and store in a tightly covered cake container.

TLC Tip: *All that sifting and folding seems like a lot of trouble, and it is, but my mother thought the results were worth it. I use a couple squares of waxed paper for the sifting process. The flour can easily be poured from the paper.*

ANNIVERSARY CAKE

This is the cake my sister, Ruth, made for a cakewalk at Blackman School, the country school we kids attended. Ruth was a winner with this cake. With a hint of orange in the layers and a fluffy orange frosting, you'll be a winner with it too.

2½ cups flour
3 teaspoons baking powder
¾ teaspoon salt
¾ cup shortening
1 tablespoon grated orange
    rind

1½ cups sugar
3 eggs
1 cup milk
1 teaspoon vanilla

Sift the flour, baking powder and salt together three times. (These days, technically, you don't have to do this step, but I think you'll notice a difference if you take the time to do it.) Blend the shortening and the orange rind. Add the sugar gradually, beating until light and fluffy. Add the eggs one at a time; beat about one minute after each addition. Add the dry ingredients alternately with the combined milk and flavoring; mix well after each addition; beat well after last addition only. Turn into 3 well-greased 8" layer cake pans. Bake in a 375 degree oven for 25 to 30 minutes. Cool in pans 5 minutes; then remove to wire racks to finish cooling. Be sure cake is completely cool before frosting with Fluffy Orange Frosting.

TLC Tip: I always line the bottom of my layer cake pans with waxed or parchment paper. It is insurance that you can remove the layer without part of it sticking to the bottom of the pan—not a pretty sight. Here's how: lay the pan on as many squares of paper as needed, in this case three. Trace around the pan with the tip of your scissors or a pencil. Remove the pan and cut out the circles. Grease the pan, lay in a circle of paper, and grease the circle. Always remove the paper before cake cools.

FLUFFY ORANGE FROSTING

2¼ cups sugar
7 tablespoons water
⅜ teaspoon cream of tartar
3 egg whites
¼ teaspoon salt
1½ teaspoons vanilla
2 teaspoons grated orange rind
Yellow food coloring, if desired

Combine first four ingredients in top of double boiler; beat slightly to mix ingredients. Place over rapidly boiling water; beat with rotary or hand beater until mixture will hold a peak (about 7 minutes). Remove from boiling water; add salt, vanilla and orange rind. Tint a delicate yellow with food coloring, if desired. Beat until thick and cooled, or until frosting holds its shape. This should make enough frosting to fill and frost three 8" layers.

OREO COOKIE CAKE

It seems that anything you can add those ever popular chocolate sandwich cookies to is a sure winner. Such is this cake—tender, white cake with bits of crumbled Oreo cookies covered with a smooth and fluffy frosting and garnished with more cookies. Wonderful!!

1 (18½-ounce) package white cake mix
1¼ cups water
⅓ cup oil
3 egg whites
1 cup coarsely crushed creme-filled chocolate sandwich cookies, such as Oreo

In a large mixer bowl, combine all cake ingredients except crushed cookies. Blend at low speed until moistened; beat 2 minutes at highest speed. Gently stir in 1 cup coarsely crushed cookies. Pour batter into two 8" or 9" round cake pans that have been greased and floured. Bake at 350 degrees for 25 to 35 minutes or until toothpick inserted in center comes out clean. Cool 10 minutes; remove from pans. Cool completely.

Fluffy White Frosting:
4 cups powdered sugar
1 cup shortening (not butter-flavored)
1½ teaspoons vanilla
2 egg whites

In a medium bowl, combine 1 cup powdered sugar, shortening, egg whites and vanilla. Beat in remaining powdered sugar until frosting is smooth and creamy. Fill and frost Oreo Cookie Cake. Garnish with Oreo cookie halves.

TLC Tip: *There should be enough frosting to generously frost the two layers. If I am going to take the time to make a layer cake, there is nothing I hate worse than not having enough frosting.*

MOUSE CAKE

This is a delicate spice cake with a yummy penuche icing. The unusual name comes from my sister, Ruth. My mother would make this cake, a favorite of my sister, and she and her friends would enjoy it after a bout of trying to ride the cows (forbidden by dad, but that's what made it more appealing). Knowing it was setting on the kitchen table was a good excuse to sneak into the kitchen after everyone was asleep. In fact, that is how it got its name. When asked about the looks of the cake the next morning, my sister would always reply, "The mice must have gotten into it". I'm sure all of your little mice will love it as much as she does.

2¼ cups cake flour	¾ teaspoon cinnamon
1 cup sugar	¾ cup brown sugar, packed
1 teaspoon baking powder	½ cup soft shortening
¾ teaspoon soda	1 cup buttermilk
1 teaspoon salt	3 eggs
¾ teaspoon cloves	

Measure the flour onto a square of waxed paper. Blend with the other dry ingredients in a large mixer bowl. Add the brown sugar, shortening and buttermilk. Beat 2 minutes using the medium speed of your mixer (or 300 strokes by hand if you are so inclined). Scrape bottom and sides of bowl occasionally. Add the eggs and beat 2 more minutes. Pour into a greased and floured 9 x 13" pan. Bake at 350 degrees for 45 to 50 minutes. Cool before frosting with Minute Penuche Frosting or Easy Penuche Icing.

TLC Tip: If you bake in a glass pan, remember to set the oven at 325 degrees.

MINUTE PENUCHE FROSTING

2 cups packed brown sugar	¼ teaspoon salt
½ cup milk	1 teaspoon vanilla
½ cup shortening	

Combine all ingredients except vanilla in small saucepan. Bring to a full rolling boil over medium heat, stirring constantly. Boil 1 minute. Remove from heat and beat until mixture is lukewarm. Stir in vanilla. Beat until smooth and of spreading consistency. Makes enough frosting to generously frost the Mouse Cake or any other 9 x 13" cake.

EASY PENUCHE ICING

½ cup butter
1 cup packed brown sugar
¼ cup milk

2 to 2½ cups sifted powdered
  sugar

Melt butter in saucepan. Stir in brown sugar. Boil and stir over low heat 2 minutes. Stir in milk. Bring to boil, stirring constantly. Cool to lukewarm. Gradually stir in powdered sugar. Place pan in ice water and stir until thick enough to spread.

TLC Tip: Regular milk will do just fine in this recipe, but if you happen to have some evaporated milk open, using it will add to the richness of the frosting.

CHOCOLATE CHIP ZUCCHINI CAKE

I discovered this cake the year we had a plentiful supply of zucchini from our garden. I used zucchini in everything from appetizers to dessert. This was requested often.

1½ cups sugar
½ cup butter, softened
¼ cup oil
1 teaspoon vanilla
2 eggs
1½ cups flour
¼ cup unsweetened cocoa

Dash of salt, optional
1 teaspoon baking soda
½ cup buttermilk
2 cups shredded zucchini
½ to 1 cup semi-sweet
  chocolate chips
½ cup chopped nuts

In a large bowl, combine sugar, butter, oil, vanilla and eggs; beat well. Measure flour, cocoa, and baking soda onto a square of waxed paper. Combine, and add to creamed mixture along with buttermilk. Blend well. Fold in the zucchini, chocolate chips and nuts. Spread in a greased and floured 9 x 13" pan. Bake at 350 degrees for 35 to 45 minutes or until toothpick inserted in center comes out clean. Cool completely. Frost or garnish as desired.

TLC Tip: I prefer the mini chips in this cake. I don't think I have ever frosted it—it just doesn't seem to need that added touch. I have also used part brown sugar which adds a slightly different taste and comes out well, and I have reduced the sugar to 1 cup, with good results.

CHOCOLATE BIRTHDAY CAKE A LA CREME

This is what I like to call an adult birthday cake. Of course the fact that it is chocolate adds to its merits. I've served it often, and besides tasting wonderful, it makes a showy presentation. I like to use those long, skinny candles, sticking them directly into the center of the cake, slanting them slightly like a bouquet of flowers. The exact number of candles usually doesn't matter for an adult birthday—just so they have something to wish over and blow out.

3 ounces unsweetened chocolate	4 eggs
2½ cups sifted cake flour	1 tablespoon grated lemon rind
1 teaspoon salt	1 cup milk
1 teaspoon baking soda	Cocoa Butter Filling
¾ cup shortening	1 cup whipping cream, whipped
1½ cups granulated sugar	

Melt the chocolate over low heat or in the microwave. Measure the flour, salt and soda on a square of waxed paper, stir together. In a large bowl, cream the shortening with the sugar; beat in the eggs one at a time, until light and fluffy. With mixer at medium speed, beat in the lemon rind, then the flour mixture alternately with the milk, beating well after each addition. Stir in the chocolate until well blended, then turn into two 9" cake pans that have been greased and bottoms lined with waxed or parchment paper. Bake at 350 degrees for 30-40 minutes. Cool in pans 10 minutes; then remove from pans and cool on wire racks. When ready to assemble cake, place one layer on plate, top with filling, add second layer. Mound whipped cream in a circle around edge of cake. Sprinkle with chocolate shot or curls.

TLC Tip: *If you want additional whipped cream to serve with the cake, plan accordingly.*

Cocoa Butter Filling:

1 cup butter	½ cup cocoa
¾ cup powdered sugar	1 teaspoon vanilla

In small mixing bowl with mixer at medium speed, cream butter. Gradually beat in powdered sugar, cocoa and vanilla. Beat until fluffy.

276

MALLO-NUT FUDGE CAKE

This is the cake my Uncle Everett raved so about. It really built my confidence as a baker, young as I was. This recipe comes from an old Spry cookbooklet published in 1949. Reminiscent of rocky road candy, you'll savor every bite.

3 ounces unsweetened
   chocolate, cut fine
¾ cup boiling water
1¾ cups cake flour
1½ cups sugar
¾ teaspoon salt
½ teaspoon baking powder
¾ teaspoon soda

½ cup shortening
⅓ cup buttermilk
1 teaspoon vanilla
2 eggs, unbeaten
18 large marshmallows,
   cut in half
½ cup coarsely chopped nuts

Put the chocolate in a large mixer bowl. Pour the boiling water over the chocolate and stir until melted. Cool. Combine the flour, sugar, salt, baking powder and soda on a square of waxed paper; add to chocolate mixture along with the shortening. Blend on low speed of mixer for 2 minutes. Add the buttermilk, vanilla and eggs and continue beating another 2 minutes on low speed. Pour into 2 greased and floured 8" square pans. Bake at 350 degrees for 30-40 minutes. Cool in pans 5 minutes, then remove and place on plate. While cake is still warm, press marshmallows on one layer, turned bottom-side up. Spread with Minute-Boil Fudge Frosting (see below), put other layer on top. Add nuts to remaining frosting, spread on top of cake only. Decorate each corner with a quartered marshmallow. Yum, yum!!

TLC Tip: Should you not have two 8" square pans, bake the cake in two 9" round pans.

MINUTE-BOIL FUDGE FROSTING

2 ounces unsweetened
   chocolate, cut fine
1½ cups sugar
7 tablespoons milk
2 tablespoons shortening

2 tablespoons butter
1 tablespoon white corn syrup
¼ teaspoon salt
1 teaspoon vanilla

Place the chocolate, sugar, milk, shortening, butter, corn syrup and salt in a saucepan. Bring slowly to a full rolling boil, stirring constantly, and boil briskly 1 minute. (If it is a rainy or very humid day, rare in these parts, boil the mixture 1½ minutes.) Cool to lukewarm. Add the vanilla and beat until thick enough to spread. If frosting becomes too thick, add a little cream or soften over hot water. Makes enough frosting for the tops of two (8") layers.

PRIZE WINNING ZUCCHINI FUDGE CAKE

Always on the lookout for new and different recipes, I copied this one while leafing through magazines at my sister-in-law's house. I would take it out and read through it ever so often, but somehow never seemed to find just the right occasion to prepare it. One year I decided to make it to enter in the Howard County Fair. I devoted the entire morning to making that cake. It was a very warm September day, and I worked right under the air conditioner vent hoping it would turn out well. I have to admit it was one beautiful cake that I carried out to the fair barn that day. I even asked my niece, Cheri, to ride along and hold the cake! I won a blue ribbon and Reserve Champion and a bottle of vanilla!! Not bad for my first try, huh? This cake has a taste that is to die for—it should, all that butter and sugar. It makes a very large cake, so prepare to share.

4 large eggs	1 teaspoon baking soda
2¼ cups sugar	¾ teaspoon salt
2 teaspoons vanilla	1 cup buttermilk
¾ cup butter, softened	3 cups coarsely shredded
3 cups flour	zucchini
½ cup unsweetened cocoa	1 cup chopped walnuts
2 teaspoons baking powder	Chocolate Frosting

In a large bowl, beat eggs with electric mixer until fluffy. Gradually add the sugar, beating until thick and lemon colored. Gradually beat in the vanilla and butter. In a large sifter, combine dry ingredients. Sift ⅓ of the dry ingredients over egg mixture. Stir together until just combined. Add ½ the buttermilk, stir just until combined. Add ½ the remaining dry ingredients, the remainder of the buttermilk, then the remaining dry ingredients, stirring just to combine after each addition. Fold in zucchini and nuts. Divide batter into three 9" greased and floured cake pans that have been lined with waxed or parchment paper. Bake until top springs back lightly when touched and/or toothpick inserted in center comes out clean, about 25-30 minutes. Cool in pans 10 minutes, then remove from pans, remove paper, and continue cooling on wire racks. Fill and frost with Chocolate Frosting. If you want to really gild the lily, you can further embellish with puffs of whipped cream and fresh raspberries.

Chocolate Frosting:

1 cup butter, softened	½ cup unsweetened cocoa
2 pounds sifted powdered	1 tablespoon vanilla
sugar	⅓ to ½ cup milk

Combine all ingredients in a large mixer bowl using the minimum amount of milk. Continue beating until smooth and creamy, adding more milk if necessary. Use to fill and frost Prize Winning Zucchini Fudge Cake.

HEATH BAR CAKE

Cleo doesn't have much of a sweet tooth, but occasionally has been known to succumb to a Heath Bar. This cake was made for him. The candy crunch topping provides just the right amount of "sweet" so no frosting is needed.

2 cups brown sugar, packed	1 teaspoon vanilla
2 cups flour	½ cup chopped nuts
½ cup butter	6 (1.4-ounce) Heath bars
1 teaspoon soda	(The original called for
½ teaspoon salt	6 (5-cent) bars so you
1 cup milk	know how long this has
1 egg, beaten	been around!)

Stir the sugar into the flour and mix well. Cut in the butter with a pastry blender. (The preceding job is a good one for your food processor.) Set aside 1 cup of this mixture. To the rest add the soda, salt, milk, egg and vanilla. Beat well. (I usually use my hand mixer for this.) Pour into a greased and floured 9 x 13" pan. Break up the Heath bars and combine with reserved mixture. Pour over the cake batter. Bake at 350 degrees for 30-35 minutes.

TLC Tip: I've tried using the pre-crushed candy and also the Heath Bar Sensations, but I prefer breaking the bars myself.

RITA JO'S CHOCOLATE CHIP DATE CAKE

This easy-to-snack-on cake comes from my sister-in-law's files. Almost like a date nut bread, it holds up well in lunch boxes, tastes great with a glass of milk, yet can be dressed up with a scoop of ice cream or spoonful of whipped cream to grace a company table.

1½ cups chopped dates	2 eggs
1½ cups boiling water	1½ cups flour
1¾ teaspoons soda, divided use	1 (6-ounce) package chocolate chips
1½ cups sugar, divided use	½ cup chopped nuts
½ cup shortening	

Combine the dates, boiling water and 1 teaspoon soda in a small bowl. Let stand until cool. Mix the sugar, eggs and shortening and cream well. Add the flour and ¾ teaspoon soda and fold in the date mixture. Pour into a greased 9 x 13" baking pan. In another small bowl, combine the chocolate chips, ½ cup sugar and chopped nuts. Sprinkle on top of batter. Bake about 40 minutes in a 350 degree oven. Remove to rack and cool in pan.

CHOCOLATE MOCHA CAKE

If you like the flavor of coffee and chocolate like I do, this just may become one of your favorite cakes.

3 cups cake flour
¾ teaspoon baking powder
1½ teaspoons baking soda
1 teaspoon salt
1½ teaspoons cinnamon
¾ cup cocoa

¾ cup shortening
2¼ cups sugar
3 eggs
1 cup buttermilk
1½ teaspoons vanilla
¾ cup strong coffee

Sift the dry ingredients together three times. (I know we don't often do this any more, but I think you will be pleased with the results if you do.) Cream the shortening; gradually add the sugar, beating well. Add the eggs, one at a time, beating about 1 minute after each. Add the dry ingredients alternately with the combined milk and flavoring, beating well after each addition. Add the cool coffee; stir until batter is smooth. Pour into 3 greased and floured 9" pans and bake at 350 degrees for about 30 minutes. Test with toothpick or cake tester after 25 minutes. Cool in pans 10 minutes, then remove to wire rack to finish cooling. Fill and frost as desired.

TLC Tip: *I like to frost this cake with the coffee variation of My Favorite Fudge Frosting (see index).*

MY FAVORITE FUDGE FROSTING

There's nothing like a good fudge frosting to set off even the simplest of cakes. This is a dependable one, you don't have to worry that it will be too stiff to spread or that you'll have to add lots more powdered sugar. This makes a generous amount of frosting for a 2-layer cake.

3 ounces unsweetened
   chocolate
¼ cup + 2 tablespoons oil
¾ cup granulated sugar
¼ cup + 2 tablespoons water

1½ teaspoons vanilla
3 cups powdered sugar
⅛ teaspoon salt
1 egg yolk

Melt the chocolate in the oil in a small saucepan over low heat. Add the granulated sugar and water; bring to a boil over medium heat, stirring constantly. Boil 1 minute or until mixture thickens. Remove from heat and stir in the vanilla, powdered sugar and salt. Beat until smooth and creamy. Add egg yolk. Beat occasionally as mixture cools and is of spreading consistency.

TLC Tip: *If you wish to frost a 9 x 13" pan cake, follow the above directions but use 2 ounces chocolate, ¼ cup oil, ½ cup granulated sugar, ¼ cup water, 1 teaspoon vanilla and 2 cups powdered sugar.*

TLC Tip Two: *For a taste change, dissolve 1 teaspoon instant coffee in the water before you add it to the chocolate and oil. Good!!*

GOLDEN CHIFFON CAKE

My husband thinks chiffon cakes are the only kind!! Usually baked in a tube pan, they are impressive and deliciously light, perfect on their own or as an accompaniment to ice cream or fresh fruit. They can be glazed, frosted or dusted with powdered sugar, but Cleo says they are best when unadorned.

2 cups flour	¾ cup cold water
1½ cups sugar	2 teaspoons vanilla
3 teaspoons baking powder	Grated rind of one lemon
1 teaspoon salt	1 cup egg whites (about
½ cup cooking oil	7 or 8)
7 unbeaten egg yolks	½ teaspoon cream of tartar

Measure the flour, sugar, baking powder and salt into a sifter or sieve. Sift into a large bowl. Make a "well" in the flour mixture and add, in order, the oil, egg yolks, water and flavorings. Beat with a spoon (I sometimes use a hand mixer, but it isn't necessary) until smooth. Set aside. Measure the egg whites and cream of tartar into a perfectly clean mixer bowl, making sure there is no trace of oil on the bowl or beaters. Whip the egg whites until they form very stiff peaks. They should be much stiffer than for angel food cake or meringue. Pour the egg yolk mixture gradually over the whipped whites, gently folding with rubber spatula just until blended. Do not stir. Pour into an ungreased 10" tube pan at once, and bake in a preheated 325 degree oven for 55 minutes; then increase the oven temperature to 350 degrees and continue baking 10 minutes. Immediately turn the pan upside down, placing the tube part over a funnel or neck of a bottle so that the edges of the pan hang free of table or counter. Let set until cold. Loosen from sides and tube with sharp knife. Remove to cake plate; stand back and admire your handiwork!

SPICY CHIFFON CAKE

I always like this variation.

1 teaspoon cinnamon

½ teaspoon nutmeg

½ teaspoon allspice

½ teaspoon cloves

Follow the directions for Golden Chiffon Cake, adding the above to the dry ingredients. Frost with Creamy Nut Icing if desired.

Creamy Nut Icing:

½ cup shortening (part butter
is wonderful)

2½ tablespoons flour

¼ teaspoon salt

½ cup milk

½ cup brown sugar

2 cups sifted powdered sugar

½ teaspoon vanilla

½ cup coarsely chopped nuts

Melt the shortening in a medium sized saucepan. Remove from heat and blend in the flour. Gradually stir in the milk. Bring to a boil, stirring constantly, and boil 1 minute. (If the mixture curdles don't worry, the icing will not be affected.) Stir in the brown sugar. Remove from heat and mix in the powdered sugar. Beat until consistency to spread. Stir in the vanilla and nuts; spread on top and sides of cake.

PEPPERMINT CHIFFON CAKE

This is one of the prettiest chiffon cakes.

Prepare Golden Chiffon Cake, substituting ½ teaspoon peppermint flavoring for the vanilla and omitting the grated lemon rind. Frost with Candy Mountain Icing.

Candy Mountain Icing:

½ cup sugar

¼ cup white corn syrup

2 tablespoons water

2 egg whites

⅓ cup coarsely crushed
peppermint candy

In a small saucepan, stir the corn syrup and water until well blended. Boil rapidly until mixture spins a 6" to 8" thread, 242 degrees on your candy thermometer. When mixture begins to boil, start beating the egg whites. Beat until stiff enough to hold a peak. Pour the hot syrup slowly in a thin steady stream into the beaten whites, beating constantly with your electric mixer until mixture stands in very stiff peaks. Blend in the peppermint candy. Frost top and sides of cake. Sprinkle with a little additional crushed peppermint candy if desired.

FRESH ORANGE CHIFFON CAKE

This is Cleo's overall favorite. If he has a choice, this is what he requests for birthdays, Father's Day, or any day. I really think this is best made with the fresh oranges, but I have, in a pinch, used frozen orange juice. Cleo prefers it plain, but the Orange Cream Icing is a nice touch.

2¼ cups cake flour
1½ cups sugar
3 teaspoons baking powder
1 teaspoon salt
½ cup cooking oil (I like
    canola)
5 unbeaten egg yolks

Juice of 2 medium oranges
    plus water to make ¾ cup
    liquid
Grated rind of 2 oranges
1 cup egg whites (7 or 8)
½ teaspoon cream of tartar

Measure the dry ingredients into a sifter or sieve. Sift into a large bowl. Make a "well" in the dry ingredients and add, in order, the oil, egg yolks, liquid and grated rind. Beat until smooth. Set aside. In a large mixer bowl, combine the egg whites and cream of tartar. Be sure the bowl and beaters are free of any trace of oil. Beat until very stiff—much stiffer than for angel food cake or meringue. Pour egg yolk mixture gradually over whipped egg whites, gently folding with rubber spatula just until blended. Do not stir. Pour at once into a 10" ungreased tube pan and bake in a 325 degree oven for 65 to 70 minutes. Immediately turn pan upside down, placing the tube over a funnel or glass bottle. Let hang until cold. Loosen from side and tube with a thin sharp knife. Remove to cake plate. Dust with powdered sugar or ice, if desired.

Orange Cream Icing:

½ cup shortening (part butter
    is nice)
4 tablespoons cake flour

¼ teaspoon salt
½ cup orange juice
3 cups sifted powdered sugar

Melt the butter in a small saucepan over medium heat. Remove from heat and stir in the flour and salt. Gradually add the orange juice. Return to heat and bring to a boil; boil for 1 minute. Remove from heat and stir in the powdered sugar. Set the saucepan in a bowl of ice water. Beat until thick enough to spread.

TLC Tip: *If I frost this cake, I like to garnish it with some thin strips of orange rind.*

COCOA CHIFFON CAKE

The collection just wouldn't be complete without a chocolate version, so here it is. I found this recipe in the Detroit Free Press *more years ago than I would care to admit. I always like making this cake because it uses the same amount of yolks and whites. This is nice served with the Chocolate Fluff that follows.*

¾ cup boiling water	1 teaspoon salt
½ cup cocoa	½ cup vegetable oil
1¾ cups cake flour	2 teaspoons vanilla
1¾ cups sugar	7 eggs, separated
1½ teaspoons soda	½ teaspoon cream of tartar

Combine the boiling water and cocoa; cool. Sift the flour, sugar, soda and salt together into a large bowl. Make a "well" and add, in order, the oil, vanilla, egg yolks, cooled cocoa mixture and vanilla. Beat until smooth. Put the egg whites and cream of tartar in a large mixer bowl. Be sure bowl is free of any trace of oil. Beat until whites are very stiff. Pour the egg yolk mixture gradually over the whites, gently folding it in with a rubber spatula just until blended. Pour into an ungreased 10" tube pan; bake at 325 degrees for 55 minutes, then increase the oven temperature to 350 degrees and continue baking for 10 to 15 minutes or until cake springs back when gently pressed. Invert pan with tube over a funnel or bottle; let hang until cold. Loosen sides and tube with a long, thin knife; remove to cake plate.

Chocolate Fluff:

2 cups whipping cream	½ cup cocoa
1 cup sifted powdered sugar	Dash of salt

Mix all ingredients together in a chilled bowl. Whip until stiff enough to hold a point. Serve on wedges of Cocoa Chiffon Cake.

APRICOT POUND CAKE

Various versions of this cake were very popular at one time, and when you make this, you will understand why. An easy cake to make, it is also easy to carry to church suppers and club meetings.

1 (18½-ounce) package lemon
    cake mix
½ cup sugar

4 eggs
½ cup vegetable oil
1 cup apricot nectar

Combine the cake mix and sugar in a large mixer bowl. Blend in the eggs, oil and apricot nectar; beat 6 minutes at medium speed. Pour into a greased and floured 10" tube pan. Bake at 350 degrees about 50 minutes. Cool on cake rack 10 minutes, then remove from pan and return cake to cake rack. Place the cake rack on a sheet of waxed paper. Pour Lemon Glaze over the hot cake, allowing icing to drizzle down the sides.

Lemon Glaze:
¼ cup lemon juice

1¾ cups sifted powdered
    sugar

Combine lemon juice and powdered sugar, beating until smooth.

TLC Tip: *I have baked this cake in a large fluted pan. Just be sure it is well greased and floured (I find a stiff pastry brush works well for this job) and that the pan holds at least 12 cups.*

THELMA'S HOLIDAY EGGNOG CAKE

In 1981, Cleo started StarCom, an electronics distribution company. My, how we worked!! The consumer satellite industry was just getting off the ground, and everything moved so quickly our heads were spinning. It seems like we were forever on the go, either to one of our seven offices, a trade show (in the early days there were five or six a year) or on a trip with a manufacturer to some foreign country. During the holidays, we always got the staff together for dinner, usually at a restaurant, and then we gathered at our home for a dessert buffet. I was in "tall cotton", as they say here in West Texas. What fun to prepare four or five desserts. My formula was simple—a cheesecake, something fruity and/or lite, a cake, a pie and always something chocolate. This cake was often the cake part of the formula. Simple to make, light in texture and taste, and easy to decorate, it has been on the menu for nearly all my open houses, teas, and family gatherings. I hope you will enjoy it as much as I have.

2 tablespoons soft butter	⅛ teaspoon nutmeg
½ cup chopped, blanched	2 eggs
almonds	1½ cups commercial eggnog
1 (18½-ounce) size yellow cake	¼ cup melted butter
mix	½ teaspoon rum flavoring

Grease a large bundt pan or tube pan with the softened butter. Sprinkle with the chopped almonds, turning pan to coat bottom and sides. Combine cake mix, nutmeg, eggs, eggnog, melted butter and flavoring. Beat until smooth, about 4 minutes on the medium speed of your mixer. Pour batter into prepared pan. Bake at 350 degrees 45 to 55 minutes. Let cool in pan 10 minutes, remove and invert on cake rack to finish cooling. Garnish as desired.

TLC Tip: *Just before serving, I like to give the cake a generous dusting of powdered sugar, and garnish with candied red and green cherries.*

287

RUM CAKE

Pixie Hughes and her husband Cosby were friends of my mother in Pryor, Oklahoma. Their daughter Kaye, and her husband Glen, Bounds played a part in Cleo and my courtship. Isn't it a small world? This is Pixie's recipe for Rum Cake. It is a real favorite of my family, often requested for birthday celebrations and holidays. Our son, Joey, is especially fond of this cake.

1 (18½-ounce) box yellow cake
    mix
½ cup vegetable oil
1 cup water

1 teaspoon rum flavoring
1 (3.4-ounce) package instant
    vanilla pudding (dry)
4 eggs

Combine all ingredients in a large mixer bowl. Blend on low speed, and continue beating for 2 minutes on medium speed. Pour into a greased and floured 12-cup bundt cake pan. Bake at 350 degrees for 45 to 50 minutes. While still warm, and before you take the cake out of the pan, pour the following glaze over the cake.

Glaze:
1 stick (½ cup) butter
⅓ cup water

1 cup sugar
1 teaspoon rum flavoring

Combine the butter, water and sugar in a small saucepan. Bring to a boil, and boil gently for 5 minutes, stirring frequently. Remove from heat and stir in rum flavoring. Pour over cake while still warm.

MRS. MOODY'S APPLE BLOSSOM CAKE

Mrs. Moody brought this cake to us at the time of my father's death. She was a friend of my mother when she lived in Anderson, Indiana. Such a thoughtful gesture; such a delicious cake! I have made this cake so many times since, and find myself reaching for this recipe for occasions such as this, especially in the fall of the year. This cake needs no icing—sometimes I give it a light dusting of powdered sugar before serving.

1½ cups canola oil
2 cups sugar
3 eggs
3 cups flour (the recipe says
    to sift three times—
    I don't always)
1½ teaspoons soda

½ teaspoon salt
2 teaspoons vanilla
½ teaspoon cloves
½ teaspoon cinnamon
½ teaspoon nutmeg
3 cups chopped, peeled apples

Mix the sugar, oil, eggs and vanilla. Add the dry ingredients and mix well. Stir in the apples. Bake in a large bundt or tube pan 1 to 1½ hours in a 350 degree oven. Cool in pan 10 minutes, then remove to wire rack.

FRESH APPLE CAKE

This recipe came to me from Rita Richards, the mother of our son-in-law, David. Rita is from Iowa Falls, Iowa, and is a delightful lady. She and her husband, Jack, spend a lot of time on the golf course, she gardens, and does needlework that's beyond belief! We enjoy talking about crafty things, and yes, food. Her apple cake is delicious on its own, but add the sauce, and WOW! When you pull out your fall clothes, pull out this recipe. It will make you a star in your own kitchen.

4 cups peeled, sliced apples	1 teaspoon salt
2 cups sugar	2 eggs
2 cups flour	¾ cup vegetable oil
1½ teaspoons baking soda	2 teaspoons vanilla extract
2 teaspoons cinnamon	1 cup chopped pecans

In a large bowl, stir together the apples and sugar. Add the dry ingredients; stir well. In a separate bowl, beat the eggs, oil, and vanilla. Stir egg mixture into the apple mixture, blending until thoroughly moistened. Stir in the pecans. Pour into a greased 9 x 13" pan. Bake at 350 degrees for 50 minutes, or until cake springs back when lightly pressed. Serve with warm Apple Dessert Sauce. Serves 12 to 15.

Apple Dessert Sauce:

1 cup sugar	½ cup whipping cream or
½ cup butter	evaporated milk
	1 teaspoon vanilla

Place all ingredients in a small saucepan; stir together. Bring to a boil over medium heat and cook three minutes. Serve warm.

TLC Tip: Rita says the sauce keeps well, but should be reheated before serving.

SWEDISH LEMON APPLE CAKE

I was first attracted to this cake because the sauce baked right along with the cake. After I tasted it, I immediately added it to my file. I've used it often—for family meals, casual get-togethers and to share with people who had new babies or were experiencing the loss of a loved one. The ingredients can easily be kept on hand so you can whip it up at a moment's notice.

1 regular sized package lemon   **1 can apple pie filling**
   cake mix

Spread the pie filling in the bottom of a 9 x 13" pan. Prepare cake batter as package directs; spread evenly over apples. Bake at 350 degrees for about 45 minutes. Serve with Tag-Along Sauce.

Tag-Along Sauce:
1 cup brown sugar   ⅛ **teaspoon salt**
2 tablespoons flour   **1 cup water**
¼ **teaspoon nutmeg**   **2 tablespoons butter**

In a small baking dish, combine dry ingredients and then gradually stir in the water. Add butter. Bake in oven along with cake. Sauce will thicken without stirring.

TLC Tip: *I have used spice cake and even yellow cake instead of the lemon cake with good results.*

AUNT EVELYN'S NEVER FAIL APPLESAUCE CAKE

A natural during the fall season, this spicy cake chock full of raisins and nuts will disappear quickly any time you serve it. Aunt Evelyn didn't serve it with the glaze, but sometimes I use it for a little showier presentation.

1 cup shortening	1½ teaspoons soda
2 cups granulated sugar	1 teaspoon cinnamon
2 cups unsweetened	1 teaspoon nutmeg
applesauce	½ teaspoon cloves
3 tablespoons hot water	1 teaspoon salt
2 eggs, unbeaten	1½ cups raisins
3 cups flour	½ cup chopped black walnuts

Cream the shortening and sugar together in a large mixer bowl. Add the applesauce, water and eggs; mix on the low speed until all are combined. Measure the flour, spices, salt and soda onto a square of waxed paper. Stir to combine, add to the creamed mixture, mixing on low until all dry ingredients are incorporated. Stir in the raisins and nuts. Pour into a well greased and floured 12-cup bundt pan. Bake on the center shelf in a 350 degree oven for 60 to 70 minutes or until a toothpick inserted in the center comes out clean. Remove to wire rack to cool for 10 to 15 minutes; remove from pan to finish cooling. Serve plain or glaze if desired.

Spicy Brown Sugar Glaze:

6 tablespoons butter	1½ cups confectioner's sugar
6 tablespoons brown sugar	1 teaspoon cinnamon
6 tablespoons whipping	1 teaspoon allspice
cream	½ teaspoon ginger

Melt the butter with the brown sugar in a small saucepan over low heat; stir in the cream, bring to a boil, and boil for 2 minutes. Sift the sugar with the spices onto a square of waxed paper. Add to the butter/brown sugar mixture, beat until smooth. Spoon over cake letting glaze drip naturally down the sides and center.

CRANBERRY ORANGE POUND CAKE

A delectable version of pound cake made all the better when served with the yummy sauce. This is worth keeping a bag of cranberries in the freezer for—it would be a shame to serve this only during the holiday season.

2¼ cups sugar
1½ cups butter, softened
1 teaspoon vanilla
1 teaspoon grated orange peel
6 eggs
3 cups flour

1 teaspoon baking powder
½ teaspoon salt
1 (8-ounce) carton sour cream
1½ cups chopped fresh or
    frozen cranberries (no
    need to thaw)

In a large mixer bowl, beat the sugar and butter until light and fluffy. Add the vanilla and orange peel. Add eggs 1 at a time, beating well after each addition. Lightly spoon flour into measuring cup; level off. In medium bowl, combine 3 cups flour, baking powder and salt; add alternately with sour cream, beating well after each addition. Gently stir in the cranberries. Pour batter into a greased and floured bundt pan. Bake at 350 degrees for 65 to 75 minutes or until toothpick inserted in center comes out clean. Cool 15 minutes; remove from pan. Serve with Butter Rum Sauce.

Butter Rum Sauce:
1 cup sugar
1 tablespoon flour
½ cup half-and-half

½ cup butter
1 teaspoon rum flavoring

In medium saucepan, combine sugar with flour. Add half-and-half and butter. Cook over medium heat until thickened and bubbly. Remove from heat and stir in rum flavoring.

LOU'S MANDARIN ORANGE CAKE

Lou Beard was one of my first roommates at Anderson College. She and Bobbi Jo Harris and I were crammed into a room on the third floor of Morrison Hall in the fall of 1953. Lou was a sophomore, and more poised and "college wise", but it was she and Bobbi Jo who gave me the nickname Tillie Belle. Thank goodness some things aren't forever! I helped at the serving table when she and Norm married during those college years. Norm and Lou still live in Anderson, Indiana, where she teaches music and is active in the church and university community, and Norm is Dean of International Studies at Anderson University. Norm is a travel expert and tour leader, and often coordinates the travel for the World Conference of the Church of God. Lou is a gracious, talented lady, and a great cook. She served this cake when I joined them for dinner during one of my visits to Anderson. It makes me think of spring, no matter what time of year I serve it.

1 (18½-ounce) package yellow
    cake mix
¾ cup oil

4 eggs
1 (11-ounce) can mandarin
    oranges, undrained

Mix all ingredients together until well blended, about 4 minutes using the medium speed on your mixer. Pour into three greased and floured 9" cake pans whose bottoms have been lined with waxed or parchment paper. Bake at 350 degrees for 18-20 minutes. Cool in pans about 5 minutes, then remove from pans to wire rack to finish cooling.

Filling and Frosting:
1 (20-ounce) can crushed
    pineapple, undrained
1 (3-ounce) package instant
    vanilla pudding

1 (8-ounce) carton whipped
    topping, thawed

Combine pineapple and pudding; fold in the whipped topping. Spread between cake layers and on top of cake. Refrigerate for several hours before serving.

TLC Tip: My experience has been that off-brand whipped toppings are not necessarily the way to go in a filling such as this. I find they do not seem to have as good a consistency, or hold up as well, as Cool Whip or Le Creme. TLC Tip Two: This cake needs to be kept cool—as in the refrigerator! Make sure the layers are completely cool before filling them, and chill the filling a bit before using it. The first time I made this cake I took it to a luncheon. The layers began to slide around. However, the taste sure wasn't affected, as everyone raved over the cake. If you wish to take it somewhere, I would suggest baking it in a 13 x 9" pan for about 30 to 40 minutes and spreading the filling on the top of the cake.

RUTH'S GRAHAM CRACKER CUPCAKES

The recipe for these delectable little goodies was given to me by my sister. They are festive enough for the holidays, but once you make them, you probably will want to enjoy them more often.

½ cup shortening
1 cup sugar
2 eggs
1 cup milk
2 teaspoons baking powder
Pinch of salt

2⅔ cups graham cracker
 crumbs (about 32 squares,
 if you are making your
 own crumbs)
½ cup chopped nuts
1 teaspoon vanilla

Cream the shortening and sugar; add the eggs and beat well. Gradually add the milk. Mix the baking powder, salt and cracker crumbs. Combine with milk mixture. Add nuts if desired. Pour into muffin tins lined with paper liners. Bake at 350 degrees for 20-25 minutes. Spread with the following topping.

Topping:
1 cup crushed pineapple,
 undrained (I have used 1
 small flat can of crushed
 pineapple and it worked
 fine)

1 cup sugar
1 cup cut-up maraschino
 cherries

Combine the pineapple and sugar in a small saucepan. Bring to a boil and boil gently for 15 to 20 minutes. Add the cherries. Put on top of cupcakes while still warm.

TLC Tip: It is not mandatory that you use cupcake liners. Also, I have baked these in the little mini pans with success. Adjust the baking time accordingly.

RUTH SIMMONS' FRUIT COCKTAIL CAKE

Ruth Simmons and her husband Ivan are friends from my days as an Army wife. They live in the panhandle of Oklahoma, and ranched for years. I was always amazed at the apparent ease with which she put meals on the table. Often she had extra farm hands to feed and lived far away from town. As I recall, she kept two freezers full. Good, hearty food and plenty of it was her goal. This cake is one that served her well, and one I have used time and time again. Note that there is no shortening in this cake.

2 cups flour	**2 eggs**
1½ cups sugar	**1 (16-ounce) can fruit cocktail**
1½ teaspoons soda	**⅓ cup packed brown sugar**
½ teaspoon salt	**Topping**

Combine the flour, sugar, soda and salt in a large bowl. Add the eggs and fruit with juice and mix well. Pour into a greased and floured 9 x 13" baking pan. Sprinkle brown sugar over the top. Bake at 350 degrees for 40 minutes. Cover with Topping while cake is still warm.

Topping:

½ cup butter	**1 cup angel flake coconut**
1 cup sugar	**1 cup chopped nuts**
1 cup cream or evaporated milk	**1 teaspoon vanilla**

Combine the butter, sugar and milk in a small saucepan. Bring to a boil over medium heat and boil for 8 minutes. Remove from heat and add coconut, nuts and vanilla. Spread over cake.

EDNA'S DATE CAKE

Edna Cates was my Grandmother Crabtree's cousin. It was this cake that my mother made every Christmas using black walnuts, when we had taken the time and energy to crack their tough shells. She used black walnuts because my father was particularly fond of them. I guess this was her answer to fruit cake. The layers do not rise much, probably because of the dates, so don't expect some lofty creation. My mother always iced this with a thin powdered sugar icing. I usually cheat a little and use a simple butter cream. Making this cake brings back wonderful memories of my mother's kitchen—eating it is even better!!

1½ cups sugar
½ cup butter
2 eggs
1 cup buttermilk
1 teaspoon soda
1½ cups flour
½ teaspoon salt (my mother
    didn't say how much,
    but that amount suits
    me fine)

¼ teaspoon cloves
1 teaspoon cinnamon
8 ounces chopped dates
    (I usually buy the kind
    that are already
    chopped)
1 cup chopped nuts

Cream the butter and sugar; add the eggs and beat well. Mix the soda and buttermilk and add to the creamed mixture. Combine flour, salt and spices on a square of waxed paper and gradually mix into the liquid mixture. Fold in the dates and nuts. Grease two 9" round cake pans; line the bottoms with waxed or parchment paper, and grease the paper. Pour in the batter and bake at 350 degrees for about 25 minutes. Cool in pans 5 minutes, then remove from pans, peel off paper and continue cooling on a wire rack. When completely cool, fill and frost with a simple butter cream frosting. Do not fill and frost too generously if you want the cake to look and taste like my mother's!!

TLC Tip: *Did you know that the dates and nuts should be coated lightly with flour before adding to the batter? After measuring the flour, you can use a tablespoon or two for this purpose.*

296

ITALIAN CREAM CAKE

Our daughter, Cyndee, and Darell were married in a lovely, memorable ceremony at the home of my sister-in-law and brother-in-law, Linda and Paul Lindell. Cyndee and Cleo came down the stairway to the altar setting in the living room, and the reception was held in the large family room. Cyndee and I made her dress—she sewing on the pearls—but I didn't attempt the wedding cake. I did, however, do the groom's cake, an Italian Cream. This is it. Baked in a bundt pan, it is much easier to serve than the usual layers.

5 eggs, separated	½ teaspoon salt
2 cups sugar	1 cup buttermilk
½ cup butter, softened	2 cups coconut
½ cup shortening	1 cup pecans, chopped
2 cups flour	1 teaspoon vanilla
1 teaspoon soda	

Cream the sugar and shortening; add the egg yolks one at a time, beating well after each. Sift the dry ingredients together onto a square of waxed paper and add alternately with the buttermilk. Add the coconut, pecans and vanilla. Beat the egg whites until stiff but not dry. Carefully fold into the cake batter, and pour into a greased and floured bundt cake pan. Bake at 350 degrees 1 hour or until a cake tester comes out clean. Cool 5 minutes in the pan, then remove from the pan to a wire rack to finish cooling.

Cream Cheese Icing:

1 (8-ounce) package cream cheese	½ teaspoon vanilla
¼ cup butter, softened	1 (1-pound) box powdered sugar

Cream butter, cheese and vanilla. Stir in the powdered sugar and beat until smooth. Spread on cooled cake.

GRAHAM CRACKER CREAM PIE

I remember my mother making Graham Cracker Cream Pie when I was a little girl. Sometimes she would make it to take to a Sunday School class party. There is something about the combination of this creamy filling and the graham cracker crust that is absolutely delicious, and definitely the kind of dessert devoured to the last crumb.

1 (9") graham cracker crust	3 large eggs, separated
1 cup sugar	2 tablespoons butter
3 tablespoons flour	2 teaspoons vanilla
3 tablespoons cornstarch	Meringue made from the 3
¼ teaspoon salt	egg whites
3 cups milk	

Bake the graham cracker crust at 350 degrees for 10 minutes. Combine the sugar, flour, cornstarch and salt in a large saucepan. Gradually whisk in the milk. Bring to a boil, stirring occasionally, over medium-high heat; boil 1 minute. Remove from heat. Beat the egg yolks lightly in a small bowl. Gradually whisk in 1 cup of the hot mixture; return to the saucepan, whisking constantly. Place over heat, return to boil, and boil 1 minute longer. Remove from heat and whisk in the butter and vanilla. Cover the surface of the filling with a piece of plastic wrap to help hold in the heat. Prepare the meringue with the remaining egg whites. (Recipe follows). Fill the pie shell with the filling, immediately top with the meringue, place in a 325 degree oven, and bake for about 20 minutes, until light golden brown.

Meringue:

1 tablespoon cornstarch	Pinch of cream of tartar
1 tablespoon + ¼ cup water	¼ cup sugar
3 egg whites	

Dissolve cornstarch in 1 tablespoon water. Bring remaining ¼ cup water to a boil. Add to boiling water and cook and stir until thickened. Cool. Combine egg whites and the cream of tartar in a mixer bowl. Beat until foamy, then add sugar a tablespoon at a time. Beat to stiff peaks, then beat in the cooled cornstarch mixture.

TLC Tip: *This makes a generous amount of filling. You may want to use a 10" crust.*

RUTH'S PEANUT STREUSEL PIE

This is another delicious recipe from my sister's kitchen. If you are a peanut butter fan, you'll love this. I have, on occasion, substituted the Lite Cream Pie Filling for this one when I was feeling a little guilty about my consumption of sugar and fat, and it is still good. But for a once-in-awhile indulgence, go for the real thing.

⅓ cup smooth peanut butter
¾ cup sifted confectioner's
   sugar
1 (9") baked pie shell
⅓ cup flour
⅛ teaspoon salt

3 eggs, separated
2 tablespoons butter
½ cup sugar
2 cups milk, scalded
½ teaspoon vanilla

Blend peanut butter and confectioner's sugar. Sprinkle ⅔ of this mixture over the bottom of the baked pie shell. Combine flour, ½ cup sugar and salt in a medium saucepan. Stir in the scalded milk. Cook over medium heat, stirring constantly, until thickened. Stir a small amount of the cooked filling into the slightly beaten egg yolks. Combine with the remaining hot mixture and cook several minutes longer. Stir in the butter and vanilla. Pour into the pie shell, and top with meringue made from the three egg whites. Sprinkle the remaining peanut butter mixture over the meringue. Bake in a 325 degree oven for 20 minutes or until lightly browned.

Ruth's Meringue:
3 egg whites, room
   temperature
¼ teaspoon cream of tartar

1 tablespoon cornstarch
½ cup sugar

Beat the egg whites until they form soft peaks. Add cream of tartar. Mix the cornstarch and sugar and gradually add the mixture to the egg whites, beating until mixture is stiff and shiny.

DATE CREAM PIE

This is a rather unusual but very delicious pie. It is rich, and you have to like dates to enjoy it. I think of serving this pie around the holidays. I got this recipe from my mother-in-law, Eula Carlile Phillips.

½ cup sugar
¼ cup cornstarch
1 teaspoon salt
2 cups sour cream
2 eggs, slightly beaten

2 cups quartered dates
¼ cup chopped pecans
1 teaspoon lemon juice
1 (9") baked pie shell

Combine sugar, cornstarch and salt. Add sour cream. Cook in a double boiler, stirring constantly, until thickened. Add eggs, return to heat, and continue cooking and stirring for another 5 minutes. Remove from heat, and add the dates and nuts. Cool. Add the lemon juice, and pour into baked pie shell. Chill slightly. Garnish with whipped cream, if desired, and you can afford the additional calories!!

CHOCOLATE CREAM PIE

A meal at the home of friends, Ron and Gloria South, always ended in dessert. It might be as simple as a piece of bread spread with a little jam, a chocolate chip cookie from her freezer stash, or something more elegant, like this delicious chocolate pie. As good friends do, we have shared some wonderful times, the birth of their twin boys is one that comes to mind. We've also shared some not-so-good times, but that's what friends are for. Gloria is a great cook—you'll enjoy her pie.

2 cups milk, scalded
2 (1-ounce) squares
    unsweetened chocolate
¼ cup cornstarch
1 cup sugar
¼ teaspoon salt

3 egg yolks, slightly beaten
2 tablespoons butter
½ teaspoon vanilla
1 (9") baked pie shell
Meringue made from 3 egg
    whites (see index)

Heat the milk in a medium saucepan over moderate heat until bubbles form around the edges. Melt the chocolate in the scalded milk. Mix the cornstarch, sugar and salt in a small bowl; stir into the milk mixture. Cook over moderate heat, stirring constantly, until it boils. Remove from heat, and add a small amount to the beaten egg yolks. Return this mixture to the mixture in the pan, place on burner and cook 2 minutes longer. Remove from heat, add the butter and vanilla. Pour at once into the pie shell, top with the meringue and bake in a 325 degree oven 20 minutes until nicely browned.

COCONUT CREAM PIE

My Aunt Máco was such a dear. She was a great housekeeper, good with needlework and crafts, kept a beautiful yard, and fixed wonderful food. She had a merry laugh and a wonderful spirit. I guess I never expected her to get old, so when she died suddenly at nearly 80, it left a very vacant space in my heart and life. One of the things she left me was this pie recipe. I think of you each time I make it, Aunt Máco!

¾ cup sugar
⅓ cup flour
¼ teaspoon salt
3 egg yolks, beaten
2 cups milk
2 tablespoons butter

1 teaspoon vanilla
1⅓ cups flaked coconut,
    divided use
1 (9") baked pie shell
Meringue made from 3 egg
    whites (see index)

In a medium saucepan, combine the sugar, flour and salt. Gradually stir in the milk. Cook over medium heat, stirring constantly, until mixture boils and thickens. Cook 2 minutes longer, then remove from heat. Add a small amount of the hot mixture to beaten egg yolks, then add this mixture to the mixture in the pan. Cook 2 minutes longer. Remove from heat. Add the butter, vanilla, and 1 cup coconut. Pour into the baked pie shell, cover with meringue, sprinkle ⅓ cup coconut over the top and bake in a 325 degree oven for 20 minutes, until nicely browned.

LEMON CREAM PIE

This pie is a favorite of mine. I like the combination of flavors, and the rich, but refreshing, taste.

1 cup sugar
⅓ cup cornstarch
¼ teaspoon salt
2¾ cups milk
4 large egg yolks, beaten
¼ cup fresh lemon juice

1 tablespoon butter
1 teaspoon vanilla
½ teaspoon grated lemon rind
Pinch of nutmeg
½ cup sour cream
1 (9") baked pie shell

Combine sugar, cornstarch and salt in a large saucepan. Gradually whisk in the milk until smooth. Bring to a boil, stirring gently, over medium high heat; boil 1 minute. Remove from heat. Gradually whisk 1 cup hot mixture into the egg yolks; return to saucepan, whisking constantly. Return to boil and boil 1 minute more. Remove from heat and stir in the lemon juice, butter, vanilla, lemon rind and nutmeg until completely smooth. Cover the surface with waxed paper and cool 15 minutes. Whisk in the sour cream and pour into the pie shell. Cover and refrigerate at least 3 hours before serving. Individual slices may be garnished with whipped cream and a small wedge of thinly sliced lemon if desired.

LITE CREAM PIE FILLING

Here is a cream pie filling that is easy and versatile. I have used it for Coconut Cream Pie, Banana Cream Pie, Banana Pudding and as a filling for cream puffs and eclairs. Cleo likes it because it is less sweet. I'm sure you'll find many uses for it, too.

3 tablespoons cornstarch	2 egg yolks
½ teaspoon salt	1 teaspoon vanilla extract
¼ cup sugar	1 tablespoon butter (optional)
2 cups skim milk	

In a large microwave safe dish, mix cornstarch, salt and sugar. Gradually whisk in milk and egg yolks. Microwave on 100% power for two minutes. Whisk thoroughly, then continue to cook on high power for 5 to 6 minutes, stirring after every minute. When filling has thickened, add vanilla and butter. Cool and use as desired. If adding coconut, now is the time to add it. This filling makes enough for an 8" or 9" pie, adequate, but not generous.

LITE COCONUT CREAM PIE

Prepare cream filling, adding 1 cup flaked coconut with the vanilla and butter. Pour into a baked 9" pie shell. Cover with a meringue made from three egg whites. (Check the index for some good recipes.) Sprinkle a little additional flaked coconut over the meringue. Bake in a 325 degree oven for 20 minutes, until lightly brown.

LITE BANANA CREAM PIE

Prepare cream filling as above recipe directs. Slice 2 or 3 ripe bananas onto the bottom of a baked 9" pie shell. Pour the filling over. Top with a meringue made from 3 egg whites (see index). Bake in a 325 degree oven for 20 minutes.

TLC Tip: *I know it's hard to wait, but these pies need to cool before slicing and serving. I think they are best served at room temperature.*

LEMON MERINGUE PIE

Just remembering the tart sweetness of my mother's Lemon Meringue Pie makes my mouth water! Piled high with fluffy meringue, it was the perfect ending to one of our country meals. Our son, Joey, is fond of this pie.

2 cups water, divided use	1 large lemon, rind and juice
7 tablespoons cornstarch	1 tablespoon butter
1¼ cups sugar	1 (9") baked pie shell
3 egg yolks, slightly beaten	Meringue (recipe follows)

Mix the cornstarch and ½ cup water to make a thin paste. Combine the remaining 1½ cups water and the sugar in the top of a double boiler and bring to a boil over direct heat. Add the cornstarch paste and cook until mixture begins to thicken; place over boiling water and continue cooking until thick and smooth, about 15 minutes. Pour over the slightly beaten egg yolks; return to double boiler, and cook 1 minute longer. Add lemon rind, juice and butter and blend well. Remove from heat and cover surface with plastic wrap to help retain heat while preparing the meringue. When meringue is ready, reheat briefly over medium-low heat and pour into pie shell, top with meringue and bake in a 325 degree oven about 20 minutes, until nicely browned.

Mom's Meringue:

3 egg whites	1 teaspoon lemon juice
9 tablespoons sugar	

Beat the egg whites until stiff but not dry. Add the sugar gradually, beating constantly. Beat in the lemon juice. Pile lightly on filling in baked pie shell. Bake as directed.

303

KEY LIME PIE

Cleo and I love cruising! Lucky for us, that turned out to be one of the perks provided by the electronics distribution business. In 1993, we won a cruise provided by the Fujitsu Company. One of the ports of call was Key West, Florida. Mark Gurvey, National Sales Manager for Fujitsu, and his wife, Karen, accompanied us on a whirl-wind tour of the island. Since we were in port during the early morning hours, eating was not on our mind—that is not until we came upon a restaurant that had just prepared 17 Key lime pies. That morning we "ate dessert first", and savored every bite. When we returned home, I knew I had to try to create that rich, creamy taste. After several unsuccessful attempts, I arrived at this version. I hope you'll enjoy it, too.

1 (9") graham cracker pie shell	½ cup Key lime juice (it will be bottled)
1 (14-ounce) can sweetened condensed milk	4 egg whites, divided use
4 egg yolks	6 tablespoons sugar
	½ teaspoon cream of tartar

Bake the graham cracker pie shell in a 350 degree oven for 8 minutes. Remove from oven and place on a wire rack to cool a little. Mix together condensed milk, egg yolks and lime juice. Beat 1 egg white until stiff. Fold into the egg/milk mixture and pour into the pie shell. Beat the remaining egg whites to a stiff peak, gradually adding sugar and cream of tartar. Spread meringue over filling to the inner edge of the crust. Bake on the middle rack in an oven heated to 350 degrees for 15 to 20 minutes or until egg whites are golden brown. Save up your calories for this one—it is worth it.

TLC Tip: If you can't find key lime juice, you can substitute regular lime juice, in which case I would use fresh limes as I feel fresh is always superior. Key limes are green on the outside and their flesh and juice are yellow. Don't expect your pie filling to be green. There is no law that says you have to use a graham cracker crust, but that is the usual way it is made.

TLC Tip Two: If you wish, you can bake the filled pie for 8-9 minutes without the meringue, chill and top with whipped cream. If I do that, I like to garnish each slice with a strawberry fan and a half slice of lime.

MICHIGAN BLUEBERRY PIE

There's no doubt about it, Michigan blueberries are a sight to behold; plump and large, and faintly frosty looking. We used to pick them by the bucket full, take them home and freeze what didn't get consumed in pie or muffins or just eating right out of hand. Today blueberries are grown in other places too, but when I find some that have the Grand Junction, Michigan, label, my hand just automatically reaches out and they make their way into my shopping cart. Our daughter, Beverly, likes Blueberry Pie. This one's for her.

1 recipe pie crust for double-crust pie
3½ cups fresh blueberries
¾ cup sugar
1 tablespoon freshly grated lemon peel
1 tablespoon freshly squeezed lemon juice
3 tablespoons minute or instant tapioca
2 tablespoons lightly salted butter

Roll out half the pie crust dough to a thickness of about ⅛". Carefully fit it into a 9" glass pie pan and trim the edge even with the pan. Place lined pie pan in the refrigerator to chill while preparing filling. Wash, drain and sort the berries. Toss with the lemon juice. In a small bowl, combine the sugar, tapioca and lemon rind. Mix gently with the berries. (Always use a wooden spoon when mixing fruit.) Let stand 15 minutes. Roll out the top crust, cut some slits for the steam to escape. Turn the berry mixture into the crust; dot with the butter. Ease the top crust over the filled bottom crust; trim the overhang to ¾". Fold the top crust over the bottom crust and press lightly to the rim of the pie pan. Crimp to seal the edges. Bake 50 to 60 minutes in a preheated 400 degree oven until filling bubbles and crust is golden. Served slightly warm with a scoop of good vanilla ice cream, this is sure to please.

TLC Tip: *If the edges of the crust seem like they are browning too fast, tear off a square of foil, cut an 8" hole in the center and lay over the pie. The top will continue to brown and the edges will be protected.*

LINDA'S CRANBERRY APPLE PIE

One of the most requested holiday pies in our family is my sister-in-law's Cranberry Apple. She tells me that she and our mutual friend, Jean McAdams, sort of invented this pie. We love the sharp taste of the cranberries with the mellow taste of the apples. The crunch of walnuts is the crowning touch.

Pastry for a (9") 2-crust pie	½ cup brown sugar, packed
2 cups cranberries, fresh or frozen	1 teaspoon cinnamon
	2 tablespoons flour
4 cups peeled and sliced apples	1 cup coarsely chopped walnuts
1 small orange	2 tablespoons butter
¾ cup granulated sugar	

Roll out the pastry and line a 9" plate; trim the edges, leaving a ½" overhang. Wash the cranberries and pick out any bad ones. Cut the cranberries in half. Grate the peel from the orange, then juice the orange. In a large bowl, combine the cranberries, apples, orange peel and juice. Mix thoroughly. Combine the sugars, cinnamon, flour and walnuts; pour over the cranberry/apple mixture and toss gently to coat. Pour into a pastry-lined pie pan and dot with small pieces of the butter. Roll out top crust and fit it over the fruit. Trim ¾" overhang; fold the edge under the bottom crust and pinch together to seal, making a raised rim all around. Cut several slits or make decorative cutouts in the top crust. Set the pie in the lower third of a preheated 425 degree oven and bake 10 to 12 minutes. Reduce the heat to 350 degrees, raise the pie to the center of the oven, and continue baking an additional 40 to 45 minutes or until the pastry is golden brown and the fruit is tender when pierced with a fork through a vent hole. Check the pie halfway through the baking time and add a foil edging if necessary to prevent the crust from overbrowning. Cool the pie on a wire rack.

CRANBERRY PEAR PIE

When the family gathers for holiday dinners, everyone knows that "Aunt Thelma will make something no one has ever heard of before". This is what I made one Thanksgiving. I can't say that it drew rave reviews, but I loved it. If you like the tartness of cranberries and the flavor of pears, I'm sure you will too. A scoop of vanilla ice cream makes a great accompaniment.

2 (12-ounce) bags fresh or
   frozen cranberries
1½ cups light brown sugar,
   packed
1 cup golden raisins
½ teaspoon freshly grated
   orange peel
¼ cup orange juice
2 tablespoons cornstarch
   mixed with 3 tablespoons
   water

1¼ pounds firm-ripe pears,
   peeled and diced, about
   2½ cups
1 tablespoon heavy cream or
   milk
1 tablespoon granulated
   sugar
Pastry for a 2-crust (10") deep-
   dish pie

Coarsely chop the cranberries, in batches, in food processor or blender. Scrape into a large, heavy pot. Stir in the brown sugar, raisins, orange peel and juice. Bring to a boil, reduce heat and simmer uncovered 5 minutes, stirring mixture until bubbling and syrupy. Stir in cornstarch mixture. Simmer 1 minute or until thickened. Stir in pears, remove from heat and let cool to room temperature. Divide the pie crust into two pieces, one a little larger than the other. Roll the larger piece of dough to a 13" circle. Line pie plate with dough. Spread filling in lined pie plate. Roll out remaining dough to a 12" circle. With a pastry wheel or sharp knife cut ten ½" wide strips. Save the scraps, arrange 5 strips evenly spaced over filling, placing longest near center. Lay remaining strips on top in opposite direction. Press ends to edge of bottom crust. Trim off excess. With fingers, roll overhang of bottom crust up over edges of strips into an even rim. Flute rim. Brush lattice and rim with cream and sprinkle with sugar. Bake in a 400 degree oven for 45 to 55 minutes until lattice and rim are golden brown. Cool; serve at room temperature.

TLC Tip: *If you are feeling creative, you can cut holly leaves and roll holly berries from dough scraps. Arrange leaves on one side of pie and place berries on leaves, using cream for "glue". Brush with additional cream, sprinkle with sugar and proceed with baking as above.*

RHUBARB PINEAPPLE PIE

I think you'll find the combination of rhubarb and pineapple very tasty. Those who think the taste of rhubarb is a little too tangy will like this variation. This is another pie from my mother's files.

3 cups cut rhubarb	Additional brown sugar for
1 cup drained crushed	sprinkling on top of fruit
pineapple	2 eggs
Red food coloring, if desired	3 tablespoons cream
⅓ cup brown sugar	3 tablespoons flour
2 tablespoons melted butter	Dash of salt
3 or 4 drops almond flavoring	Sprinkle of nutmeg
1 (10") unbaked pie shell	¾ cup sugar

Combine the rhubarb, pineapple and food coloring in a large bowl. Pour the brown sugar, butter, and almond flavoring over the fruit and mix thoroughly but gently. Pour into a 10" unbaked pie shell. Sprinkle a little additional sugar over the top, perhaps a tablespoon or two. Combine the remaining ingredients and pour over the fruit mixture. Bake at 425 degrees on bottom shelf of oven for 12 minutes, then move pie to center shelf, reduce the oven temperature to 375 degrees and continue baking for 30 to 40 minutes until bubbly in the center. Cool before serving.

BLUEBERRY BANANA PIE

Another goodie from my sister-in-law, Linda. This pie has been often requested for family get-togethers and church suppers. No one will believe you if you tell them how easy this is to make, so just let it be your little secret.

1 prepared (9") graham	1 can prepared blueberry pie
cracker crumb crust	filling
2 to 3 bananas	1 (8-ounce) container
	whipped topping, thawed

Slice the bananas into the bottom of the pie shell. Cover evenly with the blueberry pie filling. Top with the whipped topping. If you wish, you can decorate the top with banana slices that have been dipped in lemon juice to prevent browning, a few discretely arranged blueberries and some mint leaves. Even without the added touch, 6 to 8 people will be happily contented when you serve them this pie.

TLC Tip: *I have found that the outcome of recipes using bananas is in direct proportion to the ripeness of the bananas. For a recipe such as this one, or banana pudding, they do need to be ripe, as green ones don't seem to impart the right flavor. Now for cake or bread, being a little overripe doesn't make any difference.*

MOM'S RHUBARB CREAM PIE

We had a great rhubarb patch on the farm where I grew up. I loved the looks of the plant—those huge leaves and bright red stalks. We ate a lot of stewed rhubarb during the spring, but once in a while mother would treat us to this pie. In those days I don't think the word "garnish" was in my mother's vocabulary, but the pie was great in all its simplicity. The closest we ever came to embellishing it was to pour some rich Jersey cream over the top. Wow!!

3 cups diced pink rhubarb	3 egg yolks
1 cup sugar	1 tablespoon lemon juice
3 tablespoons flour	1 unbaked (9") pie shell

Arrange the rhubarb in the pie shell. Blend the sugar and flour. Whisk the egg yolks and lemon juice together and stir into the flour/sugar mixture to form a thick paste. (If mixture is too thick to pour, add a tablespoon of milk.) Pour this over the rhubarb and bake at 400 degrees for 20 minutes, then reduce the oven temperature to 350 degrees for 20 minutes. When pie is done, the top will appear a bit crusty. Cool slightly before serving. (Mother's recipe did note that you could serve this with whipped cream, or top with a meringue made from the reserved egg whites. I never use the meringue but who knows, it might be a whole new taste.)

TLC Tip: *Don't expect a cream pie as in "chocolate cream pie." I think it gets its name from the creamy rather than clear thickening.*

STREUSEL CREAM PEACH PIE

When you can get the kind of peaches that smell like peaches, in season, naturally, this pie is wonderful. Made from loose pack frozen peaches it is still good. Top this one with a little whipped cream or cinnamon flavored sour cream or yogurt if you like.

4 cups quartered peeled peaches (8 to 10)	1 egg
	2 tablespoons cream
1 (9") unbaked pastry shell	¼ cup brown sugar, packed
½ cup sugar	½ cup flour
½ teaspoon nutmeg (optional)	½ cup soft butter

Arrange peaches in pie shell. Sprinkle sugar and nutmeg over peaches. Beat egg and cream together; then pour over peaches and sugar. Mix brown sugar, flour and butter until crumbly. Sprinkle crumb mixture over fruit in pie pan. Bake in 425 degree oven for 35 to 45 minutes or until browned and bubbly. Serve slightly warm.

EVERYTHING PIE

This is a rather unusual name for a rather unusual pie. I got this recipe from a friend, Linda Bloom, many years ago. She and her husband, John, live in Duncanville, Texas. I have used it quite often as it makes 2 to 4 pies, depending on the size of pan used. If you are serving a crowd, this is definitely a plus. This is another pie that is further enhanced by a dab of whipped cream or other similar topping.

1 (16-ounce) can sour pie
   cherries
1 (20-ounce) can crushed
   pineapple
7 tablespoons cornstarch
2 cups sugar

6 bananas, sliced
1 cup pecans, chopped
1 teaspoon vanilla
1 teaspoon red food coloring,
   if desired
2 to 4 baked pie shells

Drain the fruit, saving the juice. Add enough water to the juice to make 2 cups. Pour into a saucepan and add the sugar and cornstarch. Cook, stirring constantly, over medium heat until thick. Set aside to cool, then add the reserved fruit, bananas, nuts, vanilla and food coloring. Pour into baked pie shells. Chill. Top with desired topping.

TLC Tip: *If you use the small pie shells you purchase from the frozen food case, you will probably need 4 shells. If you make your own crust, two to three 9" shells will hold the filling.*

SOUTHERN CHESS PIE

This recipe was given to my mother by Velma Forgy. Velma was a great niece of Jefferson Davis, and she said this was his favorite pie. Velma made a lovely handkerchief that my mother carried on her wedding day. I carried it on my wedding day, as did my sister, my sister-in-law, my daughters, and my nieces. It is now being saved for the next generation of weddings. As with all chess pies, this is a very sweet pie but Velma said "you can serve with whipped cream if you wish".

1½ cups sugar
½ cup butter
3 eggs
½ cup half-and-half

1 tablespoon cornmeal
1 teaspoon vanilla
Pinch of salt
1 (9") unbaked pastry shell

Cream the butter and sugar. Add the eggs, one at a time, beating well after each addition. Stir in the cream, cornmeal, vanilla and salt, using the low speed on the mixer or by hand. Pour into pie shell; bake at 350 degrees for 30 to 40 minutes, or until a table knife inserted one inch from edge of crust comes out clean.

FRESH STRAWBERRY PIE

During the 1950's, when I was in college in Anderson, Indiana, a local restaurant chain was famous for its fresh strawberry pie. In those parts, restaurants still serve a lot of this type of pie when strawberries are in season, and these days, even when they are out of season, I expect. The last time I was in Anderson, I ordered a piece of Strawberry Pie. My taste must have changed, because I think this one is better. You won't be disappointed and your friends and family will love you forever for fixing them this treat.

1 cup sugar	3 tablespoons dry strawberry
2 tablespoons white corn	gelatin
syrup	1 quart strawberries
3 tablespoons cornstarch	1 (9") baked pie shell
1 cup water	

In a medium saucepan, combine the sugar, corn syrup, cornstarch and water. Bring to a boil over moderate heat and cook, stirring constantly, until mixture is thick and clear. Remove from heat, add gelatin and mix well. Set aside to cool slightly. Meanwhile, wash strawberries thoroughly but gently, hull, and slice or cut in half, depending on the size. Carefully fold the strawberries into the cooked mixture, then pour into prepared shell. Chill several hours until firm. Of course this needs to be served with a generous dollop of whipped cream and garnished with one perfect stem-on strawberry.

TLC Tip: An alternate way to serve this is to clean and hull the berries, then place stem end down, pointed end up, in the pie shell. Fill vacant spaces with berry halves or quarters. When all berries are arranged, pour cooked filling over. This makes a gorgeous presentation.

GRANDMOTHER'S CUSTARD PIE

My husband's mother, Eula Carlile Phillips, makes great custard pies—all the grandkids rave about them, and fight over who gets the last piece at family celebrations. Her fame with custard pies began long ago, as it was the favorite pie of her first husband, Clifford, my husband's father. He was a gentle giant of a man, a minister who pastored churches in Oklahoma, Kansas and Colorado before he became ill with cancer. In the short time I was privileged to be around him, it was easy to see why he and my father were friends. Though recovering from his first surgery, he made the trip to Michigan to marry Cleo and me in December of 1969. Eula told me that she got this recipe from a friend in her Home Demonstration Club in Texhoma, Oklahoma, many years ago. I am glad she did! I must confess that I make this pie seldom, not wanting to compete with her success, I suppose.

4 eggs	**½ teaspoon almond flavoring**
½ cup sugar	**2½ cups milk, scalded**
¼ teaspoon salt	**1 (9") unbaked pastry shell**
½ teaspoon vanilla	**Dash of nutmeg, optional**

Beat eggs slightly, add sugar, salt and flavorings. Heat the milk until bubbles appear around the edge. Slowly pour the scalded milk into the egg mixture, stirring as it is added. Add a dash of nutmeg, if desired. Pour into pie shell. Place on lowest rack in 400 degree oven. Bake for 25 to 30 minutes. The tip of a silver knife inserted in center of pie will come out almost clean when custard is done. Let cool before cutting. I know, it's hard to wait, but it will be worth it!

TLC Tip: When making the filling for custard-type pies, I find it best not to use an electric mixer to beat the eggs. Somehow it beats too much air into the mixture. A wire whisk (my favorite) or wooden spoon is better.

TLC Tip Two: I have used 1 cup skim evaporated milk and 1½ cups skim milk in this recipe with good results. I doubt Grandmother would ever do that, however.

TLC Tip Three: Baking a custard pie with a flaky bottom crust can be a bit tricky. Baking it on the lowest rack of the oven does seem to help. I have baked the crust 10 minutes before pouring in the filling, then continued to bake for the regular time. If the edges of the crust start to get too brown, cover with foil for remaining baking time.

BANANAS FOSTER PECAN PIE

Who would think—bananas in a pecan pie! The flavor will remind you of the popular dessert immortalized by Brennan's Restaurant.

1 cup firmly packed light brown sugar	1 teaspoon cinnamon
	¼ teaspoon salt
3 eggs, beaten	1 large banana, cubed
½ cup light corn syrup	1 cup chopped toasted pecans
¼ cup melted butter	1 (9") unbaked pie shell
2 teaspoons rum flavoring	

In a large mixing bowl, combine the sugar, eggs, corn syrup, flavoring, cinnamon and salt. I like to use a hand mixer and low speed. Fold in the banana and pecans. Pour into the pie shell. Bake in a 375 degree oven for 45 minutes, until crust is golden brown and filling is set. Cool before serving. There are some who insist on a scoop of ice cream with this!

MOCHA PECAN PIE

For all you coffee and chocolate lovers, this pie's for you!! A great combination of these two flavors, easy to put together and easier yet to disappear. I like to garnish this with a puff of whipped cream and a few chocolate covered coffee beans.

2 tablespoons instant coffee (I like espresso)	4 large eggs
	½ cup sugar
¼ cup boiling water	1 cup dark corn syrup
2 ounces unsweetened chocolate	1½ cups coarsely chopped pecans
2 tablespoons butter	1 unbaked (9") pie shell

Dissolve coffee powder in boiling water in a small saucepan. Add chocolate and butter; stir constantly over low heat until chocolate and butter are melted and mixture is smooth. Cool slightly. In a large bowl beat the eggs slightly with a wire whisk. (Don't use an electric mixer, as this whips the eggs too much.) Beat in sugar and corn syrup until blended. Gradually stir in the chocolate mixture until well mixed. Stir in the pecans. Pour into pastry shell. Bake at 375 degrees until a knife inserted halfway between the outside and center comes out clean, about 40-45 minutes. Cool on a wire rack.

CHOCOLATE PECAN PIE

Easy to prepare, delicious to eat, what more could you ask? Serve with whipped cream or ice cream, if you dare, or try nonfat frozen yogurt. (That's a little like having a cheeseburger and fries and a diet coke!)

1 (9") unbaked pie shell	1½ teaspoons vanilla
¼ cup chopped pecans	1½ cups semi-sweet chocolate
¾ cup dark corn syrup	chips, melted
3 eggs	¾ cup pecan halves
½ teaspoon salt	

Press the ¼ cup chopped pecans into the bottom of the pie shell. Combine syrup, eggs, salt and vanilla and beat well with a wooden spoon or wire whisk. Slowly add the chocolate to the egg mixture and beat briskly until blended. Stir in the pecan halves and pour into prepared crust. Bake on the lowest rack in preheated 350 degree oven about 30 minutes. Cool. Small slices are in order here—this pie is rich.

CHERRY CREAM PIE

When you forgot about the church dinner, or are called on to bring dessert at the last minute, pull this recipe out of your hat. I guarantee that it will disappear almost before you set it on the table. It makes a large 10" pie. An added bonus is that you can serve it from a bowl for a dessert/salad or spoon it into pretty goblets. I like to prepare the latter by layering it with graham cracker crumbs, then topping with whipped topping and sprinkling a few crumbs on the topping.

1 (14-ounce) can condensed milk	2 packages Dream Whip, prepared or 1 (8- or 12-
¼ cup lemon juice	ounce) tub whipped
1 (8-ounce) can crushed pineapple, drained	topping, thawed
1 (16-ounce) can pitted sour cherries, drained	½ cup chopped nuts
	1 (10") baked pie shell or graham cracker crust

Combine milk and lemon juice, mixing with a whisk until slightly thickened. Stir in drained pineapple, cherries and the chopped nuts. Fold in the whipped topping. Spoon into a baked 10" pie shell or graham cracker crust, or prepare to serve in one of the ways suggested above. Chill several hours.

MY FAVORITE PUMPKIN PIE

*What would fall be without Pumpkin Pie, much less Thanksgiving? Pumpkin pies are not difficult to make. This one makes enough filling for a 10"
crust and even then you might have enough left over to fill a custard cup—
cook's treat!! The spice mixture in this filling seems to be just right to suit
my family. I hope your family likes it too.*

1 unbaked (10") pie shell	½ teaspoon salt
2 eggs	1 teaspoon ground cinnamon
1 (16-ounce) can solid pack	½ teaspoon ground ginger
pumpkin (I like the	¼ teaspoon ground cloves
Libby's brand)	1 (12-ounce) can undiluted
¾ cup granulated sugar	evaporated milk

Beat the eggs lightly in large bowl. Stir in the remaining ingredients in
order given. Pour into the pie shell. Bake 15 minutes at 450 degrees, then
reduce the oven temperature to 350 degrees and continue baking for 40 to
50 minutes or until knife inserted in center comes out clean. The center
may seem a little soft, but will firm up as it cools. Cool on a wire rack.

TLC Tip: *I always use glass pie pans. If you use metal, bake the pie on a
preheated baking sheet.*

SWEET POTATO PIE

*A little more dense, and I think a little richer, than a pumpkin pie, this one
is especially enjoyed by niece Lisa Hancock. I like to prepare the potatoes by
baking or boiling them in their skins, then peeling and coarsely mashing
them. This pie should have a little texture. Like its cousin, it needs a
topping of whipped cream!*

2 cups mashed cooked sweet	1 teaspoon bourbon flavoring
potatoes	¾ teaspoon cinnamon
¾ cup packed light brown	½ teaspoon allspice
sugar	¼ teaspoon nutmeg
1½ cups evaporated milk	¼ teaspoon salt
¼ cup melted butter, cooled	1 (9") unbaked pie shell
3 eggs, beaten	

In a large mixing bowl, blend the sweet potatoes, sugar, milk, butter, eggs,
flavoring, spices and salt until smooth. Pour into the pie shell. Bake in a
400 degree oven for 45 to 55 minutes. Let cool before serving.

UNBELIEVABLE LEMON PIE

This is for one of those nights when you rush home after a busy day of work or errands, and you want to spiff up a simple supper with a special dessert. No one will believe how easy this was to make! Looks make a lot of difference, so don't forget to garnish with a little whipped topping and half a thin slice of lemon.

1 (14-ounce) can condensed milk	3 eggs
1 cup water	¼ cut butter, softened
½ cup lemon juice	1½ teaspoons vanilla
½ cup biscuit mix	1 cup flaked coconut

Combine all the ingredients except the coconut in a blender container. Blend on low speed for 3 minutes. Pour mixture into a greased 10" pie plate; let set 5 minutes. Sprinkle the coconut on the top. Bake at 350 degrees for 35-40 minutes or until a knife inserted near the edge comes out clean. Cool slightly; serve warm or cool. Refrigerate the leftovers, if there are any!

CHOCOLATE BAR PIE

This is a rich pie perfect for luncheons or dessert teas. Serve it in small pieces.

10 large marshmallows	1 teaspoon instant coffee
¼ cup milk (whole milk is best)	1 (4-ounce) container whipped topping, thawed
1 (4-ounce) milk chocolate candy bar, broken into pieces	1 (9") chocolate cookie crust
	¼ cup chopped almonds, toasted

Combine the marshmallows and milk in the top of a double boiler; cook over simmering water until marshmallows are just melted. Remove from heat; add chocolate bar and coffee powder, stirring until chocolate melts. Let mixture cool to room temperature. Fold whipped topping into chocolate mixture. Pour into crust and sprinkle almonds over top of pie. Chill at least 4 hours. To make a stunning presentation, drizzle melted chocolate on the dessert plate before placing the serving of pie on it.

TLC Tip: *Skim milk doesn't seem to work well in this recipe.*

PEACH SKILLET PIE

This dessert is sort of a marriage between a cobbler and a pie. We used to make it on the farm when the peaches were at their juiciest. This is best served slightly warm and a dip of good ice cream along the side doesn't hurt either.

For the dough:

2 cups flour
4 teaspoons baking powder
½ teaspoon salt

6 tablespoons shortening or
    butter
½ to ⅔ cup milk

Combine dry ingredients in medium-sized bowl. Cut in shortening or butter. Stir in the smallest amount of milk, adding more if necessary to make a dough that is soft. Turn out onto a floured counter; knead lightly about 10 times, then roll out into a circle about ¼" thick. Place in a 10" cast iron skillet, letting dough hang over the edge.

For the filling:

6 to 8 fully ripe peaches,
    peeled and sliced
¾ cup sugar

½ teaspoon salt
½ teaspoon cinnamon
2 tablespoons butter

Put the sliced peaches in the dough-lined skillet. Combine the sugar, salt, and cinnamon; sprinkle over the peaches. Dot with small pieces of the butter. Fold the edges of the dough over the peaches, leaving the center uncovered. Bake in a 450 degree oven for 10 minutes, then reduce the oven temperature to 375 degrees and continue baking about 40 minutes.

WIN SCHULER'S WALNUT CREAM PIE

Schuler's is a well-known restaurant in lower Michigan. During my grow-
ing-up years, people would travel some distance just to experience the
wonderful food. This pie will make you wish you could go there too.

1 (3-ounce) package butterscotch pudding, cooked type	2 teaspoons vanilla
	1 (9") cookie crumb crust
	24 caramels, unwrapped
1⅔ cups milk	6 ounces semi-sweet chocolate chips
1 egg yolk	
3 tablespoons butter	½ cup butter
¾ cup whipping cream	½ cup light corn syrup
⅓ cup powdered sugar	2 cups chopped walnuts
Dash of salt	

Combine the pudding mix, milk and egg yolk in a medium saucepan. Cook over medium-high heat, stirring constantly, until mixture thickens and just comes to a boil. Remove from heat at once and stir in the butter. Chill until completely cold (covered in the freezer for 45 minutes will do it). Beat the whipping cream with powdered sugar and dash of salt and vanilla until thick and able to hold its shape. Beat chilled pudding about 1 minute, then fold in the whipped cream until thoroughly combined. Pour into prepared crust. Freeze until firm, several hours or overnight. Prepare the sauce by placing the remaining ingredients in the top of a double boiler over simmering water, stirring until smooth. Keep sauce warm or reheat gently. To serve, remove pie from freezer and let set 20 to 30 minutes at room temperature. Spoon warm sauce over individual servings. Yum!!

TLC Tip: *This is a lush dessert! The sauce is wonderful. You must serve the sauce warm, as it is very thick and chewy when cold. It keeps well, and reheats over low heat beautifully. If you don't have a double boiler, you can prepare it in a saucepan over low heat IF you stir frequently and watch carefully.*

PIÑA COLADA PIE

I like this pie for its ease of preparation. I like eating it for the way it makes me feel. Somehow the flavors of pineapple and coconut remind me of swaying palm trees and lapping waves and the sound of ukuleles being strummed as the sun sets over the water. It's like a mini Hawaiian vacation.

1 (9") graham cracker pie crust	1 (8-ounce) can crushed pineapple, drained
8 ounces cream cheese, softened	1 teaspoon rum extract
3 tablespoons sugar	1 teaspoon coconut extract
¾ cup milk	1 (8-ounce) container whipped topping, thawed

Beat the cream cheese with the sugar until fluffy; add the milk and flavoring gradually. (This step is important to the final texture of the pie, so don't cheat here.) Fold in the pineapple and whipped topping. Let set slightly before spooning into the pie shell. Chill several hours before serving. Garnish with flaked coconut and/or toasted chopped almonds if desired.

TLC Tip: *Personally, I like the added sweetness that the sweetened crushed pineapple adds to this pie. If you prefer a less sweet pie, go with the pineapple in its own juice.*

PUMPKIN CHIFFON PRALINE PIE

This is another very impressive pie!! For years, this was requested for every Thanksgiving get together, even though regular pumpkin pie was on the menu.

⅓ cup butter
⅓ cup firmly packed brown
    sugar
⅓ cup chopped nuts
1 (10") baked pie shell
¾ cup sugar
1 envelope unflavored gelatin
1½ teaspoons pumpkin pie
    spice

½ teaspoon salt
4 egg yolks, slightly beaten
1 (16-ounce) can pumpkin
¾ cup milk
4 egg whites
¼ cup sugar
½ cup cream, whipped

Cream the butter and brown sugar well in a small bowl; stir in the nuts. Spread on the bottom of the pie shell; bake 5 minutes in a 450 degree oven. Cool completely. Combine the ¾ cup sugar, gelatin, pumpkin pie spice and salt in top of double boiler; stir in egg yolks, pumpkin and milk. Cook over hot, not boiling, water, stirring constantly, 15 minutes or until completely heated through and gelatin is dissolved; chill just until mixture starts to set. Beat egg whites until foamy in large bowl; beat in the ¼ cup sugar, a tablespoon at a time, until meringue forms soft peaks; set bowl in pan of ice. Beat pumpkin gelatin mixture until fluffy; gently fold into chilled meringue, still over ice. Spoon into prepared pie shell, making deep swirls on top with tip of spoon. Chill until firm. Decorate with a crown of whipped cream and more chopped nuts before serving.

TLC Tip: Don't try to put this filling into a 9" crust—there is too much. Should you have to do this, lacking a 10" pie pan, spoon the extra filling into custard cups as an extra treat for the cook!!

LEMON CHIFFON PIE

I first made this pie soon after I was married. It is so impressive, all that fluffy filling piled high. It is also a light dessert, perfect as the ending to a spring or summer meal. Try substituting orange or lime juice and rind for the lemon juice and rind in this recipe.

½ cup sugar
1 envelope unflavored gelatin
⅔ cup water
½ cup fresh lemon juice
4 egg yolks, slightly beaten

1 tablespoon grated lemon
   rind
4 egg whites
½ teaspoon cream of tartar
½ cup sugar
1 (9") baked pie shell

Blend the sugar, gelatin, water, juice and egg yolks in a saucepan. Cook over medium heat, stirring constantly, until it boils. Add the rind. Place the pan in cold water; cool until mixture mounds slightly when dropped from a spoon. Beat the egg whites until foamy, add the cream of tartar and continue beating until soft peaks form. Gradually add the sugar, beating until stiff peaks form. Fold the gelatin mixture into the meringue until no streaks of white remain. Pile into a cooled, baked 9" pie shell. Chill several hours until set. Garnish with whipped cream and a small, thin slice of lemon if desired.

TLC Tip: *If using lime juice, you can add a drop or two of green food coloring to intensify the color if you wish. Personally, I find there is a fine line between green and too green, so proceed cautiously.*

MOCHA MACAROON PIE

This is more of a fancy dessert than a pie, in the true sense of the word, but delicious any way you look at it. It is not difficult to make, and will surely up your rating as a great cook.

6 ounces sweet baking chocolate (like German's)	Dash of salt
1¼ cups graham cracker crumbs	5 egg whites at room temperature
⅓ cup chopped pecans, toasted	2 teaspoons vanilla, divided
1 cup sugar	2 teaspoons instant coffee
1 teaspoon baking powder	1 cup whipping cream
	¼ cup powdered sugar

Grate the chocolate into a large bowl; remove and reserve 1 tablespoon for garnish. Add graham cracker crumbs and pecans to the chocolate, blending thoroughly. Combine sugar and baking powder in a small bowl. Add salt to egg whites in large mixer bowl; beat with electric mixer at high speed until foamy and double in volume. Add sugar mixture, a tablespoon at a time, until meringue forms stiff peaks. Add 1 teaspoon of vanilla to the meringue with the last addition of sugar. Fold in crumb-nut mixture. Generously butter a 10" pie plate, including the rim. Pour in the meringue mixture. Bake in a 350 degree oven for 30 minutes or until browned and firm to the touch. Cool on wire rack. Combine remaining 1 teaspoon vanilla with water and instant coffee, stir to dissolve coffee. Stir in heavy cream and powdered sugar. Chill several hours. About 1 hour before serving, whip cream mixture until soft peaks form. Spread in center of pie. Sprinkle with reserved grated chocolate. Garnish with pecan halves, if desired.

TLC Tip: *My salad shooter does a very good job of grating the chocolate. As an alternative for the heavy cream, I have used light whipped topping. I dissolved 2 teaspoons instant coffee in a small amount of hot water and folded it into the topping. Worked just fine.*

PEANUT BUTTER PIE

This is a very easy pie to make, impressive to serve, great to have in the freezer for those times you need a dessert in a hurry or to make ahead for a party or special dinner, luncheon or shower. My cousin Jean rates this A+.

1 pound cream cheese, softened	1 (12-ounce) container whipped topping, thawed
2 cups confectioner's sugar	2 cookie crumb crusts, chocolate or vanilla
1 (14-ounce) can condensed milk	Additional topping for garnish, if desired
1½ cups smooth peanut butter	

Using an electric mixer, cream the cream cheese, sugar and milk. This will take a while, be patient. Stir in the peanut butter until well mixed. Fold in the whipped topping. Pour into the prepared crusts, dividing the filling evenly. Smooth the tops, cover with foil, and freeze. To serve, remove from freezer, let stand at room temperature 15 to 30 minutes before serving. Don't let pie stand too long or it will be too soft to slice and serve. Cut into desired slices. This is a very rich pie, so servings can be small and still satisfying. Garnish with whipped topping. When I use a chocolate crust, I like to sprinkle chocolate shot or curls over the topping. If I use a vanilla crust, I like to sprinkle on chopped salted peanuts. My cousin, Jean, likes to garnish her servings with a miniature peanut butter cup. Talk about gilding the lily!!

TLC Tip: *I almost always use lite cream cheese in this recipe, and it is still plenty rich. Suit yourself.*

JAPANESE FRUIT PIE

A little like a light fruitcake baked in a crust, this unusual pie will disappear quickly from your dessert table.

1 cup sugar	2 dozen candied cherries,
½ cup melted butter	halved
½ cup flaked coconut	2 eggs, beaten
½ cup golden raisins	1 teaspoon vanilla
½ cup toasted pecans	1 teaspoon cider vinegar
½ cup crushed pineapple,	1 (9") unbaked pie shell
very well drained	

Blend all the ingredients except the crust in a mixing bowl. Pour into pie shell. Bake in a 325 degree oven for about 40 minutes, until filling is set. Let cool at least 2 hours before cutting.

FOOLPROOF PIE CRUST

For some of you, foolproof pie crust may mean purchasing the refrigerated kind that you unfold and place in the pan. And that isn't all bad, I've used it many a time. Do keep in mind that the prepared crust contains lard, which makes a flaky crust but is a saturated fat. This crust is simple to make, and makes enough for you to freeze the extra to have at a moment's notice—your very own refrigerated dough! Give it a try.

4 cups flour	½ cup water
1 tablespoon sugar	1 tablespoon vinegar
2 teaspoons salt	1 large egg
1¾ cups shortening	

In large bowl, stir together, with a fork, the flour, sugar and salt; cut in shortening until crumbly. In small bowl, beat together the water, vinegar and egg; add to flour mixture and stir until all ingredients are moistened. Divide dough into 5 portions and, with hands, shape each into a flat round patty, ready for rolling. Wrap each patty in plastic or waxed paper and chill at least ½ hour. When you are ready to use the pie crust, lightly flour both sides of the patty and roll out on lightly floured board or pastry cloth. Fold in half and transfer to pie pan. Bake as individual recipe directs. You can prevent a soggy bottom crust by baking pie on lowest rack of oven at temperature specified in individual recipe. For baked pie shell, prick bottom and sides of pastry with fork. Bake on center rack in preheated 450 degree oven 12 to 15 minutes or until golden brown. Cool on wire rack; fill as desired.

GRANDMOTHER'S PIE CRUST

This is the pie crust Grandmother makes to go with her custard pie. Somehow, I was surprised to see how this was put together, but Grandmother told me that she uses these ingredients but mixes it in the usual way, cutting in the shortening and then mixing in the water by hand. You might keep that in mind when you prepare this crust.

1½ cups sifted all-purpose
    flour
½ teaspoon salt

⅓ cup shortening (do not use
    butter, margarine or oil)
3 to 4 tablespoons ice water

Place flour and salt in large mixer bowl. Add shortening and beat on lowest speed of mixer until mixture resembles coarse crumbs, about 2 minutes, scraping bowl occasionally. Sprinkle 3 tablespoons water over flour mixture and continue beating on low speed only to blend, about ½ minute, adding more water if necessary to hold dough together. Remove from bowl, press into a ball, roll lightly on floured board from center out to edge, forming a circle about ⅛" thick. Fold in half, fit into pie pan, unfold, trim 1" beyond edge of pan. Tuck edge under and flute as desired, pressing edge to pan. Chill ½ hour. If baking without filling, prick all over with fork. After chilling time, fill and bake as recipe directs for custard type pies. For baked pie shell, place in 450 degree oven for 10 to 12 minutes until golden brown.

TLC Tip: *There are those who say that pastry flour makes the best pie crusts. You might want to try it. It can be purchased at most health food stores or my mail order. Check the sources elsewhere in this book for possibilities.*

GRAHAM CRACKER CRUST

Use this recipe for any pie needing a graham cracker crust, or other desserts using a crust of this nature.

6 tablespoons butter
1½ cups graham cracker
    crumbs (about 20 squares)

¼ cup sugar

Melt the butter. Combine crumbs and sugar. Pour in the butter and toss. Press crumbs evenly over bottom and sides of a 9" pie plate. Chill until firm or bake at 350 degrees for 8 minutes.

MIXER PIE CRUST

This is a rather unusual way to prepare pie crust, but I think you will like it. Why not give it a try?

3 cups flour	2 teaspoons salt
¾ cup shortening	2½ teaspoons powdered milk
4 teaspoons sugar	½ cup very cold water

Combine all ingredients except the water in mixer bowl. Mix until shortening is broken into small pieces. With hands, make a well in the mixture; add the water all at once. Mix just until dough is formed, adding a few drops of water if necessary. This makes enough dough for a double crust pie or 2 pie shells. Shape as desired. Bake double crust pie as recipe directs. For pie shells, bake at 450 degrees for 10 to 12 minutes. Cool before filling.

TLC Tip: *I like to use pie weights when baking a pie shell. These weights are ceramic, and can be used over and over. You can also use dry beans or rice in the same way. I line the shell with a piece of foil, add the weights, and bake for about half the total time, then remove the weights and finish baking. My shells look nicer since I have been doing this.*

LINDA'S NEVER FAIL PIE CRUST

Linda is fond of making her pie crusts with oil. That isn't such a bad idea—you still have the fat, but it isn't saturated. Some say that whatever "shortening" you use for pie crust should be cold. Linda follows through with using chilled oil.

3 cups flour	¼ cup + 2 tablespoons cold
1 teaspoon salt	milk
¾ cup cold canola oil	

Stir all ingredients together lightly. Form into a ball with your hands. Divide in half; place one half between sheets of lightly floured waxed paper and roll out to desired size. Don't chill before rolling. Once the pastry is arranged in the plate, then chill at least 30 minutes. Use the remaining dough for a top crust, or arrange in a second plate. Bake as recipe directs.

TLC Tip: *There are those who say you should butter a pie plate before pressing in the pastry. It makes the pie easier to serve.*
TLC Tip Two: *I have prepared this crust in my food processor. If you choose to use this method, use the guidelines that came with your processor. Just be sure not to overmix.*

Cookies and Candies

The cookies of my childhood were Sugar, Molasses, Peanut Butter and Oatmeal. Grandmother's sugar and molasses were large, thick, soft rounds, dusted with flour, and just great alone or with a tall glass of milk. I'm sure she used lard as the shortening! My mother's Peanut Butter Cookies were a rich, crisp yet soft cookie, with ridges on the top, not the kind with chocolate kisses stuck in the middle. Oatmeal were chunky and moist, with plenty of raisins to bite into. Fudge was popular—we always played the guessing game, would it set up? Did we cook it long enough? (We didn't own a candy thermometer—we just dropped a little bit into a cup of cold water, and watched to see if it formed a ball of the right consistency.) Would it be smooth or grainy? One of our neighbor ladies made a great grainy fudge. I loved it! It was only much later that I learned fudge really wasn't supposed to have that texture and that smooth was what you aimed for. Mother made very good divinity—often with black walnuts added to please my father. We pulled taffy occasionally, but only in the winter months. I think it had something to do with the weather. We never bought much candy, though occasionally dad would come home with a bag of orange slices. On the rare occasions we went swimming at Base Line Lake, we got a Slowpoke—that wonderful caramel on a stick.

GRANDMA'S FAVORITE MOLASSES COOKIES

I can't be positive that these are my grandmother's molasses cookies. But the recipe was in my mother's files, a brown, tattered page from an old farm magazine. If it isn't "the one" it surely is close—thick and soft—the kind that marries so well with a tall, cool glass of milk. My grandmother never bothered with fancy shapes, preferring instead the simplicity and ease of an overturned glass or a biscuit cutter. However, I have used this dough to make great little bunnies and such. The original recipe called for lard. I have substituted shortening.

½ cup shortening	½ teaspoon cinnamon
¾ cup sugar	1½ teaspoons ginger
1 egg	2 teaspoons soda
½ cup sour cream (I use lite)	½ teaspoon salt
½ cup molasses	3 to 3½ cups flour, divided

Cream the shortening and sugar. Add the egg and beat until all are well mixed. Combine the salt, ginger and cinnamon with 1½ cups of the flour; add alternately with the sour cream. Stir the soda into the molasses and add to above mixture. Add enough more flour to make a soft dough. (It will take upwards to 1½ to 2 cups more flour depending on weather conditions, etc.) Chill well at least 2 hours or even overnight, tightly covered. Roll out on lightly floured surface to ¼" thickness. (You can roll them thinner, but if you want them like my grandmother made them, ¼" is about right.) Cut into shapes with floured cutter. Place on ungreased cookie sheet and bake at 350 degrees about 9 minutes. Do not overbake. You want nice soft cookies, not rocks. Remove from pan immediately with spatula and allow to cool on wire racks. Store tightly covered—but watch carefully—these may disappear right off the cooling racks.

TLC Tip: *You can sprinkle the tops of the cookies with a little granulated sugar before baking if you wish.*

GAYLE'S SUGAR COOKIES

Gayle Charles lives in Green Bay, Wisconsin where her husband, Dave, is in the electronics and plumbing distribution business. This recipe is her family's favorite—so much so, in fact, that each year she makes two batches—always after the 15th of December so they will last through the holidays. The touch of maple syrup is unusual.

2 cups sugar	1 teaspoon vanilla
1½ cups butter	4 cups flour
3 eggs	1 teaspoon each soda, salt and
½ teaspoon maple syrup	baking powder
(the real stuff)	¼ teaspoon nutmeg

Cream butter and sugar; add the eggs and mix well. Add maple syrup, vanilla and flour. Mix in the soda, salt, baking powder and nutmeg. Batter will be stiff. Chill about 1 hour. Roll ¼" thick. Cut into shapes. Place on greased sheet in a 350 degree oven for 6-10 minutes. Remove from baking sheet to wire rack to cool. Frost and decorate as desired.

TLC Tip: *Weather affects flour—if there has been a lot of humidity, you may need a little more flour to make a dough that holds the shape well.*

SUGAR COOKIE CUT-OUTS

As a third-grade teacher I was always making treats for my class to celebrate special days. Seems like we were always celebrating something! This recipe has yielded shamrocks, hearts, Easter eggs or bunnies, pumpkins and trees depending on the holiday. You will need to make 1½ times this recipe to make 30 cookies of a decent size. These cookies are perfect for decorating.

¾ cup shortening (part butter	½ teaspoon lemon flavoring
makes a good flavor)	or 1 teaspoon vanilla
1 cup sugar	2½ cups flour
2 eggs	1 teaspoon baking powder
	1 teaspoon salt

Mix the shortening, sugar, eggs and flavoring well. Blend the flour, baking powder and salt; stir in. Chill at least 1 hour. Roll ⅛" thick on floured board. Cut into desired shapes. Place on ungreased baking sheet. Bake at 400 degrees for 6 to 8 minutes. Cool on wire racks.

TLC Tip: *Just a reminder that the cookie sheet should be cold before you place the cut-out dough on it. That is where having more than one helps— I like three. One in the oven, one cooling and one to fill with cookies.*

330

SWEDISH GINGER COOKIES

These cookies are crisp and flavorful, just crying to be dunked in a big glass of milk. I made these when I taught a unit about "Christmas Around the World" as part of my third grade curriculum. When we studied Sweden, we always chose a St. Lucy, who dressed up in a white dress (we dispensed with the wreath of lighted candles on her head) and passed out the cookies to her classmates on December 5. If you are partial to ginger snaps, this will be one of your favorites.

1 cup butter
1½ cups sugar
1 egg
1½ tablespoons grated orange
   peel
2 tablespoons dark corn syrup
1 tablespoon water

3¼ cups flour
2 teaspoons soda
2 teaspoons cinnamon
1 teaspoon ginger
½ teaspoon cloves
Blanched almonds for
   decoration

Thoroughly cream the butter and sugar. Add egg; beat until fluffy. Add orange peel, corn syrup, and water; mix well. Sift together dry ingredients; stir into creamed mixture. Chill dough thoroughly. On a lightly floured surface, roll to ⅛" thick. Sprinkle dough with sugar; press in lightly with rolling pin. Cut into desired shapes. Top each with an almond half. Bake at 375 degrees for 8 to 10 minutes. Cool slightly; remove from baking sheet to wire rack to finish cooling.

BUTTERSCOTCH STICKS

A good bar cookie is hard to beat when time is of essence. These fill the bill nicely.

½ cup butter
2 cups brown sugar, packed
2 eggs
2 cups sifted flour

2 teaspoons baking powder
½ cup chopped nuts
½ teaspoon salt
2 teaspoons vanilla

Melt the butter in a small saucepan; stir in the sugar and cool. Blend in the eggs. Stir in the remaining ingredients. Spread in a 13 x 9" pan. Bake in a slow oven, 325 degrees, for about 30 minutes. The bars may seem soft—not to worry, they will firm up as they cool. While still warm, cut into sticks about 2 x ½". Remove from pan and roll in powdered sugar if you wish. (I always wish!!)

TLC Tip: *Toasting the walnuts for this recipe really adds to the flavor.*

DREAM BARS

When you bite into one of these bars, you'll think you're dreaming, they're so good!! I first started making them in the 60's. With all the emphasis on "less" of everything, I'll admit they need to be a special occasion treat. I just know you'll remember them for your special occasions.

¼ cup soft shortening
¼ cup soft butter

½ cup brown sugar, packed
1 cup flour

Topping:
2 eggs, well beaten
1 cup brown sugar, packed
1 teaspoon vanilla
2 tablespoons flour
1 teaspoon baking powder

½ teaspoon salt
1 cup flaked coconut
1 cup slivered almonds (or
    other chopped nuts)

Mix shortening, butter and sugar thoroughly. Stir in flour. Flatten into bottom of ungreased 13 x 9" baking pan. Bake 10 minutes at 350 degrees. While crust is baking, prepare topping. Mix eggs, sugar and vanilla. Add flour, baking powder and salt. Stir in coconut and almonds. Spread over crust; return to oven and bake 25 minutes more. Cool; cut into bars.

NOEL FRUIT BARS

If you are one of those people who like fruitcake—a little, not too much—this cookie may be just what you need. I always make this cookie for the holidays, when mixed candied fruit is easy to find.

2 eggs
1 cup powdered sugar
4 tablespoons melted butter
¾ cup flour
1½ teaspoons baking powder

½ teaspoon salt
1 cup chopped walnuts
1 cup snipped dates
¾ cup mixed candied fruit

Beat the eggs until light and fluffy; gradually beat in the powdered sugar. Stir in the melted butter. Measure the flour, baking powder and salt onto a sheet of waxed paper; stir together and fold into the egg mixture with the nuts and dried fruit. Spread in a greased 9 x 9" pan. Bake at 325 degrees for 30-35 minutes. Frost with a butter cream icing and decorate with candied cherries, if desired.

FUDGEY CHOCOLATE CHUNK BROWNIES

These brownies are wonderful even if you don't use the icing. They are easily and quickly made in the processor.

4 ounces semi-sweet chocolate, broken into pieces
1 cup walnuts or pecans
1 cup sugar
2 large eggs
1¼ sticks unsalted butter, softened and cut into 5 pieces (10 tablespoons)

1½ cups unsweetened cocoa
1 tablespoon vanilla
¼ teaspoon baking powder
¼ teaspoon salt
¼ cup light corn syrup
¼ cup plus 2 tablespoons flour
Fudge Icing

Using metal blade, pulse chocolate until chopped very unevenly, about 8 times. Add the nuts and pulse until nuts are coarsely chopped, about 6 times; remove and reserve. Process sugar, eggs, butter, cocoa, vanilla, baking powder and salt until smooth and shiny, about 1 minute, stopping once to scrape work bowl. With machine running, pour corn syrup through feed tube and process 5 seconds. Spoon flour in a circle onto batter, then add chocolate and nuts. Pulse twice. Scrape down sides of work bowl and pulse just until combined, 1-2 times. Spread batter evenly into a buttered 8 x 8" pan. Bake in a 350 degree oven until a toothpick inserted in center comes out moist, but not wet, about 40 minutes. Transfer to a wire rack and cool completely. When cool, spread with Fudge Icing, if desired.

Fudge Icing:
2 tablespoons unsalted butter
1 tablespoon water
2 ounces semi-sweet or bittersweet chocolate

¾ cup powdered sugar
1 teaspoon vanilla
Pinch of salt

Melt butter with water and bring to a simmer; keep hot. Process chocolate, cut into pieces, with powdered sugar until chocolate is as fine as sugar, about 1 minute. With machine running, pour butter and water mixture through feed tube and process until smooth, stopping once to scrape down sides of work bowl. Add vanilla and a pinch of salt and process 3 seconds to blend.

CRANBERRY CRUNCH BARS

This recipe is an all time favorite around our house and especially of my husband, Cleo. The cranberry/orange flavor is delicious between the crunchy, buttery crust. These bars hold quite well, but probably should be kept refrigerated because of the fruit filling. We used to be able to purchase the cranberry orange relish in jars near the cranberry sauce. But alas times change, and now what works for me is what is called cranberry-orange sauce and it comes in a plastic tub.

1¾ cups flour	½ cup granulated sugar
¾ teaspoon salt	2 tablespoons cornstarch
1½ teaspoons cinnamon	2 (12-ounce) containers
1¼ cups packed brown sugar	cranberry orange Cran-
2 cups quick oats	Fruit
1 cup butter	1 egg
1 cup finely chopped nuts	1 tablespoon water

Combine flour, salt and cinnamon in a large bowl; stir in the brown sugar and oats. Cut in the butter with a pastry blender until mixture is crumbly. Stir in the walnuts. Press half the mixture evenly over the bottom of a lightly greased 13 x 9" baking pan. Bake in a 400 degree oven 5 minutes. Cool slightly on wire rack. While layer bakes, mix granulated sugar and cornstarch in a medium saucepan; stir in the cranberry-orange relish. Cook, stirring constantly, until mixture thickens and boils for 3 minutes. Spread evenly over partly baked layer. Sprinkle with remaining oatmeal mixture; press down firmly with hand. Beat egg well in a cup; stir in water. Brush lightly over crumb mixture. Bake in 400 degree oven for 30 minutes or until firm and golden. Cool completely on wire rack; dust with powdered sugar, if desired, and cut into bars.

TLC Tip: *I always seem to have a little trouble "brushing the egg mixture lightly over the topping". I just sort of dab away with the pastry brush and it seems to work. One could omit this step, but I do think it helps the crust to be nice and firm, so I guess it is worth the trouble.*

CHOCOLATE COOKIE BAR

An easy and delicious bar cookie for all you chocolate fans. Since this one uses cocoa and oil you can indulge with less guilt.

½ cup oil
1 cup sugar
1 egg
¼ cup cocoa
2 cups flour

1 teaspoon soda
Pinch of salt
1 cup buttermilk
1 cup chopped nuts

In a large bowl, mix the oil, sugar and egg. Add the cocoa, and mix again. Combine flour, soda and salt. Add alternately with the buttermilk to the creamed mixture. Stir in the nuts at the last. Pour into a greased 15 x 10" jelly roll pan; bake at 350 degrees for 25 minutes. Cool before cutting into bars. Frost if you wish.

TLC Tip: *I really think you'll like this cookie. Less rich than a brownie, these simple bars will satisfy most chocolate cravings and still leave you plenty to share. I seldom frost this cookie.*

APRICOT ALMOND SQUARES

If you are an apricot lover, you'll be a fan of these easily made bars.

1 (16½-ounce) package yellow
    or white cake mix
½ cup butter, melted

½ cup finely chopped almonds
1 cup apricot preserves

In a large bowl, combine cake mix and butter; mix at low speed with mixer until crumbly. Stir in almonds. Reserve 1 cup mixture for topping. Press remaining base mixture in bottom of generously greased 13 x 9" pan. Carefully spread 1 cup preserves over base. (To facilitate spreading, warm the preserves a little.)

Filling:
1 (8-ounce) package cream
    cheese, softened
¼ cup sugar
2 tablespoons flour
⅛ teaspoon salt

1 teaspoon vanilla
1 egg
⅓ cup apricot preserves
½ cup coconut

In same bowl, beat cream cheese, sugar, flour, salt, vanilla and egg until well blended. Stir in ⅓ cup preserves at low speed. Carefully spread filling mixture over base. Combine reserved 1 cup base mixture and coconut; sprinkle over filling. Bake at 350 degrees for 30 to 40 minutes or until golden brown and center is set. Cool completely. Store in refrigerator.

TOFFEE AND FUDGE BARS

What a combination—brownies with toffee bits nestled inside. Bet you can't eat just one!!

½ cup butter, softened
1 cup sugar
1 egg
1½ teaspoons vanilla
1½ cups flour
½ cup cocoa
¼ teaspoon baking powder

¼ teaspoon soda
¼ teaspoon salt
4 (1.05-ounce) chocolate-
    covered toffee candy
    bars, coarsely crushed
¼ cup chopped nuts

In a large bowl, cream butter, sugar, egg and vanilla until light and fluffy. Lightly spoon flour into measuring cup, level off. Add flour, cocoa, baking powder, soda and salt to creamed mixture; blend at low speed with electric mixer until dough forms, about 1 minute. The dough will be stiff. Stir in half of the crushed toffee bars and the nuts. Pat dough into ungreased 9" square pan. Sprinkle with the remaining candy. Bake at 350 degrees for 15 to 20 minutes or until center is set. Cool completely; cut into bars.

TOFFEE SQUARES

This is a rich cookie that looks and tastes like toffee candy. It is absolutely delicious, and especially good at holiday time.

1 cup butter (I like salted
    butter in this recipe)
1 cup brown sugar, packed
1 egg yolk
1 teaspoon vanilla

2 cups flour
¼ teaspoon salt
3 to 4 (⅞-ounce) milk
    chocolate bars
½ cup chopped nuts

Cream butter, sugar, egg yolk and vanilla. Stir in flour and salt thoroughly. Spread in a 13 x 9" rectangle on a cookie sheet, leaving about 1" around the edges. Bake 20 to 25 minutes in a 350 degree oven. It will still be soft. Remove from oven. Immediately place separated squares of chocolate on top. Let stand until soft; spread evenly over surface. Sprinkle with nuts. Cut into small squares while warm.

TLC Tip: *If you prefer a softer, cake-like cookie, spread batter in a 9 x 13" baking pan. Bake 25 to 30 minutes; finish as above.*

PAUL'S PUMPKIN BARS

Once in a while you happen upon a recipe that proves to be popular, delicious, easy, and versatile. This is one of those. Whoever Paul was, thank you. Naturally one thinks of these bars in the fall, containing pumpkin and spices as they do. My husband likes them best unfrosted, with only a light dusting of powdered sugar. I love the added touch of the frosting. It is also nice cut into larger squares and served on a plate with a puff of whipped cream and a sprinkle of cinnamon.

4 eggs
1⅔ cups sugar
1 cup cooking oil
1 (16-ounce) can pumpkin
2 cups flour

2 teaspoons baking powder
2 teaspoons cinnamon
1 teaspoon salt
1 teaspoon baking soda

In large mixer bowl, beat together the eggs, sugar, oil and pumpkin until light and fluffy. Stir together the flour, baking powder, cinnamon and salt. Add to pumpkin mixture and mix thoroughly. Spread batter in ungreased 10 x 15" baking pan. Bake at 350 degrees for 25 to 30 minutes. Cool. Frost if desired.

Frosting:
1 (3-ounce) package cream
   cheese
¼ cup butter, softened

1 teaspoon vanilla
2½ to 3½ cups powdered
   sugar

Cream together cream cheese and margarine. Stir in vanilla. Add powdered sugar—a little at a time, beating well, until mixture is smooth and of spreading consistency.

TLC Tip: I have used reduced-fat cream cheese in this frosting with good success.

337

BUTTERSCOTCH CHOCOLATE SQUARES

This is another of my mother's recipes. I guess you might call this a blonde brownie. Whatever you call it, you'll call it good.

2¾ cups flour
2½ teaspoons baking powder
½ teaspoon salt
⅔ cup shortening
2¼ cups packed brown sugar

3 eggs
1 cup broken nuts
1 (6-ounce) package chocolate
    pieces

Measure flour, baking powder and salt onto a square of waxed paper. Melt shortening in a medium saucepan; stir in the brown sugar and allow to cool slightly. Beat in the eggs one at a time, beating well after each addition. Add the flour mixture, nut meats and chocolate pieces and blend well. Pour into a greased 10 x 15" jelly roll pan. Bake at 350 degrees for 25 to 30 minutes. Cut into squares while still slightly warm.

CINNAMON NUT DIAMONDS

This is another standby—great tasting, easy to put together and no shaping to take up your time. Just mix, spread in the pan, bake and cut into diamonds for a different shape.

2 cups flour
½ teaspoon salt
1 teaspoon cinnamon
1 cup butter, softened
1 cup brown sugar, packed

1 teaspoon vanilla
1 egg yolk
1 egg, slightly beaten
½ cup finely chopped nuts

Stir together the flour, salt and cinnamon; set aside. Cream butter, sugar, vanilla and egg yolk until light and fluffy. Add flour mixture. Mix well. Spread in greased 10 x 15" jelly roll pan. Brush with slightly beaten egg. Sprinkle with chopped nuts, patting them into dough. Bake in 350 degree oven for 25 to 30 minutes. Cut into 2" diamonds. Remove to wire rack to cool.

AUNT MAVIS' CARROT COOKIES

Aunt Mavis and Uncle Earl lived under the shadow of the water tower near Grannie's house in Pryor, Oklahoma. She is a friendly red-head who played girls' basketball as a youth, and still rides her bike at 80 years old. She loves to garden and fish, and adores dogs. She says she has made these cookies for years, and always felt good about serving them to her children because they contained vegetables. She was ahead of her time, wasn't she? Perhaps you'll find yourself feeling good about serving them to your children or grandchildren, too.

1 cup shortening (Aunt Mavis uses Crisco)	1 teaspoon salt
1 cup sugar	2 cups flour
1 egg	1 teaspoon baking powder
2 cups cooked, mashed carrots	1 to 2 cups powdered sugar
	Grated rind and juice of 1 orange

Cream the shortening and sugar; add the egg and continue beating until fluffy. Mix in the carrots. Combine the salt, flour and baking powder on a square of waxed paper. Add to the creamed mixture, and combine well. Aunt Mavis says she adds a little more flour if the mixture is too thin to drop nicely. Drop heaping tablespoon-size mounds of dough on an ungreased cookie sheet (or one lined with parchment paper). Bake at 350 degrees for about 15 to 20 minutes. Cool on a wire rack. Combine the powdered sugar, with the rind and juice, beginning with 1 cup sugar, and adding enough more to make a spreadable frosting. Stir until smooth; spread on cooled cookies.

TLC Tip: These are a soft, absolutely wonderful cookie, great even without the frosting. Their color is a beautiful orange, perfect for the fall season. I'd say this a super way to get your beta carotene.

339

CHOCOLATE CHIP COOKIES

Not your usual Chocolate Chip Cookie, these from the kitchen of my friend, Michelle Dorrington, are more like a sugar cookie with chocolate chips. She says the fun of these are the size, and she often decorates the giant cookie to celebrate special holidays. I'm feeling creative already, aren't you?

1 cup butter
1½ cups granulated sugar
2 cups flour
1 teaspoon baking soda

1 teaspoon salt
1 egg
1 teaspoon vanilla
1 cup chocolate chips

Cream butter and sugar. Add egg and vanilla. Mix well. Combine flour, soda and salt. Add to butter mixture. Mix thoroughly. Stir in the chocolate chips. Form into 2" balls. Place on ungreased cookie sheet (6 to 8 to a sheet) and bake in a 350 degree oven for 15 minutes. For one giant cookie, place entire batch of cookie dough on a large ungreased pizza pan. Spread to within 1" of edge and bake in a 350 degree oven for 18 to 20 minutes. Decorate if desired. Cut into wedges to serve.

CHOCOLATE CHIP COOKIES BEAUCHAMP

Shirley Beauchamp, good friend, good cook, shares this recipe, a favorite of her family.

1 cup shortening (Shirley
    uses Crisco)
½ cup granulated sugar
1 cup brown sugar, packed
1 teaspoon vanilla
2 eggs
2 cups flour

1 teaspoon soda
1 teaspoon salt
1 (12-ounce) package
    chocolate chips
Coarsely chopped nuts,
    if desired

Beat the shortening, sugars and vanilla until creamy; add the eggs, and mix thoroughly. Combine the dry ingredients; add to the creamed mixture. Fold in the chocolate chips, and the nuts, if using. Drop by spoonfuls onto cookie sheet and bake at 350 degrees for 10 to 12 minutes. Let set on pan 1 minute before removing to wire rack to cool.

SHIRLEY'S OATMEAL DATE COOKIES

A good oatmeal cookie is hard to beat, and the addition of dates doesn't hurt a bit. My friend, Shirley Armstrong, kept the cookie jar full of these, and shared them often.

½ cup shortening
1 teaspoon salt
1 teaspoon cinnamon
1 teaspoon vanilla
1 tablespoon molasses
1 cup sugar
1 egg

1 cup flour
¾ teaspoon soda
1 cup rolled oats, quick or
   regular
½ cup chopped nuts
½ cup chopped dates

Mix the shortening, salt, cinnamon, vanilla, molasses, sugar and egg until creamy. Add the dry ingredients, nuts and dates. Drop by small spoonfuls onto a greased cookie sheet (or one lined with parchment paper). Bake at 350 degrees for about 13 minutes. Don't overbake.

MRS. SMITH'S PLYMOUTH COOKIES

The Smiths were our neighbors across the road when I was growing up. It was their hills we sledded down, and these were the cookies she handed out when she saw us playing in their yard. It was their daughter-in-law, Golda, who assisted the doctor when I was born in my parents' bedroom. I don't know why they are called Plymouth Cookies, but it really doesn't matter—I'd like them no what they were called.

1 cup shortening
⅔ cup granulated sugar
⅔ cup packed brown sugar
3 eggs
1 teaspoon soda dissolved
   in 1 tablespoon water

½ teaspoon salt
½ teaspoon baking powder
3 cups flour
½ cup raisins

Cream the shortening with the sugars; beat in the eggs. Add the soda/water mixture. Combine the dry ingredients; add to the creamed mixture. Stir in the raisins. Drop by teaspoonfuls onto a lightly greased baking sheet. Bake at 375 degrees for 12 to 15 minutes. Do not overbake; these cookies are meant to be soft.

MERINGUE COOKIES

These one-bite cookies are a real hit. I especially like the flavor combination of chocolate, nuts and peppermint. Don't try to make these when the weather is damp—a problem we don't have to deal with much here in West Texas.

2 egg whites, room temperature	1 cup semi-sweet chocolate pieces
⅛ teaspoon salt	1 cup chopped nuts
⅛ teaspoon cream of tartar	3 tablespoons crushed
¾ cup sugar	peppermint candy
½ teaspoon vanilla	

Place egg whites in mixer bowl; beat on high speed until foamy. Add salt and cream of tartar and continue beating until soft peaks form. Add sugar 1 tablespoon at a time, beating well after each addition. When meringue is stiff and white, remove bowl from mixer and fold in vanilla, chocolate pieces, nuts and candy. Drop by teaspoonfuls on lightly greased baking sheet. Bake at 250 degrees for 40 minutes. Store in airtight container.

DROPPED SUGAR COOKIES

When you want a sugar cookie but don't want to chill, roll and cut, this is the recipe to pull out.

2 eggs	¾ cup sugar
⅔ cup vegetable oil	2 cups flour
2 teaspoons vanilla	2 teaspoons baking powder
1 teaspoon grated lemon peel	½ teaspoon salt

Beat the eggs with a whisk. Stir in the oil, vanilla and lemon rind. Blend in sugar until mixture thickens. Blend the flour, baking powder and salt; stir in. Drop by teaspoonfuls onto an ungreased baking sheet. Flatten with greased bottom of glass dipped in sugar. Bake 8 to 10 minutes. Remove from pan immediately.

TLC Tip: Have you discovered the small-sized scoops made for dipping cookie dough and releasing it onto the cookie sheet? They are a great little invention. It's quick, and solves the problem of getting the cookies all the same size.

JEANINE'S OATMEAL BUTTER CRISPS

I can still vividly remember sitting in Jeanine Rogers' Benton Harbor, Michigan, kitchen and watching her put together these delectable cookies. That was many years ago, but these are still one of my favorite oatmeal cookies.

1 cup shortening	3 cups quick rolled oats
1 cup brown sugar	1½ cups flour
1 cup white sugar	1 teaspoon salt
1 teaspoon vanilla	1 (4-ounce) package flaked
2 eggs	coconut
2 teaspoons soda	

Cream the shortening and sugars; add eggs and vanilla and mix well. Measure dry ingredients onto waxed paper, stir to combine. Blend well with creamed mixture. Drop by spoonfuls onto ungreased cookie sheet. Bake in a 350 degree oven for 12-15 minutes or until lightly browned. Cool slightly before removing from pan.

TLC Tip: *Nuts, raisins or chocolate chips can be added to this dough depending on your taste or mood.*

CHOCOLATE WALNUT WAFERS

With its coating of sparkling sugar and walnut half garnish, this cookie makes a nice addition to a party or shower tray. The fact that it tastes great doesn't hurt either!

2 cups flour	2 ounces unsweetened
1 teaspoon baking powder	chocolate, melted
½ teaspoon salt	1 egg
¼ teaspoon baking soda	1 teaspoon vanilla
¾ cup butter	¼ cup milk
¾ cup packed brown sugar	Granulated sugar
	Walnut halves

Measure the flour, baking powder, salt, and baking soda onto a square of waxed paper. Beat butter and brown sugar together until fluffy; mix in the melted chocolate, egg, vanilla and milk. Stir in the dry ingredients, a third at a time, blending well to make a soft dough. Chill several hours or until firm enough to handle. Roll dough, a level teaspoonful at a time, into balls. Roll each ball in granulated sugar. Place 3" apart on ungreased cookie sheet; flatten to ¼" thickness with bottom of a glass. Top each with a walnut half. Bake in a 350 degree oven for 12 minutes or until firm. Carefully remove the wafers to wire racks to cool.

MY MOM'S PEANUT BUTTER COOKIES

I think my mother was the only one in her family to venture very far from the nest. When she decided to go to Anderson College in the early 30's, met my father, married and moved with him back to Michigan, her family actually thought they would never see her again. I'm not sure my Grandmother Crabtree ever forgave my father for "taking her away". Mom worked side by side with my father on the farm for long hours. She could milk a cow by hand, drive the tractor, and pitch hay. She was also very creative, good with handwork and sewing, and a great cook. She was a support for me when my children were little and I was a single parent, and we were good friends as well. She made wonderful Peanut Butter Cookies. I can still smell them, fresh from the oven, and see their distinctive fork creases decorating the tops. I carried them to school many times over the years. That was before "fattening" was part of my vocabulary. My mother said "these would keep well if hidden well".

1 cup butter	1 cup creamy peanut butter
1 cup brown sugar, packed	1 teaspoon vanilla
1 cup white sugar	1 teaspoon soda
2 eggs, well beaten	2½ cups flour

Cream butter and sugars; add beaten eggs, peanut butter and vanilla. Stir soda and flour together, then add to creamed mixture and combine well. Drop by teaspoonfuls onto a lightly greased baking sheet. Press into flat shapes with a fork leaving the imprint of the fork for a decorative touch. Bake in a 375 degree oven for about 10 minutes. Remove from pan while still hot; cool on wire rack.

TLC Tip: Mom's notes said these needed a little salt. I agree—maybe ¼ teaspoon.

GERT'S CANDY JAR COOKIES

Gert Bridge was the cook at Farrand School when I taught there in the 1960's. She was a very friendly lady with a deep love for food, which she definitely knew how to prepare. I often thought that the children who were privileged to eat her hot lunches probably didn't know how lucky they were. She often made us teachers feel special by greeting us in the morning with freshly baked cinnamon rolls. I can taste them yet!! With that kind of introduction, you just know these cookies will be good.

½ cup salted butter, softened
⅓ cup packed brown sugar
1 tablespoon orange juice
1 teaspoon grated orange rind
1 cup flour
⅔ cup chopped dates

½ cup chopped walnuts, or
   your choice
1 bar German's sweet
   chocolate
Additional chopped nuts

Cream the butter and sugar together; beat in the juice and rind. Blend in the flour, dates and walnuts. Roll the dough into small balls and place on an ungreased cookie sheet. Bake in a slow oven, 300 degrees, for 23-25 minutes. Remove from baking sheet and cool. Melt the chocolate in the top of a double boiler or in the microwave. Dip each cookie in the chocolate and roll in chopped nuts. Cool on waxed paper; store in a cool place. Makes about 2 dozen.

TLC Tip: *I've always had a sweet tooth, but I find that just dipping the top of these cookies in chocolate is enough to satisfy mine.*

SUGAR AND SPICE COOKIES

Another version of a molasses cookie—yummy and pretty.

¾ cup shortening
1 cup sugar
1 egg
¼ cup molasses
2 cups flour
¼ teaspoon salt

1 teaspoon cinnamon
¼ teaspoon cloves
½ teaspoon ginger
2 teaspoons baking soda
Powdered sugar

Cream shortening, sugar and egg. Stir together the flour, salt, spices and soda. Add to creamed mixture until thoroughly mixed. Shape into balls using a heaping teaspoonful of dough and place 2" apart on greased baking sheet. Bake 10-12 minutes at 375 degrees. Roll cookies in powdered sugar while they are still warm.

COCONUT GINGEROONS

It isn't often you think of coconut in a ginger cookie, but I think you will be pleasantly surprised at this combination of flavors.

2 cups flour	**½ cup unsalted butter**
½ teaspoon baking powder	**½ cup packed brown sugar**
1½ teaspoons ground ginger	**¼ cup molasses**
½ teaspoon ground cinnamon	**1 egg**
½ teaspoon ground coriander	**2 cups flaked coconut**
⅛ teaspoon salt	**½ cup granulated sugar**

Combine flour, baking soda, spices and salt on a square of waxed paper. Beat the butter with the brown sugar. Add the molasses and egg and continue to beat until mixture is fluffy. Stir in the flour mixture until smooth; stir in the coconut. Chill several hours. Roll dough by level tablespoonfuls to form balls. Quickly dip one side into water, then into the granulated sugar. Place sugar side up on a large parchment covered cookie sheet. Flatten slightly. Bake at 375 degrees for 15 minutes or until cookies are lightly browned. Transfer to wire racks; cool completely. Store airtight.

TLC Tip: I don't always chill the dough for several hours. However, there is no denying that the longer refrigerator time makes for easier shaping.

MEXICAN CINNAMON COOKIES

I'm not sure these are authentic Mexican cookies, but I am sure that they taste great. If you like cinnamon toast you'll love these.

1 cup butter	**¼ teaspoon salt**
½ cup powdered sugar	**2¼ cups flour**
1 teaspoon cinnamon	**½ cup granulated sugar**
1 teaspoon vanilla	**½ teaspoon cinnamon**

In a large electric mixer bowl, beat butter until light and fluffy. At low speed, beat in ½ cup powdered sugar, 1 teaspoon cinnamon, the vanilla and salt just until combined. Add the flour—dough will be rather stiff. Refrigerate 30 minutes. Roll dough into 1" balls, flatten with fingers to about ¼" thick. Place 1½" apart on ungreased cookie sheets. Bake in a 400 degree oven for 10 minutes or until a delicate golden brown. Combine granulated sugar and ½ teaspoon cinnamon in a small bowl. Roll the hot cookies in this mixture. Place on wire rack to cool; sprinkle with any remaining cinnamon sugar.

PIÑA COLADA MACAROONS

Cleo really likes these cookies. You'll think you've been transported to the tropics when you bite into them.

¾ cup sugar
⅓ cup butter, softened
1 (3-ounce) package cream
   cheese, softened
1½ teaspoons rum extract
1 egg yolk

1¼ cups flour
2 teaspoons baking powder
¼ teaspoon salt
8 ounces candied pineapple,
   finely chopped
4 cups flaked coconut

In a large bowl, beat sugar, butter and cream cheese until light and fluffy. Add rum extract and egg yolk; blend well. In a small bowl, combine flour, baking powder and salt. Gradually add flour mixture to creamed mixture; mix well. Stir in pineapple and 3 cups of the coconut. Cover with plastic wrap; refrigerate at least 1 hour for easier handling. Shape dough into 1" balls. Gently roll in remaining 1 cup coconut to coat. Place 2" apart on ungreased cookie sheets; flatten slightly. Bake at 350 degrees for 10 to 15 minutes or until light golden brown. Immediately remove from cookie sheets. Cool on wire racks.

RUSSIAN TEACAKES

These bite-size cookies literally melt in your mouth! They go by many names, but no matter what you call them, they are always a welcome addition to a cookie platter. One or two of these crunchy little snowballs beside a dish of fruit or sherbet really makes dessert complete.

1 cup soft butter (there really
   is no substitute in this
   recipe)
½ cup sifted powdered sugar

1 teaspoon vanilla
2¼ cups flour
¼ teaspoon salt
¾ cup finely chopped nuts

Mix butter, sugar and vanilla thoroughly. Blend flour and salt; stir in. Mix in the nuts. Chill. Roll into 1" balls (resist the urge to make them larger). Place on ungreased baking sheet. Bake at 400 degrees for 10 to 12 minutes. While still warm, roll in additional powdered sugar. Cool. Roll in sugar again.

TLC Tip: *There is no sneaking around about eating these little gems. The heavy coating of powdered sugar is sure to give you away!*

BON BON COOKIES

You bake these like cookies and eat them like candy! Though they are a little time-consuming to make, the results are so worth it for special occasions. For gift giving, why not place each cookie in a mini paper muffin cup?

½ cup soft butter
¾ cup sifted powdered sugar
1 tablespoon vanilla
   (yes, 1 tablespoon)

Food coloring, if desired
1½ cups flour
⅛ teaspoon salt

Mix butter, sugar, vanilla and food coloring, if using. Blend in flour and salt. If dough is dry, add 1 to 2 tablespoons cream or milk. Wrap level tablespoon of dough around filling—a well-drained maraschino cherry, candied cherry, pitted date piece, nut, chocolate piece, small chocolate mint, are just some suggestions. Place 1" apart on ungreased baking sheet. Bake at 350 degrees for 12 to 15 minutes. Cool. Dip tops of cookies in icing. Decorate as desired with chopped nuts, coconut, decorating sprinkles.

Icing:
1 cup powdered sugar
2 tablespoons cream

1 teaspoon vanilla
Food coloring (optional)

Mix powdered sugar, cream, vanilla and food coloring, if desired. To make a chocolate icing, add 1 ounce unsweetened chocolate, melted, and use ¼ cup cream.

SNICKERDOODLES

This is the cookie my mom is best remembered for. She always filled the cookie jar when she came to visit and the grandkids and nieces and nephews emptied it almost as fast as she filled it. To this day, I cannot eat one of these simple, homey cookies without thinking of her.

1 cup soft shortening
   (please use part butter)
1½ cups sugar
2 eggs

2¾ cups flour
2 teaspoons cream of tartar
1 teaspoon soda
¼ teaspoon salt

Mix the shortening, sugar and eggs thoroughly. Blend all dry ingredients; stir into creamed mixture. Roll into balls the size of small walnuts. Roll in a mixture of 2 tablespoons sugar and 2 teaspoons cinnamon. Place 2" apart on ungreased baking sheet. Bake at 400 degrees for 8 to 10 minutes. These cookies will puff up at first, then flatten out. Remove to wire rack to cool.

YULE MINT-WICHES

These are festive cookies just meant for the holidays. In recent years it seems that I have had difficulty finding the thin mints used as the filling. The end result is worth a search, however.

¾ cup butter	½ teaspoon baking powder
1½ cups powdered sugar	½ teaspoon salt
2 eggs, beaten	Green and/or red decorating
1 teaspoon vanilla	sugar
2-3 drops peppermint extract	Chocolate mint wafers,
2¼ cups flour	unfilled

Cream the butter with the powdered sugar. Add the eggs, vanilla, and peppermint, mixing until fluffy. Stir flour, baking powder, and salt together; blend into creamed mixture. Chill thoroughly. Make marble-sized balls. Dip half of each ball in green or red sugar. Place sugar side up on greased cookie sheet. Bake in moderate oven, 350 degrees, for 10 to 12 minutes. Quickly remove cookies from baking sheet in pairs. Place a chocolate wafer between 2 hot cookies, pressing slightly to melt the chocolate. Cool on wire racks.

TLC Tip: *It is important not to get carried away with the size of the balls. The cookies are not pretty to look at or easy to eat if they are too large.*

FESTIVE CHERRY-ETTES

These cookies melt in your mouth and can become quite addictive. My mother made these often when asked to "bring 3 dozen cookies" or she got the word we were coming home from college for the weekend with friends-in-tow.

¾ cup shortening	2 teaspoons vanilla
¼ cup butter	2 cups flour
1 teaspoon salt	1 cup finely chopped pecans
½ cup powdered sugar	20 candied cherries

Blend the first 5 ingredients. Add the flour and pecans and mix into a soft dough. Measure out level tablespoonfuls of dough and roll to form small balls. Place on a greased baking sheet. Press a little indentation in the center of each ball with finger tip and place a cherry in each one. Bake at 325 degrees for 25 minutes. Should make 40 cookies.

TLC Tip: *Instead of the cherries, you can fill each indentation with a dab of jam or jelly if desired. If you choose to do this, use regular jam or jelly, not the fruit spread. The spread just doesn't seem to work as well.*

VIENNESE ROUNDS

This makes a very pretty cookie to serve for showers or special parties, but tastes wonderful any time. Cleo likes them best just plain, without the jam or frosting.

1 cup butter	½ cup hazelnuts, ground
1½ cups sifted powdered sugar, divided use	Red food coloring
	1 cup seedless red raspberry
1½ cups flour	jam
1 teaspoon vanilla	

Cream butter and ½ cup of the sugar until well blended in a large bowl; stir in flour, vanilla, and ground nuts. Roll dough, 1 level teaspoonful at a time, into balls. Place 2" apart on greased cookie sheets. Lightly grease the bottom of a measuring cup and dip in powdered sugar; press over each ball to flatten to about 1" round. Bake in a 350 degree oven 10 minutes or until golden around the edges. Remove carefully from cookie sheets to wire racks; cool. Beat remaining 1 cup sugar with a few drops of water until smooth in a small bowl; tint pink with a drop or two of food coloring. Spread half of the cookies with raspberry jam; top with remaining cookies, sandwich style, flat side down. Attach a writing tip to a decorating set; fill with pink frosting; press out in rings on top of cookies. Let set until frosting hardens. Store in a loosely covered container with waxed paper between layers.

TLC Tip: You can put the frosting in a small zip-lock bag, snip a tiny bit off one corner, and squeeze the frosting from the bag onto the cookies.

CHOCOLATE OATMEAL NO-BAKE COOKIES

If you're in a hurry and want a good, rich cookie, this is it. Very easy and quick to make.

½ cup butter	½ cup milk
4 tablespoons cocoa, rounded	3 cups quick rolled oats
½ teaspoon salt	1 teaspoon vanilla
2 cups sugar	2 tablespoons peanut butter

Combine butter, cocoa, salt, sugar and milk in a large saucepan. Bring to a full, rolling boil, remove from heat, stir in the peanut butter and let set for 1 minute. Stir in the vanilla and the rolled oats. Drop by spoonfuls onto waxed paper. May be made large or small. Cool before serving.

TLC Tip: You can omit the peanut butter and add 1 cup of miniature marshmallows and ½ cup nuts or coconut for a different taste.

NOEL WREATHS

I just love Christmas! And I love having people in our home during the holiday season. The day after Thanksgiving I bring out the Christmas music and the Christmas dishes. I hang the "Merry Christmas Y'All" mugs on the mug tree, and start the decorating. For several years we had an Open House for our church family and other friends. With the house at its holiday best, the soft glow of lighted candles and festive music playing in the background, it is somehow easy to let the cares of the world fall away. What fun I had pouring over magazines, cookbooks and my own recipe file deciding what to serve. There is no getting around it, Christmas cookies take time and patience, but I think the results are very much worth it. This buttery cookie with its maple filling was nearly always on my cookie trays.

1 cup butter
½ cup sugar
1 egg
1 teaspoon vanilla
2½ cups flour
1 cup finely chopped nuts

¼ cup white corn syrup
¼ teaspoon maple flavoring
Red hot candies and green
   candied cherries for
   decoration

Cream the butter and sugar until fluffy; beat in egg and vanilla. Stir in the flour gradually, blending to make a soft dough. Measure out ¼ cup dough and mix with walnuts, corn syrup and maple flavoring for filling. Set aside. Fit star plate or disk in your cookie press. Fill with remaining dough; press out into 4" lengths on ungreased cookie sheets; join ends of each to form a circle. Fill center of each with about 1 teaspoon of filling. Decorate with a red hot (for berry) and slivers of green cherry (for leaves). Bake in 350 degree oven for 15 minutes or until golden. Remove carefully with spatula while still hot; cool on wire rack. Store with waxed paper between layers. Keep tightly covered.

SHIRLEY'S DATE PINWHEELS

Shirley Armstrong is a friend from my days in Michigan. We stayed with her, and her husband Chuck, when we moved back to Michigan from Oklahoma. As I recall, we slept in sleeping bags on the floor, as they lived in an apartment. I did the cooking, while everyone else was working. I have never forgotten how gracious they were to share what they had at the time. After a lifetime of teaching, they now live in Anderson, Indiana. Shirley is a great cook, and I love these cookies, one of her specialties.

2¼ cups chopped dates	1 cup brown sugar
1 cup sugar	3 eggs
1 cup water	4 cups flour
1 cup chopped nuts	½ teaspoon salt
1 cup shortening	½ teaspoon soda

Combine the dates, sugar and water in a small saucepan. Cook over medium heat for about 10 minutes, until mixture thickens. Remove from heat and add the nuts. Beat the shortening and brown sugar until well mixed and creamy. Add eggs, beating well. Measure flour, salt and soda onto a square of waxed paper. Stir to combine. Gradually add flour mixture to creamed mixture; mix well. If mixture is soft, chill an hour or so. Divide dough into two parts; roll one into a 12 x 10" rectangle. Spread with half the date mixture. Roll up from wide side as for jelly roll. Wrap in plastic wrap and chill again, from 2 to 24 hours. Repeat with remaining dough and filling. Slice into ¼" rounds; place on a greased cookie sheet and bake at 350 degrees for 10 to 12 minutes or until edges are lightly browned.

TLC Tip: *You may find it easier to roll the dough between sheets of waxed paper. In that case, you can use the paper to help with the shaping process, and wrap the roll in the waxed paper, twisting the ends to seal.*

CANDY CANE COOKIES

I began making these cookies before I was married, so they have been a part of our Christmas assortment for a long time. Buttery and a bit fragile, they take time to make, but the results are worth it.

1 cup powdered sugar	1 egg
½ cup butter, softened	2½ cups flour
½ cup shortening	½ teaspoon red food color
1½ teaspoons almond or	½ cup crushed peppermint
peppermint extract	candy
1 teaspoon vanilla	½ cup granulated sugar

Mix the powdered sugar, shortening, almond extract, vanilla and egg in a large bowl. Stir in the flour. Divide the dough in half. Tint 1 half with the red food color. For each candy cane, shape 1 teaspoon dough from each half into a 4" rope by rolling back and forth on a lightly floured surface. Place 1 red and 1 white rope side by side; press together lightly and twist. Place on an ungreased cookie sheet. Curve top of cookie down to form handle of cane. Bake in a 375 degree oven for about 9 minutes or until set and very light brown. Mix candy and granulated sugar; sprinkle over cookies immediately after removing from oven. Place the cookies on a wire rack to finish cooling.

CUPCAKE-ETTES

An unusual and festive way to prepare brownies for any occasion. I usually do these for Christmas, but there's no reason to limit them to December.

1 (1-pound) package fudge-	Red or green candied cherry
type brownie mix	halves
Frosting	

Prepare the batter from brownie mix according to package directions for fudge-type brownies. Place paper nut cups (1½" across top) on cookie sheet; grease cups. Spoon batter into cups, filling ⅔ full. Bake in 350 degree oven, about 20 minutes or until toothpick inserted in center comes out almost clean. Cool. Give each brownie cup a white frosting topknot; place a red or green candied cherry half on the frosting.

TLC Tip: Are your creative juices running yet? How about chocolate frosting with a sprinkle of chopped nuts? A pastel frosting with a jelly egg? Chocolate frosting with candy corn or a candy pumpkin?

HOMESTEADERS

I guess the reason I like these cookies so much is that they remind me of the "windmill" cookies I ate as a child. These can be kept in the refrigerator for several days, ready to slice and bake at a moment's notice. The aroma alone says "Welcome".

3 cups flour	1 well-beaten egg
½ teaspoon salt	½ cup chopped nuts
½ teaspoon soda	2 tablespoons melted butter
1½ teaspoons cinnamon	1 cup sifted powdered sugar
1 cup butter, melted	½ teaspoon vanilla
1 cup packed brown sugar	2 to 3 teaspoons warm milk

Measure dry ingredients together onto a sheet of waxed paper. Stir to combine. Mix the melted butter, sugar and egg; blend in the dry ingredients and nuts. Press into a waxed paper lined loaf pan. Chill ½ hour in freezer or overnight in the refrigerator. Be sure pan is covered tightly. When ready to bake, remove from pan and slice into ¼" thick slices, place on ungreased cookie sheet and bake at 375 degrees for 10 to 12 minutes. Cool. Arrange cookies side by side on wire racks over waxed paper. Combine melted butter, powdered sugar, vanilla and warm milk to make a frosting of pouring consistency. Drizzle back and forth over cookies; let dry. Store loosely covered with waxed paper between layers.

PECAN TASSIES

I remember the first time I bit into one of these little tarts. I thought they were the most wonderful thing I had ever eaten. They are always popular, no matter what the occasion, and much easier to make than one would suppose by observing the end result.

1 (3-ounce) package cream cheese, softened	1 egg, lightly beaten
½ cup + 1 tablespoon butter, softened, divided use	¾ cup packed brown sugar
	1 teaspoon vanilla
1 cup flour	Dash of salt
	⅔ cup chopped pecans

Blend cream cheese with ½ cup butter until smooth. Add the flour; blend well. Chill for about 2 hours or overnight. Divide dough into 24 balls; press into 1¾" muffin cups. (There is a nifty little wooden gadget that will do this with one push. You might want to check it out if you make many of this type of goodie.) Blend egg, brown sugar, vanilla, 1 tablespoon butter, salt and pecans in small bowl; fill pastry cups with egg mixture, being careful not to fill too full. (I always seem to have a little filling left over.) Bake in a preheated 375 degree oven for 20 minutes or until lightly browned. Cool before removing from tins. This recipe makes 2 dozen.

S'MORES

I don't remember the first time I ate a S'More, but I do remember the best time. It was my sixteenth birthday and I was allowed to have some girlfriends spend the night. We carted the makings for a hot dog roast all the way to the river, the end of our farm. No charcoal grill for us, this was the real thing, bonfire and all. After the main course, we spiked big, fluffy marshmallows on freshly cut saplings, and toasted (burned is more like it, but who cared) them over the glowing embers, bringing them close and blowing out the flames as they caught fire, as marshmallows are prone to do when being toasted. When it was just right, we pulled it off the stick, and plopped it onto a square of milk chocolate resting on a square of graham cracker, covered it with another cracker, and squished the whole thing together to melt the chocolate and spread the melted marshmallow. The next step was getting it to our mouths. Um-m, heaven!! I guess most 16 year old girls would not think this much of a celebration, but that night, beside the river, under the stars, with my friends, I don't think I had a care in the world. It's one of my fondest memories.

In case you don't have a river, or a farm, or a bonfire, you can still enjoy S'Mores, and imagine the rest.

Large, soft marshmallows   **Graham crackers**
Chocolate candy bars, plain is
    probably best

Place a square of candy bar on a graham cracker square. Top with one marshmallow. Put on a paper plate and cook in the microwave on high for 15 to 25 seconds, until marshmallow and chocolate are melted. Cover with another graham cracker. Enjoy. There could be many variations on a theme here— spread the top cracker with peanut butter before placing on the marshmallow, use candy bar with almonds, use cinnamon graham crackers—but I don't think you can beat the original.

RUTH'S HARD CANDY

My sister has made this candy for years. It is a colorful holiday or any-day treat, excellent for gift-giving or filling the candy jars in your own home. Easier than you'd think to make, choose your favorite flavor or make a variety.

2 cups sugar
1 cup white corn syrup
½ cup water

½ teaspoon flavoring oil, your choice
¼ teaspoon food coloring

Combine sugar, syrup and water in a large heavy saucepan. Bring to a rapid boil, and cook to the hard crack stage, 280 degrees on the candy thermometer. Remove from heat and add flavoring of choice and food coloring to correspond with flavoring. Pour onto buttered cookie sheets. When it starts to harden around the edges, twist into strips and cut with scissors. Finish cooling, then toss in a paper bag with powdered sugar, if desired.

TLC Tip: Some suggested colors and flavorings are:

peppermint - green
anise - blue
wintergreen - red
cinnamon - brown

clove - orange
lemon - yellow
spearmint - clear

ORANGE COCONUT BALLS

I first learned about these delectable goodies when I was teaching at Moss Elementary. The recipe makes a lot, and is perfect for sharing with friends or as part of a tray for an open house or party. The orange flavor makes these quite refreshing.

½ cup butter, softened
1 (6-ounce) can frozen orange
    juice, thawed
1 (1-pound) box powdered
    sugar

1 (12-ounce) box vanilla
    wafers, crushed finely
1 cup chopped nuts
2 cups flaked coconut

Cream together the butter, orange juice and powdered sugar. Add crushed vanilla wafers and nuts. Shape into balls and roll in coconut.

JELLO BALLS

You can make these confections in just about any color scheme to suit your mood or a special occasion. These are especially pretty in pastels for showers, or red and green for Christmas.

4 (3-ounce) packages Jello of one color, divided
2 cups flaked coconut

1 can condensed milk (like Eagle Brand)
1 cup chopped nuts

Place 3 packages Jello in a bowl, mix in coconut, milk and pecans. Place in refrigerator until firm. Roll in balls and then in the remaining package of Jello. These are more attractive if not made too large. Store in a plastic bag.

PEANUT BUTTER BONBONS

Since this recipe makes such a large quantity, perhaps you would like to get together with a friend to share the expense and the shaping. These make a nice gift placed in bon bon cups and arranged in a decorative box or on a tray.

2 cups peanut butter
½ cup butter
4½ cups sifted powdered sugar

3 cups crisp rice cereal
2 cups butterscotch pieces
2 cups semi-sweet chocolate pieces

In a saucepan melt the peanut butter and butter. In a large bowl combine the powdered sugar and cereal; pour peanut butter mixture over cereal mixture. Blend together with hands. Form into small balls; chill until firm. Melt butterscotch pieces and chocolate pieces over hot water in separate double boilers or in the microwave. (Check manual for your microwave.) Dip half the candies in each coating; swirl top with back of fork or teaspoon. Place on waxed paper lined baking sheet. Chill. Makes about 100.

EASY PEANUT BUTTER CUPS

No tedious shaping here. Just press in pan, top with chocolate, and try to wait until it is firm enough to cut into squares.

2 cups butter, softened	3½ cups powdered sugar
⅓ of a (1-pound) box graham crackers, crushed	2 cups semi-sweet chocolate chips
1 cup peanut butter	

In a large bowl, mix soft butter, graham cracker crumbs, peanut butter and powdered sugar. Press into a well-greased 10 x 15" jelly roll pan. Melt chocolate chips over hot water or in microwave. Spread over graham cracker and peanut butter mixture. Refrigerate until firm. Cut into squares. Try to stop at just one!!

MOLASSES POPCORN BALLS

These are the popcorn balls of my childhood, and still my favorite. I like the flavor the molasses adds to this treat.

3 quarts popped corn	½ teaspoon vinegar
⅔ cup light molasses	½ teaspoon salt
1½ cups sugar	2 tablespoons butter
½ cup water	2 teaspoons vanilla

Place popped corn in a large roasting pan and keep warm in a 200 degree oven. (A disposable foil roasting pan is good if you don't have a metal one.) Place the molasses, sugar, water, vinegar and salt in a large heavy saucepan. Bring to a boil, and continue boiling without stirring, until mixture reaches 270 degrees on a candy thermometer, or becomes brittle when dropped into cold water. Remove from heat and add butter and vanilla. Gradually pour over popped corn, mixing carefully and thoroughly with a wooden spoon. Grease your hands with a little butter and form the mixture into balls of desired size. Cool, then wrap in plastic wrap. Makes about 36.

TLC Tip: *This recipe is so old that it called for wrapping the balls in waxed paper—we didn't have plastic wrap when I was a child. Now the wrap even comes in colors so you can present these for all kinds of holidays.*

CHRISTMAS AT BLACKMAN SCHOOL

I think the Christmas celebration at the two-room country school I attended for eight years has to be near the top of my special memories. We always got to use colored chalk to fill the chalk boards with holiday scenes, and we covered the lower windows with a thick layer of Bon Ami soap, then drew designs on the dry surface letting the clear glass show through. We made yard after yard of red and green construction paper chains, and strung them up over the windows and hung them from the ceiling. The tree was always a sight to behold (most of the decorations made by the students) and was put up early enough so we could enjoy it. The excitement built as the stage was erected, and practice for the program started. Were we distracted by all this? You bet, but our teacher never seemed to be stressed out about it, or perhaps I was too preoccupied to notice. The students in all eight grades took part in the Christmas program, which always included "recitations", songs and a play. There was always a welcome "piece", usually spoken by one of the small children from the "little room" (the primary grades), perhaps a humorous poem by the school clown from the "big room" (the upper grades), and maybe a piano solo by my brother. We practiced every day until show time. Since I have taught school myself, I have a great appreciation for the teachers who endured the pre-Christmas antics of 20 to 30 children. On the day of the program, I was always too nervous to eat supper. If the weather had cooperated, there was a blanket of snow. The tires of our Model A always made a crunching sound as they made fresh tracks in the snow. Crisp air and an inky sky dotted with stars added to the magic of the night. Dressed in our Sunday best, we performed before our family and friends. Finally we all gathered on the stage to sing Jingle Bells, and I knew it was time for the arrival of Santa. We always heard the jingle of HIS sleigh bells while we were singing. Santa always scared me— I was never one to run to him with my wish list, but I admired him from afar. Santa passed out the treat sacks, filled with homemade fudge and penuche, nuts in the shell, hard candy, a tangerine and often a popcorn ball. You can be sure that when we went to sleep that night, our little heads were filled with visions of sugar plums.

MOM'S PEANUT BRITTLE

My mother's recipe for Peanut Brittle has served me well, and is still as good as the first time I made it. It is absolutely the best! One year I made 54 batches for our youth at church to sell to earn money to go to the state youth convention. I became so proficient, that I would have two batches going at once.

3 cups sugar
1 cup white corn syrup
1 cup water
1 pound raw peanuts
1 teaspoon salt

1 teaspoon vanilla
2 tablespoons soft butter
　(Mom said to always use
　butter, and I do!)
1 teaspoon soda

Combine the sugar, syrup and water in a large heavy saucepan. Bring to a boil over high heat. While mixture is coming to a boil, combine the salt, vanilla, butter and soda in a small bowl. When sugar/syrup mixture reaches boiling, reduce heat slightly and continue boiling to 250 degrees. Add the peanuts, and continue boiling, stirring constantly, until the mixture reaches 295 degrees. (Stirring constantly is important as the mixture can burn easily.) Remove from heat and add the salt-vanilla-butter-soda mixture. Mix thoroughly (mixture will foam up) and spread thinly on two buttered baking sheets. Let cool and break into pieces.

MR. DANIELS' PEANUT BUTTER FUDGE

It was my privilege to teach Laurie Daniels when she was a third grader at Moss Elementary. For Christmas, she presented me with a package of this wonderful fudge made by her father. For all you peanut butter lovers, this is to die for! Thanks, Mr. Daniels.

1 pint marshmallow cream
　(2 7-ounce jars will do)
1 cup chunk style peanut
　butter

1 teaspoon vanilla
2 cups sugar
⅔ cup milk

Combine the marshmallow creme, peanut butter and vanilla in a large, warm mixing bowl. Combine the sugar and milk in a heavy saucepan. Cook sugar/milk mixture to soft ball stage, or until candy thermometer reaches 235 degrees. Pour over the peanut butter mixture. Stir until mixed. Spread in a buttered 8" or 9" square pan. Cool, cut into small pieces.

TLC Tip: *I like to use a 12 x 8" foil pan, well buttered. This will produce a fudge that isn't quite so thick. If you line the pan with foil, you can remove the fudge from the pan which makes it easier to cut neatly into squares.*

RUTH'S PEANUT BUTTER BALLS

How can you miss with peanut butter, coconut, graham crackers and chocolate?

1 pound butter	2 (1-pound) boxes powdered
1 cup crunchy peanut butter	sugar
1 cup graham cracker crumbs	Chocolate coating
1 can flaked coconut	

Melt butter and peanut butter together. Combine with crumbs, coconut and powdered sugar, using hands if necessary to mix thoroughly. Shape into balls, chill, and dip in melted chocolate coating. Sprinkle tops with chopped peanuts while still warm, if desired. Chill thoroughly.

RITA JO'S CHOCOLATE COVERED PEANUT BUTTER BALLS

These delicious candies will take care of your peanut butter cravings in a hurry.

1½ (1-pound) boxes powdered	1 teaspoon vanilla
sugar	1 (12-ounce) package semi-
1 cup peanut butter	sweet chocolate pieces
¼ cup butter, melted	1 (2" square) paraffin wax

Mix the sugar, peanut butter, butter and vanilla in a large bowl. Melt the chocolate pieces with the paraffin over hot water. Combine well. Shape the peanut butter mixture into small balls. Chill well. Dip into the chocolate mixture. Place on waxed paper-lined cookie sheets and place in refrigerator to chill.

TLC Tip: *If you chill filling mixtures before dipping in chocolate, the chocolate mixture will begin to harden sooner, producing a nicer looking candy.*

MILLION DOLLAR FUDGE

This recipe was given to me by the mother of one of my students when I taught second grade at Farrand School in Plymouth, Michigan. I don't know how it got its million dollar name, unless it refers to the amount of chocolate it contains. This recipe will provide enough for all your holiday gift-giving and entertaining needs. A very rich fudge, I add nuts or not, depending on my mood.

2 bars German's sweet chocolate	**4½ cups sugar**
1 (12-ounce) bag semi-sweet chocolate chips	**½ teaspoon salt**
2 (7-ounce) jars marshmallow creme	**1 large (12-ounce) can evaporated milk**
	Chopped nuts, if desired

Place the sweet chocolate, chocolate chips and marshmallow creme into a large mixing bowl. Combine the sugar, salt and milk in a large, heavy saucepan. Bring to a boil over medium-high heat and boil for 6 minutes. Stir continuously, as mixture has a tendency to burn. Remove from heat, pour over the chocolate, chocolate chips and marshmallow fluff. Mix well. Add nuts if desired. Pour into a well-buttered 10 x 15" jelly roll pan. Cool. Cut into small squares. Cover well, and store in refrigerator or other cool place.

TLC Tip: *If you leave out the nuts, you can use cookie cutters to cut the fudge into interesting and fun shapes. Just cut while the mixture is still a little soft. I have made hearts, Texas shapes (place a red hot where your home town is), and Christmas shapes. Cookie cutters that are open at the top seem to work best. Place all the scraps in a plastic bag for incidental snacking.*

VANILLA FUDGE

I have prepared this recipe and the variations many times over the years when sweets are called for, and used it for party favors, gifts and indulging my own sweet tooth. Easy to make and predictable results make this a recipe you will rely on time and time again.

2½ cups sugar
½ cup butter
⅔ cup evaporated milk
1 (7-ounce) jar (2 cups) marshmallow creme

8 ounces almond bark or vanilla flavored candy coating, coarsely chopped
¾ cup chopped walnuts (optional)
1 teaspoon vanilla

Line a 9" square or 12 x 8" foil pan with foil so that the foil extends over sides of pan; butter the foil. In a large heavy saucepan, combine sugar, margarine and milk. Bring to a boil, stirring constantly. Continue boiling 5 minutes over medium heat, stirring all the while (mixture tends to burn easily). Remove from heat; add marshmallow creme and almond bark. Blend until smooth. Stir in nuts, if using, and vanilla. Pour into prepared pan. Cool to room temperature. Score fudge into small pieces, or cut into desired shapes. (See Million Dollar Fudge recipe.) Decorate as desired. Refrigerate until firm. Remove from pan by lifting foil; cut through scored lines using large knife. Store in refrigerator or other cool place, wrapped well.

TLC Tip: *One year I used a small ghost cookie cutter to cut shapes from the fudge, placing mini chocolate chips for the eyes. Cute!!*

PEPPERMINT CANDY FUDGE

The mint cuts the sweet somewhat making this version a refreshing change of pace.

Omit vanilla. Substitute ½ cup finely crushed peppermint candy for the nuts and add desired amount of red food coloring to make the mixture a soft pink.

PISTACHIO FUDGE

I especially like this fudge—in fact, it is very easy for me to eat too much.

Substitute pistachios for walnuts and add enough green food coloring to make mixture pale green.

CHOCOLATE FUDGE

This recipe makes a smaller amount than the Million Dollar Fudge. The flavor and consistency are very good, and the basic recipe can be varied in any number of ways—you can probably think up a variation of your own. With a recipe like this and the Vanilla Fudge in your files you can create your own personal fudge assortments for that special gift.

2½ cups sugar
½ cup butter
⅔ cup evaporated milk
1 (7-ounce) jar (2 cups)
   marshmallow creme

1 (12-ounce) package (2 cups)
   semi-sweet chocolate
   chips
¾ cup chopped nuts
   (if desired)
1 teaspoon vanilla

Line a 9" square or 12 x 8" foil pan with foil so that the foil extends over the sides of the pan. Butter the foil. In a large heavy saucepan, combine sugar, margarine and milk. Bring to a boil, stirring constantly. Continue boiling 5 minutes over medium heat. Stir constantly, as mixture tends to burn easily. Remove from heat, add the marshmallow creme and chocolate chips; blend until smooth. Stir in nuts and vanilla. Pour into prepared pan. Cool to room temperature. Score fudge into small squares. Garnish as desired, and refrigerate until firm. Remove fudge from pan by lifting foil; remove foil from fudge and cut along score lines with a large knife. Store, covered, in refrigerator or other cool place.

ROCKY ROAD FUDGE

This variation is yummy.

Stir in 2 cups miniature marshmallows after nuts and vanilla. (Marshmallows should not melt.) Quickly spread in prepared pan.

TLC Tip: *One year I made a variety of these fudges, and layered eight pieces in small square boxes, tied them with Christmas ribbon, tagged them and used them as place favors for a luncheon. Your local stationery store or card shop may be a source for the boxes.*

MACKINAC ISLAND FUDGE

Mackinac Island is one of the unique areas of the United States. It sits in the waters between upper and lower Michigan, and is accessible only by ferry. No motor driven vehicles are allowed on the island, so the mode of travel is bicycle, horse and carriage, or your own feet. The Grand Hotel dominates the island, and the waterfront bustles with small businesses and eateries. Long before fudge shops were common in malls and resort areas, Mackinac Island was famous for its "fudge shoppes". When we took the family there in the summer of 1974, we were fascinated by all the different flavors. This candy is reminiscent of that fudge. It is easy to make and sets up nicely.

½ cup butter
½ cup light corn syrup
Dash of salt
1 pound powdered sugar

6 ounces semi-sweet chocolate
chips
1 teaspoon vanilla

In a large saucepan, bring the butter and syrup to a boil, stirring constantly. Boil 1 minute and add half the sugar, stirring until all of the little lumps of sugar smooth out. Add remaining sugar, bring back to a boil and continue stirring until smooth. Boil gently about 2 minutes. Remove from heat and stir in chips and vanilla. Pour at once into greased 8" square pan. Cool about 10 minutes before cutting into squares.

Variation: For maple fudge, substitute butterscotch chips for chocolate and maple flavoring for vanilla.

TLC Tip: *If you line the pan with foil, the candy can be lifted out for easier cutting.*

TOFFEE FUDGE

If you are a Heath bar fan, you'll love this simple-to-prepare candy.

1 cup chopped pecans
¾ cup brown sugar
½ cup butter

½ cup milk chocolate or semi-
sweet chocolate pieces

Sprinkle pecans on the bottom of a greased 9 x 9" square pan. Combine sugar and butter in saucepan. Bring to a boil, stirring constantly; boil 7 minutes. Remove from heat and spread over nuts. Sprinkle chocolate pieces over top. Cover pan so heat will melt chocolate. Spread evenly over top. Cut in squares while still warm or break into uneven pieces when cool.

CHRISTMAS FUDGE

This fudge is so pretty with the bits of red and green cherries and pieces of nut showing through.

2¼ cups sugar
¼ cup sour cream
¼ cup milk
2 tablespoons butter
1 tablespoon light corn syrup

¼ teaspoon salt
2 teaspoons vanilla
1 cup chopped nuts
⅓ cup quartered candied
   cherries

Combine sugar, sour cream, milk, butter, corn syrup and salt in a heavy saucepan. Stir over moderate heat until sugar is dissolved and mixture reaches a boil. Boil over moderate heat 9 to 10 minutes or until mixture reaches 238 degrees on a candy thermometer. Remove from heat and allow to stand until lukewarm (110 degrees), about 1 hour. Add vanilla, and beat until mixture just begins to lose its gloss and hold shape. (Requires very little beating.) Quickly stir in nuts and cherries and turn into a buttered 12 x 8" pan. Let stand until firm before cutting.

ORANGE CREAM FUDGE

This fudge was inspired by a recipe my sister gave me. I've gotten so accustomed to the candies made with marshmallow creme that I adapted her longer-cooking recipe to this quicker, and probably more foolproof, version. The flavor is superb.

2½ cups sugar
½ cup butter
⅓ cup evaporated milk
⅓ cup orange juice
1 (7-ounce) jar (2 cups)
   marshmallow creme

8 ounces almond bark or
   vanilla flavored candy
   coating, coarsely
   chopped
1 tablespoon grated orange
   peel

Line a 12 x 8" foil pan with foil so that the foil extends over the sides of the pan; butter the foil. In a large heavy saucepan, combine sugar, butter, orange juice and milk. Bring to a boil, stirring constantly. Continue boiling 5 minutes over medium heat, stirring all the while (mixture tends to burn easily). Remove from heat; add marshmallow creme, almond bark and grated orange peel. Blend until smooth. Pour into prepared pan. Cool to room temperature. Score fudge into small pieces. Refrigerate until firm. Remove from pan by lifting the foil; cut through scored lines using large knife. Store in the refrigerator or other cool place, wrapped well. (After I cut it, I usually leave the pieces in place and put them back in the pan, foil and all. Then I place the pan in a large plastic bag.)

TLC Tip: *Should you desire to add nuts to this fudge, slivered almonds make a nice addition.*

366

FUDGEMALLOW RAISIN CANDY

This is another of Laura Furney's delectable recipes. I have been known to make a batch of this for no reason at all—except that it is so good.

1 (12-ounce) package semi-sweet chocolate chips
1 cup chunk-style peanut butter

3 cups miniature marshmallows
¾ cup raisins

Microwave the chocolate chips and peanut butter until melted. (You can also melt them in a pan on the stove using medium-low heat.) Fold in the marshmallows and raisins. Pour into a foil-lined 8 x 11" pan. Chill until firm. Cut into squares. Store where it is cool. Laura says this candy freezes well.

TLC Tip: Another neat way to form this candy is to fill mini-muffin cups with a spoonful of the mixture. Easy to eat and store this way.

RAINBOW DIVINITY

This method of making divinity takes a little bit of the chance out of the outcome. It also allows for a variety of flavors and colors, and is almost too pretty to eat.

3 cups sugar
¾ cup light corn syrup
¾ cup water
Dash of salt
2 egg whites
3 tablespoons fruit-flavored gelatin

1 teaspoon vanilla
1 cup chopped nuts (optional)
½ cup flaked coconut (optional)
Garnishes as desired

Combine sugar, corn syrup, water and salt in a large saucepan; bring to boiling, reduce heat, and cook to hard-ball stage, 250 degrees on the candy thermometer. Beat egg whites until fluffy. Add dry gelatin gradually, beating until stiff peaks form. Beat in the vanilla. Pour syrup slowly into egg white mixture, beating constantly with mixer on high speed until candy holds shape and loses gloss. Stir in nuts and coconut, if desired; pour quickly into 9" buttered pan, or drop by teaspoonfuls onto waxed or parchment paper. To cut into squares, use a knife dipped into hot water.

TLC Tip: If making for Christmas, red or green colored sugar sprinkled on the top before mixture hardens makes a nice touch. I don't have the stamina to make this without my stand mixer and some hand mixers don't have enough power. My mother, however, used to make fabulous divinity without either.

RUTH'S CARAMEL POPCORN

Ruth keeps up her image as a great cook with this delicious recipe for caramel popcorn. Ruth likes to use the lesser amount of popcorn—she says it is more yummy. I won't argue with her!!

13 to 15 cups popped corn	¼ cup light corn syrup
1 cup brown sugar	½ teaspoon salt
½ cup butter or margarine	½ teaspoon soda

Heat oven to 200 degrees. Keep popcorn warm in a large pan. In a large saucepan, combine sugar, butter, corn syrup and salt. Bring to a boil, stirring constantly. Continue cooking over medium heat for 5 minutes. Remove from heat, stir in soda until foamy. Pour over popped corn, stirring until corn is well coated. Divide between two 9 x 12" pans. Bake one hour, stirring every 15 minutes. Cool before eating—mixture is very hot.

LAURA HORN'S BAKED CARAMEL CORN

Laura Horn, a friend from Fort Worth, certainly did us a favor by giving my daughter, Cyndee, this recipe. Cyndee has made countless batches of this wonderful caramel corn. I've made my share, too. Easy and delicious— the kind of snack it is hard to stop eating.

6 quarts popped corn	1 teaspoon salt
1 cup butter	½ teaspoon baking soda
2 cups brown sugar	1 teaspoon vanilla
½ cup light or dark corn syrup	

Keep popcorn warm in a 250 degree oven. Melt butter in a large heavy saucepan. Stir in the brown sugar, corn syrup and salt. Bring to a boil, stirring constantly. Boil, without stirring, for 5 minutes. Remove from heat, stir in soda and vanilla. Pour over popped corn, mixing well. Turn into 2 large, shallow baking or roasting pans. Bake at 250 degrees for one hour, stirring every 15 minutes. Remove from oven, cool. Break apart and store in a tightly covered container or plastic bag.

TLC Tip: *I have noticed that sometimes Cyndee adds pecans, peanuts or other goodies—M & M's, raisins, etc.—to the mixture after removing from the oven but while it is still a bit sticky.*

SPICY CEREAL CRUNCH

I love this snack—I guess the combination of brown sugar and cinnamon hits the spot with me. A sweet version of the many and varied cereal snack mixtures that abound, I think you'll like this one a lot.

½ cup butter
1⅓ cups brown sugar
¼ cup light corn syrup
2 teaspoons cinnamon
½ teaspoon salt
3 cups toasted oat cereal

2 cups rice squares
2 cups corn squares
2 cups wheat squares
1 cup raisins
1 cup pecans

In a buttered bowl, toss cereal, raisins and nuts. Set aside while making syrup. Combine first 5 ingredients in a large heavy saucepan. Stir constantly over medium high heat until boiling; boil for 3 minutes. Pour hot syrup mixture over cereal mixture, stir to coat. Spread on two buttered cookie sheets. When cool and firm, break into pieces.

ZACHARY'S PEOPLE CHOW

This is the treat our 12 year old cocker spaniel, Zack, would prepare for us if he could. I just know he would serve this in a plastic dog bowl with "People Chow" written on the side. Since he is short on cooking skills, I do it for him. My sister-in-law Linda and daughter Cyndee enjoy making this, too.

1 cup semi-sweet chocolate
   chips
1 cup milk chocolate chips
1 cup peanut butter
1 stick (½ cup) butter or
   margarine

1 small box (about 13 cups)
   Crispix or Rice Chex
1 (1-pound) box powdered
   sugar

Melt the first 4 ingredients together in a large heavy saucepan. Pour the cereal into a large bowl. Pour the chocolate mixture over, stirring carefully but thoroughly. Dump into a large paper bag; pour the powdered sugar over all; shake well. Spread mixture on cookie sheet/s and let cool.

CHOCOLATE PEANUT PILLOWS

This is a rather unusual snack but surprisingly good.

1 (6-ounce) package chocolate
   pieces
1 tablespoon shortening
½ cup peanut butter

2 tablespoons powdered sugar
3 cups spoon-size shredded
   wheat
½ cup finely chopped peanuts

Melt the chocolate and shortening over low heat. Remove and stir in the peanut butter and powdered sugar. Dip shredded wheat biscuits in the chocolate mixture, coating all sides; gently shake off excess. Place on rack over waxed paper, sprinkle with chopped peanuts. Cool, then store in the refrigerator or other cool place.

RICE KRISPIE SQUARES

This is a real oldie that continues to be a goodie. I have made this sweet treat since I was a child. I grew up near the Kellogg cereal factory in Battle Creek, Michigan, and went on many a tour there. They would sometimes serve these with a cup of ice cream (they called them Dixie Cups) before we left. I love it that these squares are still popular with young and old alike. Our daughter, Deanna, is a particular fan of these, and her only problem is getting the mixture into the pan before eating it!!

¼ cup butter
10 ounces marshmallows

6 cups Rice Krispies

Melt butter in a large, microwave-safe bowl until melted. Add the marshmallows and stir to coat. Microwave butter/marshmallow mixture until melted, 1 to 2 minutes, stirring after one minute. Add the cereal, mixing thoroughly. Press into a buttered 9 x 13" pan. Cool before cutting into squares or other desired shapes—if you can wait!!

TLC Tip: *Naturally the butter and marshmallows can be melted on the stove. Just use low heat, stir often, and watch carefully.*

CANDY STRAWBERRIES

These little morsels are so cute, and make a very colorful addition to a candy tray. When strawberries are in season, save the plastic pint or half-pint boxes that you purchase them in. Line with plastic or cellophane, place these candies inside, tie on a bow and you have a pretty gift package.

2 cups finely chopped pecans
3 cups angel flake coconut
1 (6-ounce) package
    strawberry gelatin +
    additional for rolling the
    strawberries in

1 (14-ounce) can sweetened
    condensed milk
1 teaspoon vanilla
Green decorator icing

Mix nuts, coconut and gelatin in bowl; stir in milk and vanilla. If mixture isn't red enough to suit, add food coloring to beef up the color. Chill overnight. Shape into strawberries, using about 1 teaspoon mixture for each strawberry. Roll each in additional gelatin. Let stand until dry. Using a decorating tip and bag, make green frosting leaves on the top of each strawberry. Let dry before storing, loosely covered.

CHOCOLATE COVERED PRETZELS

I just love the combination of sweet and salty this snack provides. A popular item in candy and specialty shops, you can make it easily at home.

8 ounces chocolate chips or
    chocolate coating, semi-
    sweet or milk

4 ounces pretzel twists

In a medium saucepan over low heat, melt the chocolate, stirring constantly. Keep mixture warm. Dip pretzels into coating; allow excess to drip off. Place on waxed paper to harden. Store in a covered tin placing waxed paper between the layers.

TLC Tip: You can sprinkle cookie decorations on the pretzels before the chocolate hardens for a little pizazz.

WHITE CHOCOLATE PRETZELS

8 ounces almond bark or vanilla flavored candy coating	¼ teaspoon peppermint extract, if desired 4 ounces pretzel twists Crushed peppermint candy

In a medium saucepan over low heat, melt the almond bark, stirring constantly. Add the peppermint extract, blending gently. Keep mixture warm. Dip pretzels into coating, allowing excess to drip off. Place on waxed paper. Sprinkle tops of pretzels with crushed candy. Allow to cool. Store in tightly covered container, placing waxed paper between layers.

TLC Tip: While looking through a specialty catalog, I saw dipped pretzels that were sprinkled with all sorts of things—cookie crumbs, toffee pieces, chocolate sprinkles. Use your imagination and come up with your own special treat.

Desserts

The most common dessert I remember as a child was some kind of fruit—fresh during season, or canned in the winter. We had access to strawberries, raspberries (I made my spending money picking berries during the summer), peaches, pears, cherries, grapes, plums and apples. We never had much citrus—probably it was too expensive. Strawberry shortcake was the summer dessert of choice, and peach shortcake a close second.

Mother made Cottage Pudding—I remember this homey dessert as part of nearly every meal she fixed for the thrashing crew or silo fillers. It is not what you would call glamorous, but is very tasty and satisfying. Adding to its merits is the fact that it is made with ingredients readily available. I remember it best served with lemon or vanilla sauce. In later years, sauces with a little more pizazz, such as chocolate or sour cherry were served with it.

When mother entertained for Sunday dinner (rarely did she entertain at other times) she would sometimes serve Orange Pineapple Bavarian cream. I thought it the height of elegance at the time, chilled and served in the green, stemmed dessert dishes.

Ice cream was the ultimate. It seems like we never had it except on Sunday. I guess it would have meant an extra trip into town for the ice. We would stop at the ice house after church and dad would purchase a chunk of ice, crystal clear and diamond bright, wrap it in a couple of gunny sacks, and we would hurry home, where the vanilla custard mom had already made was waiting, probably keeping cool in the milk house.

Now mom's ice cream was a heart doctor's nightmare. No one had heard of cholesterol and so it contained fresh milk from our Jersey cows, probably at least ¼ cream, whole eggs and no doubt a few extra yolks for richness, plus pure vanilla extract, all cooked up to a smooth, rich custard.

Dad would chip the ice into small chunks with the ice pick, then further reduce it to a fine crush with the side of his trusty axe. We kids always started the turning of the freezer with much vim and vigor, losing interest as it became harder and harder to make the crank go around.

When it was frozen, the dasher was removed and spoons appeared for a first, wonderful taste. Then the cover was replaced, more ice and salt were mounded on top, and the whole thing shrouded in more gunny sacks. We kids always wondered what was so magical about letting the ice cream "ripen", and found it very difficult to wait, but the results were the stuff memories are made of.

When I was small, I don't remember having any flavor other than vanilla, nor were our servings embellished with chocolate or nuts. In later years I do remember adding fresh sliced peaches or strawberries.

Allegan had a wonderful dairy, and they made great tasting ice cream. My father's favorite flavor was Orange Pineapple, so if we bought ice cream, that is probably what we had. Sometimes we would stop on our way home after church on Sunday night for a cone. They piled them high then, and I can still taste it. The dairy would also pack up a five-gallon container for church picnics and such. They used a heavy, padded canvas container which kept the ice cream at just the right dipping consistency. Waiting in line for a cone filled with ice cream from that "magic" container was one of the best reasons to attend the Sunday School Picnic.

COTTAGE PUDDING

Over the years, I had almost forgotten what a homey, delicious dessert this was. We prepared it often in our farm kitchen, and served it to everyone from farm hands to visiting preachers. I have resurrected it in recent years, and our son-in-law, David, has taken a special liking to it. It can be served very simply, or "gussied up" in any number of ways with various toppings and garnishes. This dessert brings back the warmest memories of my mother and grandmother. My favorite topping is the Vanilla Sauce (see index), but the Lemon runs a close second. Chocolate lovers can have a heyday with this also.

¼ cup shortening
⅔ cup sugar
1 egg
½ cup milk

½ teaspoon flavoring (Here you might think about the kind of sauce you are going to put on it. For vanilla, I would use vanilla flavoring. For lemon, a little lemon would be nice, or a combination of lemon and vanilla. You get the point.)
1½ cups cake flour
2 teaspoons baking powder
½ teaspoon salt

Cream the shortening and sugar together. Add the egg and beat until smooth. Add the milk and the flavoring, then the flour, baking powder and salt. Mix until smooth and pour into a greased and floured 9 x 9" baking pan. Bake in a 350 degree oven for 25 minutes. While warm, cut into squares and serve with your choice of sauce. (Need I say that this is just heavenly when served when the cake and sauce are both slightly warm?)

APPLE CRISP

I've tried many variations of Apple Crisp through the years, and I always come back to this one. I guess you could say it is my favorite. It is rare that there is any left, so it must be the favorite of my friends and family too.

4 cups pared, cored and sliced baking apples
⅔ to ¾ cup brown sugar, packed
½ cup flour

½ cup rolled oats, quick or regular
½ teaspoon cinnamon
¾ teaspoon nutmeg
⅓ cup soft butter

Place the sliced apples in a greased square pan, 8 x 8". Blend remaining ingredients until mixture is crumbly. Spread over apples. Bake in a 375 degree oven for 30 to 35 minutes or until apples are tender and topping is golden brown. You'll also notice the apple mixture bubbling up through the crumbly top. Serve as is or with ice cream or pour on light or whipping cream. Yum!!

TLC Tip: *I most often use a metal pan, don't ask me why. If you choose to use a glass baking dish, reduce the oven temperature by 25 degrees. As for the apples, I use whatever I have on hand if I haven't planned ahead. Otherwise, I like Granny Smith or a mixture of baking and all-purpose apples. The food processor surely helps to make the topping in a jiffy. Just pour in the dry ingredients, pulse briefly to mix. Drop in the butter, which you have cut into pieces, and pulse until large crumbs form. Easy.*

TLC Tip Two: *For a slightly different taste, stir ¼ cup butterscotch flavored chips into the crumb mixture before sprinkling on the apples.*

CRANBERRY APPLE CASSEROLE

When I think of casserole, I think of a main dish. This definitely breaks that rule, as this is a dessert. My Cleo thinks this is one of the greatest, and I must admit, when the mornings begin to be crisp, the mums start to bloom and the smell of fireplace smoke is in the air, I get out this recipe. Served warm with a scoop of vanilla ice cream on the top, it is the perfect ending to a fall meal. Or serve it with steaming mugs of coffee for a casual get-together.

3 cups peeled, chopped apples
2 cups fresh cranberries
2 tablespoons flour
1 cup sugar
3 individual packages instant oatmeal with cinnamon and spices

¾ cup chopped pecans
½ cup flour
½ cup firmly packed brown sugar
½ cup butter, melted

Combine apples, 2 cups cranberries and the 2 tablespoons flour, tossing to coat. Add 1 cup sugar, mixing well. Pour into a 2-quart casserole. Combine oatmeal, pecans, ½ cup flour and the brown sugar; stir in the melted butter and mix until crumbly. Spoon over the fruit mixture. Bake, uncovered, at 350 degrees for 45 minutes. Garnish with additional pecan halves and more cranberries, if desired.

TRADITIONAL BANANA PUDDING

Banana pudding is always popular. There is a good recipe on the vanilla wafer box, but I usually use my Lite Cream Pie Filling (see index). I think this is best made with bananas that are fully ripe—not overripe, but definitely not on the green side. It is always best when freshly made, but leftovers have a way of disappearing even so.

1 recipe Lite Cream Pie Filling
3-4 bananas, sliced

Vanilla wafers
Meringue made with 3 egg whites (See index)

In a 1½-quart casserole, place a layer of vanilla wafers, then a layer of banana slices. Top with half the cream filling. Make another layer of wafers and banana slices, and top with the remainder of the cream filling. Cover completely with the meringue, and bake in a 350 degree oven for 15 minutes. Watch carefully so meringue does not get too brown.

TAPIOCA PUDDING

Tapioca Pudding is probably the most common dessert around our house. It is simple to put together, not too sweet, and totally comforting. My husband, Cleo, does not claim to be a cook, but he thinks the secret to a pudding that is not pasty is just to heat it to the boiling point, not to actually let it boil. It sets up as it cools. I have to admit he is probably right, so it takes a bit of watching to catch it at the right point to remove it from the heat. These days I prepare it in the microwave. If you prefer to cook it on the stove, you certainly can.

⅓ cup sugar
3 tablespoons Minute tapioca
2 pinches of salt (can be omitted)

1 egg
2¾ cups milk (I use skim)
1 teaspoon vanilla

Mix the sugar, tapioca and salt in a large microwave-safe bowl. Stir in the egg with a small amount of the milk until the egg is well combined. Add the remainder of the milk. Let set for 5 minutes. Microwave on high for 2 minutes. Stir. Microwave on high another 2 minutes. Stir. Continue microwaving on high, stopping every minute to stir. The pudding will puff up and look and feel slightly thick when it is done, about 6-8 minutes total. Remove from the microwave and add the vanilla. Cool slightly, stir well, and divide into serving dishes. Makes 4 large or 5 or 6 smaller servings. Garnish with a little whipped cream if you wish—that's Cleo's favorite way—but we usually eat it plain.

TLC Tip: *This pudding is at its best when served slightly warm, but tapioca lovers will eat the chilled leftovers with nary a complaint.*

GRANDMOTHER YERDEN'S PUDDING

My Grandmother Yerden lived in my parents' home from the time they were married until her death in 1960. Or perhaps they lived in her home. Anyway, I grew up close to this grandmother. She was a "fleshy" woman, quiet, a hard worker, avid reader and taught the older adult Sunday School Class for many years. My cousin, Jean, and I have always given her the blame for our thin hair, and I just know I got the "tearing-articles-out-of-magazines gene" from her. She married when she was sixteen, and always encouraged me to "have some butterfly years" before I married. This is the pudding she made for us children when we were little. It is the height of comfort food, plain and simple, and puts a packaged mix to shame.

2 cups milk, divided use	**2 eggs**
2 tablespoons flour	**1 teaspoon vanilla**
½ cup sugar	

Heat 1½ cups of the milk over medium heat. Combine the sugar and flour; mix in the remaining ½ cup milk. Add the sugar, flour, milk mixture to the heated milk. Continue to cook over medium heat until thick, about 5 minutes. Add a small amount to the beaten eggs, mix well, and return to saucepan. Continue to cook for another minute or so. Remove from heat and add vanilla.

TLC Tip: *There is no mention of salt in this recipe. Add a pinch if you wish—I think it adds to the flavor somewhat. This pudding is quite sweet—you might be able to get by with ⅓ cup sugar.*

AUNT SMYRNA'S BLACKBERRY COBBLER

Aunt Smyrna Crabtree's cobbler was a much sought after dessert for family gatherings in Pryor, Oklahoma. Whether a birthday dinner, holiday feast or picnic in the park, just knowing her cobbler was waiting in the wings brought a smile to our faces. At 92, my aunt says she doesn't do much cooking any more. When I pressed her for the cobbler recipe, she laughed and said she "just put it together". She did say she used fresh or frozen berries, and never did like a dry cobbler—she wanted lots of juice. She put pastry on the bottom of the pan, and on top of the berries but never on the sides. Make this one, and think of her.

3 (16-ounce) packages frozen blackberries, thawed	½ teaspoon cinnamon
1½ cups sugar	2 tablespoons butter
3 tablespoons flour	Pastry for double-crust pie

Pour the berries with their juice into a large bowl. In a small bowl, combine the sugar, flour and cinnamon. Pour over the berries and stir gently with a wooden spoon. Divide the pastry in half. Roll one half to fit the bottom of an 8 x 11" glass baking dish. Pour in the berries. Dot with the butter. Roll the remaining pastry to fit over the berries, cutting slits to let the steam escape. Carefully lay over the berries, crimp around edge if you wish, or leave loose. Sprinkle a little sugar over the top. Bake on the middle shelf in a 425 degree oven for 40 minutes, or until crust is golden and juices are bubbly and thick.

TLC Tip: Probably Aunt Smyrna never did this, but sometimes I add a little orange or lemon zest to the berry mixture.

TLC Tip Two: I don't live in an area where blackberries are plentiful, so I use the frozen berries. If you are fortunate enough to be able to get fresh ones, you will need to add a little water—maybe ½ cup.

MOM ALBRIGHT'S PEACH COBBLER

This easy cobbler is a favorite dessert of nephew Brad Albright, and comes from his Grandmother Albright.

¼ cup butter
1½ cups sugar, divided use
2 teaspoons baking powder
½ cup milk
1 cup flour

1 (28-ounce) can peach slices, drained (I use the kind packed in juice)
1 cup water

Beat together with an electric mixer, the butter, ½ cup sugar, baking powder, milk and flour. Pour into a lightly greased 8 x 11" baking dish. Arrange the peach slices over the batter. Sprinkle with the remaining 1 cup sugar, and pour the water over. Bake in a 350 degree oven for 30 minutes or longer. (My sister says it will take longer.) Delicious with a drizzle of cream on top.

TLC Tip: *The original recipe called for butter the size of an egg. My sister and I decided that ¼ cup was about right.*
TLC Tip Two: *I find that ¾ cup sugar sprinkled on top of the fruit is enough for our tastes. The addition of ¼ teaspoon salt and ½ teaspoon vanilla added to the batter makes a richer tasting cobbler. I like to use the juice drained from the peaches for part of the water, also.*

CHERRY TORTE

This torte is especially nice to serve during the Christmas season—red cherries, white whipped cream and glistening red sauce.

½ cup soft butter
5 tablespoons powdered sugar
1 cup cake flour
1 (1-pound) can sour cherries
2 eggs, beaten
1 cup sugar

¼ cup flour
¾ teas baking powder
½ cup chopped nuts
1 teaspoon vanilla
¼ teaspoon salt

Cream the butter with the powdered sugar and cake flour. Pat flour mixture on bottom of an ungreased 13 x 9" baking pan and bake at 350 degrees for 15 minutes. Drain the cherries, reserving the juice. Blend the remaining ingredients well and fold in the drained cherries. Pour over the crust and bake at the same temperature for 30 minutes. Remove from oven and cool. While the torte is baking, prepare the sauce by combining 2 tablespoons cornstarch with ¼ cup sugar in a small saucepan. Add enough water to the reserved cherry juice to make 1 cup. Stir into the cornstarch mixture; bring to a boil, stirring constantly, and continue boiling until thickened and clear. To serve, cut into squares, top with sweetened whipped cream and cherry sauce.

CHERRY CAKE COBBLER

This is another dessert we enjoyed when I was a child. Grandmother baked it in a granite pan of unusual proportion, and used home-canned cherries. Those two facts have made it a little hard to make in "modern" times. I have adjusted the recipe slightly to fit a 12 x 8" baking dish. This is wonderful served warm with a bit of vanilla ice cream on top.

1½ cups sugar, divided use
1 cup flour
¼ teaspoon salt
2 teaspoons baking powder
1 tablespoon butter or
  shortening
½ cup milk

1 teaspoon vanilla or almond
  extract (or ½ teaspoon
  each)
2 (1-pound) cans sour pie
  cherries, drained, and
  juice reserved
Reserved cherry juice plus
  enough water to make 2
  cups

Combine ½ cup sugar, flour, salt and baking powder in a large mixing bowl; add butter, milk and flavoring. Beat on medium speed for 2 minutes. Pour into greased 8 x 12" baking dish. Cover batter with drained cherries; sprinkle remaining 1 cup sugar over cherries. Heat cherry juice and water until steaming; pour over cherries. Bake at 375 degrees about 40 minutes. Lay a piece of foil lightly over the top after 20 minutes if necessary to prevent overbrowning.

TLC Tip: *If, like me, you no longer use granite baking pans, don't forget to reduce the oven temperature to 350 degrees to allow for the glass baking dish.*

FRESH PEACH COBBLER

I love this cobbler. Just writing about it brings a smile to my face. When I was a little girl living in Michigan, we lived near the peach orchards. I will always remember when dad would bring home the peaches—two or three bushel at a time—for mother and grandmother to can. The aroma was heady. We would take out the ripest ones to eat out of hand, the juice dripping down our chins and arms, or to slice, sprinkle with a little sugar and cover with cream. Of course some of them ended up in cobbler. To this day, if a peach doesn't smell like a peach, I don't buy it.

2 tablespoons quick tapioca	1 cup water
1 cup sugar	2 tablespoons lemon juice
¼ teaspoon salt	¼ teaspoon grated lemon rind
¼ teaspoon nutmeg	2 tablespoons butter
4 cups sliced fresh peaches	

Combine tapioca, sugar, salt and nutmeg; blend well, and fold into peaches. Add water, lemon juice and lemon rind. Turn into an 8 x 12" baking dish and dot with the butter.

Crust:

1½ cups flour	½ teaspoon salt
2 teaspoons baking powder	½ cup shortening or butter
2 tablespoons sugar	½ cup milk

Measure the flour, baking powder, sugar and salt into a bowl. Cut in the shortening with a pastry blender and stir in the milk. Continue to stir until a soft dough forms. Turn onto a sheet of waxed paper that has been dusted with flour. Pat into a rectangle to fit baking dish. Use the waxed paper to help you place the dough on top of the peaches. (It isn't necessary for the dough to touch the edges or be perfectly even along the edges.) Cut several slashes in the dough. Bake in a 425 degree oven for 30 minutes. This is heavenly served slightly warm. Some people think the addition of ice cream makes it even better.

TLC Tip: This is a very soft dough so the use of waxed paper is important.

EASY PUMPKIN SWIRL

Rolled desserts always look difficult and a little mysterious, but actually they aren't if you know what to do. This is an especially tasty one that will add points to your reputation as a cook.

¾ cup buttermilk baking mix
3 eggs
1 cup sugar
⅔ cup canned solid pack
   pumpkin
2 teaspoons cinnamon
1 teaspoon pumpkin pie spice

½ teaspoon nutmeg
1 cup powdered sugar
8 ounces softened cream
   cheese
6 tablespoons butter, softened
1 teaspoon vanilla
1 cup chopped nuts

Grease a 15 x 10" jelly roll pan. Line with waxed or parchment paper. Grease the paper. Beat the eggs and sugar until fluffy. Beat in the pumpkin; stir in the dry ingredients. Pour into pan and spread evenly. Sprinkle with nuts. Bake in a 375 degree oven for 13 to 15 minutes. Invert onto a towel that has been dusted with powdered sugar. Peel off the paper. Roll up cake and towel together from short side. Place seam side down on wire rack. Cool completely. Prepare filling by beating together the powdered sugar, cream cheese, butter and vanilla. Unroll cake. Spread with filling; re-roll cake. Refrigerate until ready to serve. Cut into slices to serve.

TLC Tip: This is wonderful as is, but a dollop of whipped cream is a nice addition. If I am serving this as part of a dessert buffet, I like to slice the cake but leave it arranged as a whole. I spread puffs of whipped cream down the center of the roll and dust lightly with cinnamon.

GLORIA'S LEMON DESSERT

This is one of the all-time favorite desserts in our family! Easy and inexpensive, this comes from my friend Gloria South. She and her husband, Ron, have lived in Germany for several years, where they teach with the American Schools. I think I've immortalized this dessert for her, but when we met at the train station in Frankfort, Germany, a few years ago, she could scarcely remember it!

1 (12-ounce) can evaporated
  milk
1 (3-ounce) package lemon
  gelatin
1¾ cups boiling water

½ cup lemon juice
1 cup sugar
A double recipe of graham
  cracker crumb crust

Chill the milk until cold. (I like to put it in my metal mixer bowl along with the beater, and put it all in the freezer for an hour or two.) Dissolve gelatin in boiling water and chill until it begins to set. Whip gelatin until light and fluffy; add lemon juice and sugar. Whip the milk until stiff; fold into gelatin mixture. Press the graham cracker crumb mixture into a 9 x 13" pan, reserving a small amount for garnish. Pour gelatin mixture on top of crumbs, smoothing the surface. Sprinkle reserved crumbs over. Chill until set; cut into squares to serve.

TLC Tip: *I've tried this using sugar-free Jello, and I just don't like it as well. My daughters use evaporated skim milk and it works just fine. I always use freshly squeezed lemon juice, but years ago I didn't, and people still liked it.*

PINEAPPLE ORANGE BAVARIAN CREAM

This is the only "fancy" dessert I can remember my mother making when I was a small child. The saying that you "eat with your eyes as much as your mouth" must be true, as I can remember exactly how it looked almost more than I can remember how it tasted. I have even scoured antique stores to find green dessert dishes like my mother had. Of course any pretty clear dish will show off the soft peach color nicely, as will a topping of whipped cream and a mint leaf.

1 (20-ounce) can crushed
   pineapple (about 2 cups)
1 tablespoon sugar

1 (3-ounce) package orange
   gelatin
⅛ teaspoon salt
1 cup whipping cream

Combine the pineapple with juice and the sugar in a small saucepan; heat to boiling. Remove from heat and stir in the gelatin and salt, stirring until gelatin is thoroughly dissolved. Chill until mixture begins to set. Whip the cream until stiff peaks form; fold into gelatin mixture. Spoon into serving dishes. Chill until set. Garnish as desired before serving.

TLC Tip: *I don't mess around with this recipe. Somehow I can't bring myself to do it. But since you don't have the emotional attachment, you may want to try pineapple in juice, sugar-free gelatin and whipped topping. I can't guarantee the results.*

YERDEN FAMILY VANILLA ICE CREAM

When my brother's family drags out the ice cream freezer, they fill it with this wonderfully rich mixture. Smooth and creamy, it really needs no embellishing, but topped with lightly-sweetened fresh fruit, you'll think you're in paradise!!

4 eggs
2¼ cups sugar
5 cups milk—whole milk is
   best, of course

2 cups whipping cream
2 cups half-and-half
3 teaspoons vanilla
½ teaspoon salt

In a large mixer bowl, beat the eggs until fluffy. Add the sugar gradually, continuing to beat until mixture is very thick and pale in color. Reduce the mixer speed and add the milk, whipping cream, half-and-half, vanilla and salt. Pour into freezer container. Freeze according to manufacturer's directions.

EASY ICE CREAM PIES

It's nice to have a dessert that you can put together quickly, is showy, and tastes like "more". This just might be it. Not only does it fit all the above criteria, but it allows you to use your creativity. I've listed some of my favorite combinations, you take it from there.

Basic Directions:

1 prepared crumb crust	Topping
1 quart ice cream or frozen yogurt (you might like more)	Garnishes

Spoon the ice cream into the crumb crust. Pour the topping over, garnish as desired. Cover lightly; place in freezer until serving time. Remove from freezer about 10 minutes before serving. Cut into wedges to serve.

Easy Pie 1: Use a chocolate crumb crust, coffee ice cream, fudge sauce and top with crushed toffee bars.

Easy Pie 2: Use a graham cracker crumb crust, butter pecan ice cream, caramel sauce and more pecans for a topping.

Easy Pie 3: Use a chocolate crumb crust, rocky road ice cream, and top with marshmallow topping.

Easy Pie 4: Use a chocolate crumb crust, vanilla ice cream, chocolate sauce and top with salted Spanish peanuts. This version brings back wonderful memories of the Kandy Kitchen in Allegan, Michigan. It was THE place to go for hand made and shaped candies and wonderful ice cream treats when I was growing up. My favorite was the Tin Roof Sundae, a concoction of vanilla ice cream, chocolate sauce (not hot fudge sauce, just chocolate sauce) and topped with Spanish peanuts. Alas, the Kandy Kitchen has gone the way of so many other soda fountains, but the memory lingers on.

Easy Pie 5: Chocolate crumb crust, peppermint ice cream, fudge sauce and crushed peppermint candy topping.

I think you get the idea—have fun!

RUTH'S HOMEMADE ICE CREAM

In the Albright household, ice cream is real ice cream. Simple to put together, with few ingredients, you'll be licking your lips and begging for more in no time.

3 cups whipping cream	½ of an (8-ounce) bottle
3 cups sugar	vanilla
Pinch of salt	Milk to fill freezer container
	¾ full

Combine cream, sugar, salt and vanilla. Pour into freezer container; fill container ¾ full with milk (whole milk is best). Freeze according to freezer directions.

CARLILE FAMILY ICE CREAM

This is the ice cream our family enjoyed for birthdays, cookouts, church socials and as a background for my husband's favorite—blackberries. It is not rich, more like an ice milk.

6 eggs (be sure to use good quality eggs with no chips or cracks)	1 package whipped topping mix (like Dream Whip), dry
1⅓ cups granulated sugar	4 teaspoons vanilla
Pinch of salt	Milk
1 (14½-ounce) can evaporated milk	

In a large mixer bowl, beat the eggs until very light, gradually adding the sugar and salt. Turn the mixer speed to low and add the evaporated milk, whipped topping mix and vanilla. Add about 2 cups milk. Pour mixture into freezer can. Add dasher and fill with more milk until mixture is about 3 inches from top of can. Cover, freeze according to the directions that came with your freezer. We often can't wait, so serve immediately, but you can remove the dasher, re-cover can and pack with ice and salt to serve later.

MY MOTHER'S NEW YORK ICE CREAM

This is the ice cream referred to at the beginning of this dessert section. She must have doubled the recipe, as 1½ quarts of ice cream wouldn't have gone very far at our house!!

1 cup sugar
1 tablespoon cornstarch
¼ teaspoon salt
2 cups milk, scalded

3 eggs, beaten
1 cup whipping cream
2 teaspoons vanilla

Blend the sugar, cornstarch and salt. Add the scalded milk and cook over hot water for 10 minutes, stirring often. Add a small amount to the beaten eggs; blend and return to the double boiler and continue to cook for 3 minutes. Chill. Add the whipping cream and vanilla. Pour into container of ice cream freezer and freeze according to freezer directions.

TLC Tip: *Fill the can only ⅔ to ¾ full to allow for expansion—you'll have a smoother ice cream.*

CHOCOLATE CHERRY CORDIAL ICE CREAM

In the early 1970's, Cleo and I published a TV guide called TV Facts. *We often ran a recipe from a reader or advertiser. This one comes from Bill Schaffner. I taught his youngest son, Kyle, in the third grade—the older son, Shane, married our niece, Cynthia. Small world. This is a delicious ice cream—loaded with fat and calories, but worth a once-in-a-Blue-Moon splurge.*

6 eggs
1 (14-ounce) can sweetened
  condensed milk
1 (12-ounce) can chocolate
  syrup

1 (16-ounce) can dark sweet
  cherries, drained, juice
  reserved
2 pints whipping cream
1 quart half-and-half

Beat the eggs until well mixed. Add the milk and chocolate syrup and stir until smooth. Quarter the cherries and add with ½ cup of the cherry juice to the egg/chocolate mixture. Stir. Pour into freezer container. Add the whipping cream and half-and-half. Freeze, following the directions that came with your ice cream freezer.

TLC Tip: *Bill's original recipe called for maraschino cherries. I rarely use these cherries because of the preservatives and coloring they contain, so I have substituted sweet cherries.*

WESTERN GINGERBREAD

This gingerbread was a favorite of my mother, who made it often to serve when friends came by or to take to church socials. It is difficult to think about gingerbread without whipped cream—so it is usually the crowning glory when I serve it. However, it is also good to eat out of hand when the urge for a little something extra hits.

2 cups flour	½ cup shortening
1¼ cups sugar	1 egg
1 teaspoon baking powder	2 tablespoons molasses
1 tablespoon cinnamon	1 teaspoon soda
1½ teaspoons ginger	1 cup buttermilk
¼ teaspoon salt	1 tablespoon butter

Mix together in a bowl the flour, sugar, baking powder, cinnamon, ginger and salt. Cut in the shortening with a pastry blender until particles are fine. Reserve ½ cup. To the remaining crumb mixture, add the egg, molasses, and the soda which has been dissolved in the buttermilk. Beat 2 minutes with an electric mixer at low speed. Pour into a 9 x 13" pan that has been greased and floured. Cut the butter into the reserved crumbs. Sprinkle over the batter. Bake at 350 degrees for 30-35 minutes. Serve as desired.

APPLE KUCHEN

This is a homey dessert that you apple lovers will really enjoy. The convenience products make it a snap to prepare. Need I say this is especially good served warm?

½ cup butter, softened	½ cup sugar
1 (16½-ounce) yellow cake mix	1 teaspoon cinnamon
½ cup flaked coconut	1 cup sour cream
1 (20-ounce) can pie-sliced	2 egg yolks
apples, well drained	
(not apple pie filling)	

Cut the butter into the dry cake mix until crumbly. Mix in the coconut. Pat the mixture lightly into an ungreased 9 x 13" pan, building up slightly on the sides. Bake 10 minutes in a 350 degree oven. Arrange the apples on the warm crust. Mix sugar and cinnamon; sprinkle on the apples. Blend the sour cream and egg yolks; drizzle over the apples. (The topping will not completely cover the apples.) Bake 25 minutes more or until edges are light brown. Do not overbake.

RUTH'S FRUIT PIZZA

This dessert always brings compliments. Every time I serve it, people think it is the greatest. My sister gave me this recipe, and naturally I think of her each time I prepare it.

1 package Duncan Hines sugar cookie mix	3 tablespoons strawberry gelatin
1 (8-ounce) package cream cheese	Fruit pieces, such as halved strawberries, fresh
1 cup powdered sugar	blueberries, kiwi slices,
1 cup granulated sugar	banana slices (dipped in
3 tablespoons cornstarch	lemon water to prevent
1 cup water	browning) mandarin
	orange slices, etc.

Mix the cookie mix as directed on the package. Lightly grease a pizza pan or cookie sheet; press the dough into the pan and bake in a 350 degree oven for 8 to 10 minutes. Do not overbake. Cool. Whip the cream cheese and powdered sugar. Spread on the cool crust. In a small saucepan, combine the granulated sugar, cornstarch and water. Cook over medium heat until thick and clear, stirring constantly. Stir in the dry gelatin while still boiling. Remove from heat and cool. Spread over cream cheese, arrange desired fruit pieces in an attractive pattern over the glaze. Chill in the refrigerator. Cut into wedges to serve.

TLC Tip: Light cream cheese seems to work well with this. You might want to arrange the fruit atop the cream cheese and pour the glaze over the fruit, but I think the fruit shows up better when it is on top of the glaze.
TLC Tip Two: Be sure the glaze is cool before spreading over the cheese and / or fruit.

ALMOND CHEESECAKE

Smooth and rich, as a cheesecake should be, this cheesecake has a delicious almond flavor. It has been served for many special occasions, including the 25th Anniversary Celebration the children hosted for Cleo and me. Other goodies that shared the dessert table were Peppermint Eggnog Punch, Ruby Punch, and Orange Chiffon Cake. Check the index for the recipes.

1½ cups graham cracker
   crumbs
2 tablespoons sugar
1 teaspoon ground cinnamon
½ cup plus 2 tablespoons
   butter, melted
3 (8-ounce) packages cream
   cheese, softened
1 cup sugar
4 eggs

1¼ teaspoons almond
   flavoring
1 (8-ounce) carton sour cream
1 tablespoon plus 1 teaspoon
   sugar
¼ teaspoon almond flavoring
¼ cup sliced almonds, toasted
1 small chocolate candy bar,
   grated

Combine the graham cracker crumbs, 2 tablespoons sugar, cinnamon and butter; mix well. Press mixture into bottom and ½" up the sides of a 9" spring form pan. Beat the cream cheese with an electric mixer until light and fluffy. Gradually add 1 cup sugar, mixing well. Add eggs, one at a time, beating well after each addition. Stir in 1¼ teaspoons almond flavoring; pour into prepared pan. Bake at 375 degrees for 45 to 50 minutes, or until set. Combine sour cream, 1 tablespoon plus 1 teaspoon sugar, and ¼ teaspoon almond flavoring; stir well, and spoon over the cheesecake. Bake at 500 degrees for 5 minutes. Let cool to room temperature; then refrigerate 24 to 48 hours. Garnish with the almonds and the grated chocolate.

TLC Tip: *I have used reduced-fat cream cheese and sour cream in this recipe with excellent results.*

PUMPKIN AMARETTO CHEESECAKE

Cheesecake is high on my list of favorite desserts. I suppose some would argue that a plain cheesecake with perhaps a bit of fruit sauce cannot be improved upon. However, the creative part of me insists I be adventurous and try variations on the theme. I like this one with its combination of pumpkin and almond flavors. I hope you do too.

11 graham cracker squares, crushed
¼ cup sugar
⅓ cup unsalted butter, melted
2 (8-ounce) packages cream cheese, softened
1 cup packed light brown sugar

2 cups solid pack pumpkin
4 eggs
1½ teaspoons cinnamon
½ teaspoon nutmeg
1 tablespoon flour
1 teaspoon almond flavoring
2 tablespoons heavy cream

In a 9" spring form pan, mix cracker crumbs, sugar and melted butter. Using the back of a spoon or your fingers, press the mixture evenly onto the bottom and sides of the pan. Bake 8 minutes at 325 degrees. Remove from oven and cool. In a large bowl, whip cream cheese until smooth. Stir in the brown sugar; blend thoroughly. Stir in the pumpkin. Add the eggs, one at a time, beating well after each addition. Stir in the remaining ingredients. Pour mixture onto prepared crust. Set filled pan on a large square of heavy duty foil. Shape the foil tightly around the edge of the pan. Set the pan in a large roasting pan filled with ½" of boiling water. Bake 1 hour or until knife inserted in center comes out clean. Remove from oven; cool. Top with whipped cream for a spectacular finish!!

TLC Tip: You may think there is nothing you can do to further enhance this wonderful dessert but think again—how about setting each slice in a pool of caramel sauce? Wow!

STRAWBERRY CREAM CHEESE CAKE

This is one of the first cheesecakes I ever made. I found the recipe years ago in a Seventeen *magazine. I thought it sounded good, and I was right—it is good. The delicate pink color makes a very pretty presentation and lends itself to occasions such as showers and luncheons.*

1 cup corn flake crumbs
½ cup butter, melted
½ cup brown sugar
½ teaspoon cinnamon
2 (10-ounce) packages frozen
   sweetened strawberries,
   thawed and drained,
   juice reserved
1 (14-ounce) can crushed
   pineapple, drained
2 envelopes unflavored
   gelatin

1½ cups granulated sugar
1 teaspoon salt
2 eggs, beaten
2 teaspoons vanilla
2 teaspoons grated lemon peel
1 tablespoon lemon juice
6 drops red food coloring
   (optional)
3 (8-ounce) packages cream
   cheese, softened
1 cup heavy cream

Combine the butter with the crumbs, brown sugar and cinnamon. Press on the bottom of a 9" spring form pan. Mix the gelatin, sugar, salt, strawberry juice and eggs. Stir and cook over medium heat for 5 minutes. Remove from heat and add vanilla, lemon juice and peel and food coloring. Beat cheese until fluffy, add gelatin mixture, beating until smooth. Whip the cream, and fold into the gelatin mixture, then gently fold in the strawberries and pineapple. Pour into prepared pan. Chill several hours or overnight. This looks pretty served on a clear dessert plate with a spoonful of whipped cream and a fresh strawberry as a garnish.

J. L. HUDSON'S CHEESECAKE CHIFFON

What fun it was to eat in the J. L. Hudson restaurant. This Detroit area department store had a huge "downtown" store, and several branches in area shopping centers. I used to take the girls shopping for school clothes (in those days, girls didn't wear pants to school, so it meant at least 5 dresses, plus play clothes for after school) and we would treat ourselves to lunch or supper, often in this restaurant. I doubt the store is the same, being bought by the Dayton chain, and times and menus change. You'll like this lighter version of cheesecake.

16 ounces cream cheese
8 ounces sour cream
2 (3.4-ounce) boxes regular vanilla pudding (the kind you cook)

4 tablespoons butter
1 tablespoon vanilla
20 Lorna Doone butter cookies, crushed

Beat the cream cheese and sour cream until fluffy. Prepare the pudding as package directs, but reducing the milk to 3½ cups. Remove from heat and add butter and vanilla, then the cheese mixture. Pour into a greased 9" spring form pan that has been lightly dusted with Lorna Doone crumbs. Cover and chill 24 hours before serving.

CHOCOLATE GRAHAM CRACKER DELIGHT

This is a lush dessert that is a special favorite of our daughter, Deanna. Since it is frozen, it is wonderful to make ahead when you are expecting guests.

1½ packages German sweet chocolate
⅓ cup milk
2 tablespoons sugar

1 (3-ounce) package cream cheese
3½ cups whipped topping
1 graham cracker pie shell

Finely chop ½ package of chocolate. Heat the remaining chocolate and 2 tablespoons of the milk in a saucepan over low heat. Stir until melted. Beat the sugar into the cream cheese; add remaining milk and chocolate mixture. Beat until smooth. Fold in the whipped topping. Blend until smooth. Fold in the chopped chocolate. Spoon into the pie shell. Freeze until firm, about 4 hours. Let stand a few minutes—maybe 15 or so—at room temperature before serving. Store any leftover pie in the freezer.

TLC Tip: *This pie is also good made with a chocolate crumb crust.*

MOCHA SOUFFLÉ

*Soufflés are something you think about ordering in a fancy restaurant—
you know, you have to order when you choose the main course so it can be
prepared while you eat and served the minute it comes out of the oven. The
waiter places it in front of you, makes a hole in the top with a flourish and
spoons in some wonderful sauce. It's marvelous. You can do it yourself for
your family and friends with a little planning. The best thing about this
soufflé, besides its rich, satisfying taste, is that it is low in calories. Don't
tell—your guests will never guess.*

6 egg whites	**2 teaspoons instant coffee**
¼ cup sugar	**1 cup evaporated skim milk**
3 tablespoons unsweetened	**1 teaspoon orange flavoring**
cocoa powder	**1½ teaspoons vanilla**
2 tablespoons cornstarch	**½ teaspoon cream of tartar**

Bring the egg whites to room temperature. In a saucepan, stir together the
sugar, cocoa, cornstarch and coffee. Stir in the milk. Cook and stir over
medium heat until thickened and bubbly. Cook 2 minutes more. Remove
from heat. Stir in flavorings, turn into a large bowl and cover surface with
clear plastic wrap. In a large mixer bowl, beat the egg whites and cream of
tartar until stiff peaks form. Stir about ¼ of the egg whites into the
chocolate mixture to lighten, then fold in the remaining whites. Turn into
a 2- to 2½-quart soufflé dish. (If using a 2-quart soufflé dish , cut a strip of
foil 6 x 30", fold in half lengthwise. Wrap around top of soufflé dish,
forming a collar. Tape to hold in place.) Bake in a 375 degree oven 20 to 25
minutes or until knife inserted off-center comes out clean. Serve immediately. Makes 6 servings, about 100 calories each.

SOUFFLÉ AU CHOCOLAT

This is one of those desserts you prepare when you want to make a terrific impression. It is absolutely gorgeous to look at and decadent to eat.

4 eggs, separated
2 envelopes unflavored
  gelatin
2¼ cups cold water, divided
2 cups sugar, divided
1 (8-ounce) package cream
  cheese, softened

3 ounces unsweetened
  chocolate, melted
1 teaspoon chocolate
  flavoring
1 to 2 teaspoons instant coffee
  dissolved in ¼ cup water
1 (8-ounce) container
  whipped topping, thawed

Beat the egg yolks and set aside. Soften gelatin in 1 cup water; stir over low heat until dissolved. Add remaining water, 1 cup sugar and the beaten yolks. Cook, stirring constantly, for 5 minutes over low heat. Combine cream cheese, chocolate, flavoring and coffee liquid, mixing until well blended. Gradually add gelatin mixture, blending well. Chill until mixture mounds slightly. Beat egg whites until foamy; gradually add remaining 1 cup sugar, beating until stiff peaks form. Fold egg whites and whipped topping into cream cheese mixture. Wrap a 3" collar of foil around the top of a 1½-quart soufflé dish; secure with tape. Pour mixture into dish; chill until firm. Remove collar before serving.

TLC Tip: This can also be chilled in a trifle dish. I like to garnish this with a ring of whipped cream sprinkled with chocolate shavings, chocolate sprinkles or chocolate covered coffee beans.
TLC Tip Two: Always use care when using uncooked egg whites.

TANGY LEMON TRIFLE

This is not your usual trifle, but looks elegant in a trifle bowl. This makes a large dessert so it is great for entertaining or carrying to potluck meals.

1 envelope unflavored gelatin
1 cup freshly squeezed lemon
  juice
6 eggs, separated
1½ cups sugar, divided

1 purchased angel food cake
  (about 9" round) cut or
  torn into 1" pieces
1 (8-ounce) carton whipped
  topping, thawed

Soften gelatin in lemon juice; let stand 5 minutes. Beat the egg yolks until thick and lemon colored. Combine egg yolks, ½ cup sugar and the gelatin mixture in a small saucepan; cook over low heat until thickened, stirring constantly. Set aside to cool completely. Beat the egg whites until soft peaks form. Gradually add 1 cup sugar; continue to beat until peaks are stiff and glossy. Fold lemon mixture into egg whites. Gently fold in whipped topping. Carefully fold cake pieces into mixture, coating all pieces well. Spoon into trifle dish; cover tightly and chill overnight.

TLC Tip: *This looks pretty garnished with lemon twists or slices and mint leaves.*
TLC Tip Two: *Always use care when using uncooked egg whites.*

CHOCOLATE TOFFEE TRIFLE

Every now and then you need a dessert that's a real show-stopper. This is it, and so easy to make. Keep it a secret if you want—your guests will rate you one terrific cook.

1 (19.8-ounce) package fudge
  brownie mix
4 tablespoons strong brewed
  coffee mixed with 1
  teaspoon sugar

3 (3.9-ounce) packages
  chocolate instant
  pudding mix
1 (12-ounce) container
  whipped topping, thawed
6 (1.4-ounce) English toffee
  candy bars, crushed

Prepare the brownie mix, and bake according to package directions in a 13 x 9" pan. Prick the top of the warm brownies at 1" intervals using a fork; drizzle with the coffee mixture. Let cool and crumble. Prepare the pudding mix according to package directions, omitting chilling. Place ⅓ of the crumbled brownies in bottom of a 3-quart trifle dish. Top with ⅓ each of pudding, whipped topping and crushed candy bars. Repeat layers twice with remaining ingredients, ending with crushed candy bars. Chill 8 hours. Let your guests view this luscious dessert before they indulge.

TEXAS TRIFLE

My wonderful husband, Cleo, doesn't claim to know his way around the kitchen. But put him in his office, give him a teaching assignment, or place him on the tennis court and he is perfectly at home. He is a loving and caring husband and father, and generous to a fault. Besides all that, he has been my chief tester for these 25 years—lavish with praise and gentle with criticism. Cleo has a great attitude about food—he eats to live. He does not feel cheated if a meal does not include dessert, and if it does, the less sweet the better. This trifle, which takes its name from the colors of the Texas flag—or the American flag, for that matter—is one of his favorites. The red strawberries, blue blueberries and white whipped cream make it a natural for the 4th of July or any other occasion with a patriotic theme. Once you prepare this colorful dessert, you'll join him in singing its praises.

½ cup butter, softened
½ cup sugar
2 eggs
1 teas baking powder
½ cup self-rising flour
1 teaspoon vanilla
2 cups prepared custard, cooled (I like my Lite Cream Pie Filling—see index—or use Bird's custard powder)

½ cup orange juice, divided use
2 cups sliced, fresh strawberries
2 cups fresh blueberries
2 tablespoons sugar, divided use
1 cup whipping cream
½ cup slivered almonds

Combine the butter, ½ cup sugar and eggs and beat until fluffy. Stir in the baking powder. Add the flour and mix well. Stir in the vanilla. Pour into a greased and floured 9" cake pan. Bake for 20 minutes and allow to cool. Cut cake into bite-size pieces and place in the bottom of trifle bowl or large glass bowl. Pour ¼ cup orange juice over the cake pieces. Top with strawberries, then blueberries, reserving a few for garnish if desired. Sprinkle with 1 tablespoon sugar, and pour the remaining ¼ cup orange juice over all. Spoon the custard over the fruit, cover and refrigerate at least 2 hours or overnight. Shortly before serving, combine the 1 tablespoon sugar with the whipping cream, and whip until stiff peaks form. Spoon over top of cold trifle. Garnish with slivered almonds and reserved fruit, if desired. This is simply delicious and very elegant.

TLC Tip: *The sponge cake is very buttery and rich but rather coarse. Don't despair, it tastes fine. I have simplified this at times by using purchased pound cake, but I feel it is really best using the homemade cake. I don't make this with frozen fruit. You just can't beat the fresh for looks and texture, let alone taste. Needless to say, this is a seasonal dessert—enjoy!!*

PUNCH BOWL CAKE

Once you make this dessert you will understand the title. It makes a large amount, so you really do need to use a large punch bowl. It is easy to prepare and very yummy.

1 (16½-ounce) box yellow cake mix, prepared as directed and baked in a 9 x 13" pan

2 (16-ounce) cans cherry pie filling

1 (16-ounce) can chunk pineapple

4 bananas, sliced

2 (8-ounce) containers whipped topping, thawed

4 (3.4-ounce) boxes instant vanilla pudding, prepared as directed

Pecans, cherries, coconut as desired

Crumble the cooled cake. Layer ½ the cake cubes in a clear punch bowl. Top with 1 can cherry pie filling, 2 boxes of pudding, half the pineapple, half the bananas and half the whipped topping. Repeat layers using rest of ingredients. Garnish with chopped pecans, chopped cherries and coconut if desired. Spoon into serving dishes to serve.

TLC Tip: *This recipe can quite easily be divided in half by baking the cake in two 9" layers. Layer the ingredients in a trifle dish.*

PECAN PUMPKIN CRUMBLE

This easily prepared pumpkin dessert will leave your friends and family begging for more. A topping of whipped cream is almost a must.

1 cup sugar

1½ teaspoons pumpkin pie spice

2 eggs

1 (16-ounce) can pumpkin

1 (12-ounce) can evaporated milk

1 (16½-ounce) package yellow cake mix

½ cup butter, melted

¾ cup chopped nuts

In a large bowl, combine sugar, spice, eggs, pumpkin and evaporated milk; mix well. Pour into an ungreased 9 x 13" pan. Sprinkle evenly with the dry cake mix; drizzle evenly with melted butter. Sprinkle the nuts over the top. Bake at 350 degrees for 40 to 50 minutes. Cut into squares to serve topped with a dollop of whipped cream. Refrigerate leftovers if there are any!!

PUMPKIN PIE SQUARES

This is pumpkin pie for a crowd. With an unusual crust, the familiar filling and a crunchy topping, this dessert will bring raves from all your pumpkin-loving friends.

Crust:

1 cup flour	½ cup packed brown sugar
½ cup quick oats, uncooked	½ cup butter

In a small bowl, combine the flour, oats and brown sugar. Cut in the butter until mixture resembles coarse crumbs. Press into bottom of a greased and floured 9 x 13" pan. Bake at 375 degrees for 12 to 15 minutes or until light brown. Reduce oven temperature to 350 degrees.

Filling:

1 (16-ounce) can pumpkin	1 teaspoon cinnamon
1 (12-ounce) can evaporated	½ teaspoon ginger
milk	¼ teaspoon cloves
2 eggs	½ teaspoon salt
¾ cup sugar	

In medium mixer bowl, place all the filling ingredients. Beat at low speed until mixed. Increase speed to medium; beat 3 minutes. Pour over baked crust. Bake 15-20 minutes until set.

Topping:

1 cup packed brown sugar	¼ cup butter
1 cup chopped walnuts	2 tablespoons flour

Combine all ingredients in a small bowl using a pastry blender or fork. Mixture should be crumbly. Remove pumpkin mixture from oven, sprinkle with topping and continue baking for 10-15 minutes more until topping is golden brown. Cut into 15 pieces to serve.

TLC Tip: *Pumpkin pie seems a little incomplete without whipped cream, so don't be shy about garnishing each piece with a small spoonful. You might want to serve the dessert and pass a bowl of whipped cream so those who wish may add it.*

MINT BROWNIE PIE

I love the combination of chocolate and mint. Somehow the refreshing flavor of the mint makes me feel better about eating the chocolate. Oh well! This is a simple dessert to make, but if you don't tell, no one will ever suspect. It is so rich and chocolate-y.

1 (19-ounce) package brownie mix	6 ounces thin mints (the Andes brand is good)
1 quart chocolate chip ice cream	1 tablespoon milk

Prepare the brownie mix as directed on the package but bake in two 9" glass pie plates for 20 to 25 minutes at 325 degrees. (Save extra brownie base for another time, or fix two pies.) Let cool completely. Scoop the ice cream on top of the cooled brownie-pie. I like to use a large heavy flat scoop for this. Work quickly, so the ice cream doesn't melt too much, but you can pop it in the freezer for a few minutes if it does. Melt the thin mints with milk over low heat. Stir often. Cut the pie into wedges to serve. Spoon the warm mint sauce over.

TLC Tip: *Did you know there are lite brownie mixes? You might want to try it in this recipe to reduce the fat somewhat.*

NEIMAN MARCUS CAKE

I doubt that Neiman Marcus had anything to do with this cake, but the fact that it is rich makes the name appropriate.

1 (16½-ounce) package German chocolate cake mix	½ cup chopped nuts
4 eggs, divided use	1 (8-ounce) package cream cheese, softened
½ cup butter, softened	1 teaspoon vanilla
	1 pound powdered sugar

Combine the cake mix, 2 eggs, butter and chopped nuts in a large mixer bowl. Beat for about 2 minutes on medium speed. Spread in a 9 x 13" baking pan. Beat the remaining 2 eggs into the softened cream cheese until well blended and fluffy; add the vanilla. Gradually add the powdered sugar, mixing until smooth. Spread over the cake mixture and bake at 350 degrees for about 35 minutes. Cut into small pieces to serve.

APPLE DUMPLINGS

I guess the first "complicated" dessert I ever made was Apple Dumplings. It is still one of my personal favorites. There may be fancier recipes, but I don't think this one can be beat.

**Pastry for double-crust (9")
   pie
6 medium tart juicy apples
1½ cups sugar, divided use**

**2 cups water
4 tablespoons butter
1¾ teaspoons cinnamon,
   divided use**

Roll out pastry a little less than ⅛" thick and cut into 7" squares. Pare and core an apple for each dumpling. Boil 1 cup sugar, 2 cups water, 3 tablespoons butter, and ¼ teaspoon cinnamon together for 3 minutes. Place an apple on each square of pastry. Combine ½ cup sugar and 1½ teaspoons cinnamon in a small bowl. Fill the cavities of the apples with the cinnamon/sugar mixture. Dot each with a little of the remaining butter. Bring opposite points of the pastry up over the apple. Overlap, moisten and seal. Lift carefully, place a little apart in a 8 x 12" (or similar) baking dish. Pour hot syrup around dumplings. Bake immediately in a 425 degree oven for 40 to 45 minutes or until crust is nicely browned and apples are cooked through. (Test with a fork.) Serve warm with the syrup and heavy cream.

TLC Tip: *If I have any leftover pastry, I like to cut out some little leaves to decorate the tops of the dumplings.*

LEMON CAKE PUDDING

This dessert is like magic—you put it in the pan and during the baking, a sauce forms on the bottom while a delicate cake rises to the top. Lemon lovers will adore this dessert.

**¼ cup flour
1 cup sugar
¼ teaspoon salt
1 tablespoon grated lemon
   rind**

**¼ cup lemon juice
2 egg yolks, well beaten
1 cup milk
2 egg whites, stiffly beaten**

Blend flour, sugar, and salt in a mixing bowl. Stir in lemon rind and juice, egg yolks and milk. Fold in the beaten egg whites. Pour into a 1-quart baking dish or 6 custard cups. Set in a pan of hot water. Bake at 350 degrees for 50 minutes.

GINGERBREAD WITH WARM APPLE TOPPING

This dessert is reminiscent of Grandmother's kitchen. Wonderful served warm.

1 (9") pan gingerbread, your own or a mix	¼ cup sugar
2 medium cooking apples, peeled, cored and sliced	¼ cup butter
	½ teaspoon ground cinnamon
½ cup light corn syrup	½ teaspoon cornstarch

Place the apples, corn syrup, sugar, butter and cinnamon in a large glass bowl; microwave on high for 3 to 4 minutes or until apples are tender. Add the cornstarch to the apple mixture; stir until smooth. Microwave on high for 2 to 3 minutes or until thickened and bubbly. Cut gingerbread into 3" squares; spoon apple mixture over gingerbread.

CHOCOLATE MACADAMIA NUT TART

The ultimate dessert!! Better make sure it follows a light meal, and serve small portions, even to skinny people!

¾ cup sugar	½ cup dark chocolate chips
1½ cups light brown sugar	½ cup macadamia nuts, coarsely chopped
1 pinch salt (about ⅛ teaspoon)	
½ cup flour	Unbaked crust for (9" or 10") pie
6 eggs	
6 tablespoons melted butter	Dark and white chocolate for garnish
¾ cup whipping cream	

In a large bowl, mix the sugars, salt and flour together. Using a wire whisk, slowly add the eggs, then the melted butter and finally the whipping cream. Blend only until smooth; do not whisk air into the batter. Distribute the chocolate chips and macadamia nuts over the bottom of the unbaked pie shell, then pour the batter over the nuts. Be sure not to overfill the crust. Bake in a preheated 350 degree oven for about 1 hour or until golden brown. Cool. Decorate top with melted dark or white chocolate, or go for it, and use both!! Chill at least 3 hours.

TLC Tip: *I like to use a 9 or 10" tart pan with a removable bottom for this dessert, but a regular pie shell will work just fine.*

FROSTED PINEAPPLE SQUARES

My mother said these were "very good" and she was telling the truth. Though not what you would call a quick recipe, you'll be rewarded by plenty of compliments when you serve these. Thanks, Mom.

Filling:

½ cup sugar
3 tablespoons cornstarch
¼ teaspoon salt

1 egg yolk, slightly beaten
1 large can pineapple chunks, undrained

Mix the sugar, cornstarch and salt in a small saucepan. Stir in the egg yolk and pineapple with juice. Cook over medium heat, stirring constantly, until thick and smooth, about 7 minutes. Remove from heat, and cool to lukewarm while preparing dough.

Dough:

⅔ cup milk
1 teaspoon sugar
1 package active dry yeast
¼ cup very warm water

4 egg yolks, lightly beaten
4 cups flour
1 cup butter

Scald the milk; add the sugar and cool to lukewarm. Dissolve the yeast in the warm water; add to the milk mixture. Stir in the beaten egg yolks. Measure the flour into a large bowl. Cut in the butter using a pastry blender until mixture resembles coarse meal. Stir in the yeast and milk mixture; blend thoroughly. Dough will be soft and moist. Divide dough in half. Roll one half out on floured surface to fit a 10 x 15" jelly roll pan with some overhang. Place dough in pan and spread with cooled pineapple filling. Roll remaining dough large enough to cover filling. Seal edges. Snip top of dough with scissors to let steam escape. Cover; let rise in warm place until double, about 1 hour. Bake at 375 degrees 35 to 40 minutes. Frost with a powdered sugar icing. Nice served warm.

PERSIMMON PUDDING

My brother-in-law, John Albright, is a minister in the Detroit area. He has pastored churches in Indiana, Illinois and Ohio, and served as National Youth Director. John likes to camp, work with plants, and in his younger years, ride motorcycles. This is his favorite dessert. He often requests it for his December 26 birthday. Since persimmons are a seasonal fruit, my sister usually uses frozen purée to fulfill his request. Be sure the persimmons you select are very soft, like a very ripe tomato. This glorious fall dessert is heavenly served warm with a scoop of vanilla ice cream on the top.

2 cups persimmon purée (cut
    off the top of the
    persimmon and squeeze
    out the pulp; don't use
    the skins)
2 eggs, slightly beaten
1½ cups sugar
2 cups flour

2 teaspoons baking powder
1 teaspoon soda
2 teaspoons cinnamon
2 cups buttermilk
¼ cup melted butter
¼ cup water
2 tablespoons butter
¼ cup brown sugar

Beat the eggs with the sugar in a large mixer bowl. Stir the dry ingredients together on a square of waxed paper. Add the buttermilk and melted butter to the egg mixture; stir in the flour mixture until smooth. Pour into a greased 13 x 9" pan (I usually use a glass one). Combine the water, 2 tablespoons butter and brown sugar in a small saucepan. Bring to a boil; then pour over the batter. Bake in a 350 degree oven for about 1 hour. What a treat!

TLC Tip: The finished product will be soft, like a pudding, and not like a cake.

CHOCOLATE CUPS OLÉ

Our son-in-law, David Gross, especially likes this dessert and has been known to indulge in more than one. Your family and guests will like it too, with its creamy texture and hint of cinnamon.

1 (14-ounce) can sweetened condensed milk	½ cup toasted, chopped almonds
⅔ cup chocolate flavored syrup	1 teaspoon vanilla
	¼ teaspoon ground cinnamon
	2 cups whipping cream

Combine the condensed milk, chocolate syrup, chopped almonds, vanilla and cinnamon. In a large mixing bowl, beat the whipping cream until soft peaks form; fold in the chocolate mixture. Spoon into small custard cups or parfait dishes, cover with plastic and freeze until firm, about 4 hours. This can also be frozen in muffin tins lined with paper bake cups. Remove paper cups to serve. This is nice garnished with a little additional whipped cream and a sprinkle of cinnamon or shaved chocolate.

TLC Tip: Please take the time to toast the almonds. It makes such a difference in the flavor. You can remove this from the freezer a few minutes before serving, but it is at its best when slightly frozen.

RUTH'S BANANA SPLIT DESSERT

This is a wonderful dessert that will serve a lot of people. It is made ahead which is helpful when guests are expected. As my sister is the wife of a minister, she has many occasions when this is appropriate.

2 cups graham cracker crumbs	1 (20-ounce) can crushed pineapple, drained, juice reserved
¼ cup sugar	
½ cup melted butter	3 or 4 bananas, sliced
1 (1-pound) box powdered sugar	1 (8-ounce) container whipped topping
1 cup soft butter	Chopped nuts
2 eggs	Maraschino cherries
1 teaspoon vanilla	

Mix the crumbs, ¼ cup sugar and butter; press into a 9 x 13" pan. Bake at 350 degrees for 8-10 minutes and let cool. Beat the powdered sugar, 1 cup butter, eggs and vanilla together and spread over the cooled crust. Spread drained pineapple over egg/sugar mixture. Dip each banana slice in the reserved pineapple juice and arrange over pineapple. Spread whipped topping over all, and sprinkle with chopped nuts. Garnish with maraschino cherries if desired. Chill at least 24 hours before serving.

STRAWBERRY FLUFF AND STUFF

When my sister, Ruth, told me about this recipe, I thought the procedure sounded a little strange. Well, the procedure may be strange but the end result is anything but. If you don't have a stand mixer, I recommend you rush right out and get one so you can make this divine dessert! I don't think you should try it with a hand mixer.

Crunch Stuff:

½ cup butter	1 cup flour
⅓ cup brown sugar	1 cup chopped nuts

Cream the butter; stir in the brown sugar and flour. Finally add the nuts. Spread in a 9 x 13" pan. Bake at 400 degrees for 8 to 10 minutes. Crumble in the bottom of the pan.

Fluff Stuff:

2 egg whites	1 teaspoon lemon juice
1 cup sugar	1 teaspoon vanilla
1 large container frozen	1 cup whipping cream,
strawberries in syrup,	whipped
partially thawed	

In a large bowl of an electric mixer, beat the egg whites until stiff; add the sugar gradually. Add the lemon juice, vanilla and strawberries; whip at high speed for 5 minutes. (I told you you needed a stand mixer!) Fold in the whipped cream and spread the mixture over the crumb crust. Freeze for 6 hours or overnight. Cut into squares to serve.

TLC Tip: *Wouldn't this be pretty set on clear glass dessert plates with strawberry purée drizzled over the top, a small fluff of whipped cream and a strawberry half?*

TORTONI DELIGHT

A delightful make-ahead dessert to serve at the end of your next Italian meal.

1½ cups soft macaroon cookie crumbs	1 cup whipping cream, whipped
2 eggs, separated	¼ cup finely chopped toasted almonds
½ cup powdered sugar	
1 teaspoon sherry flavoring	12 maraschino cherries with stems (optional)
1 teaspoon vanilla	

Line 12 medium muffin cups with paper or foil baking cups. Divide ½ cup of the crumbs evenly among the muffin cups. In a small bowl, beat egg yolks with powdered sugar until smooth and fluffy; stir in sherry and vanilla flavorings. In a large bowl, beat egg whites until stiff peaks form; gently fold in egg yolk mixture. (Always use care when using uncooked eggs.) Fold in whipped cream, then almonds and 1 cup crumbs until well combined. Spoon into muffin cups, mounding slightly. Top with cherries, if desired. Freeze until firm—at least 4 hours, overnight is OK. Remove paper liners to serve.

TLC Tip: *These look nice served on small dessert plates lined with a lace paper doily.*

MOM'S PINEAPPLE MARSHMALLOW DESSERT

This light, fluffy dessert became one of my mother's most requested recipes. It is amazing how so few ingredients can result in a mouth-watering creation.

1 pound marshmallows	1 (20-ounce) can crushed pineapple, very well drained
1 cup milk (I wouldn't go lower than 2% here)	
1 pint whipping cream	Graham cracker crumbs

Melt the marshmallows with the milk in the top of a double boiler or the microwave. Cool. (Don't rush this step. Either start in plenty of time to let the mixture cool naturally, or help it along a bit by setting the bowl in a pan of ice water.) Whip the cream until stiff peaks form. Add the drained pineapple to the marshmallow mixture, then fold in the whipped cream. Cover the bottom of a 9 x 13" pan with graham cracker crumbs. (About ½ cup should be enough.) Spoon the marshmallow mixture on top. Cover with a thin layer of crumbs. Chill thoroughly until set. Cut into squares to serve.

TLC Tip: *Use pineapple in syrup for a sweeter dessert.*

COCONUT DELIGHT

Aunt Lodema Crabtree likes to serve this luscious dessert when she and Uncle Neil get together with friends on Friday nights for Canasta and conversation. Once you make it, you'll know why their friends rave over it— it's everything a dessert should be.

1 cup flour
½ cup butter, softened
1 cup finely chopped nuts
   (Aunt Lodema uses
   pecans)
1 large box of instant vanilla
   pudding
2½ cups milk

1 (8-ounce) package cream
   cheese
1 cup confectioner's sugar
1 teaspoon vanilla
1 cup flaked coconut plus a
   little more for garnish
1 (12-ounce) container
   whipped topping,
   thawed, divided use

Mix the flour, butter and nuts to form a soft dough; press in a 13 x 9" pan. Bake in a 375 degree oven for 15 minutes. Cool. In a large bowl, combine the pudding mix and milk. Beat until slightly thickened. In another bowl, combine the cream cheese, sugar and vanilla. Beat this mixture into the pudding mixture. Add 1 cup coconut. Fold in 1 cup whipped topping. Pour over the cooled crust. Cover and chill. Just before serving, spread the remaining whipped topping over the pudding. Sprinkle with a little coconut. Makes 12 generous, delectable servings.

TLC Tip: *I usually use skim milk, lite cream cheese, and lite whipped topping and my family and friends still smack their lips.*

STRAWBERRY SWIRL

Margaret Kruithoff was a member of our church in Allegan, Michigan. Her boys were our friends, and we spent many a Sunday afternoon playing at each other's homes. Her Strawberry Swirl is a pretty, refreshing and delicious dessert.

1 cup graham cracker crumbs
1 tablespoon sugar
¼ cup melted butter
1 (3-ounce) package
   strawberry gelatin
1 cup boiling water
1 cup cold water (or
   strawberry juice)

½ pound marshmallows
½ cup milk (don't go below 2%
   here)
1 cup whipping cream
2 cups sliced fresh
   strawberries

Combine the crumbs, sugar and melted butter; press in a 9" square pan. Set aside. Dissolve the gelatin in 1 cup boiling water. Add the 2nd cup water; set in refrigerator to cool slightly. Melt the marshmallows with the milk in the top of a double boiler or microwave. Cool. Whip the cream until stiff peaks form, fold into the marshmallow mixture. When the gelatin is partially set, fold in the sliced strawberries. Swirl the marshmallow mixture through the Jello. Pour over the graham cracker crust. Chill until firm. Cut into squares to serve.

TLC Tip: *This can be made using frozen, sweetened strawberries. Drain well, use the juice as part of the cold water; use the berries instead of the sliced strawberries.*

RUTH'S CHOCOLATE DELIGHT

OR

THE ONLY THING BETTER THAN ROBERT REDFORD

This dessert goes by a host of names, but The Only Thing Better Than Robert Redford is what my sister and her friends called it. It's simple, showy, and delicious. Now as for the sub-title, you'll have to be the judge of that!

1 cup flour	4½ cups milk
½ cup butter	2 (3.4-ounce) packages instant
½ cup pecans	chocolate pudding
1½ cups powdered sugar	1 (3.4-ounce) package instant
1 (8-ounce) + 1 (3-ounce)	vanilla pudding
packages cream cheese	1 small chocolate bar
1 (12-ounce) carton whipped	
topping, thawed	

Mix flour, butter and pecans; press into a 9 x 13" pan and bake at 375 degrees for 15 minutes. Cool. Cream the cheese and powdered sugar until fluffy; fold in 1 cup whipped topping and spread over cooled crust. Combine milk and pudding mixes; spread over cheese layer. Chill. Before serving, spread whipped topping over all, and decorate with shaved chocolate bar. Cut into squares to serve.

TLC Tip: *I have used light cream cheese, skim milk, and light whipped topping with good results. I do not use sugar-free instant pudding. One can get really creative here with other flavors of pudding—butterscotch, lemon, pistachio, to suggest a few. Amazingly this dessert does not taste "instant".*

FLUFFY CHEESE TORTE

This is another recipe from my Michigan days. It is so pretty. I like to serve it around the February holidays. It is delicious, light but rich, if such a thing is possible.

1½ cups flour
¼ cup brown sugar, packed
½ cup finely chopped nuts
¾ cup butter, softened
8 ounces cream cheese
1 cup powdered sugar

1½ teaspoons vanilla
2 envelopes Dream Whip,
 prepared as directed on
 package
1 can cherry pie filling

Combine the flour, brown sugar and chopped nuts; cut in the softened butter. Press into a 9 x 13" pan and bake at 400 degrees for 12-15 minutes. Cool. Beat cheese, sugar and vanilla together, then beat in the prepared Dream Whip. Pour over cooled crust. Let set briefly; top with cherry pie filling. Chill. Cut into squares to serve.

CITRUS DELIGHT

This dessert lives up to its name. It is delightful to serve for a springtime brunch or summer luncheon. Clear serving dishes set this off beautifully.

2 tablespoons minute tapioca
1½ cups water
⅛ teaspoon salt
⅓ cup sugar
1 (6-ounce) can frozen orange
 juice concentrate,
 thawed
1 orange, peeled and chunked

1 banana, sliced
1 (20-ounce) can chunk
 pineapple, drained
1 (16-ounce) can sliced
 peaches, drained
Mint leaves and/or cherries
 for garnish

Combine the tapioca and water in a small saucepan and let stand for 15 minutes. Cook and stir over medium heat until mixture comes to a boil. Remove from heat; add salt, sugar and orange juice concentrate. Stir to blend. Put mixture into a refrigerator container, cover and chill. Before serving add fruit and garnish as desired.

FROSTY ICE CREAM SANDWICH

This is my variation of T.G.I. Friday's adult version of a chocolate freeze. I like to serve this dessert to end a casual meal, perhaps hamburgers or other sandwich fare. Once you make it, you'll do it again.

2 scoops vanilla ice cream	½ teaspoon instant coffee
4 Oreo cookies, crushed	(I like instant espresso)
½ cup crushed ice	2 tablespoons water
½ teaspoon chocolate extract	4 tablespoons half-and-half
	Oreo cookie for garnish

In a blender container, put the ice cream, crushed Oreo cookies, and crushed ice. Dissolve the instant coffee and chocolate flavoring in the 2 tablespoons water. Add to the blender container with the half-and-half. Whirl until smooth and creamy. Pour into a large balloon glass or tumbler, garnish with the Oreo cookie and serve with a straw. Heaven!!

SUMMER FRUIT COMPOTE

When a light ending is called for, this fills the bill nicely. Fresh fruit really is necessary for optimum taste.

¼ cup sugar	1 medium nectarine
½ teaspoon rum flavoring	1 medium plum
mixed with 2 tablespoons	1 small pear
water	1 small peach
1 teaspoon grated lime rind	4 small strawberries
2 tablespoons fresh lime juice	

Combine the sugar, flavoring mixture, lime rind and juice. Seed and slice the fruit, except the strawberries. Pour dressing over fruit in a medium mixing bowl; toss lightly. Cover and chill. Spoon into individual serving bowls; garnish each with a whole strawberry.

TLC Tip: *Did you know that fresh fruit should always be mixed with a wooden or other non-metal spoon?*

SOURCES

Bob's Red Mill Natural Foods, Inc.
5209 SE International Way
Milwaukie, Oregon 97222
503 654-3215

This company offers many kinds of baking flour that have not been treated with chemicals. They also carry whole grains, beans, a wide variety of baking products and mixes. I am especially fond of their 10-Grain Pancake and Waffle Mix. They also have a high protein whole wheat flour that is great for use in your bread machine recipes. All this, and the people are very nice to deal with, too.

The King Arthur Flour Baker's Catalogue
PO Box 876
Norwich, VT 05055-0876
1 800 827-6836

Everything you need for baking up a storm, from untreated flours to flavorings to pans and appliances. They carry a white wheat flour that combines all the fiber and nutritional benefits of whole wheat flour and the sweeter, lighter taste and appearance of all-purpose flour. Amazing!

Cook Flavoring Company
PO Box 890
Tacoma, WA 98401
206 472-1361

High quality flavorings, including a vanilla especially formulated for use in cookie dough. They also carry some flavorings not readily available, such as Kona coffee, hazelnut and blackberry.

Walnut Acres
Penns Creek, PA 17862
1 800 433-3998

If you're into organic, this is a good place to get it. They carry whole grain pasta, cheeses, unsulphured dried fruit, flours and mixes, and more.

Gaze Crystal Kitchen
1515 E. FM 700
Big Spring, TX 79720
915 267-8206

One of the best-kept secrets in West Texas is this little shop tucked away in the corner of Harris Lumber and Hardware, Inc. You'll find all kinds of kitchen gadgets, baking pans, cookie cutters, coffees, bread mixes, cookbooks and appliances, as well as fine china and crystal. If you aren't close enough to drive in, just call, they'll ship.

A

African Chow Mein 192
ALMOND(S)
Almond Cheesecake 392
Almond Pudding Loaf 77
Spiced Holiday (or Any Day) Nuts 35
Amazing Fried Chicken 216
Anniversary Cake 272
APPETIZERS
Dips
  Beverly's Guacamole 26
  Cyndee's Lo-Cal Cheese Dip 23
  Deviled Ham Dip 24
  Garlic Yogurt Dip 24
  Mexicana Bean Dip 25
  Rio Grande Dip 25
  Spinach Dip 23
Finger Foods
  Aunt Virginia's Nuts and Bolts 33
  Barbecued Pecans 33
  Crunchy Party Mix 37
  Crunchy Topping Mix 36
  Cyndee's Party Snack 34
  Down on the Ranch Mix 35
  Spiced Holiday (or Any Day)
    Nuts 35
  Spicy Cereal Crunch 369
  Sugared and Spiced Nuts 36
  Thel's Texas Trash 34
Hot Hors d'oeuvres
  Cheddar Puffs 30
  Chili Cheese Squares 29
  Crab Meat Appetizers 31
  Sauce (for Spicy Appetizer
    Meatballs) 32
  Sausage Balls 31
  Spicy Appetizer Meatballs 32
  Spinach Parmesan Quiches 30
Spreads and Molds
  90's Butter 78
  Caviar Pie Romanoff 26
  Chutney and Cheese 29
  Fake Clotted Cream 57
  Ham and Cheese Ball 28
  Honey-Lemon Butter 75
  Orange Marmalade Spread 80
  Seafood Cheese Spread 27
  Smoky Bacon Cheese Spread 27
  Smoky Salmon and Cheese Ball ... 28
  Yogurt Cheese 79
Apple Dessert Sauce 289
APPLE(S)
Apple Cinnamon Jelly 80
Apple Crisp 376
Apple Dumplings 403
Apple Kuchen 390
Apple Syrup 94
Applesauce Oatmeal Bread 70
Aunt Evelyn's Never Fail
  Applesauce Cake 291

Country Skillet Apples 250
Cranberry Apple Casserole 377
French Apple Coffee Cake 66
Fresh Apple Cake 289
Fried Apples 249
Gingerbread with Warm
  Apple Topping 404
Hot Applesauce 94
Jan's Southern Fried Apples 249
Linda's Cranberry Apple Pie 306
Mrs. Moody's Apple Blossom Cake ... 288
Swedish Lemon Apple Cake 290
APRICOT(S)
Apricot Almond Squares 335
Apricot Glazed Cornish Hens 219
Apricot Pound Cake 286
Apricot Salad Ring 124
Apricot Sunburst Muffins 51
Brandied Apricot Sauce 94
Artichoke Rice Salad 106
ASPARAGUS
Asparagus Soup 145
Asparagus With Milk 250
Athlete's Burgers 172
Aunt Edna Hitsman's Crisp Pickles 92
Aunt Elsie's Candle Salad 111
Aunt Lodema's Buffle Loaf 65
Aunt Máco's Delicious Salad 125
Aunt Máco's Featherbed Rolls 58
Aunt Máco's Luscious Punch 39
Aunt Máco's Taco Pie 193
Aunt Mavis' Carrot Cookies 339
Aunt Smyrna's Blackberry Cobbler 380
Aunt Virginia's Nuts and Bolts 33
AVOCADO(S)
Avocado Dressing 132
Beverly's Guacamole 26
Chicken Avocado Salad 129
Citrus Avocado Salad 118
Curried Avocado Soup 152
Southern Citrus Salad 119

B

Baked Doughnut Twists 67
Baked Honey Wheat Cakes 85
BANANA(S)
Banana Wheat Quick Bread 73
Bananas Foster Pecan Pie 313
Best Banana Muffins 50
Blueberry Banana Pie 308
Frosted 7-Up Salad 127
Laura Horn's Frozen Fruit Punch 42
Lite Banana Cream Pie 302
Ruth's Banana Split Dessert 407
Traditional Banana Pudding 377
Whole Wheat Banana Pancakes 86
Barb Taylor's Pasta Salad 135
Barbecued Baby Back Ribs 211
Barbecued Beef Pita Sandwiches 174
Barbecued Beef Sandwiches 174

Barbecued Pecans 33
BEANS
Black Bean Soup 153
Chuckwagon Beans 251
Cornbread Salad 115
Four Bean Salad 103
Frankfurter Supper Dish 208
Garbanzo Bean Salad 107
Juanita's Green Beans 251
Mexicana Bean Dip 25
Navy Bean Soup Carlile 141
Rena Farnum's Bean and
  Vegetable Salad 106
Rio Grande Dip 25
Three Bean Stew 159
Western Zucchini 266
Zucchini, Rice and Beans 267
BEEF
African Chow Mein 192
Athlete's Burgers 172
Aunt Máco's Taco Pie 193
Barbecued Beef Pita Sandwiches 174
Barbecued Beef Sandwiches 174
Beef Chow Mein Bake 199
Beef Rice Soup 146
Beef Stroganoff 187
Best of the Southwest Taco Salad 132
Bev's Mexican Hash 193
Bologna with Kraft Dinner 207
Broiled Flank Steak 183
Buckaroo Stew 157
Cabbage Patch Stew 155
Cheeseburger Pie 206
Chicken Fried Steak 186
Connecticut Beef Supper 188
Daniel's Cheeseburger Pie 192
Deanburgers 172
Easy Deep-Dish Pizza 205
Edith's Cabbage Rolls 203
Flank Steak Sandwiches 173
Fluffy Meatloaf 190
Frankfurter Supper Dish 208
Good Brown Stew 158
Hearty Beef and Potato Casserole ... 197
Impossible Main Dish Pies 206
Linda's Green Beef Enchiladas 196
Mañana Beef Bake 201
Mediterranean Stir-Fried Beef 189
Mom's Chili for Twenty-five 161
Paul's Texas Red 160
Pizza Burgers 171
Rita Jo's Western Chili Casserole 195
Savory Rump Roast 182
Savory Swiss Steak 184
Shirley's Brisket 183
Sloppy Joes 173
Spaghetti Sauce, My Own 202
Spicy Appetizer Meatballs 32
Suggested Pizza Toppings 204
Sunday Morning Pot Roast 181
Swiss Steak, The Family's Favorite ... 185

Tater Tot Casserole 198
Waikiki Meatballs 191
World's Greatest Pizza 204
Yankee Doodle Macaroni 200
Best Banana Muffins 50
BEVERAGES
Cold
  Aunt Máco's Luscious Punch 39
  Celebration Punch 43
  Fruit Smoothie 40
  Jean's Christmas Punch 37
  Kay Shaw's Pink Punch 41
  Laura Horn's Frozen Fruit Punch ... 42
  Lime Punch 43
  Mock Sangría 46
  Peppermint Eggnog Punch 42
  Ruby Punch 40
  Sparkling Lemonade 38
  Tea Syrup 39
  Yvonne's Almond Tea 43
Hot
  Dee's Favorite Cocoa Mix 44
  Holiday Wassail 45
  Shirley's Hot Grape Punch 44
  Spiced Cranberry Punch 45
  Spiced Russian Tea 46
Beverly's Guacamole 26
Bev's Fajitas 221
Bev's Mexican Hash 193
Biscuits Supreme 55
Black Bean Soup 153
Blackberry Cobbler, Aunt Smyrna's ... 380
BLUEBERRY(IES)
Blueberry Banana Pie 308
Blueberry Sauce 96
Dee's Favorite Blueberry Muffins 54
Michigan Blueberry Pie 305
Texas Trifle 399
Bologna with Kraft Dinner 207
Bon Bon Cookies 348
Brandied Apricot Sauce 94
Bread and Butter Pickles 93
BREADS
Biscuits
  Biscuits Supreme 55
  Butter Biscuit Sticks 56
  Cloud Biscuits 55
  Onion Parsley Butterfingers 56
  Tea Party Scones 57
Coffee Cakes, etc.
  Baked Doughnut Twists 67
  Crunchy Coffee Kuchen 67
  French Apple Coffee Cake 66
  Fruit Swirl Coffee Cake 68
  Raisin Coffee Cake 69
  Aunt Lodema's Buffle Loaf 65
  Butterscotch Coffee Ring 70
  Easy and Elegant Kolaches 62
  Swedish Tea Ring 62
  Pecan Coffee Ring 66

Cornbread
  Grandma's Cornbread 72
Miscellaneous
  Cornmeal Mush 88
  Dean's Honey Wheat Bread 59
  Eggnog French Toast 87
  Fried Mush 89
  Garlic Herb Bread 61
  Quick Pizza Dough 204
Muffins
  Apricot Sunburst Muffins 51
  Best Banana Muffins 50
  Chocolate Cheesecake Muffins 52
  Cyndee's Oatmeal Muffins 52
  Dee's Favorite Blueberry
    Muffins 54
  Honey Bran Muffins 49
  Jennie Brink's Graham Gems 49
  Mini Brunch Puffs 54
  Oatmeal Raisin Muffins 51
  Prune Wheat Muffins 50
  Pumpkin Streusel Muffins 53
  Super Cheese Muffins 53
Pancakes and Waffles
  Baked Honey Wheat Cakes 85
  Buttermilk Whole Wheat Waffles . 86
  Multi-Grain Pancakes 83
  Oat Wheat Waffles 87
  Quick Buckwheat Pancakes 84
  Simply Wonderful Pancakes 85
  Whole Wheat Banana Pancakes ... 86
  Whole Wheat Pancakes 86
Rolls
  Aunt Máco's Featherbed Rolls 58
  Chocolate Chip Party Rolls 64
  Londa's Whole Wheat Rolls 61
  Mom Mizell's Hot Rolls 60
  My Mother's Parkerhouse Rolls 60
  Pat's Cinnamon Rolls 64
Sweet Breads
  Almond Pudding Loaf 77
  Applesauce Oatmeal Bread 70
  Banana Wheat Quick Bread 73
  Cherry Chip Bread 76
  Cherry Nut Bread 71
  Chocolate Zucchini Bread 71
  Cranberry Cheese Bread 74
  Cranberry Oatmeal Bread 78
  Dorothy Mason's Hobo Bread 73
  Fig and Honey Loaf 75
  Gloria's Date Bread 77
  Norwegian Holiday Bread 63
  Ruth's Pumpkin Raisin
    Nut Bread 76
  Zucchini Oatmeal Bread 74
BROCCOLI
  Broccoli and Crab Bisque 163
  Chicken 'N Broccoli Pie 206
  Creamy Broccoli and
    Cauliflower Salad 102
  Impossible Main Dish Pies 206

Jean's Broccoli Sausage Chowder 166
Joan's Broccoli Casserole 252
Ruth's Broccoli Casserole 252
Scarecrow Country Inn
  Broccoli Salad 108
  Seafood Divan 240
Broiled Flank Steak 183
Brunch Egg Casserole 89
Buckaroo Stew 157
Butter Biscuit Sticks 56
Butter Rum Sauce 93, 292
Buttermilk Whole Wheat Waffles 86
Butterscotch Chocolate Squares 338
Butterscotch Coffee Ring 70
Butterscotch Sticks 331

C

CABBAGE
  Cabbage Patch Stew 155
  Edith's Cabbage Rolls 203
  Fresh Vegetable Salad 101
  German Red Cabbage 253
  Hush Puppy Cole Slaw 108
  Mock Oysters 148
  My Granny's Coleslaw 109
  Caesar Salad Dressing 104
CAKES
  Anniversary Cake 272
  Apricot Pound Cake 286
  Aunt Evelyn's Never Fail
    Applesauce Cake 291
  Chocolate Birthday Cake
    a la Creme 276
  Chocolate Chip Zucchini Cake 275
  Chocolate Mocha Cake 280
  Cocoa Chiffon Cake 285
  Cranberry Orange Pound Cake 292
  Edna's Date Cake 296
  Fresh Apple Cake 289
  Fresh Orange Chiffon Cake 284
  Golden Chiffon Cake 282
  Heath Bar Cake 279
  Italian Cream Cake 297
  Lou's Mandarin Orange Cake 293
  Mallo-Nut Fudge Cake 277
  Mom's Angel Food Cake 271
  Mouse Cake 274
  Mrs. Moody's Apple Blossom Cake ... 288
  Neiman Marcus Cake 402
  Oreo Cookie Cake 273
  Peppermint Chiffon Cake 283
  Prize Winning Zucchini
    Fudge Cake 278
  Rita Jo's Chocolate Chip
    Date Cake 279
  Rum Cake 288
  Ruth Simmons' Fruit Cocktail
    Cake 295
  Ruth's Graham Cracker Cupcakes ... 294
  Spicy Chiffon Cake 283

Swedish Lemon Apple Cake 290
Thelma's Holiday Eggnog Cake 287
Candy Cane Cookies 353
Candy Mountain Icing 283
CANDY(IES)
Candy Strawberries 371
Chocolate Covered Pretzels 371
Chocolate Fudge 364
Chocolate Peanut Pillows 370
Christmas Fudge 366
Easy Peanut Butter Cups 358
Fudgemallow Raisin Candy 367
Jello Balls 357
Laura Horn's Baked Caramel Corn . 368
Mackinac Island Fudge 365
Million Dollar Fudge 362
Molasses Popcorn Balls 358
Mom's Peanut Brittle 360
Mr. Daniels' Peanut Butter Fudge ... 360
Orange Coconut Balls 356
Orange Cream Fudge 366
Peanut Butter Bonbons 357
Peppermint Candy Fudge 363
Pistachio Fudge 363
Rainbow Divinity 367
Rice Krispie Squares 370
Rita Jo's Chocolate Covered
   Peanut Butter Balls 361
Rocky Road Fudge 364
Ruth's Caramel Popcorn 368
Ruth's Hard Candy 356
Ruth's Peanut Butter Balls 361
Spicy Cereal Crunch 369
Toffee Fudge 365
Vanilla Fudge 363
White Chocolate Pretzels 372
Zachary's People Chow 369
Carlile Family Ice Cream 388
CARROT(S)
Aunt Mavis' Carrot Cookies 339
Carrots Ambrosia 253
Fresh Vegetable Salad 101
Ginger Glazed Carrots 253
Cashew Rice Pilaf 262
CAULIFLOWER
Cream of Cauliflower Soup 152
Creamy Broccoli and
   Cauliflower Salad 102
Caviar Pie Romanoff 26
Celebration Punch 43
Celery Dill Sauce 237
CEREAL(S)
Cornmeal Mush 88
Fried Mush 89
Fruited Oatmeal 88
Hot Three-Grain Cereal 88
CHEESE
Bologna with Kraft Dinner 207
Brunch Egg Casserole 89
Cheddar Puffs 30
Cheeseburger Pie 206

Chicken Spaghetti 223
Chili Cheese Squares 29
Chutney and Cheese 29
Cornbread Salad 115
Crab Meat Appetizers 31
Cranberry Cheese Bread 74
Cyndee's Lo-Cal Cheese Dip 23
Daniel's Cheeseburger Pie 192
Easy Deep-Dish Pizza 205
Garlic Yogurt Dip 24
Ham and Cheese Ball 28
Ham 'N Swiss Pie 207
Impossible Breakfast Pie 90
Impossible Main Dish Pies 206
Kansas Corn Scallop 254
Lite and Easy Cheese Sauce 98
Orange Marmalade Spread 80
Pimiento Cheese Sandwich 178
Pizza Burgers 171
Sausage Balls 31
Seafood Cheese Spread 27
Smoky Bacon Cheese Spread 27
Smoky Salmon and Cheese Ball 28
Spinach Parmesan Quiches 30
Spinach Pie 207
Super Cheese Muffins 53
Tuna Melts 175
Turkey Enchilada Bake 231
World's Greatest Pizza 204
Yogurt Cheese 79
CHEESECAKE (See DESSERTS:
Cheesecake)
CHERRY(IES)
Cherries Jubilee Fruit Salad 122
Cherry Cake Cobbler 382
Cherry Chip Bread 76
Cherry Cream Pie 314
Cherry Nut Bread 71
Cherry Torte 381
Chocolate Cherry Cordial
   Ice Cream 389
Festive Cherry-ettes 349
Fluffy Cheese Torte 413
Garnetta's Cherry Preserves 83
Jewel Jam 81
Razzle-Dazzle Jam 81
CHICKEN
Amazing Fried Chicken 216
Apricot Glazed Cornish Hens 219
Bev's Fajitas 221
Chicken A La King 222
Chicken Almond Stir-Fry 225
Chicken and Mushroom Lo Mein 228
Chicken Avocado Salad 129
Chicken Fajitas 221
Chicken Fillet Sandwich 176
Chicken 'N Broccoli Pie 206
Chicken Pasta Salad 136
Chicken Salad Sandwiches 176
Chicken Spaghetti 223

INDEX

Citrus Glazed Rock Cornish
Game Hens 220
Creamy Parmesan Chicken 214
Crunchy Oven Fried Chicken 217
Dustyn's Favorite Oven-fried
Chicken Legs 215
Great Chicken Salad 133
Hot Chicken Salad 224
Lemon Roasted Chicken 218
Mexican Chicken Soup 142
Michelle's White Chili 162
Party Chicken 217
Pepperidge Farm Chicken 226
Rita Jo's Chicken Rice Casserole 224
Rita Jo's Country Chicken
Chowder 169
Rita Jo's Viva Chicken 227
Simply Delicious Fried
Chicken Livers 220
Waldorf Chicken Salad on
Raisin Bread 176
Chicken Fried Steak 186
Chili Cheese Squares 29
Chili Mayonnaise 129
Chilled Zucchini Soup 156
CHOCOLATE
Butterscotch Chocolate Squares 338
Cherry Chip Bread 76
Chocolate Bar Pie 316
Chocolate Birthday Cake
a la Creme 276
Chocolate Cheesecake Muffins 52
Chocolate Cherry Cordial
Ice Cream 389
Chocolate Chip Cookies 340
Chocolate Chip Cookies
Beauchamp 340
Chocolate Chip Party Rolls 64
Chocolate Chip Zucchini Cake 275
Chocolate Cookie Bar 335
Chocolate Covered Pretzels 371
Chocolate Cream Pie 300
Chocolate Cups Olé 407
Chocolate Fluff 285
Chocolate Frosting 278
Chocolate Fudge 364
Chocolate Graham Cracker Delight . 414
Chocolate Macadamia Nut Tart 404
Chocolate Mocha Cake 280
Chocolate Oatmeal
No-Bake Cookies 350
Chocolate Peanut Pillows 370
Chocolate Pecan Pie 314
Chocolate Toffee Trifle 398
Chocolate Walnut Wafers 343
Chocolate Zucchini Bread 71
Cocoa Butter Filling 276
Cocoa Chiffon Cake 285
Cupcake-ettes 353
Easy Ice Cream Pie 1 387
Easy Ice Cream Pie 3 387

Easy Ice Cream Pie 4 387
Easy Ice Cream Pie 5 387
Easy Peanut Butter Cups 358
Frosty Ice Cream Sandwich 414
Fudge Icing 333
Fudgemallow Raisin Candy 367
Fudgey Chocolate Chunk Brownies . 333
Gert's Candy Jar Cookies 345
Heath Bar Cake 279
Mackinac Island Fudge 365
Mallo-Nut Fudge Cake 277
Meringue Cookies 342
Million Dollar Fudge 362
Mint Brownie Pie 402
Minute-Boil Fudge Frosting 277
Mocha Macaroon Pie 322
Mocha Pecan Pie 313
Mocha Soufflé 396
My Favorite Fudge Frosting 281
Neiman Marcus Cake 402
Oreo Cookie Cake 273
Peanut Butter Bonbons 357
Prize Winning Zucchini
Fudge Cake 278
Rita Jo's Chocolate Chip
Date Cake 279
Rita Jo's Chocolate Covered
Peanut Butter Balls 361
Rocky Road Fudge 364
Ruth's Chocolate Delight or
The Only Thing Better Than
Robert Redford 412
Ruth's Peanut Butter Balls 361
Sanders Hot Fudge Sauce 95
S'Mores 355
Soufflé au Chocolat 397
Thel's Famous Chocolate Sauce 95
Thick Hot Chocolate Sauce 96
Toffee and Fudge Bars 336
Toffee Fudge 365
Toffee Squares 336
White Chocolate Pretzels 372
Win Schuler's Walnut Cream Pie 318
Yule Mint-wiches 349
Zachary's People Chow 369
Christmas Fudge 366
Christmas Morning Sausage Ring 90
Christmas Ribbon Ring 123
Christmas Salad 119
Chuckwagon Beans 251
Chutney and Cheese 29
Cindy's Pork Chops 213
Cinnamon Nut Diamonds 338
Citrus Avocado Salad 118
Citrus Delight 413
Citrus Glazed Rock Cornish
Game Hens 219
Clam Chowder, Potato 165
Cloud Biscuits 55
COCONUT
Candy Strawberries 371

Coconut Cream Pie 301
Coconut Delight 410
Coconut Gingeroons 346
Dream Bars 332
Jeanine's Oatmeal Butter Crisps 343
Jello Balls 357
Lite Coconut Cream Pie 302
Orange Coconut Balls....................... 356
Piña Colada Macaroons.................... 347
Ruth's Peanut Butter Balls.............. 361
Unbelievable Lemon Pie 316
Coffee Butterscotch Sauce 98
Connecticut Beef Supper 188
COOKIES
Apricot Almond Squares 335
Aunt Mavis' Carrot Cookies............. 339
Bon Bon Cookies 348
Butterscotch Chocolate Squares....... 338
Butterscotch Sticks........................... 331
Candy Cane Cookies......................... 353
Chocolate Chip Cookies.................... 340
Chocolate Chip Cookies
   Beauchamp.................................... 340
Chocolate Cookie Bar 335
Chocolate Oatmeal No-Bake
   Cookies 350
Chocolate Walnut Wafers 343
Cinnamon Nut Diamonds 338
Coconut Gingeroons 346
Cranberry Crunch Bars 334
Cupcake-ettes 353
Dream Bars 332
Dropped Sugar Cookies 342
Festive Cherry-ettes 349
Fudgey Chocolate Chunk Brownies . 333
Gayle's Sugar Cookies 330
Gert's Candy Jar Cookies................. 345
Grandma's Favorite Molasses
   Cookies... 329
Homesteaders 354
Jeanine's Oatmeal Butter Crisps 343
Meringue Cookies 342
Mexican Cinnamon Cookies............. 346
Mrs. Smith's Plymouth Cookies 341
My Mom's Peanut Butter Cookies 344
Noel Fruit Bars 332
Noel Wreaths 351
Paul's Pumpkin Bars 337
Pecan Tassies 354
Piña Colada Macaroons.................... 347
Russian Teacakes 347
Shirley's Date Pinwheels 352
Shirley's Oatmeal Date Cookies 341
S'Mores 355
Snickerdoodles 348
Sugar and Spice Cookies 345
Sugar Cookie Cut-outs 330
Swedish Ginger Cookies................... 331
Toffee and Fudge Bars 336
Toffee Squares 336
Viennese Rounds 350

Yule Mint-wiches 349
CORN
Corn 'n Turkey Bake 230
Cornbread Salad 115
Kansas Corn Scallop 254
Prairie Corn Chowder 167
Cornmeal Mush.................................... 88
Cottage Pudding 375
Country Pea Soup 154
Country Skillet Apples...................... 250
CRAB
Broccoli and Crab Bisque 163
Crab Meat Appetizers 31
Fabulous Shrimp Crab Casserole 242
Seafood Cheese Spread 27
CRANBERRY(IES)
Cran-Raspberry Mold 123
Cranberry Apple Casserole 377
Cranberry Cheese Bread 74
Cranberry Crunch Bars 334
Cranberry Oatmeal Bread 78
Cranberry Orange Pound Cake 292
Cranberry Pear Pie........................... 307
Cranberry Strawberry Jam 80
Linda's Cranberry Apple Pie 306
Cream Cheese Icing 297
Cream Gravy 186
Cream of Cauliflower Soup 152
Creamy Apricot Dressing.................. 124
Creamy Broccoli and Cauliflower
   Salad 102
Creamy Buttermilk Dressing 103
Creamy Glaze 77
Creamy Nut Icing............................. 283
Creamy Parmesan Chicken 214
Crisp and Tangy Salad 112
Crispy Baked Fish 232
Crunchy Coffee Kuchen 67
Crunchy Oven Fried Chicken 217
Crunchy Party Mix............................ 37
Crunchy Topping Mix 36
Crunchy Turkey Supreme 230
Cupcake-ettes 353
Curried Avocado Soup....................... 152
Custard Mixture (for Impossible
   Main Dish Pies) 206
Cyndee's Lo-Cal Cheese Dip 23
Cyndee's Oatmeal Muffins 52
Cyndee's Party Snack 34

D

Daniel's Cheeseburger Pie 192
Date Cream Pie 300
De-Lite-ful Tuna Salad 134
Deanburgers 172
Dean's Honey Wheat Bread............... 59
Dee's Favorite Blueberry Muffins 54
Dee's Favorite Cocoa Mix................... 44
Dennis' Creamy Italian Dressing 138
DESSERTS (See Individual Listings)
Apple Dumplings 403

Cheesecake
Almond Cheesecake 392
Fluffy Cheese Torte 413
J. L. Hudson's Cheesecake
Chiffon 395
Pumpkin Amaretto Cheesecake .. 393
Strawberry Cream Cheese Cake . 394
Chocolate Macadamia Nut Tart 404
Cobbler
Apple Crisp 376
Apple Kuchen 390
Aunt Smyrna's Blackberry
Cobbler 380
Cherry Cake Cobbler 382
Cherry Torte 381
Cranberry Apple Casserole 377
Fresh Peach Cobbler 383
Mom Albright's Peach Cobbler 381
Coconut Delight 410
Easy Pumpkin Swirl 384
Frosted Pineapple Squares 405
Frozen
Carlile Family Ice Cream 388
Chocolate Cherry Cordial
Ice Cream 389
Chocolate Cups Olé 407
Chocolate Graham Cracker
Delight 414
Easy Ice Cream Pie 1 387
Easy Ice Cream Pie 2 387
Easy Ice Cream Pie 3 387
Easy Ice Cream Pie 4 387
Easy Ice Cream Pie 5 387
Easy Ice Cream Pies 387
Frosty Ice Cream Sandwich 414
My Mother's New York
Ice Cream 389
Ruth's Homemade Ice Cream 388
Strawberry Fluff and Stuff 408
Tortoni Delight 409
Yerden Family Vanilla
Ice Cream 386
Gingerbread with Warm
Apple Topping 404
Gloria's Lemon Dessert 385
Mint Brownie Pie 402
Mocha Soufflé 396
Mom's Pineapple Marshmallow
Dessert 409
Neiman Marcus Cake 402
Pecan Pumpkin Crumble 400
Pineapple Orange Bavarian Cream . 386
Pudding
Citrus Delight 413
Cottage Pudding 375
Grandmother Yerden's Pudding . 379
Lemon Cake Pudding 403
Persimmon Pudding 406
Tapioca Pudding 378
Traditional Banana Pudding 377
Pumpkin Pie Squares 401

Punch Bowl Cake 400
Ruth's Banana Split Dessert 407
Ruth's Chocolate Delight or
The Only Thing Better Than
Robert Redford 412
Ruth's Fruit Pizza 391
Soufflé au Chocolat 397
Strawberry Swirl 411
Summer Fruit Compote 414
Trifles
Chocolate Toffee Trifle 398
Tangy Lemon Trifle 398
Texas Trifle 399
Western Gingerbread 390
Deviled Ham Dip 24
Dorothy Mason's Hobo Bread 73
Down on the Ranch Mix 35
Dream Bars 332
DRESSINGS
Avocado Dressing 132
Caesar Salad Dressing 104
Chili Mayonnaise 129
Creamy Apricot Dressing 124
Creamy Buttermilk Dressing 103
Dennis' Creamy Italian Dressing 138
Honey Mustard Dressing 105
Lime Vinaigrette 116
Lite Ranch Dressing Mix 137
Oregano Vinaigrette Dressing 112
Poppy Seed Dressing
a la Barb Taylor 137
Southern Citrus Dressing 119
Thomas' Restaurant Roquefort
Dressing 138
Yogurt Dressing 107
Dropped Sugar Cookies 342
Dustyn's Favorite Oven-fried
Chicken Legs 215

E

Easy and Elegant Kolaches 62
Easy Deep-Dish Pizza 205
Easy Ice Cream Pie 1 387
Easy Ice Cream Pie 2 387
Easy Ice Cream Pie 3 387
Easy Ice Cream Pie 4 387
Easy Ice Cream Pie 5 387
Easy Ice Cream Pies 387
Easy Peanut Butter Cups 358
Easy Penuche Icing 275
Easy Pumpkin Swirl 384
Edith's Cabbage Rolls 203
Edna's Date Cake 296
EGGPLANT
Eggplant Casserole 254
Ratatouille 262
EGGS
Brunch Egg Casserole 89
Christmas Morning Sausage Ring 90
Eggnog French Toast 87
Fried Egg Sandwiches 175

422

Impossible Breakfast Pie 90
Everything Pie 310
Extra Point Pork Chops 212

F

Fabulous Shrimp Crab Casserole 242
Fake Clotted Cream 57
Favorite Lentil Soup 150
Favorite Salmon Patties 236
Festive Cherry-ettes 349
Fettuccine Alfredo 245
Fiesta Tamale Pie 194
Fig and Honey Loaf 75
FISH
  Crispy Baked Fish 232
  Golden Fish Bake 234
  Norwegian Fish Chowder 164
  Seafood Thermidor 239
  Vegetable Topped Orange Roughy ... 233
Flank Steak Sandwiches 173
Fluffy Cheese Torte 413
Fluffy Meatloaf 190
Fluffy Orange Frosting 273
Fluffy White Frosting 273
Four Bean Salad 103
Frankfurter Supper Dish 208
French Apple Coffee Cake 66
Fresh Apple Cake 289
Fresh Orange Chiffon Cake 284
Fresh Peach Cobbler 383
Fresh Strawberry Pie 311
Fresh Vegetable Salad 101
Fried Apples....................................... 249
Fried Egg Sandwiches 175
Fried Mush 89
Fried Okra 257
Frosted 7-Up Salad 127
Frosted Pineapple Squares 405
Frosty Ice Cream Sandwich 414
Fruit and Cheese Danish 65
Fruit of the Sea Casserole 235
FRUIT(S)
  Aunt Elsie's Candle Salad 111
  Christmas Ribbon Ring 123
  Christmas Salad 119
  Citrus Avocado Salad 118
  Citrus Delight 413
  Fruited Oatmeal 88
  Fruit Smoothie 40
  Fruit Swirl Coffee Cake 68
  Hot Fruit Compote 255
  Mom's Famous Overnite Salad 117
  Punch Bowl Cake 400
  Ruth's Fruit Pizza 391
  Southern Citrus Salad 119
  Summer Fruit Compote 414
  Summertime Delight 116
  Tangy Fruit Compote 255
Fudge Icing 333
Fudgemallow Raisin Candy 367
Fudgey Chocolate Chunk Brownies 333

G

Garbanzo Bean Salad 107
Garlic Herb Bread 61
Garlic Yogurt Dip 24
Garnetta's Cherry Preserves 83
Gayle's Sugar Cookies 330
German Red Cabbage 253
Gert's Candy Jar Cookies 345
Ginger Glazed Carrots 253
Gingerbread with Warm
  Apple Topping 404
Gingered Pear Mold 126
Glaze (for Rum Cake) 288
Glenda's Salad 113
Gloria's Date Bread 77
Gloria's Lemon Dessert 385
Golden Chiffon Cake 282
Golden Fish Bake 234
Good and Easy Caesar Salad 104
Good Brown Stew 158
Graham Cracker Cream Pie 298
Graham Cracker Crust 325
Grandma's Cornbread 72
Grandma's Favorite Molasses
  Cookies 329
Grandmother Yerden's Pudding 379
Grandmother's Custard Pie 312
Great Chicken Salad 133
Greek Salad 112

H

Ham and Cheese Ball 28
Ham 'N Swiss Pie 207
Hearty Beef and Potato Casserole 197
Heath Bar Cake 279
Heavenly Pineapple Mold 128
Hill's Resort BBQ Sauce 211
Holiday Peas 256
Holiday Wassail 45
Homesteaders 354
Honey Bran Muffins 49
Honey Mustard Dressing 105
Honey-Lemon Butter 75
Hot Applesauce 94
Hot Chicken Salad 224
Hot Fruit Compote 255
Hot Three-Grain Cereal 88
Hush Puppy Cole Slaw 108

I

ICINGS
  Candy Mountain Icing 283
  Chocolate Fluff............................... 285
  Chocolate Frosting.......................... 278
  Cocoa Butter Filling 276
  Cream Cheese Icing......................... 297
  Creamy Glaze................................... 77
  Creamy Nut Icing 283
  Easy Penuche Icing 275
  Fluffy Orange Frosting 273

Fluffy White Frosting 273
Fudge Icing 333
Glaze (for Rum Cake) 288
Lemon Glaze 286
Minute Penuche Frosting 274
Minute-Boil Fudge Frosting 277
My Favorite Fudge Frosting 281
Orange Cream Icing 284
Spicy Brown Sugar Glaze 291
Vanilla Glaze 62
Impossible Breakfast Pie 90
Impossible Main Dish Pies 206
Italian Cream Cake 297
Italian Vegetable Soup 144

J

J. L. Hudson's Cheesecake Chiffon 395
J. L. Hudson's Maurice Salad 130
JAMS & JELLIES
  Apple Cinnamon Jelly 80
  Cranberry Strawberry Jam 80
  Garnetta's Cherry Preserves 83
  Jewel Jam 81
  Mom's Peach Marmalade 82
  Peach Conserve 79
  Pineapple-Orange Marmalade 82
  Razzle-Dazzle Jam 81
Jan's Southern Fried Apples 249
Japanese Fruit Pie 324
Jeanine's Oatmeal Butter Crisps 343
Jean's Broccoli Sausage Chowder 166
Jean's Christmas Punch 37
Jean's Sausage Spaghetti Primavera . 209
Jelled Peach Mold 125
Jello Balls 357
Jennie Brink's Graham Gems 49
Joan's Broccoli Casserole 252
Juanita's Green Beans 251

K

Kansas Corn Scallop 254
Kay Shaw's Pink Punch 41
Key Lime Pie 304

L

Laura Horn's Baked Caramel Corn 368
Laura Horn's Frozen Fruit Punch 42
Lemon Cake Pudding 403
Lemon Chiffon Pie 321
Lemon Cream Pie 301
Lemon Glaze 286
Lemon Meringue Pie 303
Lemon Roasted Chicken 218
Lemon Sauce 97
Lemon Spareribs 212
Lentil Soup 151
Lime Punch 43
Lime Vinaigrette 116
Linda's Cranberry Apple Pie 306

Linda's Famous Strawberry
  Pretzel Salad 122
Linda's Green Beef Enchiladas 196
Lisa's Layered Salad 101
Lite and Easy Cheese Sauce 98
Lite and Easy White Sauce 98
Lite Banana Cream Pie 302
Lite Coconut Cream Pie 302
Lite Cream Pie Filling 302
Lite Ranch Dressing Mix 137
Londa's Whole Wheat Rolls 61
Lou's Mandarin Orange Cake 293

M

Mackinac Island Fudge 365
Mallo-Nut Fudge Cake 277
Mañana Beef Bake 201
Mashed Potatoes 259
Mediterranean Stir-Fried Beef 189
Meringue 298
Meringue Cookies 342
Meringue, Mom's 303
Meringue, Ruth's 299
Mexican Chicken Soup 142
Mexican Cinnamon Cookies 346
Mexicana Bean Dip 25
Michelle's White Chili 162
Michigan Blueberry Pie 305
Million Dollar Fudge 362
Mini Brunch Puffs 54
Mint Brownie Pie 402
Minute Penuche Frosting 274
Minute-Boil Fudge Frosting 277
Mixed Vegetable Stir-Fry 265
Mocha Macaroon Pie 322
Mocha Pecan Pie 313
Mocha Soufflé 396
Mock Oysters 148
Mock Sangría 46
Molasses Popcorn Balls 358
Mom Albright's Peach Cobbler 381
Mom Mizell's Hot Rolls 60
Mom's Angel Food Cake 271
Mom's Candied Sweet Potatoes 261
Mom's Chili for Twenty-five 161
Mom's Famous Overnite Salad 117
Mom's Peach Marmalade 82
Mom's Peanut Brittle 360
Mom's Pineapple Marshmallow
  Dessert 409
Mom's Rhubarb Cream Pie 309
Mouse Cake 274
Mr. Daniels' Peanut Butter Fudge 360
Mr. Mac's Potato Cakes 260
Mrs. Moody's Apple Blossom Cake 288
Mrs. Smith's Plymouth Cookies 341
Multi-Grain Pancakes 83

MUSHROOM(S)
  Chicken and Mushroom Lo Mein 228
  Parmesan Mushroom Soup 146

My Favorite Fudge Frosting 281
My Favorite Pumpkin Pie 315
My Granny's Coleslaw 109
My Mom's Peanut Butter Cookies 344
My Mother's New York Ice Cream 389
My Mother's Parkerhouse Rolls 60

N

Navy Bean Soup Carlile 141
Neiman Marcus Cake 402
New Year's Gathering Seafood Mold .. 121
Noel Fruit Bars 332
Noel Wreaths 351
Norwegian Fish Chowder 164
Norwegian Holiday Bread 63

O

OATMEAL
  Applesauce Oatmeal Bread 70
  Chocolate Oatmeal No-Bake
    Cookies 350
  Cranberry Crunch Bars 334
  Cranberry Oatmeal Bread 78
  Cyndee's Oatmeal Muffins 52
  Fruited Oatmeal 88
  Hot Three-Grain Cereal 88
  Jeanine's Oatmeal Butter Crisps 343
  Multi-Grain Pancakes 83
  Oat Wheat Waffles 87
  Oatmeal Raisin Muffins 51
  Shirley's Oatmeal Date Cookies 341
  Zucchini Oatmeal Bread 74
Okra, Fried 257
Old Fashioned Lemon Sauce 97
Onion Parsley Butterfingers 56
Onion Sandwiches 177
Open Face Summer Squash 265
ORANGE(S)
  Carrots Ambrosia 253
  Fluffy Orange Frosting 273
  Fresh Orange Chiffon Cake 284
  Lou's Mandarin Orange Cake 293
  Orange Coconut Balls 356
  Orange Cream Fudge 366
  Orange Cream Icing 284
  Orange Marmalade Spread 80
  Pineapple-Orange Marmalade 82
  Spinach Orange Salad 116
Oregano Vinaigrette Dressing 112
Oreo Cookie Cake 273
Outstanding Oven Browned
  Potatoes 257
Oven Black-Eyed Peas 256
Oven Fried Potatoes 258
Oven Fried Zucchini 268
Oysters, Scalloped 243

P

Parmesan Mushroom Soup 146
Party Chicken 217

PASTA
  Barb Taylor's Pasta Salad 135
  Bologna with Kraft Dinner 207
  Chicken Pasta Salad 136
  Chicken Spaghetti 223
  Fettuccine Alfredo 245
  Fruit of the Sea Casserole 235
  Jean's Sausage Spaghetti
    Primavera 209
  Mañana Beef Bake 201
  Mediterranean Stir-Fried Beef 189
  Pasta With Ham 246
  Penne and Peeled Shrimp 243
  Thel's Terrific Pasta Primavera 244
  Turkey Tetrazzini 229
  Yankee Doodle Macaroni 200
Pat's Cinnamon Rolls 64
Paul's Pumpkin Bars 337
Paul's Texas Red 160
PEA(S)
  Country Pea Soup 154
  Holiday Peas 256
  Lisa's Layered Salad 101
  Oven Black-Eyed Peas 256
PEACH(ES)
  Fresh Peach Cobbler 383
  Jelled Peach Mold 125
  Mom Albright's Peach Cobbler 381
  Mom's Peach Marmalade 82
  Peach Conserve 79
  Peach Skillet Pie 317
  Streusel Cream Peach Pie 309
PEANUT BUTTER
  Chocolate Oatmeal No-Bake
    Cookies 350
  Chocolate Peanut Pillows 370
  Easy Peanut Butter Cups 358
  Fudgemallow Raisin Candy 367
  Mr. Daniels' Peanut Butter Fudge ... 360
  My Mom's Peanut Butter Cookies 344
  Peanut Butter Bonbons 357
  Peanut Butter Pie 323
  Rita Jo's Chocolate Covered
    Peanut Butter Balls 361
  Ruth's Peanut Butter Balls 361
  Ruth's Peanut Streusel Pie 299
  Zachary's People Chow 369
PEAR(S)
  Cherries Jubilee Fruit Salad 122
  Cranberry Pear Pie 307
  Gingered Pear Mold 126
PECAN(S)
  Bananas Foster Pecan Pie 313
  Barbecued Pecans 33
  Candy Strawberries 371
  Chocolate Pecan Pie 314
  Easy Ice Cream Pie 2 387
  Mocha Pecan Pie 313
  Pecan Coffee Ring 66
  Pecan Pumpkin Crumble 400
  Pecan Tassies 354

Spiced Holiday (or Any Day) Nuts 35
Spicy Cereal Crunch 369
Sugared and Spiced Nuts 36
Penne and Peeled Shrimp 243
Pepperidge Farm Chicken 226
Peppermint Candy Fudge 363
Peppermint Chiffon Cake 283
Peppermint Eggnog Punch 42
Persimmon Pudding 406

PICKLES & RELISHES
Aunt Edna Hitsman's Crisp Pickles ... 92
Bread and Butter Pickles 93
Picnic Party Potato Salad 110

PIES
Bananas Foster Pecan Pie 313
Blueberry Banana Pie 308
Cherry Cream Pie 314
Chocolate Bar Pie 316
Chocolate Cream Pie 300
Chocolate Pecan Pie 314
Coconut Cream Pie 301
Cranberry Pear Pie 307
Date Cream Pie 300
Everything Pie 310
Fresh Strawberry Pie 311
Graham Cracker Cream Pie 298
Graham Cracker Crust 325
Grandmother's Custard Pie 312
Japanese Fruit Pie 324
Key Lime Pie 304
Lemon Chiffon Pie 321
Lemon Cream Pie 301
Lemon Meringue Pie 303
Linda's Cranberry Apple Pie 306
Lite Banana Cream Pie 302
Lite Coconut Cream Pie 302
Lite Cream Pie Filling 302
Meringue 298
Meringue, Mom's 303
Meringue, Ruth's 299
Michigan Blueberry Pie 305
Mint Brownie Pie 402
Mocha Macaroon Pie 322
Mocha Pecan Pie 313
Mom's Rhubarb Cream Pie 309
My Favorite Pumpkin Pie 315
Peach Skillet Pie 317
Peanut Butter Pie 323
Pie Crust, Foolproof 324
Pie Crust, Grandmother's 325
Pie Crust, Linda's Never Fail 326
Pie Crust, Mixer 326
Piña Colada Pie 319
Pumpkin Chiffon Praline Pie 320
Rhubarb Pineapple Pie 308
Ruth's Peanut Streusel Pie 299
Southern Chess Pie 310
Streusel Cream Peach Pie 309
Sweet Potato Pie 315
Unbelievable Lemon Pie 316
Win Schuler's Walnut Cream Pie 318

Pimiento Cheese Sandwich 178
Pimiento Mushroom Sauce 226

PINEAPPLE
Apricot Salad Ring 124
Aunt Máco's Delicious Salad 125
Cherry Cream Pie 314
Frosted 7-Up Salad 127
Frosted Pineapple Squares 405
Fruit Smoothie 40
Heavenly Pineapple Mold 128
Mom's Pineapple Marshmallow
  Dessert 409
Piña Colada Macaroons 347
Piña Colada Pie 319
Pineapple Orange Bavarian Cream . 386
Pineapple-Orange Marmalade 82
Pistachio Pudding Salad 118
Rhubarb Pineapple Pie 308
Ruth's Banana Split Dessert 407
Pistachio Fudge 363
Pistachio Pudding Salad 118
Poppy Seed Dressing
  a la Barb Taylor 137

PORK
Barbecued Baby Back Ribs 211
Bologna with Kraft Dinner 207
Christmas Morning Sausage Ring 90
Cindy's Pork Chops 213
Deanburgers 172
Deviled Ham Dip 24
Extra Point Pork Chops 212
Frankfurter Supper Dish 208
Ham and Cheese Ball 28
Ham 'N Swiss Pie 207
Impossible Breakfast Pie 90
Impossible Main Dish Pies 206
Jean's Broccoli Sausage Chowder 166
Jean's Sausage Spaghetti
  Primavera 209
Lemon Spareribs 212
Mexicana Bean Dip 25
Pasta With Ham 246
Pizza Burgers 171
Pork Chops with Mushroom Gravy .. 213
Sausage Balls 31
Scalloped Potatoes and Roasty
  Sausages 210
Southern Ham Bake 214
Suggested Pizza Toppings 204
World's Greatest Pizza 204

POTATO(ES)
Hearty Beef and Potato Casserole ... 197
Impossible Breakfast Pie 90
Mashed Potatoes 259
Mom's Candied Sweet Potatoes 261
Mr. Mac's Potato Cakes 260
Outstanding Oven Browned
  Potatoes 257
Oven Fried Potatoes 258
Picnic Party Potato Salad 110
Potato Clam Chowder 165

Potato Soup 149
Scalloped Potatoes and Roasty
  Sausages 210
Sweet Potato Pie 315
Sweet Potato Puff 260
Tater Tot Casserole 198
POULTRY (See CHICKEN and
  TURKEY)
Prairie Corn Chowder 167
Prize Winning Zucchini Fudge Cake .. 278
Prune Wheat Muffins 50
PUMPKIN
  Easy Pumpkin Swirl 384
  My Favorite Pumpkin Pie 315
  Paul's Pumpkin Bars 337
  Pecan Pumpkin Crumble 400
  Pumpkin Amaretto Cheesecake 393
  Pumpkin Chiffon Praline Pie 320
  Pumpkin Pie Squares 401
  Pumpkin Streusel Muffins 53
Punch Bowl Cake 400

Q

Quick Buckwheat Pancakes 84
Quick Ground Turkey Stroganoff 231
Quick Pizza Dough 204

R

Rainbow Divinity 367
Raisin Coffee Cake 69
Ratatouille 262
Razzle-Dazzle Jam 81
Rena Farnum's Bean and
  Vegetable Salad 106
RHUBARB
  Mom's Rhubarb Cream Pie 309
  Rhubarb Pineapple Pie 308
RICE
  African Chow Mein 192
  Artichoke Rice Salad 106
  Beef Rice Soup 146
  Cashew Rice Pilaf 262
  Crunchy Turkey Supreme 230
  Fabulous Shrimp Crab Casserole 242
  Rice-Bulgar Pilaf 263
  Rita Jo's Chicken Rice Casserole 224
  Turkey Rice Casserole 232
  Zucchini, Rice and Beans 267
Rice Krispie Squares 370
Rio Grande Dip 25
Rita Jo's Chocolate Chip Date Cake ... 279
Rita Jo's Chocolate Covered Peanut
  Butter Balls 361
Rita Jo's Country Chicken Chowder ... 169
Rita Jo's Viva Chicken 227
Rita Jo's Western Chili Casserole 195
Rocky Road Fudge 364
Ruby Punch 40
Rum Cake 288
Russian Teacakes 347

Ruth Simmons' Fruit Cocktail Cake ... 295
Ruth's Banana Split Dessert 407
Ruth's Broccoli Casserole 252
Ruth's Caramel Popcorn 368
Ruth's Chocolate Delight or The Only
  Thing Better Than Robert Redford .. 412
Ruth's Fruit Pizza 391
Ruth's Graham Cracker Cupcakes 294
Ruth's Hard Candy 356
Ruth's Homemade Ice Cream 388
Ruth's Korean Salad 114
Ruth's Peanut Butter Balls 361
Ruth's Peanut Streusel Pie 299
Ruth's Pumpkin Raisin Nut Bread 76

S

SALADS (Also see DRESSINGS)
  Apricot Salad Ring 124
  Artichoke Rice Salad 106
  Aunt Elsie's Candle Salad 111
  Aunt Máco's Delicious Salad 125
  Barb Taylor's Pasta Salad 135
  Best of the Southwest Taco Salad 132
  Cherries Jubilee Fruit Salad 122
  Chicken Avocado Salad 129
  Chicken Pasta Salad 136
  Christmas Ribbon Ring 123
  Christmas Salad 119
  Citrus Avocado Salad 118
  Cornbread Salad 115
  Cran-Raspberry Mold 123
  Creamy Broccoli and Cauliflower
    Salad 102
  Crisp and Tangy Salad 112
  Crunchy Topping Mix 36
  De-Lite-ful Tuna Salad 134
  Four Bean Salad 103
  Fresh Vegetable Salad 101
  Frosted 7-Up Salad 127
  Garbanzo Bean Salad 107
  Gingered Pear Mold 126
  Glenda's Salad 113
  Good and Easy Caesar Salad 104
  Great Chicken Salad 133
  Greek Salad 112
  Heavenly Pineapple Mold 128
  Hush Puppy Cole Slaw 108
  J. L. Hudson's Maurice Salad 130
  Jelled Peach Mold 125
  Linda's Famous Strawberry
    Pretzel Salad 122
  Lisa's Layered Salad 101
  Mom's Famous Overnite Salad 117
  My Granny's Coleslaw 109
  New Year's Gathering
    Seafood Mold 121
  Picnic Party Potato Salad 110
  Pistachio Pudding Salad 118
  Rena Farnum's Bean and
    Vegetable Salad 106

Ruth's Korean Salad 114
Scarecrow Country Inn
  Broccoli Salad 108
Southern Citrus Salad 119
Southwestern Couscous Salad 131
Spinach Orange Salad 116
Stauffer's Spinach and Egg Salad 111
Strawberry Salad 126
Summertime Delight 116
Tickled Trout House Salad
  with Honey Mustard Dressing 105
Tossed Salad with Creamy
  Buttermilk Dressing 103
SALMON
Favorite Salmon Patties 236
New Year's Gathering
  Seafood Mold 121
Salmon Chowder 168
Salmon Loaf 237
Salmon Supper 235
Smoky Salmon and Cheese Ball 28
Sanders Hot Fudge Sauce 95
SANDWICHES
Athlete's Burgers 172
Barbecued Beef Pita Sandwiches 174
Barbecued Beef Sandwiches 174
Chicken Fillet Sandwich 176
Chicken Salad Sandwiches 176
Deanburgers 172
Flank Steak Sandwiches 173
Fried Egg Sandwiches 175
Onion Sandwiches 177
Pimiento Cheese Sandwich 178
Pizza Burgers 171
Sloppy Joes 173
Tuna Melts 175
Turkey Burgers 170
Waldorf Chicken Salad on
  Raisin Bread 176
SAUCES
Apple Dessert Sauce 289
Apple Syrup 94
Blueberry Sauce 96
Brandied Apricot Sauce 94
Butter Rum Sauce 93, 292
Celery Dill Sauce 237
Coffee Butterscotch Sauce 98
Cream Gravy 186
Hill's Resort BBQ Sauce 211
Hot Applesauce 94
Lemon Sauce 97
Lite and Easy Cheese Sauce 98
Lite and Easy White Sauce 98
My Own Spaghetti Sauce 202
Old Fashioned Lemon Sauce 97
Pimiento Mushroom Sauce 226
Sanders Hot Fudge Sauce 95
Sauce (for Spicy Appetizer
  Meatballs) 32
Savory Gravy 182
Special Sauce 170

Tag-Along Sauce 290
Thel's Famous Chocolate Sauce 95
Thel's Special Pizza Sauce 204
Thick Hot Chocolate Sauce 96
Vanilla Sauce 97
Sausage Balls 31
Savory Rump Roast 182
Savory Swiss Steak 184
Scalloped Oysters 243
Scalloped Potatoes and Roasty
  Sausages 210
Scalloped Tomatoes 264
SCALLOPS
Scallops Florentine 240
Seafood Supper a la New Orleans 241
Scarecrow Country Inn
  Broccoli Salad 108
SEAFOOD (See Individual Listings)
Broccoli and Crab Bisque 163
Caviar Pie Romanoff 26
Crab Meat Appetizers 31
Crispy Baked Fish 232
De-Lite-ful Tuna Salad 134
Fabulous Shrimp Crab Casserole 242
Favorite Salmon Patties 236
Fruit of the Sea Casserole 235
Golden Fish Bake 234
New Year's Gathering
  Seafood Mold 121
Norwegian Fish Chowder 164
Penne and Peeled Shrimp 243
Potato Clam Chowder 165
Salmon Chowder 168
Salmon Loaf 237
Salmon Supper 235
Scalloped Oysters 243
Scallops Florentine 240
Seafood Cheese Spread 27
Seafood Divan 240
Seafood Supper a la New Orleans 241
Seafood Thermidor 239
Smoky Salmon and Cheese Ball 28
Tuna Melts 175
Tuna St. Jacques 233
Vegetable Topped Orange Roughy ... 233
Shirley's Brisket 183
Shirley's Date Pinwheels 352
Shirley's Hot Grape Punch 44
Shirley's Oatmeal Date Cookies 341
SHRIMP
Fabulous Shrimp Crab Casserole 242
Penne and Peeled Shrimp 243
Seafood Cheese Spread 27
Seafood Divan 240
Seafood Supper a la New Orleans 241
Seafood Thermidor 239
Shrimp Chow Mein 238
Simply Delicious Fried
  Chicken Livers 220
Simply Wonderful Pancakes 84
Sloppy Joes 173

Smoky Bacon Cheese Spread 27
Smoky Salmon and Cheese Ball 28
S'Mores 355
SNACKS
    Aunt Virginia's Nuts and Bolts 33
    Barbecued Pecans 33
    Chocolate Covered Pretzels 371
    Chocolate Peanut Pillows 370
    Crunchy Party Mix 37
    Crunchy Topping Mix 36
    Cyndee's Party Snack 34
    Down on the Ranch Mix 35
    Spiced Holiday (or Any Day) Nuts 35
    Spicy Cereal Crunch 369
    Sugared and Spiced Nuts 36
    Thel's Texas Trash 34
    Zachary's People Chow 369
Snickerdoodles 348
Soufflé au Chocolat 397
SOUPS
    Asparagus Soup 145
    Beef Rice Soup 146
    Black Bean Soup 153
    Broccoli and Crab Bisque 163
    Buckaroo Stew 157
    Cabbage Patch Stew 155
    Chilled Zucchini Soup 156
    Country Pea Soup 154
    Cream of Cauliflower Soup 152
    Curried Avocado Soup 152
    Favorite Lentil Soup 150
    Good Brown Stew 158
    Italian Vegetable Soup 144
    Jean's Broccoli Sausage Chowder 166
    Lentil Soup 151
    Mexican Chicken Soup 142
    Michelle's White Chili 162
    Mock Oysters 148
    Mom's Chili for Twenty-five 161
    Navy Bean Soup Carlile 141
    Norwegian Fish Chowder 164
    Parmesan Mushroom Soup 146
    Paul's Texas Red 160
    Potato Clam Chowder 165
    Potato Soup 149
    Prairie Corn Chowder 167
    Rita Jo's Country Chicken
        Chowder 169
    Salmon Chowder 168
    Three Bean Stew 159
    Tina's Potassium Broth 145
    Tortellini Vegetable Soup 147
    Turkey Soup 143
Southern Chess Pie 310
Southern Citrus Dressing 119
Southern Citrus Salad 119
Southern Ham Bake 214
Southwestern Couscous Salad 131
Spaghetti Sauce, My Own 202
Sparkling Lemonade 38
Special Sauce 170

Spiced Cranberry Punch 45
Spiced Holiday (or Any Day) Nuts 35
Spiced Russian Tea 46
Spicy Appetizer Meatballs 32
Spicy Brown Sugar Glaze 291
Spicy Cereal Crunch 369
Spicy Chiffon Cake 283
SPINACH
    Impossible Main Dish Pies 206
    Lisa's Layered Salad 101
    Ruth's Korean Salad 114
    Scallops Florentine 240
    Spinach Dip 23
    Spinach Orange Salad 116
    Spinach Parmesan Quiches 30
    Spinach Pie 207
    Stauffer's Spinach and Egg Salad 111
SQUASH
    Open Face Summer Squash 265
    Summer Squash Casserole 263
STEW (See SOUPS)
STRAWBERRY(IES)
    Cranberry Strawberry Jam 80
    Fresh Strawberry Pie 311
    Fruit Smoothie 40
    Jewel Jam 81
    Linda's Famous Strawberry
        Pretzel Salad 122
    Strawberry Cream Cheese Cake 394
    Strawberry Fluff and Stuff 408
    Strawberry Salad 126
    Strawberry Swirl 411
    Texas Trifle 399
Streusel Cream Peach Pie 309
Sugar and Spice Cookies 345
Sugar Cookie Cut-outs 330
Sugared and Spiced Nuts 36
Suggested Pizza Toppings 204
Summer Fruit Compote 414
Summertime Delight 116
Sunday Morning Pot Roast 181
Super Cheese Muffins 53
Swedish Ginger Cookies 331
Swedish Lemon Apple Cake 290
Swedish Tea Ring 62
SWEET POTATO(ES) (Also see
POTATOES)
    Mom's Candied Sweet Potatoes 261
    Sweet Potato Pie 315
    Sweet Potato Puff 260
Swiss Steak, The Family's Favorite 185

T

Tag-Along Sauce 290
Tangy Fruit Compote 255
Tangy Lemon Trifle 398
Tapioca Pudding 378
Tater Tot Casserole 198
Tea Party Scones 57
Tea Syrup 39

Texas Trifle 399
Thelma's Holiday Eggnog Cake 287
Thel's Famous Chocolate Sauce 95
Thel's Terrific Pasta Primavera 244
Thel's Texas Trash 34
Thick Hot Chocolate Sauce 96
Thomas' Restaurant Roquefort
  Dressing 138
Three Bean Stew 159
Tickled Trout House Salad
  with Honey Mustard Dressing 105
Tina's Potassium Broth 145
TLC Equipment Tips 10
TLC Health Tips 14
TLC Hospitality Tips 16
TLC Ingredient Tips 12
TLC Meal Planning Tips 15
TLC Preparation Tips 19
Toffee and Fudge Bars 336
Toffee Fudge 365
Toffee Squares 336

TOMATO(ES)
  Ratatouille 262
  Scalloped Tomatoes 264
  Thel's Special Pizza Sauce 204
Tortellini Vegetable Soup 147
Tortoni Delight 409
Tossed Salad with Creamy
  Buttermilk Dressing 103
Traditional Banana Pudding 377

TUNA
  De-Lite-ful Tuna Salad 134
  Fruit of the Sea Casserole 235
  Tuna Melts 175
  Tuna St. Jacques 233

TURKEY
  Athlete's Burgers 172
  Brunch Egg Casserole 89
  Corn 'n Turkey Bake 230
  Crunchy Turkey Supreme 230
  Easy Deep-Dish Pizza 205
  Fiesta Tamale Pie 194
  Quick Ground Turkey Stroganoff 231
  Suggested Pizza Toppings 204
  Turkey Burgers 170
  Turkey Enchilada Bake 231
  Turkey Rice Casserole 232
  Turkey Soup 143
  Turkey Tetrazzini 229
  World's Greatest Pizza 204

U

Unbelievable Lemon Pie 316

V

Vanilla Fudge 363
Vanilla Glaze 62
Vanilla Sauce 97
Vegetable Topped Orange Roughy 233
VEGETABLES (See Individual Listings)
  Mixed Vegetable Stir-Fry 265
  Suggested Pizza Toppings 204
Viennese Rounds 350

W

Waikiki Meatballs 191
Waldorf Chicken Salad on
  Raisin Bread 176
Western Gingerbread 390
Western Zucchini 266
White Chocolate Pretzels 372
Whole Wheat Banana Pancakes 86
Whole Wheat Pancakes 86
Win Schuler's Walnut Cream Pie 318
World's Greatest Pizza 204

Y

Yankee Doodle Macaroni 200
Yerden Family Vanilla Ice Cream 386
Yogurt Cheese 79
Yogurt Dressing 107
Yule Mint-wiches 349
Yvonne's Almond Tea 43

Z

Zachary's People Chow 369
ZUCCHINI
  Chilled Zucchini Soup 156
  Chocolate Chip Zucchini Cake 275
  Chocolate Zucchini Bread 71
  Oven Fried Zucchini 268
  Prize Winning Zucchini
    Fudge Cake 278
  Ratatouille 262
  Summer Squash Casserole 263
  Western Zucchini 266
  Zucchini Casserole 264
  Zucchini Oatmeal Bread 74
  Zucchini, Rice and Beans 267
  Zucchini Rounds 266

Sunline, Inc.
P. O. Box 1287, Big Spring, TX 79720

Please send me ____ copies of **Mealtimes and Memories** @ $16.95_____
Postage and handling (per book)   @ $ 3.00_____
Texas residents add appropriate sales tax   _____
Total _____

Name _____

Address _____

City _____ State _____ Zip _____

Make check payable to *Sunline, Inc.* • No C.O.D.'s
Prices subject to change • We accept Credit Card orders

Sunline, Inc.
P. O. Box 1287, Big Spring, TX 79720

Please send me ____ copies of **Mealtimes and Memories** @ $16.95_____
Postage and handling (per book)   @ $ 3.00_____
Texas residents add appropriate sales tax   _____
Total _____

Name _____

Address _____

City _____ State _____ Zip _____

Make check payable to *Sunline, Inc.* • No C.O.D.'s
Prices subject to change • We accept Credit Card orders

Sunline, Inc.
P. O. Box 1287, Big Spring, TX 79720

Please send me ____ copies of **Mealtimes and Memories** @ $16.95_____
Postage and handling (per book)   @ $ 3.00_____
Texas residents add appropriate sales tax   _____
Total _____

Name _____

Address _____

City _____ State _____ Zip _____

Make check payable to *Sunline, Inc.* • No C.O.D.'s
Prices subject to change • We accept Credit Card orders